GENEALOGICAL RESEARCH IN HIO

Kip Sperry

Third Edition

Third Edition Copyright © 2023
Kip Sperry
All rights reserved. No part of this publication
may be reproduced, in any form or by any means,
including electronic reproduction or reproduction
via the Internet, except by permission of the author.

Published by Genealogical Publishing Company
Baltimore, Maryland
2023

ISBN 9780806321295

Table of Contents

Preface iv
Abbreviations vi
Ohio Capsule... xiii
Chronology... 1
Early Settlement 12
Historical Guides 15
Libraries and Archives 17
    Ohio Network of American History
        Research Centers 20
    FamilySearch...................................... 21
    FamilySearch Centers 29
    FamilySearch Affiliates.......................... 32
    Ohio Genealogical Society 38
    Ohio Genealogical Society Chapters............... 40
    Ohio Genealogical Society Lineage Societies...... 43
    Ohio Genealogical Society Selected Holdings 45
    Ohio History Connection.......................... 47
    State Library of Ohio............................ 51
    Columbus Metropolitan Library 56
    Public Library of Cincinnati and Hamilton County...... 60
    Western Reserve Historical Society 61
    Other Major Genealogical Collections 66
    Guides to Repositories........................... 72
Major Sources
    Birth and Death Records 74
    Cemetery Records 77
    Census Records and Census Substitutes 79
    Church Records 84
    Court Records 87
    Directories 89
    Divorce Records 91

Major Sources (continued)
- Ethnic Records 93
- Family and Home Sources 96
- Institutional Records and Lodges 98
- Internet Addresses 99
- Land and Property Records 106
- Local Histories and Biographies 114
- Maps, Atlases, and Gazetteers 117
- Marriage Records 119
- Migration and Immigration Records 121
- Military Records 124
- Naturalization Records 141
- Newspapers 143
- Periodicals 158
- Photographs 167
- Probate Records 169
- School Records 171
- Tax Records 173
- Township Records 175
- Vital Records 176
- Substitutes for Civil Vital Records Information in Ohio 179

Ohio Counties 183
Ohio County Records 188
Addresses —Ohio 193
Addresses—Outside Ohio 227
Bibliography
- Bibliographies, Guides, and Finding Aids 229
- Biographies and Genealogies 240
- Churches and Religious Organizations 252
- Ethnic Sources 261
- Guidebooks and Methodology 265
- History 269
- Indexes and Genealogical Sources 284

Maps, Atlases, Gazetteers, and Geographical
    Finding Aids 294
Migration, Emigration, and Immigration 300
Military Records and Military History 309
Periodicals and Newsletters 318
Ohio Maps
    Index to Ohio Maps 322
    Ohio Maps 324
General Index 345

Preface

Ohio has numerous resources available for genealogical and historical research — biographies, cemetery records, census schedules, church records, county and other local histories, court records, directories, ethnic records, genealogical manuscript collections, land and property records, military records, naturalization records, newspapers, periodicals, probate records, tax records, township records, vital records (births, marriages, and deaths), statewide and local personal name indexes, and many others described in this guidebook.

Many valuable Ohio records and research aids have been published by genealogical, historical, and other organizations, including the Ohio Genealogical Society and their county and other local chapters. Numerous original records and personal name indexes of genealogical value are available on the Internet. It should be noted that many genealogical resources are also available on microfilm, microfiche, and compact discs (CD-ROM) and can be found in many public and university libraries, historical societies, and other institutions, although increasingly resources on the Internet are replacing these formats.

This research guide describes Ohio resources for family history and genealogical research. It also includes extensive footnotes and bibliographies of Ohio titles, addresses of repositories that house Ohio genealogical and historical records, oral histories, photographs, many online Ohio Internet websites, and addresses of chapters of the Ohio Genealogical Society. Valuable Ohio maps conclude this work.

This new third edition is an expanded and revised version of *Genealogical Research in Ohio*, second edition, published in 2003 by Genealogical Publishing Company (now known as Genealogical.com), Baltimore, Maryland, and supersedes much of the information in that edition. The author expresses appreciation to colleagues, archivists, reference librarians, and other individuals who were cited in earlier Prefaces to the first and second editions.

Regarding this third edition, the author was assisted by Jana Sloan Broglin of Swanton, Fulton County, Ohio, whose work was greatly appreciated. Jana is a Fellow of the Ohio Genealogical Society, former Ohio Genealogical Society trustee, author of Ohio genealogical books and periodical articles, author of nine online Legacy Family Tree Webinars, and has been a frequent presenter at national, state, regional, and local genealogy conferences.

Appreciation is also extended to Linda Swanson, Ohio Genealogical Society Collections Manager, Bellville, Ohio; and Ann K. Sindelar, Library Reference Supervisor, Cleveland History Center of the Western Reserve Historical Society, Cleveland. Also helpful were archivists, reference librarians, and others at Ohio History Connection, Columbus; Bowling Green State University, Center for Archival Collections, Jerome Library, Bowling Green; Ohio Department of Health, Vital Statistics Customer Service, Columbus; and the State Library of Ohio, Columbus; and other archivists, and other reference librarians at other institutions.

Although some of the footnotes and bibliographies cited in this third edition may appear outdated, they are included here for their historical reference value—some of the information is still relevant today. This third edition includes many references to computer resources available on the Internet. It is realized that some website addresses change frequently.

Appreciation is given to Joe Garonzik, Marketing Director, and Eileen Perkins, Designer, Genealogical.com, Baltimore, for their work getting this new edition published.

– Kip Sperry
Accredited Genealogist (Midwestern States)
Fellow, American Society of Genealogists
Fellow, National Genealogical Society
Fellow, Utah Genealogical Association

Abbreviations

ACPL	Allen County Public Library, Ft. Wayne, IN
ALAO	Academic Library Association of Ohio
ALICE	Ohio University's online library catalog
AO	Auditor's Office
APG	Association of Professional Genealogists
BBS	Bulletin Board System
BCG	Board for Certification of Genealogists, Washington, DC
BGSU	Bowling Green State University, Bowling Green, OH
BLM	Bureau of Land Management
BLM-ESO	Bureau of Land Management, Eastern States Office
BLW	Bounty Land Warrant
CAAO	County Auditors' Association
CAC	Center for Archival Collections, Bowling Green, OH
CAGG	Computer Assisted Genealogy Group (e.g. Cleveland Area)
CALICO	Columbus Area Library and Information Council of Ohio, Columbus, OH
CAMLS	Cleveland Area Metropolitan Library System
CAR	Cleveland Archival Roundtable
CC	Clerk of Courts
CCAO	County Commissioners Association of Ohio
CCPL	Cuyahoga County Public Library
CFO	Century Families of Ohio (Ohio Genealogical Society, Bellville, OH)
CH	County courthouse
CHC	Cleveland History Center
CHS	Cincinnati Historical Society, Cincinnati, OH
CINCH	Computerized Information Network for Cincinnati and Hamilton County (online catalog)
CLIO	County Library Information Online
CML	Columbus Metropolitan Library, Columbus, OH
CO	Company, county, county office, county officer
COIN	Central Ohio Interlibrary Network
Comp.	Compiler
CONSORT	Combined online library catalog of College of Wooster, Denison University, Kenyon College, and Ohio Wesleyan University

CP	Common Pleas Court
CPCt	Common Please Court (record)
CR	Criminal, criminal court case
CPL	Cleveland Public Library, Cleveland, OH
CRL	Center for Research Libraries
CSU	Cleveland State University, Cleveland, OH
CW	*Ohio Civil War Genealogy Journal*
CWRT	Civil War Roundtable
CWRU	Case Western Reserve University, Cleveland, OH
DAR	*see* NSDAR
DMC	Digital Media Center (i.e., Ohio LINK)
DPLA	Ohio Digital Network
EFIC	Early Families of Cleveland (OH)
EOA	*Encyclopedia of Ohio Associations*
ERC	Educational Resources Center
FFO	First Families of Ohio (Ohio Genealogical Society, Bellville, OH)
FHS	Firelands Historical Society, Norwalk, OH
FOGS	Fellow, Ohio Genealogical Society
FPR	Fairview Park Regional Library, Fairview Park, OH
FSC	FamilySearch Centers (formerly Family History Center)
FSL	FamilySearch Library (formerly Family History Library)
FSLC	FamilySearch Library Catalog (formerly Family History Library Catalog)
GAR	Grand Army of the Republic
CGLC	Greater Cincinnati Library Consortium
GIS	Geographic Information System
GLO	General Land Office
GLHS	Great Lakes Historical Society, Toledo, OH
GNIS	Geographic Names Information System
GRC	Genealogical Records Committee(s), National Society Daughters of the American Revolution
GSC	Genealogy Services Collection, State Library of Ohio, Columbus, OH
GTTW	*Gateway to the West*
HCCOGS	Hamilton County Chapter, Ohio Genealogical Society
HCGL	Historical Collections of the Great Lakes
HPLM	Rutherford B. Hayes Presidential Library & Museum, Fremont, OH
HRS	Historical Records Survey
HUC	Hebrew Union College, Cincinnati, OH

ICAPGen	International Commission for the Accreditation of Professional Genealogists
IGI	International Genealogical Index
IGLR	Institute for Great Lakes Research (Bowling Green State University)
INS	Immigration and Naturalization Service
JP	Justice of the Peace
KSL	Kelvin Smith Library, Case Western Reserve University, Cleveland, OH
KSU	Kent State University, Kent, OH
LC	Library of Congress, Washington, DC
LDS	The Church of Jesus Christ of Latter-day Saints
LEECA	Lake Erie Educational Computer Association
LGR	Local Government Records
LHG	Local History and Genealogy
LRS	Library Research Service, Western Reserve Historical Society, Cleveland, OH
MC	Municipal Court
MG	Minister of the Gospel
MGC	Midwest Genealogy Center, Mid-Continent Public Library, Independence, MO
MILO	Miami Valley Library Association
ML	Morley Library, Painesville, OH
MLW	Military Land Warrant
MM	Monthly Meeting (Society of Friends/Quakers)
MODSO	Military Order of Daughters and Sons of Ohio (Ohio Genealogical Society)
MOLO	Regional Library System (Eastern Ohio)
MS/MSS	Manscript/manuscripts
MVAR	Miami Valley Archival Roundtable
MVGI	Miami Valley Genealogical Index
MVL	Miami Valley Libraries
NA	Naturalized, naturalization
NARA	National Archives and Records Administration, Washington, DC
n.d.	no date (s)
NDNP	National Digital Newspaper Program
NEHGS	New England Historic Genealogical Society, Boston, MA
NEOCAG	Northeast Ohio Computer-Aided Genealogy
NGS	National Genealogical Society, Falls Church, VA
NOECA	Northern Ohio Educational Computer Association
NOLA	Northeastern Ohio Library Association

NORWELD	Northwest Library District
n.p.	no publishing information
NSDAR	National Society Daughters of the American Revolution
NUCMC	*National Union Catalog of Manuscript Collections*
NW	Northwest
NWOCA	Northwest Ohio Computer Association
NWT	Northwest Territory
NYPL	New York Public Library, New York, NY
OA	*Ohio Archivist*
OAC	Ohio Administrative Code
OAH	Ohio Academy of History, Delaware, OH
OAHQ	*Ohio Archaeological and Historical Quarterly*
OAHSM	Ohio Association of Historical Societies and Museums
OANG	Ohio Air National Guard
OCA	Oberlin College Archives, Oberlin, OH
OCA	Ohio College Association
OA	Ohio Court of Appeals Reports
OCC	Online Collections Catalog (Ohio History Connection's online catalog)
OCLC	Online Computer Library Center, Dublin, OH
OCP	Ohio Company Purchase
OCPS	Ohio Cemetery Preservation Society
OCWGJ	*Ohio Civil War Genealogy Journal* (Ohio Genealogical Society, Bellville, OH
OD	Ohio Decisions
ODCI	Ohio Death Certificate Index (Ohio History Connection, Columbus, OH)
ODH	Ohio Department of Health, Columbus, OH
ODNR	Ohio Department of Natural Resources
OFD	Ohio Federal Decisions
OFDA	Ohio Funeral Directors Association
OFL	Ohio Friends of the Library
OGN	*OGS Genealogy News* (Ohio Genealogical Society, Bellville, OH)
OGS	Ohio Genealogical Society, Bellville, OH
OGSQ	*Ohio Genealogical Society Quarterly* (formerly *The Report*)
OGSRP	Ohio Genealogical Society, *The Report*
OH	Ohio
OH	*Ohio History*
OHC	Ohio History Connection (formerly Ohio Historical Society)

OHC	Ohio Humanities Council
OhGEN	Ohio GenWeb Project
OhioLINK	Ohio Library and Information Network
OHLF	*Ohio's Last Frontier* (newsletter)
OHN	Ohio History Network
OHO	*Ohioana*
OHP/OHPO	Ohio Historic Preservation Office, Columbus, OH
OHQ	*Ohio Historical Quarterly*
OhR	Ohio River
OHRAB	Ohio Historical Records Advisory Board
OHS	*see* OHC
OhSL	State Library of Ohio, Columbus, OH
OI	Ohio Infantry
OIB	Ohio Independent Battery
OL	Laws of Ohio; Ohio Laws
OLA	Ohio Law Abstract
OLA	Ohio Library Association
OLC	Ohio Library Council
OLJ	*Ohio Law Journal*
OLR	*Ohio Law Reporter*
OLTA	Ohio Library Trustees Association
OMA	Ohio Museum Association
OML	Ohio Municipal League
ONAHR	Ohio Network of American History Research Centers
ONG	Ohio National Guard
ONGQ	*Old Northwest Genealogical Quarterly*
ONU	Ohio Northern University, Ada, OH
OO	Ohio Opinions
OPAC	Ohio Public Access Catalog
OPAL	Ohio Private Academic Libraries
OPC	Ohio Preservation Council
OPLIN	Ohio Public Library Information Network
OR	Ohio Roster of Soldiers of 1812
ORC	*Ohio Revised Code*
ORPF	*Ohio Records and Pioneer Families* (Ohio Genealogical Society, Bellville, OH)
ORVF	Ohio River Valley Families
OS	Ohio State Reports
OSCAR	Ohio State University Libraries online catalog
OSL	State Library of Ohio
OSSO	Ohio Soldiers' & Sailors' Orphans' Home
OSU	Ohio State University, Columbus, OH

OSCD	Ohio Supreme Court Decisions
OTA	Ohio Township Association
OU	Ohio University, Athens, OH
OVA	Ohio Volunteer Artillery
OVAL	Ohio Valley Areacan Libraries
OVC	Ohio Volunteer Cavalry
OVHA	Ohio Volunteer Heavy Artillery
OVI	Ohio Volunteer Infantry
OVIL	Ohio Vital Information for Libraries Center
OVLA	Ohio Volunteer Light Artillery
OVM	Ohio Volunteer Militia
OVSS	Ohio Volunteer Sharpshooters
OVVI	Ohio Veterans Volunteer Infantry
Pal-Am	Palatines to America, Columbus, OH
PC	Probate Court
PERSI	*Periodical Source Index*
PLCH	Public Library of Cincinnati and Hamilton County, Cincinnati, OH
PM	Prime Meridian
PRF	Pedigree Resource File
RLS	Regional Library Systems (Ohio)
RS	Revised Statutes of Ohio
SAN	Sanborn Fire Insurance Maps
SAR	Sons of the American Revolution
SBO	Settlers and Builders of Ohio (Ohio Genealogical Society, Bellville, OH)
SCDL	Stark County District Library, Canton, OH
SCWFO	Society of Civil War Families of Ohhio (Ohio Genealogical Society, Bellville, OH)
SEO	Southeastern Ohio Regional Library Center
SFONT	Society of Families of the Old Northwest Territory (Ohio Genealogical Society, Bellville, OH)
SLO	State Library of Ohio, Columbus, OH
SOA	Society of Ohio Archivists
SOLO	Southeastern Ohio Regional Library Center
TAGS	Toledo Area Genealogical Society
TCGC	Theological Consortium of Greater Columbus
TIGER	Toledo' Information Gateway to Electronic Resources (Toledo-Lucas County Public Library, web browser-based electronic catalog, Toledo, OH)
TPL	Toledo Public Library, Toledo, OH
TWP	Township

UA	University of Akron, Akron, OH
UC	University of Cincinnati, Cincinnati, OH
UCLID	University of Cincinnati Libraries online catalog
UGRR	Underground Railroad
UMC	United Methodist Church
USGS	United States Geological Survey
UTMOST	University of Toledo online catalog
VMD	Virginia Miliary District (Ohio)
WCTU	Woman's Christian Temperance Union of Ohio
WorldCat	Global online network of library content and services
WPA	Works Progress Administration
WRHS	Western Reserve Historical Society, Cleveland, OH
WSU	Wright State University, Dayton, OH
YHCIL	Youngstown Historical Center of Industry and Labor, Youngstown, OH
YSU	Youngstown State University, Youngstown, OH

For Further Reference

Evans, Barbara Jean. *A to Zax: A Comprehensive Dictionary for Genealogists and Historians*. 3rd ed. Alexandria, VA: Hearthside Press, 1995.

Sperry, Kip, comp. *Abbreviations and Acronyms: A guide for Family Historians*. 2nd rev. ed. Orem, UT: Ancestry, 2003.

Note:
While some of these abbreviations are found in this book, additional abbreviations are included in this list since they may be useful to Ohio genealogical and historical researchers, reference librarians, and others.

Ohio Capsule

Capital:	Columbus (since 1816)
Cities (largest):	Akron, Canton, Cincinnati, Cleveland, Columbus, Dayton, Hamilton, Lorain, Parma, Toledo, and Youngstown
Counties:	88 (largest Ashtabula; smallest Lake)
Crops:	Soybeans, corn, wheat, others
Economy:	Agriculture, manufacturing, mining
Land area:	41,328 square miles
Libraries (largest):	Cleveland Public, Cleveland; Columbus Metropolitan, Columbus; Ohio History Connection, Columbus; Ohio State University, Columbus; Public Library of Cincinnati and Hamilton County, Cincinnati; State Library of Ohio, Columbus; Toledo-Lucas County Public Library, Toledo; Western Reserve Historical Society, Cleveland
Local government:	Aproximately1,324 townships, 688 villages, 250 cities
Migration to Ohio:	Ohio River and other rivers, canals, Lake Erie National (Cumberland) Road, Zane's Trace, railroads
Motto:	With God, All Things Are Possible
Natural resources:	Coal and limestone
Newspapers (major):	*Akron Beacon Journal, The Cincinnati Enquirer, The Cincinnati Post, The Columbus Dispatch, Dayton Daily News, Plain Dealer* (Cleveland), *Springfield News-Sun, The Toledo Blade, The Vidicator* (Youngstown)
Nickname:	The Buckeye State
Population (2020):	11,799,448 **https://www.census.gov** 282.3 persons per square mile in 2020
Postal abbreviation:	OH
Presidents:	Seven former U.S. presidents were born in Ohio: James Abram Garfield, Ulysses S. Grant, Warren Gamaliel Harding, Benjamin Harrison, Rutherford Birchard Hayes, William McKinley, and William Howard Taft.

Religions (major):	Baptist, Congregational, Episcopal, Jewish, Lutheran, Methodist, Presbyterian, and Roman Catholic
Rivers (major);	Cuyahoga, Grand, Great Miami, Hocking, Huron, Little Miami, Maumee, Muskingum, Ohio, Portage, Sandusky, Scioto, Vermilion
Statehood granted:	1 March 1803, the 17th state and the first state admitted in the Northwest Territory

Chronology

1669-1670	The first exploration in what is now Ohio is made by the French between Lake Erie and the Ohio River. The French later claim the entire Ohio Valley.
1744	King George II charters the first Ohio Company which was organized by Virginians and London merchants who traded with Virginia.
1747	Ohio Company of Virginia is organized to settle the Ohio River Valley
1748	Ohio Land Company is organized.
1750	Christopher Gist, from Virginia's Ohio Company explores Ohio.
1754	The Ohio company constructs a fort at the forks of the Ohio River.
1754-1763	French and Indian War.
1763	Treaty of Paris ends French and Indian War. France gives Great Britain most of its lands east of the Mississippi River.
1772	A Moravian settlement is established near present-day New Philadelphia; it is abandoned in 1776.
1773	First school in Ohio opens for Native American Indians at Schoenbrunn, near New Philadelphia.
1775-1783	Revolutionary War.
1778	First American Army post in Ohio territory built at Fort Laurens.
1780	George Rogers Clark defeats the Shawnee Indians.
1781	New York cedes its claims to Ohio to the United States government.
1782	8 March. Massacre of Delaware Indians at Gnadenhutten, a village located nar the Tuscarawas River in Tuscarawas County.
1783	3 September. Treaty of Paris ends the American Revolution. Great Britain formally relinquishes its right and interest in the Northwest Territory. Ohio Valley is given to the United States.
1784	Virginia cedes its claims to Ohio and other western lands to the United States.

1784	Congress passes an ordinance designed to guide the development of government of the Northwest Territory (Ordinance of 1784).
1784-1786	Native American Indians sign treaties giving up southern Ohio.
1785	Massachusetts grants its western claims, including Ohio, to the United States government. Congress passes the Land Ordinance of 1785. Townships are established. A section of each township is reserved for school development. Seven Ranges in Ohio are surveys. Fort Harmar established at the mouth of the Muskingum River.
1786	Connecticut relinquishes its western land claims, including Ohio, to the United States (except the Connecticut Western Reserve in Northeastern Ohio). Ohio Company of Associates, established at Boston, to settle lands along the Ohio River.
1787	13 July. The United States Congress enacts the Northwest Ordinance of 1787, establishing a government in the area north of the Ohio River. It encourages education; freedom of speech, press, and assembly; and prohibition of slavery. It becomes the basic instrument of government in the Northwest Territory. Ohio becomes part of the Northwest Territory. Connecticut and Virginia retain title to Ohio land - the Connecticut Western Reserve and the Virginia Military District. Congress authorizes the Ohio Company Purchase. Scioto Company is created.
1788	The first territorial government is formed at Marietta. Ohio Company of Associates establishes settlement at Marietta at the Muskingum and Ohio Rivers. Marietta is the first permanent white settlement in Ohio. It is the first capital of the Northwest Territory. Campus Martius is built as a fortress against the Native American Indians. Washington County established. 25 July. Ohio National Guard organized at Marietta.
1789	The Symmes Company is organized at Cincinnati. Fort Washington established at Cincinnati.
1790	Hamilton County established. A large French settlement is established at Gallipolis.

1793	The first newspaper north and west of the Ohio River, *The Centinel of the Northwestern Territory*, is published at Cincinnati (it was published 1793-1796).
	Fort Recovery built by General. Anthony Wayne.
1794	Battle of FallenTimbers ends the Indian Wars in Ohio.
	Native American Indians are defeated by General Anthony Wayne.
1795	Treaty of Greenville ends Native American wars and opens two-thirds of Ohio to settlers. Greenville Treaty Line separates Native American lands in Northwest Ohio from settlers' lands in the east and south.
	Connecticut Land Company created.
	A subscription library opens at Belpre.
1796	Chillicothe established in the Virginia Military District.
	General Moses Cleaveland leads a group of settlers from Connecticut and founds the city of Cleveland at the mouth of the Cuyahoga River.
	Freeman's Journal published at Cincinnati, 1796-1799.
	Youngstown established.
	Land act creates Pittsburgh and Cincinnati land offices and the United States Military Tract.
	Zane's Trace, which extends from Wheeling, Virginia (now West Virginia), to Zanesville and Lancaster, Ohio, and Limestone (now Maysville), Kentucky, on the Ohio River opens for migrants.
1797	Adams and Jefferson counties established.
	Migrants continue to use Zane's Trace.
	Muskingum Academy (now Marietta College) established (the first institution of higher learning in the Northwest Territory).
1798	Ross County established.
1799	Territorial government established in Ohio with Cincinnati as the capital.
	The *Western Spy and Hamilton Gazette* is published at Cincinnati.
1800	First territorial census taken in Ohio: population 45,365 people.
	Clermont, Fairfield, and Trumbull counties established.
	Land office opens at Steubenville.
	Connecticut gives up jurisdiction of the Western Reserve in Northeastern Ohio.
	The Scioto Gazette begins publication at Chillicothe.

1800	Chillicothe is the capital of the Territory of Ohio. Congress passes the Division Act, which creates Indiana Territory.
1801	Belmont County established.
1802	45,028 people residing in the Northwest (Ohio and Michigan). Ohio University is chartered as American Western University in Athens, renamed Ohio University in 1804. Constitutional convention held at Chillicothe.
1803	1 March. Ohio admitted to the Union as the 17th state. Edward Tiffin is the first governor. State capital is at Chillicothe from 1803-1810. Butler, Columbiana, Franklin, Gallia, Greene, Montgomery, Scioto, and Warren counties establised. Louisiana Purchase lands purchased by the United States from France. Ohio population approximately 50,000 people.
1804	18 February. Ohio University established at Athens. Muskingum County established. Coonskin Library organized at Ames (Amesville); books are distributed on horseback.
1805	Athens, Champaign, and Highland counties established. Many settlers migrate to Ohio.
1806	Geauga County established.
1807	Miami County established.
1808	Ashtabula, Cuyahoga, Delaware, Knox, Licking, Portage, Preble, Richland, Stark, and Wayne counties established.
1809	Miami University established as a state-supported university at Oxford; first classes held in 1824. Darke and Huron counties established.
1810	Population: 230,760 people in Ohio (U.S. census). State capital temporarily moved from Chillicothe to Zanesville (until 1812). Partial 1810 census survives. Clinton, Coshocton, Fayette, Guernsey, Madison, and Pickaway counties established.
1811	The *New Orleans* is the first steamboat to travel down the Ohio River.
1812	Capital transferred from Zanesville back to Chillicothe until 1816. Medina County established.
1812-1815	War of 1812. Ohio militia mobilizes in 1812. 26,280 Ohioans take an active part in this conflict.

1813	Commodore Oliver Hazard Perry wins a significant naval victory during the War of 1812, the Battle of Lake Erie, on the Ohio side of the boundary line defeating the British fleet on Lake Erie. Harrison and Monroe counties established.
1815	Thousands of settlers arrive in Ohio, often known as the "Great Migration" [to Ohio]. Lawrence and Pike counties established.
1816	State capital established at Columbus, Franklin County. Jackson County established.
1817	Treaty of Maumee Rapids allows many settlers into Northwest Ohio. State Library of Ohio established at Columbus. Zoar Village organized near New Philadelphia by a group of Germans. *The Philanthropist*, the country's first anti-slavery newspaper, is published at Mount Pleasant. Morgan County established.
1818	National Road reaches Wheeling, (West) Virginia. *Walk-in-the-Water*, the fist steamboat on Lake Erie, stops at Cleveland and Sandusky on route from Buffalo, New York, to Detroit, Michigan. Brown, Clark, Hocking, Logan and Perry counties established.
1819	University of Cincinnati established at Cincinnati as a municipal college. Cincinnati receives its city charter. Meigs and Shelby counties established.
1817/1819	Society of Separatists at Zoar (German separatists in Tuscarawas County) is an experiment in communal living which lasts until 1898.
1820	Population: 581,434 (U.S. census) Federal census of Ohio taken and is now indexed. Ohio is the fifth most populous state. Land Act changes purchase of land from the federal government to a cash basis. Allen, Crawford, Hancock, Hardin, Henry, Marion, Mercer, Paulding, Putnam, Sandusky, Seneca, Union, Van Wert, Williams, and Wood counties established.
1822	Lorain County established.
1823	Decline in sales of western Ohio lands. First Methodist mission established at Upper Sandusky.

1824	*Rufus Putnam*, the first steamboat on the Muskingum River, travels from Marietta to Zanesville.
	Kenyon College (Gambier) organized by Episcopalians (the first denominational college in Ohio).
	Holmes County established
1825	New York state's Erie Canal connects the Hudson River with Lake Erie. Western migration to Ohio and other Midwestern states increases.
	Work begins on the Miami and Erie Canal in Ohio.
1825	State law requires counties to fund education. Ohio public school system begins.
1826	Western Reserve Academy established by Congregationalists at Hudson.
1827	Akron-Cleveland branch of Ohio and Erie Canal opened.
	Daily Gazette, the first daily newspaper west of Philadelphia, begins publication at Cincinnati.
1829	Boat service on the Miami and Erie Canal begins with the arrival of the *Governor Brown* from Cincinnati to Dayton.
1830	Population: 937,903 (U.S. census).
1830-1860	Many mills and factories are built in Ohio.
1831	Joseph Smith, Jr., arrives in Kirtland, Ohio, and begins a settlement for the Latter-day Saints (Mormons).
	Xavier University created by Jesuit Order at Cincinnati.
1831-1838	Kirtland, Geauga Co. (now Lake Co.) serves as headquarters of The Church of Jesus Christ of Latter-day Saints. LDS Church units are established in Northeastern Ohio and elsewhere.
1832	Ohio and Erie Canal completed. Its route extends from Cleveland (Lake Erie) to Portsmouth near the Ohio River and links Lake Erie and the Ohio River.
1833	Ottawa Indians removed by Maumee Treaty.
	Oberlin College established—the first college in the U.S. to admit African Americans and women. It is the first co-educational college in the U.S. for both men and women and is a center of the anti-slavery movement.
	National (Cumberland) Road opens to Columbus.
	Cholera epidemic in Columbus claims some 200 lives.
	Carroll County established.
1835	Lucas County established.
1836	The Erie and Kalamazoo, Ohio's first railroad, is completed from Toledo to Adrian, Michigan.
	Ohio-Michigan boundary dispute settled.

1836	Kirtland Temple dedicated by Joseph Smith, Jr., leader of the Latter-day Saints in Kirtland, Ohio. The Kirtland Temple is now owned by the Community of Christ.
1837	Oberlin College becomes coeducational after opening its doors to women. Muskingum College established by United Presbyterian Church at New Concord.
1838	National Road completed to Vandalia. Latter-day Saints leave Kirtland for western Missouri. Erie County established.
1840	Census of pensioners for Revolutionary War for military services taken. Population: 1,519,467 (U.S. census). Ohio is one of the leading corn and wheat producing states. Lake, Ottawa and Summit counties established.
1842	Ohio Wesleyan University established in Delaware, Ohio, by the Methodists.
1843	Wabash and Erie Canal links Lafayette, Indiana, to Toledo, Ohio. Miami and Erie Canal, connecting Toledo and Cincinnati, is completed. 20 December. Baldwin-Wallace College is chartered as Baldwin Institute at Berea. Founded by Methodists, it becomes Baldwin University in 1854 and granted its first degrees in 1858. The Institution joins with German Wallace College in 1914 to form Baldwin-Wallace College. Wittenberg University (Springfield) established by Lutherans.
1845	Defiance and Wyandot counties established.
1846	Mount Union College established at Alliance by members of the Methodist Episcopal Church. Ashland and Mahoning counties established.
1846-1848	Mexican War. Many Ohioans serve in this conflict.
1847	Otterbein University established by United Brethren Church at Westerville (now Otterbein College). 11 February. Thomas Alva Edison born in Milan.
1848	Oxford College for Women established at Oxford. Ohio's African American laws repealed. Auglaize and Morrow counties established.
1849	Cholera kills about 7,500 people in Cincinnati during the years 1849-50. Cholera spreads across Ohio. Cholera kills about 400 people at Sandusky.

1850	Population: 1,980,329 (U.S. census).
	Many Ohio residents in 1850 are foreign born—Germany, Ireland, England, France, Wales, Canada, Scotland, Switzerland, and other foreign countries (source: 1850 U.S. census).
	Catholic Archdiocese created at Cincinnati.
	Heidelberg College created at Tiffin by the Ohio Synod of the Reformed Church in the United States.
	Dayton-Sandusky railroad begins.
	Capital University (Columbus) established.
	University of Dayton established.
	Fulton and Vinton counties established.
1851	Probate Court assumes responsibility for recording probate and estate matters.
	New Constitution of Ohio adopted.
	Noble and Vinton counties established.
1852	The railroad reaches Cleveland from Pittsburgh. Virginia relinquishes and cedes to the U.S. government its claim to any unsettled land in the Virginia Military District in Ohio.
1853	Public high schools in Ohio authorized.
1856	Wilberforce University becomes the nation's first college for African Americans.
1856-1857	Some county registration of births and deaths recorded.
1859	Ohio has 22 colleges and universities.
1860	Population: 2,339,511 (U.S. census).
	Ohio is the third most populous state in the U.S.
1861-1865	Civil War. Over 310,000 Ohio men serve for the Union.
	The Underground Railroad in Ohio helps slaves from the Southern states migrate to Canada.
1862	Homestead Act.
	Mary Jane Patterson becomes the first African-American woman to receive a B.A. degree from Oberlin College.
1863	July. Some 3,000 Confederate soldiers, under the command of General John Morgan, enter Southwestern and Southern Ohio.
1867	County level registration of civil births and deaths (some county birth and death records begin in 1868).
1869	G.A.R. (Grand Army of the Republic) establishes the Ohio Soldiers' and Sailors' Orphans' Home at Xenia.
1870	Population: 2,665,260 (U.S. census).
	Buchtel College established, later the University of Akron.

1870	Ohio Agricultural and Mechanical College established at Columbus (later Ohio State University), a land-grant college.
	University of Cincinnati incorporated as a municipal university.
	John D. Rockefeller organizes Standard Oil Company in Cleveland.
1872	University of Toledo established at Toledo.
1873	Ohio Agricultural and Mechanical College in Columbus (later Ohio State University) opens for students.
1876	Ohio has 6,400 churches and 35 church-supported colleges.
1880	Population: 3,198,062 (U.S. census).
1884	Western Reserve University chartered in Cleveland.
1886	American Federation of Labor organized at Columbus.
	College of Wooster established by Presbyterians.
1890	Population: 3,672,329 (U.S. census; later destroyed by fire).
	Special Union Veterans and Widows Census taken.
1890s	Akron becomes a major tire manufacturing center.
1898	Spanish-American War. 14,255 Ohioans contribute to this conflict.
	Zoarites abandon their communal lifestyle.
1899	Bluffton College, Bluffton, organized by Mennonites.
1900	Population: 4,157,545 (U.S. census).
	There are approximately 11,000 one-room schoolhouses in Ohio.
1905	Dayton. Orville and Wilbur Wright build the first practical airplane, the Wright Flyer.
1908	20 December. Birth and death records kept on a state level.
1910	Population: 4,767,121 (U.S. ceneus).
	Kent State University established at Kent.
	Bowling Green State University established.
1913	Many Ohioans suffer from severe floods, which kill over 400 people.
1917-1918	World War I. Over 240,000 Ohioans serve in the war; some 7,000 are killed.
1917	Selective Service Act
1919	Ohio ratifies the 19th Amendment providing for women's suffrage.
1920	Population: 5,759,394 (U.S. census).
1921	School becomes mandatory for youth between the ages of 6 and 18 years.
1930	Population: 6,646,697 (U.S. census).

1938	Ohio has about 1,674 one-room schoolhouses.
1939-1945	World War II. Many Ohioans serve in this war.
1940	Population: 6,907,612 (U.S. census).
1949	7 September. Marriage records are kept on a state basis. Abstracts of Ohio marriage records after 7 September 1949 are available from the Ohio Department of Health, Columbus, OH. Many marriage records are also available at the Ohio History Connection, Columbus, OH.
1950	Population: 7,946,627 (U.S. census).
1960	Population: 9,706,397 (U.S. census).
1969	20 July. Ohioan Neil Armstrong first person to set foot upon the Moon.
1970	4 May. Shootings at Kent State University by Ohio National Guard during a large Vietnam War protest. Population: 10,657,423 (U.S. census).
1980	Population: 10,797,624 (U.S. census).
1990	Population: 10,847,115 (U.S. census).
2000	Population: 11,353,140 (U.S. census).
2010	Population: 11,539,449 (U.S. census).
2020	Population: 11,799,448 (U.S. census).

Chronology References

Academic American Encyclopedia. Danbury, CT: Grolier, Inc., 1998. 14:356-62.

Along the Ohio Trail
https://ohio.gov/government/resources/along-the-ohio-trails

Brown, Jeffrey P. and Andrew R.L. Cayton, eds. *The Pursuit of Public Power: Political Culture in Ohio, 1787-1861.* Kent, OH: Kent State University Press. 1994.

Burke, Thomas Aquinas. *Ohio Lands: A Short History.* 9th ed. Columbus: Auditor of State, 1997.
https://freepages.rootsweb.com/~maggie/history/ohio-lands/ohl7.html

Hatcher, Harlan. *The Western Reserve: The Story of New Connecticut in Ohio.* Kent, OH: Kent State University Press, 1991

Shriver, Phillip R. And Clarence E. Wunderlin., Jr., eds. *The Documentary Heritage of Ohio.* Athens, OH: Ohio University Press, 2000.

The Encyclopedia Americana. Danbury, CT: Grolier, 2000.

Knepper, George W. *The Official Ohio Lands Book.* Columbus: Auditor of State, 2002. **https://www.auditor.state.oh.us**

The Ohio Almanac. Wilmington, OH: Orange Frazer Press, 1992/1993.

U.S. Bureau of the Census. *Census of Population, Ohio.* Washington, DC: U.S. Government Printing Office, 1900-2001.

___. *U.S. Census of Populations, 1950: Volume 11, Characteristics of the Population, Part 35, Ohio.* Washington, DC: U.S. Government Printing Office, 1952.

Vexler, Robert I. and William F. Swindler, eds. *Chronology and Documentary Handbook of the State of Ohio.* Dobbs Ferry, NY: Oceana Publications, 1978.

Writers' Program (Ohio). *The Ohio Guide.* New York: Oxford University Press, 1940; reprinted 1973.

Early Settlement

Ohio, historically known as the Gateway to the West, is an important state for westward migration in America. Although there were explorations and settlements in the Ohio country as early as the seventeenth century, principally by French Canadians, the earliest permanent white settlement in the present bounds of this state occurred late in the eighteenth century. Following creation of the Northwest Territory in 1787, land companies were formed by various Anglo-American groups and settlement of the Ohio country began in earnest.[1]

The territory's first permanent white settlement, Marietta, was established in 1788 under direction of General Rufus Putnam, who arrived there from New England.[2] Marietta was named in honor of Marie Antoinette, then queen of France. Early settlements were clustered in southern and northeastern areas of Ohio and along the many waterways. As frontier settlement advanced in Ohio, northwestern counties were settled last.

---

1. An indispensable history treating the American frontier, with maps and bibliographies, is Ray Allen Billington and Martin Ridge, *Westward Expansion: A History of the American Frontier*, 5th ed. (New York: Macmillan, 1982). A valuable collection of U.S. maps is contained in *Atlas of American History*, 2nd rev. ed. (New York: Charles Scribner's Sons, 1984). See also R. Douglas Hurt, *The Ohio Frontier: Crucible of the Old Northwest, 1720-1830* (Bloomington, IN.: Indiana University Press, 1996), the basic reference, *History of the Ordinance of 1787 and the Old Northwest Territory* (Marietta, OH: Northwest Territory Celebration Commission, 1937), and Peter S. Onuf, "From Constitution to Higher Law: The Reinterpretation of the Northwest Ordinance," *Ohio History* 94 (Winter-Spring I 985): 5-33.

2. Julia P. Cutler, *The Founders of Ohio* (Cincinnati: Robert Clarke & Co., 1888). This work includes historical background and a brief biographical sketch of Rufus Putnam and others.

Washington County was created in 1788, with Marietta as the county seat. As the first county to be organized in the Northwest Territory, it covered all the eastern limits of present Ohio as far west as the Scioto River. Hamilton County was established in 1790, Adams and Jefferson counties in 1797, and Ross County in 1798. The formation of other counties soon followed.

Ohio was admitted to the Union in 1803 as the seventeenth state and the first state created from the Northwest Territory. Soon new settlers poured into the region. The 1825 completion of New York State's Erie Canal, a mostly man-made waterway, linked New England and New York to Lake Erie. Settlers could travel to Ohio's northern shores and west to Michigan and beyond. The 1830s opening of the National Road, which originated in Maryland and crossed westward through Columbus and central Ohio, provided a similarly convenient highway to Ohio, Indiana, and Illinois. In addition, by 1832 Ohio created its own network of canals linking Lake Erie and Ohio towns with the Ohio River.

Beginning where the Allegheny and Monongahela rivers converge in southwestern Pennsylvania, the Ohio River was one a major waterway in America, connecting Pennsylvania and Ohio with the Mississippi River. Ohio River travelers could connect to the Muskingum, Scioto, and Miami rivers, and later Ohio's canals-Ohio and Erie Canal, Miami and Erie Canal, and other smaller canals. Within the Ohio country, settlers traveled the Ohio and Erie Canal, which extended from Cleveland to Portsmouth, and Miami and Erie Canal, which connected Toledo with Cincinnati.

Migration studies of early Ohio show considerable diversity among early heterogeneous populations. Many settlers came from New England states, especially Connecticut, Massachusetts, and Vermont. A significant number were also from Middle Atlantic states of New York, Pennsylvania (particularly western Pennsylvania), and New Jersey. Virginia, Kentucky, Maryland, Carolinas, and other Southern states also provided early settlers to Ohio. Immigrants from foreign countries came principally from England, Ireland, Wales, Scotland, Germany, Eastern and Southern Europe, and Canada, mostly as a result of industrial development and urbanization. As an example, a large group of Manx, from the Isle of Man in the Irish Sea, settled in Northeastern Ohio. Larger Ohio cities attracted Italians, French, and other Europeans. Many African Americans migrated to Ohio beginning in mid-nineteenth century.

Five major early nineteenth-century migration routes into Ohio were: (1) by Lake Erie's shores and on Lake Erie, (2) across western Pennsylvania, (3) through southeastern Ohio to Marietta and up the Muskingum River, (4) through south-central Ohio and up the Scioto River, and (5) into Cincinnati and up the Great and Little Miami rivers.[3] Some migration from Michigan, Indiana, and other Midwestern states also occurred later in the nineteenth century. The Ohio River, which comprises Ohio's southern border, was the most important migration route into southern Ohio, while Lake Erie was an important migration route in northern Ohio. Migrants passed through Ohio using roads, canals, railroads, and the Ohio River as they moved west, north, and south. Ohio is bordered by Pennsylvania on the east, West Virginia on the southeast (Virginia before 1863), Michigan and Lake Erie on the north, Indiana on the west, and Kentucky on the southwest. Leonard Peacefull's *A Geography of Ohio* is an important geographical resource for Ohio genealogists and historians.[4]

---

3. "How We Came to Ohio," *The Report* 19 (Summer 1979): 61. This article includes an excellent map of major migration routes to Ohio; see the map section at the end of this volume. See also pp. 62-67 of this same issue of *The Report*.

4. Leonard Peacefull, ed., *A Geography of Ohio,* rev. ed. (Kent, OH: Kent State University Press, 1996). Consult also Andrew R.L. Cayton, *The Frontier Republic: Ideology and Politics in the Ohio Country, 1780-1825* (Kent, OH: Kent State University Press, 1986) and Norris Franz Schneider, *The National Road: Main Street of America* (Columbus: Ohio Historical Society, 1975). See also Kevin F. Kern and Gregory S. Wilson, *Ohio: A History of the Buckeye State* (Malden, MA; Wiley-Blackwell, a John Wiley & Sons, Inc., Publication, 2014), pp. 129-137.

Historical Guides

Numerous histories and guides exist for genealogists who seek to understand Ohio's early settlement and development of various counties from which records must be sought. George W. Knepper's *Ohio and Its People*, 2nd edition, is an impressive and well-illustrated work that includes several maps of interest to genealogists; it is a scholarly historical treatise.[5] Another valuable history is Henry Howe's *Historical Collections of Ohio*, a popular state history with social and political background describing Ohio's counties, together with maps, illustrations, population statistics, and biographical sketches of many early Ohio settlers.[6] See Henry Howe's work online.
https://www.archive.org/details/historicalcollec01inhowe

---

5. George W. Knepper, *Ohio and Its People*, 2nd ed. (Kent, OH: Kent State University Press, 1997). See especially the bibliographical essay therein.

6. Henry Howe, *Historical Collections of Ohio*, 2 vols. (Cincinnati: State of Ohio, 1888, 1900); this work is indexed separately. Several other Ohio state histories of general interest are John Stevens Cabot Abbott, *The History of the State of Ohio from the Discovery of the Great Valley to the Present Time*, 2 vols. (Detroit: Northwestern Publishing Co., 1875); Simeon D. Fess, *Ohio: A Four-Volume Reference Library on the History of a Great State*, 5 vols. (Chicago: Lewis Publishing Co., 1937) [note that Fess' series actually contains more volumes than the title states]; Charles Burleigh Galbreath, *History of Ohio*, 5 vols. (Chicago: American Historical Society, 1925), separately indexed by Robertalee Lent (Post Falls, ID: Genealogical Reference Builders, 1969); Emilius Oviatt Randall and Daniel J. Ryan, *History of Ohio: The Rise and Progress of An American State*, 6 vols. (New York: Century History Co., 1912-15); Eugene H. Roseboom and Francis P. Weisenburger, *A History of Ohio* (Columbus: Ohio Historical Society, 1986), and Carl Frederick Wittke, ed., *The History of the State of Ohio*, 6 vols. (Columbus: Ohio Archaeological and Historical Society, 1941-44). Two useful general histories of the Buckeye State are Walter Havighurst, *Ohio: A Bicentennial History* (New York: W.W. Norton & Co., 1976), and George W. Knepper, *An Ohio Portrait* (Columbus: Ohio Historical Society, 1976). Also valuable is R. Carlyle Buley, *The Old Northwest: Pioneer Period, 1815-1840*, 2 vols. (Bloomington, IN: Indiana University Press, 1978), which provides historical background of the Northwest Territory.

The Newberry Library's *Historical Atlas and Chronology of County Boundaries, 1788-1980,* is an important reference source, that shows Ohio's interior and exterior boundary changes and offers an excellent collection of state maps.[7] A valuable guide to Ohio's counties is *Jurisdictional Histories for Ohio's Eighty-Eight Counties, 1788-1985.*[8] Additionally, *Evolution of Ohio County Boundaries* gives historical background of boundary changes and includes maps of Ohio county-boundary lines.[9] A valuable study of Ohio's nineteenth-century migration is Hubert G.H. Wilhelm's *The Origin and Distribution of Settlement Groups: Ohio, 1850.*[10] Wilhelm offers tabular statistics to show birthplaces of non-native Ohioans and establishes regional patterns of ethnic settlements based on the 1850 U.S. census.

---

7. Newberry Library, *Historical Atlas and Chronology of County Boundaries, 1788-1980,* John H. Long, ed. and Stephen L. Hansen, comp. (Boston: G.K. Hall, 1984), pp. 275-383. This scholarly work, arranged by counties, shows the date on which each area was created or changed and includes regional history maps along with a boundary history of Illinois, Indiana, and Ohio. This is an essential reference source for American genealogists, historians, and demographers. A state atlas for the Buckeye State is Henry Francis Walling, *Atlas of the State of Ohio* (1868; reprint, Knightstown, IN: Bookmark, 1983), which includes a section describing the evolution of Ohio counties. Another valuable map reference is William Thorndale and William Dollarhide, *Map Guide to the U.S. Federal Censuses, 1790-1920* (Baltimore: Genealogical Publishing Co., 1987), which shows Ohio county boundaries at the time of each federal census superimposed over modern county lines. In addition to the above titles, Ohio place name directories can be obtained from the Department of Natural Resources, Division of Geological Survey, Fountain Square, Columbus, OH 43224. A catalog of publications is available. A useful early gazetteer is *The 1833 Ohio Gazetteer,* 11th ed. (1833; reprint, Knightstown, IN: Bookmark, 1981).

8. W. Louis Phillips, *Jurisdictional Histories for Ohio's Eighty-Eight Counties, 1788-1985* (Bowie, MD: Heritage Books, 1986), shows the names of current counties and governing counties as well as significant dates. Two additional references are Lawrence J. Marzulli, *The Development of Ohio's Counties and Their Historic Courthouses* (Columbus: County Commissioners Association of Ohio, n.d.), and John Clements, *Ohio Facts: A Comprehensive Look at Ohio Today, County by County* (Dallas: Clements Research, 1988).

9. Randolph C. Downes, *Evolution of Ohio County Boundaries* (1927; reprint, Columbus: Ohio Historical Society, 1970). Errors have been corrected by Phillips in his *Jurisdictional Histories for Ohio's Eighty-eight Counties, 1788-1985.*

10. Hubert G.H. Wilhelm, *The Origin and Distribution of Settlement Groups: Ohio, 1850* (Athens, OH: Ohio University, 1982). This well-illustrated work should be carefully studied by genealogists doing nineteenth-century Ohio migration research.

Libraries and Archives

Ohio has an exceptional array of genealogical libraries, historical societies, and archives of major importance. Principal among these are Ohio History Connection and State Library of Ohio, both in Columbus; Ohio Genealogical Society Library, Bellville; Western Reserve Historical Society Library, Cleveland; and Cincinnati Historical Society Library. The Cleveland Public Library, Public Library of Cincinnati and Hamilton County, and Columbus Metropolitan Library are the largest public libraries in Ohio, although large genealogical collections may be found in libraries in Akron, Dayton, Toledo, Xenia, and elsewhere. The public library at Toledo has a particularly strong New England collection. Academic libraries also house significant collections, particularly Ohio State University's Thompson Library, among others, and Campus Martius Museum at Marietta. Regional libraries with strong genealogical collections are available, for example, Fairview Park Regional Branch, Cuyahoga County Public Library, Fairview Park, Ohio.

Ohio provides an abundance of library services, including computer catalogs and OhioLINK (Ohio Library and Information Network). OhioLINK is a statewide library and information network that links universities, colleges, academic libraries, and other institutions. A state-funded consortium of university and college libraries and State Library of Ohio, this online catalog provides access to research databases in many subject areas and gateways to the Internet through numerous search engines. It offers access to millions of library items statewide. Digital images include historic Ohio city maps. Access to research databases is restricted to OhioLINK member users. In summary, it is an online computer catalog of the holdings of member libraries and is available from the Internet, OhioLINK Central Catalog:
http://www.ohiolink.edu

Various government records, as well as more general genealogical aids, are available throughout the state. As in most states, county courthouses basic repositories of genealogical records. Cuyahoga, Delaware, Geauga, Montgomery, and other counties have their own county record centers (county archives) where local records are housed. The Ohio History Connection in Columbus (formerly Ohio Historical Society) organized the Ohio Network of American History Research ONAHR in 1970. These centers are valuable for preservation of local government records including land, probate, tax, vital records, and many others. At its original founding, there were eight such centers; however, ONAHR is now comprised of four state universities as well as Ohio's two largest historical organizations. Current center members are the University of Akron's Archival Services, Blegan Library at University of Cincinnati, Ohio History Connection in Columbus, Western Reserve Historical Society, Cleveland, Wright State University's Paul Laurence Dunbar Library, and Youngstown Historical Center of Industry and Labor. Universities previously in listed as research centers Center for Archival Collections at Bowling Green State University and Ohio University. The last two mentioned still have and collect local records.[11]

---

11. See, for example, Ohio Historical Society, *Guide to Local Government Records at the Ohio University Library,* rev. ed. (Athens, OH: Ohio University Library, 1992). The records at Ohio University cover eighteen counties. See also Jeanne Lacy Pramaggiore, "The Ohio Historical Society: American History Research Centers," *The Report* 33 (Spring 1993): 2-4, and *Ohio County Government Microfilm: Microfilm Available from the Ohio Historical Society* (Columbus: Ohio Historical Society, 1987). Ohio inventories identify court, land, military, probate, and other local government records.

Regarding Ohio Network of American History Research Centers, check the following website:

Ohio History Connection Online:
https://www.ohiohistory.org/research/local-government-records-program/

Many early Ohio records have been transferred to regional network centers, such as county government records, vital records, university records, and many others. Regional centers also have original newspapers or microfilm copies of newspapers for counties in their region. As an example of local records, many genealogical records for Cincinnati and Hamilton County have been computerized and are available at the University of Cincinnati.

For Bowling Green State University use this link for Center for Archival Collections:
https://www.bgsu.edu/library/cac.html

For Ohio University use:
https://www.ohio.edu/library/

Ohio Network of American History Research Centers

Ohio History Connection, Archives/Library Division, 800 E. 17th Ave., Columbus, OH 46211
https://www.ohiohistory.org/resource/local-government-records-program/

University of Akron, Archival Services, Polsky Bldg., Akron, OH 44325
https://www.uakron.edu/libraries/archives/collecions/local-government-records.dot

University of Cincinnati, Archives and Rare Books Department, Blegen Library, 8th Floor, Cincinnati, OH 45221
https://libraries.uc.edu/libraries/aarb/collections/local-government.html

Western Reserve Historical Society, Library, 10825 East Blvd., Cleveland, OH 44106
https://www.wrhs.org/research/library

Wright State University, Special Collections and Archives, Paul Laurence Dunbar Library, Dayton, OH 45435
https://www.libraries.wright.edu/special/localgovernment/

Youngstown Historical Center of Industry and Labor, Archives/Library, 151 W. Wood St., P.O. Box 533, Youngstown, OH 44501
https://www.youngstownohiosteelmuseum.org/

FamilySearch

The Genealogical Society of Utah (GSU) was organized on 13 November 1894 in Salt Lake City, Utah, with the purpose of gathering, preserving, and sharing genealogical information. Starting with a collection of 300 books, it was sponsored by The Church of Jesus Christ of Latter-day Saints (LDS Church) with the purpose to establish and maintain a genealogical library for use by its members and others. The library changed its name over the years and is now known as the FamilySearch Library. It has the largest collection of genealogical materials, and FamilySearch is the largest genealogical organization in the world. Opened in its new location in 1985, The FamilySearch Library is located in Salt Lake City. Use of the library and its many services, both in person and online, is free and open to the public.

FamilySearch Library's collection includes over 2.4 million rolls of microfilmed genealogical records, 727,000 microfiche, 555,009 digital books online, over 4,500 periodicals, access to 3,725 electronic resources and major online genealogical databases, 4.84 billion searchable genealogical and historical records, maps, pedigree charts, yearbooks, and other free genealogical materials. It is estimated the library had names of over 8 billion deceased individuals from over 100 countries. The library offers free online consultations and free lookup services. FamilySearch Library Welcome page:
https://www.familysearch.org/en/library

FamilySearch Library Collection:
https://www.familysearch.org/en/library/library-collection

The Genealogical Society of Utah began microfilming records of genealogical value in 1938, first in the United States and then internationally.[12] The scope of GSU was expanded during the use of the Internet and the founding of online genealogical services. A new website went live in May 1999, with the announcement of FamilySearch, now known as FamilySearch International.[13] FamilySearch is the name used to describe its family history efforts, products, and services. FamilySearch began digitizing its genealogical land historical records in 1998 and shifting from capturing microfilm images to digital images.

Images of original records (for example, births, marriages, death, church records, etc.) are digitized by some 300 digital cameras throughout the world. Digital images are then added to the Records section at the Search website and to the Catalog. See "Browse Records" section of the Search site. Once digital images are cataloged and indexed, minimal cataloging information is included—date, type of record, geographic jurisdiction and other data. After the images are cataloged and indexed, they are added to FamilySearch Catalog and appear in Historical Record Collections. Users are able to attach a link or copy records to individuals in FamilySearch Family Tree or as sources and Memories.

FamilySearch works with major genealogical partner services, family history websites, and online resources to accelerate the indexing of record collections, assist users to search more databases and records, and help connect generations:
https://www.familysearch.org/campaign/partneraccess

---

12. James B. Allen, Jessie L. Embry, and Kahile B. Mehr, *Hearts turned to the Fathers: A History of the Genealogical Society of Utah. 1894-1994.* (Provo, UT: BYU Studies, Brigham Young University, 1995).

13. FamilySearch is a nonprofit organization, sponsored and operated by The Church of Jesus Christ of Latter-day Saints and is free to the public. Appreciation to David E. Rencher, Chief Genealogical Officer, for his assistance.

FamilySearch partners include:
- Ancestry.com, has billions of online records of genealogical value and integrates its data with FamilySearch Family Tree. Ancestry includes Fold3.com (with an emphasis on military records); Newspapers.com; online family trees; U.S. census records since 1790; thousands of birth, marriage, and death records and related indexes; immigration records; Ohio Births and Christening Index, 1774-1973; church records and histories; family and local history books; U.S. passport applications, 1795-1925; naturalization records; biographical resources; land records; probate records; school yearbooks; city directories; and many other online genealogical and historical records.
- MyHeritage has billions of online genealogical records in over forty-two languages and offers unique matching technologies; millions of online family trees; billions of online genealogical and historical records; U.S. census records; vital records; animate family photos; colorized and restored family photos; and many other features.
- Findmypast.com's emphasis is on genealogical records from the British Isles; family trees; online vital records; British and Irish newspapers; many Irish resources; U.S. Catholic parish registers; and many other records.
- AmericanAncestors (New England Historic Genealogical Society) originally had an emphasis on New England families and immigration research, but has expanded its scope to include research throughout the U.S. It also has New England online databases and publications; journals; genealogies; biographies; local histories; The Great Migration Study Project; and other genealogical and historical resources.
- Filae.com: French archival records dating to the year 1500.

- Geneanet.org focuses on Continental Europe research, family trees, and indexed records.
- FamilySearch works with online genealogical databases, including several offering DNA testing services and analysis.

FamilySearch is closely associated with FamilySearch Library in Salt Lake City. The FamilySearch website contains:
- Digital Images and Personal Name Indexes
- FamilySearch Family Tree
- FamilySearch Genealogies
- FamilySearch Catalog
- FamilySearch Research Wiki

Digital Images and Personal Name Indexes. Most FamilySearch digital images, databases, and personal name indexes are available online for free, but some restricted images can only be viewed at a local FamilySearch Family History Center, FamilySearch Affiliate Library, or in Salt Lake City at the FamilySearch Library. There are over 5,700 local FamilySearch Centers and over 1,750 FamilySearch Affiliate Libraries, which include public, special, and university libraries. By using FamilySearch, users are able to Search Historical Records, browse Genealogical Collections, explore Historical Images, and FamilySearch Digital Library, search FamilySearch Genealogies, and use the FamilySearch Catalog. There are more than 13.7 million registered FamilySearch.org users.

FamilySearch Digital Library:
https://www.familysearch.org/library/books/
https://www.familysearch.org/en/library/digital-library

FamilySearch Family Tree helps users organize their genealogy, link to living and deceased family members, display and print family charts, including a fan chart, use Record Hints to learn more about families, and access billions of online genealogical records. Descendants can contribute to a single shared public profile or lineage on a global family tree where descendants can work together and share genealogical information using collaboration tools: **https://www.familysearch.org/tree/overview**

There are over 1.46 billion personal names in the free online FamilySearch Family Tree website and over 2.48 billion sources in the Family Tree.[14] Users are able to submit records, photos, stories, and audio recordings for inclusion in Memories and link them to family profiles in the online Family Tree. Two mobile apps are available: FamilySearch Memories mobile app and FamilySearch Tree app, where genealogical information can be uploaded to FamilySearch Family Tree. Memories saved in an online gallery can be organized into albums.

FamilySearch Genealogies has thousands of family trees, personal genealogies, lineages, and other histories, many submitted to FamilySearch. See "FamilySearch Genealogies" in the FamilySearch Research Wiki. Accuracy of genealogical data should be verified in original records, such as church and vital records.
https://www.familysearch.org/search/genealogies

Ancestral File: compiled genealogies submitted to FamilySearch before 2003.

International Genealogical Index (IGI): over 430 million names of ancestors containing birth, baptism (christening), marriage, or death dates.

Community Trees: lineage-linked genealogies for specific communities (e.g., residents of a town).

Guild of One-Name Studies: a collection of lineage-linked sourced genealogies.

Oral Genealogies: spoken lineage-linked genealogy interviews (For example, from Samoa).

Partner Trees: lineage-linked ancestor trees submitted before 2020 by users of MyTrees.com.

Pedigree Resource File (PRF): a growing collection of compiled genealogies submitted by users.

---

14. "FamilySearch.org Facts" (FamilySearch Newsroom, Nov. 2022) https://www.familysearch.org/en/newsroom/company-facts.

FamilySearch Catalog identifies and describes genealogical and historical records and materials held by the FamilySearch Library (formerly known as the Family History Library) in Salt Lake City, FamilySearch online records, and materials available at many FamilySearch Centers worldwide:
>   https://www.familysearch.org/search/catalog

The FamilySearch Catalog identifies place names (records by localities) where records have been acquired (usually digitized), surnames (family names), titles (of records), authors, subjects (topics), keywords (words or phrases), FamilySearch Library call numbers, microfilm/microfiche call numbers, and DGS Image Group Numbers. The online FamilySearch Catalog has over 1.72 billion digital images. Entries in FamilySearch Catalog are also identified in OCLC World Cat (the world's largest network of library content and services). Another useful resource is ArchiveGrid, a collection of some two million archival material descriptions.

Search Results from Historical Records: Users are able to combine keywords and surnames (for example, a surname and a locality). Some digitized images are only an indexed or transcribed records. Digital items and records are identified in the catalog with a camera icon, which means users can view images of original documents. A camera with a key icon means access to images are restricted for use in a Family History Center, an Affiliate Library, or FamilySearch Library in Salt Lake City. An Affiliate Library may have access to additional genealogical records not available in a Family History Center, such as digital images and personal name indexes. Searching the Library Catalog:
>   https://www.familysearch.org/en/library/searching-the-library-catalog

FamilySearch Research Wiki has over one hundred thousand articles that help users learn about genealogical records and resources in Ohio, other states, and countries internationally:
>   https://www.familysearch.org/en/wiki/Main_Page

FamilySearch Research Wiki is a free guide to hundreds of articles offering links to online genealogical articles, databases, and websites, along with suggested research strategies. Historical background and maps of localities, examples of genealogical records, and recommended research strategies help add to the usefulness of this resource. Also included are guidelines for using the FamilySearch Catalog and how to locate genealogical records of interest. Guided Research by localities is a useful feature which helps identify online resources, such as birth, marriage, and death records and online indexes. Community members are able to submit new information, update content, make changes, and offer suggestions to content in the Research Wiki. (It is not a website where users search for a single surname or given name, family names, or compiled genealogies). The Research Wiki may be translated to several non-English languages, such as French, Spanish, and Swedish. Example Ohio Wiki topics include "Ohio, United States Genealogy," "Guided Research," "Research Strategies," and "Record Finder." See also individual Ohio counties and other Ohio topics. Research Wiki provides information regarding the holdings of various libraries and record repositories in Ohio and elsewhere, including archives, public libraries, and historical societies.

Summary

FamilySearch has published the following statistics:[15]

- Total Digital images published in Historical Records section: 1.1718 billion. An image is a graphical representation (photograph) of an original, physical document.

---

15. FamilySearch.org Records and Partners by the Numbers (FamilySearch Newsroom, 5 Dec 2022), and "FamilySearch.org Facts" (FamilySearch Newsroom, Nov 2022)
https://www.familysearch.org/en/newsroom/company-facts.

- Total digital images published in Catalog viewer section: 4.935 billion. Digital images visible online via the catalog viewer only.
- Total records published in Historical Records section: 6.486 billion. A record is the information documented (transcribed) for a single life event.
- Total searchable names in Historical Records section: 11.95 billion Searchable names are all (transcribed) names contained on a record.
- Total collections on FamilySearch: 3,254 collections. A collection is a group of records and/or digital images published together.

Ohio FamilySearch Centers

Adams Ohio FamilySearch Center
    1185 Run Rd., Winchester, OH 45697
Akron Ohio FamilySearch Center
    106 E. Howe Rd., Tallmadge, OH 44278
Ashtabula Ohio FamilySearch Center
    571 Seven Hills Rd. Ashtabula, OH 44004
Athens Ohio FamilySearch Center
    7795 Lemaster Rd., The Plains, OH 45780
Canton Ohio FamilySearch Center
    735 Easthill Dr. NE, North Canton, OH 44720
Centerville Ohio FamilySearch Center
    901 E. Whipp Rd., Centerville, OH 45459
Cherry Grove/Eastgate Ohio FamilySearch Center
    695 Clough Pike, Cincinnati, OH 45245
Chillicothe Ohio FamilySearch Center
    1918 N. Bridge St., Chillicothe, OH 45601
Cincinnati Ohio East FamilySearch Center
    8250 Cornell Rd., Montgomery, OH 45249
Cincinnati Ohio FamilySearch Center
    5505 Bosworth Pl., Cincinnati, OH 45212
Clear Fork Ohio FamilySearch Center
    250 S. Street Rd., Galion, OH 44833
Columbus Ohio FamilySearch Center
    240 Red Rock Blvd., Grove City, OH 43123
Columbus Ohio North FamilySearch Center
    7135 Coffman Rd., Dublin, OH 43017
Columbus Ohio South FamilySearch Center
    2135 Baldwin Rd., Reynoldsburg, OH 43068
Dayton Ohio East FamilySearch Center
    3060 Terry Dr., Fairborn, OH 45324
Dayton Ohio FamilySearch Center
    1500 Shiloh Springs Rd., Dayton, OH 45326
Fairfield/Hamilton Ohio FamilySearch Center
    4831 Pleasant Ave. Fairfield, OH 45014

Findlay Ohio FamilySearch Center
   2800 Crystal Rd., Findlay, OH
Kirtland Ohio FamilySearch Center
   8751 Kirtland Rd (Route 306) Kirtland, OH 44094
Lima Ohio FamilySearch Center
   1195 Brower Rd., Lima, OH 45801
Lisbon Ohio FamilySearch Center
   7250 Market St., Lisbon, OH 44432
Mansfield Ohio FamilySearch Center
   1651 Middle Bellville Rd., Mansfield, OH 44904
Marion Ohio FamilySearch Center
   1725 Marion Edison Rd., Marion, OH 43302
Medina Ohio FamilySearch Center
   4411 Windfall Rd. Medina, OH 44256
Middletown Ohio FamilySearch Center
   4930 Central Ave., Middletown, OH 45044
Mount Vernon Ohio FamilySearch Center
   1010 Beech St., Mount Vernon, OH 43050
National Underground Railroad Freedom Center FamilySearch Center
   50 E. Freedom Way, Cincinnati, OH 45202
New Albany Ohio FamilySearch Center
   5835 Central College Rd., New Albany, OH 43054
Oxford Ohio FamilySearch Center
   6600 Contreras Rd., Oxford, OH 45056
Rootstown Ohio FamilySearch Center
   2776 Hartville Rd., Rootstown, OH 44272
Sandusky Ohio FamilySearch Center
   4511 Galloway Rd., Sandusky, OH 44870
Solon Ohio FamilySearch Center
   5825 Liberty Rd., Solon, OH 44139
St. Marys Ohio FamilySearch Center
   925 Glenbrook, St. Marys, OH 45885
Toledo Ohio FamilySearch Center
   State Rt. 795, Perrysburg, OH 43551
Wauseon Ohio FamilySearch Center
   858 S. Shoop Ave., Wauseon, OH 43567

West Chester Ohio
    7118 Dutchland Pkwy, Middletown, OH 45044
Westlake Ohio FamilySearch Center
    25000 Westwood Rd., Westlake, OH 44145
Wilmington Ohio FamilySearch Center
    2343 Wayne Rd., Wilmington, OH 45177
Wintersville Ohio FamilySearch Center
    437 Powells Ln., Wintersville, OH 43953
Wooster Ohio FamilySearch Center
    1388 Liahona Dr., Wooster, OH 44691
Youngstown Ohio FamilySearch Center
    2205 Tibbits-Wick Rd., Girard, OH 44420
Zanesville Ohio FamilySearch Center
    3300 Kearns Dr., Zanesville, OH 43701

Ohio FamilySearch Affiliate Libraries

Akron-Summit County Public Library FamilySearch Affiliate
    60 S. High St., Akron, OH 44326
Ashtabula County District Library FamilySearch Affiliate
    4335 Park Ave., Ashtabula, OH 44004
Avon Lake Public Library FamilySearch Affiliate
    32649 Electric Blvd., Avon Lake, OH 44012
Briggs Lawrence County Public Library FamilySearch Affiliate
    321 S. Fourth St., Ironton, OH 45638
Brunswick Library FamilySearch Affiliate
    3649 Center Rd., Brunswick, OH 44212
Buckeye Library FamilySearch Affiliate
    6625 Wolff Rd., Medina, OH 44256
Carroll County Genealogy Library FamilySearch Affiliate
    24 Second St., Carrollton, OH 44615
Champaign County Library FamilySearch Affiliate
    1060 Scioto St., Urbana, OH 43078
Clermont County Public Library FamilySearch Affiliate
    180 S. 3rd St., Batavia, OH 45103
Cleveland Public Library FamilySearch Affiliate
    325 Superior Ave., Cleveland, OH 44114
Columbus Metropolitan Library FamilySearch Affiliate
    96 S. Grant Ave., Columbus, OH 43215
Cuyahoga County Archives FamilySearch Affiliate
    3951 Perkins Ave., Cleveland, OH 44114
Cuyahoga County Public Library - Fairview Park Branch
    FamilySearch Affiliate
    21255 Lorain Rd., Fairview Park, OH 44126
Findlay-Hancock County Public Library FamilySearch Affiliate
    206 Broadway, Findlay, OH 45840
Garnet A. Wilson Public Library FamilySearch Affiliate
    207 N. Market St., Waverly, OH 45690
Geauga County Public Library FamilySearch Affiliate
    12701 Ravenwood Dr., Chardon, OH 44024

Greenville Public Library FamilySearch Affiliate
    520 Sycamore St., Greenville, OH 45331
Hardin County Genealogy Society - Robert Reed Library
    FamilySearch Affiliate
    211 W. Franklin St., Kenton, OH 43326
Highland Library FamilySearch Affiliate
    4160 Ridge Rd., Medina, OH 44256
Holmes County District Public Library FamilySearch Affiliate
    3102 Glen Dr., Millersburg, OH 44654
Lebanon Public Library FamilySearch Affiliate
    101 S. Broadway St., Lebanon, OH 45036
Licking County Genealogical Society FamilySearch Affiliate
    101 W. Main St., Newark, OH 43055
Lodi Library FamilySearch Affiliate
    635 Wooster St., Lodi, OH 44254
Lorain Public Library System - Avon Branch FamilySearch
    Affiliate
    37485 Harvest Dr., Avon, OH 44011
Lorain Public Library System - Columbia Branch FamilySearch
    Affiliate
    13824 W. River Rd., N, Columbia Station, OH 44028
Lorain Public Library System - Domonkas Branch FamilySearch
    Affiliate
    4125 E. Lake Rd., Sheffield Lake, OH 44054
Lorain Public Library System - Main Branch FamilySearch
    Affiliate
    351 W. Sixth St., Lorain, OH 44052
Lorain Public Library System - North Ridgeville Branch
    FamilySearch Affiliate
    35700 Bainbridge Rd., North Ridgeville, OH 44039
Lorain Public Library System - South Lorain Branch
    FamilySearch Affiliate
    2121 Homewood Dr., Lorain, OH 44055
Luckey Branch Library FamilySearch Affiliate
    228 Main St., Luckey, OH 43443
Mansfield - Richland County Public Library - Bellville Branch
    FamilySearch Affiliate
    97 Bell St., Bellville, OH

Mansfield - Richland County Public Library - Butler Branch
FamilySearch Affiliate
21 W. Elm St., Butler, OH 44822
Mansfield - Richland County Public Library - Crestview Branch
FamilySearch Affiliate
1575 State Rt. 96, East Ashland, OH 44805
Mansfield - Richland County Public Library - Lexington Branch
FamilySearch Affiliate
25 Lutz Ave., Mansfield, OH 44904
Mansfield - Richland County Public Library - Lucas Branch
FamilySearch Affiliate
34 W. Main St., Lucas, OH 44843
Mansfield - Richland County Public Library - Madison Branch
FamilySearch Affiliate
1395 Grace St., Mansfield, OH 44908
Mansfield - Richland County Public Library - Main Library
FamilySearch Affiliate
43 W. 3rd St., Mansfield, OH 44902
Mansfield - Richland County Public Library - Ontario Branch
FamilySearch Affiliate
2221 Village Mall Dr., Ontario, OH 44906
Mansfield - Richland County Public Library - Plymouth Branch
FamilySearch Affiliate
29 W. Broadway St., Plymouth, OH 44865
Marysville Public Library FamilySearch Affiliate
231 S. Plum St. Marysville, OH 43040
Massillon Public Library FamilySearch Affiliate
208 Lincoln Way East, Massillon, OH 44646
Medina County District Library FamilySearch Affiliate
210 S. Broadway, Medina, OH 44256
Morley Library FamilySearch Affiliate
184 Phelps St., Painesville, OH 44077
Oberlin Public Library FamilySearch Affiliate
66 S. Main St., Oberlin, OH 44074
Ohio Genealogical Society FamilySearch Affiliate
611 St. Route 97 West, Bellville, OH 44813
Pemberville Public Library FamilySearch Affiliate
375 E. Front St., Pemberville, OH 43450

Piqua Public Library FamilySearch Affiliate
116 W. High St., Piqua, OH 45356
Portsmouth Public Library FamilySearch Affiliate
1120 Gallia St., Portsmouth, OH 45662
Preble County District Library FamilySearch Affiliate
450 S. Barron St., Eaton, OH 45320
Public Library of Steubenville & Jefferson County FamilySearch Affiliate
407 S. 4th St., Steubenville, OH 43952
Public Library of Youngstown & Mahoning County FamilySearch Affiliate
305 Wick Ave., Youngstown, OH 44503
Seville Library FamilySearch Affiliate
45 Center St., Seville, OH 44273
Stark County District Library FamilySearch Affiliate
715 Market Ave. North, Canton, OH 44702
Stony Ridge Branch Library FamilySearch Affiliate
5805 Fremont Pike, Stony Ridge, Ohf 43463
Stow-Munroe Falls Public Library FamilySearch Affiliate
3512 Darrow Rd., Stow, OH 44224
The Rutherford B. Hayes Presidential Center FamilySearch Affiliate
Spiegel Grove, Fremont, OH 43420
Toledo Lucas County Public Library - Birmingham FamilySearch Affiliate
203 Paine Ave., Toledo, OH 43605
Toledo Lucas County Public Library - Heatherdowns FamilySearch Affiliate
3265 Glanzman Rd., Toledo, OH 43614
Toledo Lucas County Public Library - Holland FamilySearch Affiliate
1032 S. McCord Rd., Holland, OH 43528
Toledo Lucas County Public Library - Kent FamilySearch Affiliate
3101 Collingwood Blvd., Toledo, OH 43610
Toledo Lucas County Public Library - King Road FamilySearch Affiliate
3900 King Rd., Toledo, OH 43617

Toledo Lucas County Public Library - Lagrange FamilySearch Affiliate
3422 Lagrange, Toledo, OH 43606

Toledo Lucas County Public Library - Locke FamilySearch Affiliate
703 Miami St., Toledo, OH 43605

Toledo Lucas County Public Library - Maumee FamilySearch Affiliate
501 River Rd., Maumee, OH 43537

Toledo Lucas County Public Library - Mott FamilySearch Affiliate
1085 Dorr St., Toledo, OH 43607

Toledo Lucas County Public Library - Oregon FamilySearch Affiliate
3340 Dustin Rd., Oregon, OH 43616

Toledo Lucas County Public Library - Point Place FamilySearch Affiliate
2727 117th St., Toledo, OH 43611

Toledo Lucas County Public Library - Reynolds Corners FamilySearch Affiliate
4833 Dorr St., Toledo, OH 43615

Toledo Lucas County Public Library - Sanger FamilySearch Affiliate
3030 W. Central Ave., Toledo, OH 43606

Toledo Lucas County Public Library - South FamilySearch Affiliate
1736 Broadway, Toledo, OH 43609

Toledo Lucas County Public Library - Sylvania FamilySearch Affiliate
6749 Monroe St., Sylvania, OH 43560

Toledo Lucas County Public Library - Toledo Heights FamilySearch Affiliate
423 Shasta Dr., Toledo, OH 43609

Toledo Lucas County Public Library - Washington FamilySearch Affiliate
5560 Harvest Ln., Toledo, OH 43623

Toledo Lucas County Public Library - Waterville FamilySearch
   Affiliate
   800 Michigan Ave., Waterville, OH 43566
Toledo Lucas County Public Library - West Toledo
   FamilySearch Affiliate
   1320 W. Sylvania Ave., Toledo, OH 43612
Toledo Polish Genealogical Society FamilySearch Affiliate
   420 Sandusky St., Toledo, OH 43611
Toledo-Lucas County Public Library FamilySearch Affiliate
   325 N. Michigan St., Toledo, OH 43604
Warren-Trumbull County Public Library FamilySearch Affiliate
   444 Mahoning Ave., NW, Warren, H 44483
Washington County Public Library FamilySearch Affiliate
   Washington St., Marietta, OH 45750
Wayne County Public Library FamilySearch Affiliate
   220 W. Liberty St., Wooster, OH 44691
Western Reserve Historical Society FamilySearch Affiliate
   10825 East Blvd., Cleveland, OH 44106
Worthington Libraries - Northwest Branch FamilySearch
   Affiliate
   2280Hard Rd., Columbus, OH 43235
Worthington Libraries - Old Worthington Library FamilySearch
   Affiliate
   820 High St., Worthington, OH 43085
Worthington Libraries - Washington Park Branch FamilySearch
   Affiliate
   1389 Worthington Centre Dr., Worthington, OH 43085

Ohio Genealogical Society

The Ohio Genealogical Society (OGS) located in Bellville, the largest state genealogical organization in the United States, maintains an expanding library of Ohio source materials that is open to the public. OGS members may use the library at no cost. Here researchers will find a valuable collection of over 5,000 family histories (compiled genealogies), county and other local histories, atlases, census indexes, 4,000 indexed family Bible records, cemetery records, genealogical periodicals, city and county directories, First Families of Ohio (FFO), Society of Civil War Families of Ohio (SCWFO), Century Families of Ohio (CFO), Settlers and Builders of Ohio (SBO), Society of the Families of the Old Northwest Territory (SFONT), and Military Order of Daughters and Sons of Ohio (MODSO) application papers, published Ohio genealogical source materials, and some manuscript material. Collection emphasis includes Ohio, the thirteen colonies, and states surrounding Ohio. OGS maintains an extensive Ancestor Card File with over 250,000 cards (submitted by OGS members), ancestor charts, and a growing microfilm collection. The Ancestor Card File is a major statewide research aid and should be searched for all early Ohio families. A selected listing of OGS library holdings follows.

The Society will answer correspondence or e-mail that relates to its holdings and general Ohio reference questions. They provide a research and copy service into their library holdings for OGS members and also the public. OGS publishes Ohio source material, periodicals, and sponsors a large annual genealogy conference and annual meeting each spring.

OGS chapters are found in most Ohio counties as well as Florida. A current list of OGS chapters and their addresses is published in *Ohio Genealogical Society Quarterly, OGS Genealogy News,* and the OGS website
https://ogs.org/about/chapters-2/

Most OGS chapters publish records for their respective geographical areas, such as ancestor charts, family Bible records, newspaper obituaries, gravestone inscriptions and cemetery records, military records, and many other local Ohio records for their particular area. See **https://www.ogs.org/about/chapters-2/** for a current list of chapters.

OGS also publishes *Ohio Records and Pioneer Families*, quarterly which includes Bible records, vital records, gravestone inscriptions, tax lists, military records, newspaper abstracts, queries, and other published Ohio records of genealogical value (surname indexes). Society information, genealogical indexes, links to other Ohio websites, the OGS library catalog, and much more are available on the OGS home page. OGS has a Lending Library of duplicate books for its members available for a small fee, and a Lending Library catalog is available. A history of OGS was compiled by Hartien S. Ritter, *History of the Ohio Genealogical Society, 1959-1984.*[16] OGS projects include collecting ancestor cards and pedigree charts from its members, obtaining copies of family Bible records, statewide church records survey, publishing Ohio records, identifying Ohio cemeteries, and posting data to their website.

The Society's website is **https://www.ogs.org**

The address of the OGS Library and headquarters is:

**Ohio Genealogical Society
611 State Route 97 West
Bellville, OH 44813**

---

16. Hartien S. Ritter, *History of the Ohio Genealogical Society, 1959-1984* (Mansfield, OH: Ohio Genealogical Society, 1984).

Ohio Genealogical Society Chapters

Allen County, 620 W. Market St., Lima, OH 45801
Ashland County, P.O. Box 681, Ashland, OH 44805
Ashtabula County, Ashtabula County District Library, 4335 Park Ave., Ashtabula, OH 44004
Athens County, Southeast Ohio History Center, 24 W. State St., Athens, OH 45701
Auglaize County, P.O. Box 2021, Wapakoneta, OH 45895
Belmont County, P.O. Box 285, Barnesville, OH 43713
Brown County, P.O. Box 83, Georgetown, OH 45121
Butler County, P.O. Box 13006, Hamilton, OH 45013
Carroll County, 24 Second St. NE, P.O. Box 36, Carrollton, OH 44615
Clark County, 117 S. Fountain Ave. P.O. Box 2524, Springfield, OH 45501
Clermont County, P.O. Box 394, Batavia, OH 45103
Cleveland: Greater Cleveland, P.O. Box 40254, Cleveland, OH 44140
Clinton County, P.O. Box 529, Wilmington, OH 45177
Columbiana County, P.O. Box 861, Salem, OH 44460
Coshocton County, P.O. Box 128, Coshocton, OH 43812
Crawford County, P.O. Box 1033, Bucyrus, OH 44820
Cuyahoga East, P.O. Box 24182, Lyndhurst, OH, 44124
Cuyahoga: Greater Cleveland, P.O. Box 40254, Cleveland, OH 44140
Cuyahoga Valley, P.O. Box 31074, Independence, OH 44131
Cuyahoga West, P.O. Box 45607, Westlake, OH 44145
Darke County, 205 N. Broadway, Greenville, OH 45331
Defiance County, P.O. Box 7006, Defiance, OH 43512
Delaware County, 84 E. Winter Street, Delaware, OH 43015
Fairfield County, 503 Lenwood Dr., Lancaster, OH 43130
Fayette County, P.O. Box 342, Washington C.H., OH 43160
Firelands Genealogical Society, P.O. Box 923, Norwalk, OH 44857
Florida Chapter, 211 Woodbury Ave. Mount Dora, FL 32757
Franklin County, 96 S. Grant Ave., Columbus, OH 43215

Fulton County, P.O. Box 337, Swanton, OH 43558
Gallia County, 459 Second Ave., P.O. Box 1007, Gallipolis, OH 45631
Geauga County, 110 E. Park St., Chardon, OH 44024
Greene County, P.O. Box 706, Xenia, OH 45385
Guernsey County, 125 N. Seventh St., Cambridge, OH 43725
Hamilton County, P.O. Box 15865, Cincinnati, OH 45215
Hancock County, P.O. Box 672, Findlay, OH 45839
Hardin County, 211 W. Franklin St., P.O. Box 520, Kenton, OH 43326
Harrison County, P.O. Box 301, Cadiz, OH 43907
Henry County, c/o Edwin Wood Memorial Library, 208 Northeast Ave., Deshler, OH 43516
Highland County: Southern Ohio Genealogical Society, P.O. Box 414, Hillsboro, OH 45133
Hocking County, 64 N. Culvert St., Logan, OH 43138
Holmes County, P.O. Box 136, Millersburg, OH 44654
Hudson Library and Historical Society, 22 Aurora Street, No. G, Hudson, OH 44236
Huron County, P.O. Box 923, Norwalk, OH 44857
Jackson County, P.O. Box 807, Jackson, OH 45640
Jefferson County, 501 Fifth St., Stratton, OH 43961; P.O. Box 2367, Wintersville, OH 43953
Knox County, P.O. Box 1098, Mt. Vernon, OH 43050
Lake County, Morley Library, 184 Phelps St., Painesville, OH 44077
Lawrence County, P.O. Box 1035, Proctorville, OH 45669
Licking County, 101 West Main St., Newark, OH 43055
Logan County, 521 E. Columbus Ave., Bellefontaine, OH 43311
Lorain County, P.O. Box 865, Elyria, OH 44036
Lucas County, 325 N. Michigan St., Toledo, OH 43624
Madison County, P.O. Box 102, London, OH 43140
Mahoning County, P.O. Box 9333, Boardman, OH 44513
Marion Area, P.O. Box 844, Marion, OH 43301
Medina County, P.O. Box 804, Medina, OH 44258
Meigs County, 34465 Crew Rd., Pomeroy, OH 45769
Mercer County, P.O. Box 437, Celina, OH 45822

Miami County Historical and Genealogical Society, P.O. Box 808 Piqua, OH 45356
Monroe County, P.O. Box 641, Woodsfield, OH 43793
Montgomery County, P.O. Box 1584, Dayton, OH 45401
Morgan County, P.O. Box 418, McConnelsville, OH 43756
Morrow County, P.O. Box 401, Mt. Gilead, OH 43338
Muskingum County, P.O. Box 2427, Zanesville, OH 43702
Noble County, P.O. Box 174, Caldwell, OH 43724
Ottawa County, P.O. Box 193, Port Clinton, OH 43452
Paulding County, 205 S. Main St., Paulding, OH 45879
Perry County, P.O. Box 275, Junction City, OH 43748
Pickaway County Historical Society, 210 N. Court St., Circleville, OH 43113
Pike County, P.O. Box 224, Waverly, OH 45690
Portage County, P.O. Box 821, Ravenna, OH 44266
Richland County, c/o OGS, 611 State Rt. 97 West, Bellville, OH 44813
Richland-Shelby Genealogical Society, P.O. Box 766, Shelby, OH 44875
Ross County, P.O. Box 6352, Chillicothe, OH 45601
Sandusky County Kin Hunters, Spiegle Grove, Fremont, OH 43420
Scioto County, P.O. Box 812, Portsmouth, OH 45662
Seneca County, P.O. Box 157, Tiffin, OH 44883
Southern Ohio Genealogical Society, P.O. Box 414, Hillsboro, OH 45133
Stark County, P.O. Box 9035, Canton, OH 44711
Summit County, P.O. Box 2232, Akron, OH 44309
Trumbull County, P.O. Box 309, Warren, OH 44482
Tuscarawas County, 307 Center St., Dennison, OH 44621
Union County, P.O. Box 438, Marysville, OH 43040
Vinton County, P.O. Box 306, Hamden, OH 45634
Warren County, 406 Justice Dr., Lebanon, OH 45036
Washington County, P.O. Box 2174, Marietta, OH 45750
Wayne County, P.O. Box 856, Wooster, OH 44691
Williams County, P.O. Box 293, Bryan, OH 43506
Wood County, P.O. Box 722, Bowling Green, OH 43402
Wyandot County, P.O. Box 414, Upper Sandusky, OH 43351

Ohio Genealogical Society
Lineage Societies

OGS created First Families of Ohio in 1964 for its members to honor their Ohio pioneer ancestors. As a result, published annual FFO rosters are useful research aids for locating early Ohioans.[17] A major genealogical reference source for the state is *First Families of Ohio Roster, 1964-2000.* Rosters are regularly listed in the *Ohio Genealogical Society Quarterly.* To be eligible for membership in FFO, OGS members must prove direct descent and residence of an ancestor who lived in Ohio before 1 January 1821 and submit documented application papers and a fee.

OGS also sponsors for its members the Society of Civil War Families of Ohio (SCWFO), a lineage society with the purpose of honoring participants in the Civil War, 1861-65. Either Union or Confederate service is acceptable, but the ancestor must have lived, served in Ohio, or died there; applicants must be a direct descendant or a collateral relative. SCWFO rosters are published annually in *Ohio Genealogical Society Quarterly.* As a result of interest in Ohio and Civil War, OGS publishes *Ohio Civil War Genealogy Journal* quarterly, which features Civil War-related material pertaining to Ohio soldiers and their units. Ohio's portion of the Civil War Soldiers System, a national database, is complete:
https://www.nps.gov/civilwar/soldiers-and-sailors-database.htm

---

17. Ohio Genealogical Society, *First Families of Ohio Roster, 1964-2000,* Sunda Anderson Peters and Kay Ballantyne Hudson, eds. (Mansfield, OH: Ohio Genealogical Society, 2001). Names of OGS members accepted are also identified in *The Report,* along with name of Ohio pioneer, FFO number, county, date, birth and death dates, spouse's name, name of FFO member, and membership numbers. See Amy Johnson Crow, "First Families of Ohio Roster, 2001-2002," *The Report* 42 (Summer 2002): 64-71.

Some FFO records are on microfilm at the FamilySearch Library, Salt Lake City and accessed at an affiliate library.

Settlers and Builders of Ohio (SBO) follows FFO's cut-off year 1820 with eligible years 1 January 1821 to 31 December 1860. Again, this is for direct descendants.

OGS also has Century Families of Ohio (CFO) which is open to direct descendants of any person living in Ohio from 1861 to a century prior to the current application.

The Society of the Families of the Old Northwest Territory (SFONT) is open to direct descendants of any person who lived in the Old Northwest Territory prior to Ohio statehood of 3 March 1803. This covers those persons who lived in what is now Indiana, Illinois, Wisconsin, or Eastern Minnesota (east of the Mississippi) between 13 July 1787 and 7 May 1800 (when Indiana Territory was created), as well as ancestors who lived in what is now Ohio or Michigan between 13 July 1787 and 3 March 1803, which is Ohio statehood. Also eligible are descendants of persons in what is now Ohio, Michigan, Indiana, Illinois, Wisconsin, or Eastern Minnesota prior to 13 July 1787 as a citizen of either France or Great Britain, or as a Native American, you may qualify.

Another lineage society offered by OGS is MODSO, the Military Order of the Daughters and Sons of Ohio. This ancestor must have been a resident of the State of Ohio who served in the armed forces of the United States or the British colonial forces of the original thirteen colonies prior to the American Revolutionary War. Any member of OGS who can prove honorable service in the armed forces of the United States as veterans or who is a current military service members with residency of the State of Ohio is eligible to become a member.

All applications must have the application form, the application fee, and full documentation.

See the following link for further information regarding each of these societies: **https://www.ogs.org/about/lineage/**

Other lineage societies dealing with Ohio include: Ohio Society, Colonial Dames; Mayflower Descendants; Ohio Society United States Daughters of 1812; Sons of Union Veterans, and others.

Ohio Genealogical Society Library: Selected Holdings [18]

1880 Ohio census (original schedules)
Ancestor Card File-250,000 card index to ancestors on member charts: ancestral cards submitted by OGS members giving name, birth, death, and marriage information for each person
Archives with 500 collections
Bible Records Card Index (every-name index to 4,000 Bible records at OGS) available as part of the database search on ogs.org
Biographies (for Ohio counties and other localities in the U.S.)
Census schedules (Ohio), 1820-1930, and many census indexes
Church and religious records
City and county directories for Ohio, 1825 to date
Court records for many Ohio counties
Databases with over 120 online and searchable through One Search
Digital genealogical records
Family Bible Records-photocopies of actual Ohio family Bible records of births, marriages, and deaths, plus an every-name index
Family Card Catalog-cross-referenced by family name if the genealogy covers surnames additional to those found in the title
Family Group Records indexed online
Family Histories over 5,000 located at OGS
Family Vertical Files-pamphlets, newsletters, correspondence, clippings, short articles, arranged alphabetically by family surname

---

18. This information is adapted from a handout available from the Ohio Genealogical Society, Bellville, OH. Appreciation is extended to Linda Swanson, OGS Collections Manager, for her valuable assistance and suggestions.

Genealogies: over 4,000 published family histories (compiled genealogies), alphabetically arranged on open shelves by surname
Lineage societies with over 6,000 applications for FFO, SBO, CFO, SCWFO, SFONT, and MODSO
Local histories and biographies, with emphasis on Ohio localities
Maps and atlases, cadastral maps for Ohio counties
Military records and rosters, especially for the Civil War Newspaper abstracts
Online Library Catalog-entered by author, title, subject, and county
Periodicals (Ohio emphasis) and OGS chapter newsletters
Resources for African American, Native American, and other under-represented groups
Tax records, 1801-1814 (and for other years) for Ohio localities
Transcriptions of wills, cemeteries, marriages, births, and deaths for Ohio counties
USGS complete set of Topographical maps for Ohio
Vital records (births, marriages, and deaths for Ohio counties for various time periods)
Yearbooks, the largest known collection with over 22,000 school and college yearbooks, alumni directories, and annuals

Manuscripts available at the Ohio Genealogical Society Library include the following (refer to the "OGS Manuscript Register" for further details): family Bible records, cemetery records, church records, correspondence, court records, diaries, family papers, funeral home records, genealogy charts, military records, newspaper clippings and newspaper obituaries, photographs, and others. Most of the OGS manuscript collections pertain to Ohio families.

Ohio Genealogical Society online searchable databases include the following at the OGS website: **https://www.ogs.org/search-databases/**. OGS online databases are available to Society members and several are available to non-members:

- OGS Bible Records Index
- Miami Valley Genealogical Index (Computerized Heritage Association, Miami County, OH)
- Online OGS Library catalog

Ohio History Connection

One of the finest collections of genealogical and historical records is available at the Ohio History Connection, formerly Ohio Historical Society and formerly Ohio State Archaeological and Historical Society, incorporated in 1885. With headquarters in Columbus, Ohio, the Ohio History Connection is responsible for preserving historically significant records, serving as the archives of Ohio.

Ohio History Connection Archives & Library holds an excellent collection of manuscripts and unpublished materials, books, maps and atlases, microfilms, microfiche, newspapers (including hundreds of digitized newspapers), oral histories, periodicals, and many other materials.

https://www.ohiohistory.org/research/archives-library/

Online databases include Chronicling America, Ohio Memory, OhioPix, Ohio History Central and Ohio History Journal. The Archives & Library provides in-library access to subscription databases Ancestry Library Edition, Fold3, and Newspapers.com, as well as Akron Newspapers Premium Access.

https://www.ohiohistory.org/research/

Archives & Library has created research guides to popular research topics, including Land Records, Military Records, Naturalization Records, Newspaper Research, Prison Records, Religious Records, Vital Records, Wills and Estate Research, among others.

https://www.ohiohistory.libguides.com/home/guides

Archives and Library Research Room is available to all researchers by appointment only.

https://ohiohistory.libcal.com/

Limited research services are available by email and correspondence. A list of private researchers for hire is also available.
https://ohiohistory.libguides.com/home/services

As the State Archives for the state, Ohio History Connection preserves the historical records of Ohio's legislative, executive, and judicial branches and works with state and local governments to preserve Ohio's history and its citizens.
https://www.ohiohistory.org/research/archives-library/state-archives/

In addition to a magnificent collection of Ohio newspapers, OHC has large holdings of compiled genealogies (family histories), county and other local histories, Ohio vital records, land records, tax lists, city directories, atlases and maps, military records, manuscript collections, genealogical and historical periodicals, biographies, state and local government records, naturalization records, quadrennial enumerations, and many other resources.

Researchers should begin by searching the online catalogs that describe the collections of the Ohio History Connection.

Print items in the collections are described in their library catalog:
https://ohiohistory.on.woldcat.org/discovery

Manuscripts, State Archives, and Audio-Visual Materials are described in the archives catalog:
https://aspace.ohiohistory.org/

Major Ohio History Connection websites and databases include:
"Ohio History Journal"
https://resources.ohiohistory.org/ohj/

"Ohio Death Records Index Search"
https://resources.ohiohistory.org/death/

"Ohio Memory"
https://ohiomemory.org/

"OhioPix"
https://ohiopix.org

Although partially dated, several important guides published by Ohio Historical Society and others may be useful to access their holdings.[19] The *Genealogical Researcher's Manual with Special References for Using the Ohio Historical Society Library* describes many Ohio sources among the genealogical and historical holdings of the society.[20] Although published some years ago, *A Guide to Manuscripts at the Ohio Historical Society* provides a catalog of collections of mostly private papers as of 1972.[21] For more current information, consult OCC and manuscripts catalog at the library. *Ohio County Records Manual* describes many local government records for Ohio.[22] *Ohio Municipal Records Manual* is an informative guidebook for municipal officials and will help genealogists understand records created and maintained at this level.[23] The OHC Library has a copy of the *Abstract of County Archives Inventory, 1803-1977*, an inventory of county records housed by regional research centers in Ohio.

---

19. Carol Willsey Flavell [Bell], "Research at the Ohio Historical Society," *Genealogy Journal* 6 (June 1977): 55-58. This article describes many genealogical sources available at OHS; however, it is now partially outdated.

20. Suzanne Wolfe Mettle, et al., comps., *Genealogical Researcher's Manual with Special references for Using the Ohio Historical Society Library* (Columbus: Franklin County Chapter, Ohio Genealogical Society, 1981). This volume s also useful for locating Ohio sources in other libraries. County township maps are included as well as other illustrations. This guide is now partially outdated.

21. Ohio Historical Society, *A Guide to Manuscripts at the Ohio Historical Society*, edited by Andrea D. Lentz and Sara S. Fuller (Columbus: The Society, 1972). Although this guide is dated, it gives useful descriptions of many manuscript collections at the Ohio History Connection.

22. Ohio Historical Society, *Ohio County Records Manual*, rev. ed. (Columbus: Ohio Historical Society, 1983).

23. *Ohio Municipal Records Manual*, rev. ed. editor David Levine, comp. George Bain (Columbus: Ohio Historical Society, 1986).

A summary of Ohio History Connection holdings includes audiovisuals, books, local government records, manuscripts, maps and atlases, microfilms and microfiche, newspapers, records of the State Archives, and many other records of genealogical and historical value.

Ohio History Connection provides free access to over one million full-text searchable Ohio newspaper pages through Ohio Memory and Library of Congress Chronicling America.

Ohio History Connection has an outstanding homepage on the internet which includes research guides, finding aids, indexes, and also describes many of its holdings and services.[24]

    https://www.ohiohistory.org

See also the Ohio Memory Project:
https://www.ohiomemory.org

Ohio History Connection address:
    Ohio History Connection
    Archives & Library
    800 E. 17th Ave.
    Columbus, OH 43211

---

24. Appreciation to Tutti Jackson, Reference Archivist, Ohio History Connection, for her reference assistance.

State Library of Ohio

The State Library of Ohio provides a variety of services to Ohio state government organizations, libraries in the state, and also Ohio residents. As a state agency organized in 1817, it coordinates and collaborates library services in Ohio.

State Library houses over one million items, including genealogical and local history items, microfilms, and microfiche.[25] Access to Internet sites, online digital collections, and electronic resources are available to library patrons. They also house rare books in Special Collections and rare government documents. Other resources include county and other local histories, newspapers, journals, and magazines—many which are digital and on microfilm. State Library houses military rosters for Ohio soldiers and sailors, and include rosters for the Revolutionary War, War of 1812, Civil War (Union), Spanish-American War, World War I, Ohio regimental histories, as well as pension indexes. Other items of interest include maps, library reference materials, Ohio Revised Code and Ohio Administrative Code, Sanborn Fire Insurance Maps for Ohio, 1867-1970 (digital collection), academic databases, county and local histories, Ohio county atlases, cemetery records, city directories, genealogical guidebooks, journals, magazines, newspapers, tax records, vital records (including marriage and death records), reference materials, and others. A number of genealogy materials were transferred to the Columbus Metropolitan Library (CML) in 2007. State Library houses a large collection of Ohio state government publications and federal government documents. They are a regional federal depository for federal government documents.

---

25. Appreciation to Nicole Merriman, head of Research & Catalog Services, State Library of Ohio, Columbus, for her library research and reference assistance.

The genealogy staff at the State Library compiled a valuable reference guide, *County by County in Ohio Genealogy*, which lists genealogical materials available at this library for each Ohio county.[26] This volume is arranged alphabetically by county and indicates whether titles are on microfilm. Petta Khouw compiled *Genealogy: Helping You Climb Your Family Tree*, which is a useful, but partially outdated, overview of Ohio sources and a description of the genealogical holdings at the State Library of Ohio.[27]

For many years the State Library was the depository for transcribed records generated by the Ohio Society of the Daughters of the American Revolution (DAR). Records included copies of vital records, church records, family Bibles, gravestone inscriptions, wills, military records, and many other valuable genealogical records. The DAR records were transferred to the Columbus Metropolitan Library (CML) in 2007.

In addition to the DAR collection, most printed genealogical, family history, and local history books and related materials were transferred to the Columbus Metropolitan Library (CML) in 2007.

---

26. Petta Khouw, et al., *County by County in Ohio Genealogy*, rev. ed. (Columbus: State Library of Ohio, 1996). Although partially outdated, this reference guide serves as a listing of some 16,000 volumes and 15,000 microforms in the former genealogy collection of the State Library of Ohio. It also identifies many DAR titles now housed at the Columbus Metropolitan Library. Website address for Khouw's book: **https://ohiomemory.org/digital/collectio/p267401ccp2/id1756**

27. Petta Khouw, *Genealogy: Helping You Climb Your Family Tree*, Occasional Paper, series 3, no. 2 (Columbus: State Library of Ohio, 1990). Although partially outdated, this is a valuable summary of Ohio genealogical sources. Consult also Petta Khouw, "Finding Roots at the State Library of Ohio," *Ohio Libraries* 9 (1996): 4-7.

In addition to the DAR collection, most printed genealogical, family history, and local history books and related materials were transferred to the Columbus Metropolitan Library (CML) in 2007 including the following resources:

- Joy Wade Moulton Collection, including her genealogy columns published in the *Columbus Dispatch* citing records from England, Ireland, Scotland, and Wales, and other records.
- Palatines to America (German Genealogy Society Collection).
- Huguenot Collection (French Protestants).
- Microfilm collection of U.S. federal population census schedules.
- City Directories

State Library has maintained a small collection of family history, genealogical, and historical records. They will distribute most of their circulating books to Ohio residents and other libraries participating in interlibrary loan. However, non-residents of Ohio are not eligible for a State Library card. Many of the genealogy and local history books that were not transferred to CML are available in the circulating book collection to libraries participating in interlibrary loan. State Library is a major reference and interlibrary loan source for other Ohio libraries, although their genealogy collection of books, microfilms, and microfiche is non-circulating. Some of the family and local history books that were not transferred to CML are now circulating books. State Library maintains directories of Ohio libraries, including all libraries in 251 public library systems, at Find An Ohio Library:

https://library.ohio.gov/using-the-library/find-an-ohio-library

In addition to Ohio materials, the State Library also houses collections of resources for most states that preceded Ohio into the Union, notably the New England states. An article by the library's staff, published in *The Report*, describes the holdings of the State Library.[28] A number of these materials were transferred to the Columbus Metropolitan Library (CML) in 2007.

In addition to the State Library's online catalog, major online genealogical databases and digital collections are available at the State Library, including Ancestry Library Edition, FamilySearch.org, Fold3.com (by Ancestry), HeritageQuest (library version), Civil War Research Database, academic databases, Genealogy and Local History Online (ProQuest), New England Ancestors (New England Historic Genealogical Society), African American Heritage, academic databases, and several other online electronic resources. Also available access to online resources at the Ohio History Connection—see especially Archives & Library website:
https://www.ohiohistory.org/research/archives-library/

Staff at the State Library offers free limited research service. They will check their reference sources if a researcher will provide an ancestor's name and county of residence. There is a fee for photocopies.

Ohio Library and Information Network, known as OhioLINK, was established in 1992 as a statewide library consortium consisting of 117 Ohio libraries, including 88 OhioLINK institutions—mostly college and university libraries in Ohio. It allows users to identify resources in the State Library of Ohio:

> **https://www.ohiolink.edu/content/ohiolink_resources**
> OhioLink Library Catalog:
> **https://www.ohiolink.edu/content/ohiolink_library_catalog**

---

28. "The State Library of Ohio," *The Report* 23 (Winter 1983): 187-88. Consult also Petta Khouw, "The State Library of Ohio," *Genealogy* 82-83 (January-February 1984): 20-22. Both of these articles are now partially outdated.

OhioLINK connects library services and provides access to over 44 million books, over 100 digital research collections and databases, over 37 million electronic journal articles, and other resources. OhioLINK is a member of the Ohio Technology Consortium (OH-TECH).

Established in 2000, Ohio Memory is a collaborative statewide digital library program of the Ohio History Connection and State Library of Ohio. It contains over one million digital images from primary and secondary sources, including photographs, maps, manuscripts, newspapers, books, and many other Ohio resources.
https://ohiomemory.org/

The Ohioana Library Association is a non-profit organization with headquarters housed in another part of the State Library's building in Suite 300. Ohioana Library holds books by or about Ohioans and biographical files of prominent Ohioans, periodicals, personal papers, scrapbooks, pamphlets, photos, and other Ohio resources. Ohioana Library's books and other collections are organizationally separate from the State Library; however, many of their resources are catalogued in the State Library's online catalog.

State Library of Ohio's website should be searched for updated information regarding their holdings and services. See especially State Library's Online Catalog, "Using the [State]Library":

Discovery Layer:	**https://library.ohio.gov** Keywords, titles or authors
Classic Catalog:	**https://catalog.library.ohio.gov**
Using the Library:	**https://library.ohio.gov/using-the-library**
State Library of Ohio website:	**https://library.ohio.gov**

Location and mailing address of the State Library:

**State Library of Ohio
274 East First Avenue, Suite 100
Columbus, OH 43201**

Columbus Metropolitan Library

The Local History and Genealogical Division (LHG) of the Columbus Metropolitan Library (CML) is located on the third floor of the main library at 96 South Grant Avenue in Columbus. The library began collecting genealogical and local history materials in 1873 when the library was created. The Local History and Genealogy Division was formed in 2015 and today holds over 83,000 published genealogical sources, which includes over 25,000 microfilms and many archival collections. The collection grew considerably in 2007 when the State Library of Ohio donated most of their genealogy books and related materials to the CML. The State Library of Ohio also donated their large collection from the Ohio Daughters of the American Revolution (DAR) Genealogical Records Committee.

The following genealogical and historical collections housed in the LHG include:[29]

- Local History and Genealogy Division houses family histories and compiled genealogies, local histories, military unit histories and other military records, Civil War sources, cemetery records, periodicals, many genealogical reference sources, and other resources, especially for central Ohio counties.
- Franklin County Genealogical and Historical Society Library genealogical records
- Huguenot Collection consisting of many historical items, including family histories, church, and naturalization records.[30]

---

29. "Local History & Genealogy Collection Guide" (dated April 2021) is available online. Appreciation is extended to Megan Sherran, librarian, for her reference assistance regarding the Columbus Metropolitan Lbrary's Local History & Genealogy division in Columbus, OH.

30. Huguenots were French Protestants exiled from France in 1685 when King Louis XIV revoked the Edict of Nantes. Many early immigrants settled in New York, Pennsylvania, Virginia, and South Carolina.

- Joy Wade Moulton Collection was received in 2005 from the State Library of Ohio. Joy Moulton was a professional genealogist who wrote a genealogy column for the *Columbus Dispatch* for over thirty years. Her collection covers genealogical records from England, Ireland, Scotland, and Wales, including directories, public records, and periodicals.
- Palatines to America Collection which emphasizes Germanic immigration to North America.[31] Records donated from the PalAm Society include ethnic genealogy, history, immigration and emigration, geography, travel, foreign language topics, and German farm histories compiled from original German farm and family documents.
- DAR Genealogical Records Committee of genealogy books and transcriptions from Ohio counties, including vital records, cemetery records, family and Bible records, church records, lineage books, and many other of genealogical value for Ohio.[32]
- Local history collection relating to the history of Columbus, Franklin County, and other central Ohio counties. Records include published histories, annual reports, documents, correspondence, school yearbooks, city and county directories, microfilms, local government records, photographs, and others.
- Ohio Biography Collection containing biographical materials relating to many prominent Ohioans.
- Department of Development historical materials from the City of Columbus Department of Development.
- Ohio Depository Library of Ohio state government publications.[33]

---

31. Palatines to America Society was founded 12 July 1975 in Columbus, OH.

32. DAR transcriptions should be used cautiously since these are not original records but are mostly typed copies from primary and other sources.

33. Columbus Metropolitan Library does not participate in the Federal Depository Library Program.

- Sanborn Fire Insurance Maps for Columbus from 1887 to ca. 1962. Digital copies of Sanborn maps for other Ohio localities are available through OPLIN.
- Columbus and Ohio Map Collection has cartographic materials regarding changes and growth in the city of Columbus and the state of Ohio.

Columbus Metropolitan Library website:
https://www.columbuslibrary.org/

Columbus Metropolitan Library online resource for searching articles, online catalog, and others:
https://www.columbuslibrary.org/search/

Local History and Genealogy Division's online website is:[34]
https://www.columbuslibrary.org/history-genealogy/

"Local History & Genealogy Collection Guide" describes genealogical records at LHG[35]
https://www.columbuslbrary.org/wp=content/uploads/2021/04/Collecton-Guide.pdf

Local History and Genealogy Division offers a free service for their reference staff to search recent online U.S. newspaper obituaries. Researchers may request copies for up to six newspaper obituaries per month:
https://www.columbuslibrary.org/request-obituary/

---

34. Individuals visiting the main library may request a one hour in-person consultation. Online reference assistance is also available.

35. Local History and Genealogy Division is digitizing much of their genealogical collections.

"My History," the library's digital collection with an emphasis on central Ohio, has over 1.5 million items, including artifacts, family histories, historical photographs, images, maps, local and neighborhood history, newspapers, yearbooks, and other valuable genealogical and local history materials:
https://www.columbuslibrary.org/myhistory/

Users with a Columbus Metropolitan Library card are able to check out materials and access library services throughout central Ohio. CML has twenty-three branch libraries located throughout Franklin County serving the Columbus metro area and is one of the largest public libraries in Ohio.

Public Library of Cincinnati and Hamilton County

One of the largest public libraries in the state, this library houses one of the largest genealogy collections in a public library in the country. Emphasis is on Ohio and surrounding states, including Virginia, but the collection covers all states and several foreign countries as well. With an extensive book and microform collection, the History and Genealogy Department houses over 100,000 genealogy books, including 11,000 compiled genealogies, state and local histories, a large newspaper collection with some 10,000 bound volumes, over 45,000 bound periodicals, city directories, church and cemetery records, published vital records, military histories, maps and atlases, and many others. The map and atlas collections are particularly valuable and include nineteenth-century land ownership maps. The collection at the main library includes some 100,000 rolls of microfilm (over 50,000 genealogy rolls and some 50,000 reels of newspapers) some 200,000 microfiche; passenger lists; city directories, military histories, maps, church and cemetery records, and slave and freedmen records and other sources. The Civil War collection–U.S. pension application indexes, regimental histories, Civil War narratives and diaries–are particularly strong for both Union and Confederate units. Newspapers are housed in the Magazines and Newspapers Department. For a description of their holdings, begin by searching the CINCH online library catalog (author, title, subject, and keyword) and the Family Surname (genealogy) index—a surname index to many printed compiled genealogies housed in this public library. Also useful is NEWSDEX (index to local newspapers).

> Public Library of Cincinnati and Hamilton County
> History and Genealogy Department
> 800 Vine Street
> Cincinnati, OH 45202
> https://chpl.org/genealogy-history/

Western Reserve Historical Society

Western Reserve Historical Society (WRHS) Library, Cleveland History Center, in Cleveland, Ohio, houses one of the largest genealogical and historical collections in America. Holdings include over 250,000 books, over 18,000 published family histories (books, pamphlets, and manuscripts), 25,000 volumes of newspapers, over 31,000 microfilm rolls, one million prints and historical photographs, 10,000 linear feet of processed personal papers and records (more than 34,000 images), ethnic records, over 3,000 unpublished manuscript collections, historic post card collections, and records of family associations.[36]

WRHS is particularly strong in original records of Cuyahoga County and other Northeastern Ohio counties, but also holds records for all counties. The library has a significant book collection, biographies, city directories, family histories, genealogical indexes, local histories, maps and atlases, newspapers (including ethnic newspapers), periodicals, microfilm copies of U.S. census non-population schedules from 1850 to 1880, census indexes, land and property records (including land ownership atlases), local histories; maps (including land surveys, plats, and field notes), military records and regimental histories, passenger lists, social history, and many other genealogical and historical resources. A large microfilm and microfiche collection and several valuable card files are available.

---

36. An excellent history of the Western Reserve is Harlan Hatcher's *The Western Reserve: The Story of New Connecticut in Ohio*, rev. ed. (Cleveland: World Publishing Co., 1966). For an overview of genealogical sources, consult Meredith B. Colket Jr., *The Widely Known "Western Reserve" in Ohio* (Cleveland: Western Reserve Historical Society Genealogical Committee, 1976), and George R. Griffiths, "The Western Reserve," *The Report* 17 (Spring 1977): 30-36, although these publications are partially outdated. A major biographical and historical reference for Western Reserve researchers is Mary Lou Conlin's *Simon Perkins of the Western Reserve* (Cleveland: Western Reserve Historical Society, 1968)). Consult also Harry F. Lupold and Gladys Haddad, eds., *Ohio's Western Reserve: A Regional Reader* (Kent, OH: Kent State University Press, 1988).

Online genealogical databases are available in the Reading Room. WRHS is a FamilySearch Affiliate Library providing online access to many resources from FamilySearch, including digitized original records and genealogical databases including Ancestry Library Edition, HeritageQuest Online, and American Ancestors (New England Historic Genealogical Society), and other online subscriptions. The library does not lend materials; all research items must be used in the Library Reading Room.

The library's manuscript collections include account books, church records, Civil War Records (diaries and photographs), diaries and journals, ethnic records for Cleveland and other localities, cemetery records and gravestone inscriptions, church and Jewish synagogue records, correspondence, deeds, funeral homes, immigration records and passenger lists, local government records (many records from county courthouses), military records, personal and family papers, photographs, newspapers and clippings, oral histories, probate records, school records, tax duplicates, township records, vital records (births, marriages, and deaths), and other genealogical and historical materials. These records are identified in the online catalog, manuscript guides available at the library, finding aids, and printed guides. Manuscript records are house in closed stacks and must be searched in person.[37]

·Researchers can search for keywords, titles, authors, subjects, library call numbers, and other search terms in the WRHS online Library Collections Catalog. Keyword searches are usually the best option for locating genealogical and historical library materials. For example, library materials can be identified by names of counties, cities and towns, and family names. See the search options on the main page: Manuscript Collections, Photograph Collections, Visual Materials, Map, Books, Periodicals and Newspapers, Analytics, Vertical Files, and Computer Files. Many larger manuscript collections include a finding aid describing contents of the collection.

---

37. Digital Cleveland Starts Here portal includes historical photographs for Cleveland and Northeast Ohio and other subjects.

https://www.wrhs.org/search-collections
(Library Collections Search)

http://catalog.wrhs.org/collections/search
(WRHS Library Collections)

Many collections emphasize Cleveland, Cuyahoga County, and especially Northeastern Ohio; however, the library collections are statewide in scope and also include areas outside Ohio. Library reference staff can provide copies of reference sources for those individuals who are unable to visit the library.[38]

In addition to collecting records for Ohio counties, the library houses many New England materials (especially for Connecticut), British records, and genealogical records for other localities as well. It houses the largest Shaker manuscript collection in America, covering the years from 1723 through 1952, together with a membership card file, manuscripts, and printed sources.[39] A descriptive published guide to the Shaker manuscript collection is available.[40]

The Research Library has a valuable online "Genealogy Index" which provides references to many of its indexed genealogical resources, church records, funeral home records, Cuyahoga County cemetery inscriptions, Jewish marriage and death notices, 1907 Cleveland voter registrations, and other records. With over 320,000 entries, it is a personal name index and combining the "Bible Records Index" and 'Biographical Sketch Name Index."

---

38. Appreciation to Ann K. Sindelar, Library Reference Supervisor, Cleveland History Center, for her library research and reference assistance at the WRHS Library Research Center in Cleveland.

39. Shakers are also known as the United Society of Believers in Christ's Second Appearing (Coming). Members of this movement live a celibate and communal lifestyle, although only a few Shakers exist today, mostly residing in Maine.

40. Kermit J. Pike, *A Guide to Shaker Manuscripts in the Library of the Western Reserve Historical Society* (Cleveland: Western Reserve Historical Society, 1974). This work includes an inventory of Shaker photographs in the WRHS. See also Shaker records housed in Archives and Manuscripts, New York Public Library, New York, NY.

WRHS has several auxiliaries for members, including African American Archives Auxiliary and the Genealogical Committee which provides lectures, meetings, seminars, workshops, and assists with genealogical collection development. The Genealogical Committee publishes a quarterly publication, *WRHS Genealogy Bulletin*, which contains articles and lists regarding library collections, general genealogy interest articles, online resources, obituaries, and other articles. *Family History News* is a monthly online publication to individuals who request it.

Major WRHS websites include:

Western Reserve Historical Society[41]
https://www.wrhs.org

Research Library
https://www.wrhs.org/research/library/
https://www.wrhs.org/research/library/services

Family History & Genealogical Research
https:/www.wrhs.org/research/library/genealogy

---

41. See especially "Research & Collections" and "Library Collections Search." Also available is the Cleveland History Center's "Cleveland Starts Here," which includes many exhibits, images, interviews, maps, photographs, and various digital Cleveland and Northeast Ohio local history resources.

A major publication for using the WRHS Library is Kermit Pike's *A Guide to the Manuscripts and Archives at the Western Reserve Historical Society*, which gives a description of many voluminous manuscript collections found at the library in Cleveland, including

- General Collections, associations, account books, church and religious records, correspondence, court records, diaries, family and personal papers, journals, military records (especially War of 1812 and Civil War), notebooks, scrapbooks;
- Special Collections;
- Collections on Microfilm—Connecticut Land Company records and Shaker Manuscripts;
- Recent Accessions; and
- Ohio Government Archives arranged by county—court records and other county records, diaries, family papers, Civil War Records, school records, township records, and others. See the online WRHS Library Collections Search for updated information.[42]

The Society's address is:

Western Reserve Historical Society
Cleveland History Center Library
10825 East Boulevard
Cleveland, OH 44106

---

42. Kermit J. Pike, comp., *A Guide to the Manuscripts and Archives of the Western Reserve Historical Society* (Cleveland: Western Reserve Historical Society, 1972). Two related guides to the library are available: Kermit J. Pike, comp., *A Guide to Major Manuscript Collections Accessioned and Processed by the Library of the Western Reserve Historical Society Since 1970* (Cleveland: Western Reserve Historical Society, 1987), and Bari Stith, comp., *A Guide to Local Government Records in the Library of the Western Reserve Historical Society* (Cleveland: Western Reserve Historical Society, 1987). For historical material consult Robert A. Wheeler, ed., *Visions of the Western Reserve: Public and Private Documents of Northeastern Ohio, 1750–1860* (Columbus: Ohio State University Press, 2000)—a scholarly collection describing primary source documents for Northeastern Ohio before the Civil War.

Other Major Genealogical Collections

The following libraries have the federal population schedules from 1790 through 1950 online. Check the library for other online genealogical databases that they may have.

Allen County Public Library, Genealogy Center
900 Library Plaza
Fort Wayne, IN 46802
www.acpl.lib.in.us/genealogy

The Genealogy Center features more than 1.2 million physical items making it the largest genealogy library located in a public library. Over 72,000 compiled family histories; local histories; a large collection of genealogical and historical periodicals; gravestone inscriptions; all U.S. census schedules including agricultural, Indian (First Nations), mortality and slave; largest collection of Polk and other city and county directories; published vital records; military records; immigration records; and many other printed sources and microfilms. Emphasis is on Indiana, Ohio, and other Midwestern states, but the genealogy library collection is national in scope. The Center also offers many millions of record images presented on numerous online databases.

Brigham Young University
Harold B. Lee Library
Provo, UT 84602
http://www.lib.byu.edu

The Harold B. Lee Library, and the Utah Valley Regional Family History Center (the largest Family History Center of the FamilySearch Library in Salt Lake City), house one of the largest genealogical and historical collections in America—many of these resources pertain to Ohio and other Midwestern states. Here researchers will find over 650,000 rolls of microfilm, over 2 million microfiche, over 3 million books, many compact discs, some 250,000 maps, electronic databases, newspapers, genealogical reference books, indexes, manuscripts, and many other resources.

Cleveland Public Library
325 Superior Avenue, NE
Cleveland, OH 44114
https://www.cpl.org

An excellent collection of Ohio local histories and biographies, compiled genealogies, city directories, newspapers, vertical files, and other resources. Especially valuable is CPL's Cleveland Necrology File database, taken from an alphabetical card file (with records dating from the early 1800s to ca. 1975). For necrology data after 1975 refer to the *Cleveland News Index* **https://www-catalog.cpl.org/CLENIX**. Unless specified, resource databases may be available to all in Ohio who have a library card from any public library in Ohio. Many genealogical sources at the CPL have been placed on microfiche.

Cuyahoga County Public Library
Fairview Park Regional Library
21255 Lorain Road
Fairview Park, OH 44126
https://cuyahogalibrary.org/branches/fairview-park

This regional library has a strong collection of compiled genealogies, Ohio local histories, periodicals, printed Ohio genealogical records, indexes and abstracts of some Ohio vital records (such as the Cleveland Necrology File and Cuyahoga County Marriage License Index), general interest biographies, city directories for major U.S. cities, microfilms and microfiche (census schedules and other records), genealogical indexes, and many other resources. Emphasis is on Cleveland and Northeastern Ohio, but they also have sources for other areas of the state as well. A Genealogy/Local History Source File is a subject index to books, periodical articles, and microfilms available in the collection (however, this file is no longer maintained). This library is an example of one of the larger regional libraries in the state. See the "Addresses - Ohio" section later in this volume for additional addresses of other libraries in Ohio.

National Archives and Records Administration
Great Lakes Region
7358 South Pulaski Road
Chicago, IL 60629
https://www.archives.gov /facilities/il/chicago. html
https://www.archives.gov/facilities/great_lakes
_region.html

Original federal records for Ohio and other states in the region (Illinois, Indiana, Michigan, Minnesota, and Wisconsin); microfilms of genealogical records; census indexes; military service and pension records; immigration records; historical records received by federal agencies and courts in Ohio and other states; records of District Courts of the United States (bankruptcy, civil-law, equity, and admiralty) and criminal cases; naturalization records of the U.S. District Courts in Ohio from ca. 1850s to 1960s (Cincinnati, Cleveland, Dayton, and Toledo); naturalization papers (declarations of intention, petitions for naturalization, depositions, naturalization stubs); records of the Bureau of Land Management for land offices in Ohio, ca. 1800-1828; records of the Veterans Administration; records of the U.S. Customs Service; records of the U.S. Courts of Appeals; and other federal records. They do not house pension or service records for the twentieth century, and only limited pension and service records for the nineteenth century. See their website for descriptions of their holdings and finding aids. Consult also National Archives and Records Administration, *Guide to Records in the National Archives-Great Lakes Region,* compiled by Glenn Longacre and Nancy Malan (Chicago: National Archives and Records Administration, 1996).

Cleveland State University
Michael Schwartz Library
2121 Euclid Avenue
Cleveland, OH 44115
https://library.csuohio.edu

This library houses large collection of historical newspapers, local history collections, and other history resources.

Ohioana Library
274 East First Avenue, Suite 300
Columbus, OH 43201
https://www.ohioana.org

The Ohioana Library is located in the State Library of Ohio building near downtown Columbus in the Linda R. Hengst Room. Ohioana Library Association was founded in 1929 as a non-profit organization. Ohioana Library publishes *Ohioana Quarterly*, confers the Ohiana Book Awards presented to Ohio authors since 1942, and supports the Ohioana Book Festival. It is organizationally separate from the State Library.

Ohioana Library goals are to collect and preserve Ohio literature, including works by Ohio authors, artists, and musicians. Their collection includes over 45,000 books by or about Ohioans, and over 20,000 biographical files on prominent Ohioans, periodicals, personal papers, scrapbooks created by Ohio civic and cultural organizations, post cards, correspondence, newspaper clippings, personal papers, pamphlets, photos, and sheet music. Resources at the Ohioana Library include Ohio genealogy, local history, and church histories. Most of their collections are catalogued in the State Library's searchable online catalog, but their materials do not circulate to other libraries. Finding aids are available online. Researchers also have access to the OhioLINK Catalog and the online SearchOhio Catalog. Research is by appointment only.

State Library's online catalog:
https://catalog.library.ohio.gov/

Ohio State University Library
1858 Neil Avenue Mall
Columbus, OH 43210
https://www.lib.osu.edu

One of the largest libraries in the state, Ohio State University's Thompson Library houses many genealogical and historical resources and indexes, electronic databases, guides, bibliographies, Ohio local and regional histories, city directories, newspapers, published genealogical sources, periodicals and periodical indexes, biographies, legal references, and many other sources of interest to genealogists and historians. (See their website for online research tools and online catalog.) OSU's libraries are primarily academic libraries and not genealogical repositories. The Thompson Library is the main library on campus, although there are other libraries as well. OSCAR is OSU's online electronic catalog.

Toledo-Lucas County Public Library
Local History and Genealogy Department
325 North Michigan Street
Toledo, OH 43624
https://www.toledolibrary.org

This library owns a large genealogical book collection of over 35,000 volumes, including compiled genealogies, state and local histories, periodicals, newspapers and newspaper indexes, city directories, genealogical reference books, microfilms, electronic databases, biographies, published genealogical sources, vital records, church and cemetery records, military records, ancestor charts, maps, and many other resources. The *Toledo Blade* is on microfilm from 1835 to the present, as well as a comprehensive obituary file comprised of notebooks and index cards. The Toledo-Lucas County Public Library houses many printed sources for Northwest Ohio, for other areas of Ohio, and also for the six New England states, but also has records for other states as well.

The Newberry
60 W. Walton St.
Chicago, IL 60610
https://newberry.org
https://newberry.org/genealogy-and-local-history

The Newberry has over 17,000 published genealogies, with strong coverage of Colonial America and New England. Local history collections include county, city, town, church, and local histories from all areas of the U.S. as well as Canada and the British Isles. Published indexes, abstracts or transcriptions of pre-twentieth century records of birth, death, and marriage, probate, deed, court, tax, and cemetery records are available primarily for the Mississippi Valley to the Eastern Seaboard. The Newberry's collections of Civil War unit histories and genealogical periodicals are one of the country's best.

Xenia Community Library
76 E. Market St.
Xenia, OH 45385
https://greenelibrary.info/resources/history/

The History and Genealogy Department at the library contains cemetery records from over 130 cemeteries in Greene County, OH, the newspapers the *Cincinnati Enquirer* and the *Dayton Daily News*, census records, birth and death records 1869-1909, Sanborn Fire Insurance Maps, Ohio Soldiers' & Sailors' Orphans' Home inventory of surnames from Applications for Admission (later called the Ohio Veteran's Children's Home) in Xenia, and online computer databases. Xenia Library is one of the community libraries in the Greene County public library system.

Guides to Repositories

Numerous guides exist on both the state and national levels to help researchers explore Ohio repositories. The *American Library Directory* is the standard reference on the subject of the United States and Canada and includes addresses of Ohio libraries.[43] Addresses of historical and genealogical societies, museums, and similar organizations in Ohio are listed in *Directory of Historical Organizations in Ohio*, 5th edition (1996).[44] Addresses of genealogical societies exclusively, both in Ohio and in other states, are listed in *Meyer's Directory of Genealogical Sources in the U.S.A. and Canada*,[45] although this work is partially outdated. *Guide to Manuscripts Collections and Institutional Records in Ohio* lists addresses of many church archives, college archives, public libraries, historical societies, and other libraries in the state.[46]

---

43. *American Library Directory*, 2 vols. 54th ed. (New Providence, NJ; Bowker, 2001)

44. Ohio Historical Society, *Directory of Historical Organizations in Ohio* 5th ed. (Columbus: Ohio Historical Society, 1996). This is a significant reference source for identifying Ohio historical societies, museums, and similar libraries and societies in the state. See also American Association for State and Local History, *Directory of Historical Organizations in the United States and Canada*, 15th ed. (Walnut Creek, CA: Alta Mira Press, 2002).

45. Mary Keysor Meyer, ed., *Meyer's Directory of Genealogical Societies in the U.S.A. and Canada*, 10th ed. (Mt. Airy, MD; Libra Publications, 1994). See also Dina C. Carson, ed., *Directory of Genealogical and Historical Societies in the U.S. and Canada* (Niwot, CO; Iron Gate Publishing, 1992)

46. David R. Larson, ed. *Guide to Manuscripts Collections and Institutional Records in Ohio* (Columbus: Society of Ohio Archivists, 1974). This work is now partially outdated.

Other references of value are Paul D. Yon's *Guide to Ohio County and Municipal Records for Urban Research,* which can be used to identify many of the municipal records in Ohio, provide inclusive dates for them and give their location.[47] Although partially outdated, Elizabeth Bentley's two reference guidebooks, the *County Courthouse Book* and *The Genealogist's Address Book,*[48] are valuable for locating addresses of interest to genealogists. The above guides are available at major libraries in Ohio and elsewhere.

Guides to regional and local libraries are also available for the state. See, for example, Dorothy Smith and Maggie Yax, *A Guide to Manuscripts, Special Collections and Archives, Paul Laurence Dunbar Library,* revised edition, a fine example of an Ohio regional archives inventory.[49]

---

47. Paul D. Yon, *Guide to Ohio County and Municipal Records for Urban Research* (Columbus: Ohio Historical Society, 1973). This guide gives the location of many local Ohio records, although it is partially outdated.

48. Elizabeth Petty Bentley, *County Courthouse Book* 2nd ed. Baltimore: Genealogical Publishing Co., 1995) and *The Genealogist's Address Book,* 4th ed. (Baltimore: Genealogical Publishing Co., 1998).

49. Dorothy Smith and Maggie Yax, comps., *A Guide to Manuscripts, Special Collections, and Archives, Paul Laurence Dunbar Library,* rev. ed. (Dayton, OH: Special Collections and Archives. Wright State University Libraries, 1996).

MAJOR SOURCES

Birth and Death Records

County-level registration of civil births and deaths in Ohio date from 1867 (record of births and record of deaths reported to the Probate Court). Some earlier records are sometimes available but are incomplete; however, even after mandated by law. Less systematic recording for some counties occurred as early as the 1850s (1856-1857), and a few such registrations may be found for even earlier years in the records of townships or other local governing bodies. The obligatory recording of Ohio's births and deaths on the state level began 20 December 1908.

Pre-1908 civil vital records on the county level—births, marriages, and deaths—are found in the Probate Court at each county courthouse, or they may be housed at the responsible Ohio regional center or county archives. Most early Ohio vital records are available on microfilm at the FamilySearch Library or they are available online at **https://www.FamilySearch.org**. Many vital records are available at the Ohio History Connection. Virginia E. McCormick's 1982 article in *The Report* provides a useful discussion of death—related sources in Ohio.[50]

Ohio death certificates for the period 20 December 1908 through 31 December 1944 are housed at the Ohio History Connection and may be accessed by mail. An index to deaths on microfiche and microfilm is also housed at OHC. The FamilySearch Library (Genealogical Society of Utah) has microfilmed indexes to Ohio death certificates for the period 1908-44, and the death certificates themselves, 1908-1953. The *Ohio Death Certificate Index* online database for the period 1913-1937, may be searched on the Internet at the Ohio History Connection site **https://www.ohiohistory.org/dindex**. This website is one of the major personal name indexes for the state.

---

50. Virginia E. McCormick, "Sources of Information about Death: A Strategy for searching by Mail," *The Report* 22 (Fall 1982): 125-29.

State level recording of birth certificates since 20 December 1908 and death certificates since 1 January 1945 are available from the Ohio Department of Health (Vital Statistics Office) in Columbus. The local health department will have birth and death certificates from 1908 to the present. Most government offices in Ohio respond to mail requests, and most records are open to the public. (See "Marriage Records" later in this volume.)

Delayed birth records may also be found in Ohio. These are described by the Ohio Revised Code as "Any birth certificate submitted for filing eleven or more days after the birth occurred constitutes a delayed birth registration."[51] In 1935 with the advent of Social Security, many Ohioans who were of age to receive it, had no birth certificate and needed one to apply.[52] Many times the delayed birth certificates will have births from the late 1800s and early 1900s recorded, well before the state registration requirements.

For adoption records prior to 1964, adults born and adopted in Ohio, and their lineal descendants, may access their records with proper identification. For the period of 1 January 1964 to 18 September 1996, adults can access their records. Adoptees brorn on or after 18 September 1996, who have reached the age of 21 may access their records if their birth parents consented and the consents are on file. If the adopted person is between 18-21 years old, his or her adoptive parents may access the adoption records.[53] Records of some nineteenth-century adoptions are available in county courthouses.

Other rich sources for locating birth and death records are family Bibles, military records, newspaper announcements, probate records, the 1900 U.S. federal population schedule (month and year of birth), and gravestones. These items will be discussed in further detail within their sections.

---

51. https://www.codes.ohio.gov/ohio-revised-code/section-3705.10

52. https://www.ssa.gov/policy/docs/ssb/v70n3/v70n3p27.html

53. https://www.adopteerightslaw.com/ohio-obc/

Ohio vital records have been transcribed by the DAR, and copies may be found at the DAR Library in Washington, DC, the FamilySearch Library, and many libraries in Ohio. Because of some transcription and typing errors, however, DAR records should be used with some caution.

The Ohio Genealogical Society Library in Bellville also has many family Bible records. Sometimes Bibles and family records were taken outside the state by family members or others making them more difficult to locate. However, when family Bibles and other family records are located, the effort may well be worth it. Information found in home sources—scrapbooks, newspaper clippings, correspondence, photographs, genealogies, and in published sources—should be verified by performing research into original records.

Cemetery Records

Gravestones and cemetery records are an important source for birth and death dates, names of spouses and children, and (sometimes) age, birthplace, parents' names, relationships, references to military service, and other genealogical and family history information. Occasionally a place of birth is given on a gravestone, for example, if a birth was in another state or a foreign country.

Many of the state's gravestones have been copied by the DAR, local genealogical organizations, and interested individuals. Additionally, the records of sextons, morticians, churches, and coroners may prove helpful in locating burial information in township, city, denominational, family, or private cemeteries. A variety of transcribed cemetery records are available at the Ohio Genealogical Society Library, Ohio History Connection, Columbus Metropolitan Library, Western Reserve Historical Society Library, public and other libraries in the states, as well as the FamilySearch Library in Salt Lake City.

Ohio genealogists and OGS chapter volunteers have done and exceptional job of providing published records of cemeteries and guides to locating such records. The major reference guidebook, *Ohio Cemeteries, 1803-2003*, identifies the location of cemeteries throughout Ohio and indicates if inscriptions have been published.[54] This guidebook does not include individual gravestone inscriptions or names of people who are buried in Ohio. The Ohio Genealogical Society has an active Cemetery Committee that continues to survey cemeteries and works with local OGS chapters.

---

54. Ohio Genealogical Society, Cemetery Committee, comp., *Ohio Cemeteries, 1803-2003*, (Mansfield, OH: Ohio Genealogical Society, 2003). Earlier titles were Ohio Genealogical Society, *Ohio Cemeteries*, Maxine Hartmann Smith, ed. (Mansfield, OH: The Society, 1978) and *Ohio Cemeteries Addendum* (Baltimore: Gateway Press, 1990).

A comprehensive and updated directory of Ohio cemeteries 1803-2003, was an OGS Ohio Bicentennial project.

Another useful work, *Ohio Cemetery Records*, provides actual inscriptions, conveniently bringing together those previously published in *The "Old Northwest" Genealogical Quarterly*.[55] These records may prove helpful to researchers working northeastern and central Ohio counties.

Other gravestone inscriptions have been published in genealogical periodicals and elsewhere. One fine example is the enormous cemetery compilation entitled *A Monumental Work: Inscriptions and Interments in Geauga County, Ohio, through 1983*, a 732-page indexed volume that includes maps of cemeteries and townships in Geauga County located in northeastern Ohio.[56]

Several online sites are useful for locating cemeteries:

Ohio Cemeteries (OPLIN)
https://www.oplin.ohio.gov

BillionGraves
http://www.billiongraves.com

Find A Grave
http://www.findagrave.com

Ohio Cemetery Records by state and county
https://ldsgenealogy.com/OH/Cemetery-Records.htm

---

55. *Ohio Cemetery Records Extracted from the "Old Northwest" Genealogical Quarterly* (Baltimore: Genealogical Publishing Co., 1984). This work comprises all the cemetery records in the fifteen volumes of the cited quarterly and is a companion to Marjory Smith's *Ohio Marriages*. *Ohio Cemetery Records*, has an excellent every-name index compiled by Elizabeth P. Bentley.

56. Violet Warren and Jeannette Grosvenor, comps, *A Monumental Work: Inscriptions and Interments in Geauga County, Ohio, through 1983* (Evansville, IN: Whipporwill Publications, 1985).

Census Records and Census Substitutes

United States census population schedules are one of the basic sources American genealogists use. For Ohio, the first extant federal census is 1820, however, Wood County is missing which encompassed much of Northwestern Ohio. A collection of federal population schedules from 1790 through 1950 is widely accessible on microfilm at the National Archives and Records Administration and its regional archives as well as Ancestry.com and FamilySearch.org. The Ohio Genealogical Society has Ohio census population schedules on microfilm for the years 1820-1930.

Researchers using the Ohio federal census schedules may wish to consult William Thorndale and William Dollarhide's *Map Guide to the U.S. Federal Census, 1790-1920*.[57]

A proxy "1790 Census" listing heads of household, mainly in Hamilton, Washington, and other early Ohio counties was published by Accelerated Indexing Systems.[58] Also by the same publisher are the census reference works, *Early Ohio Census Records* and *Ohio Early Census Index* covering various years before 1820.[59]

---

[57]. William Thorndale and William Dollarhide, *Map Guide to the U.S. Federal Censuses, 1790-1920* (Baltimore: Genealogical Publishing Co., 1995).

[58]. Ronald Vern Jackson, *First Census of the United States, 1790, Ohio North West Territorial Census Index* (North Salt Lake: Accelerated Indexing Systems, 1984). See also *Ohio, 1790, Volume Two* (North Sale Lake: Accelerated Indexing Systems, 1986).

[59]. Ronald Vern Jackson, Gary Ronald Teeples, and David Schaefenneyer, eds., *Early Ohio Census Records*, 2nd ed. (Bountiful, UT: Accelerated Indexing Systems, 1975-80), and Ronald Vern Jackson, et al., eds., *Ohio Early Census Index*, 2 vols. (Salt Lake City: A.G.E.S., 1980).

A Census of Pensioners of the Revolutionary War or Military Services was taken in 1840 and is published.[60] It shows pensioner's name, age, name of head of family with whom the pensioner resided on 1 June 1840, and town and county of residence. Remnants of the 1890 census, which suffered general destruction by fire in Washington, DC in 1921, include a special schedule of surviving Union Civil War veterans or their widows and are available for Ohio counties at the Ohio Historical Society, FamilySearch Library, and other libraries as well.

Statewide indexes to the federal population schedules of Ohio have been published for the years 1820 through 1880. Census indexes serve as major research aids for locating heads of households, although they do not index all names in households. Several large cities-notably Akron, Cincinnati, Cleveland, Columbus, Dayton, and Toledo-and an increasing number of counties have printed 1870 census indexes.

In addition to the more commonly known federal population census schedules, several auxiliary schedules were taken in early years-principally schedules of mortality (1850-80), agriculture, commerce and industry, and mining. All have genealogical significance, even though they do not intrinsically identify relationships.

---

60. *A Census of Pensioners for Revolutionary or Military Services* (Washington DC: Blari and Rives, 1841). Ohio pensioners are listed on pages 168-181. This work is indexed separately.

The most frequently used of these auxiliary enumerations, the mortality schedules, identify persons who died during within the twelve months immediately preceding the official census date of 1 June. Although some Ohio mortality schedules have not survived, they are extant for the years 1850 (Ohio counties alphabetically H-W), 1860 (all Ohio counties), 1870 (incomplete), and 1880 (counties A through Geauga County only). They are available on microfilm at the State Library of Ohio, the FamilySearch Library, and other libraries, and some are published.[61] Original mortality schedules and microfilm copies are housed at the Ohio History Connection. Various Ohio auxiliary census schedules are discussed by Dr. William B. Saxbe, Jr., in a useful article in *The Report*.[62]

Although Ohio did not take an official state census (as did Illinois, Massachusetts, Michigan, New Jersey, New York, and several other states), some local census substitutes are extant. Quadrennial enumerations listing adult males over twenty-one years of age as eligible voters were taken by township. Lists were compiled by county assessors at the same time that they assessed taxable property; they cover various years from approximately 1803 to 1911.[63] Prior to 1863 they recorded white males only. Quadrennial enumerations are records of potential voters-they are not complete for all Ohio townships but are very valuable when extant.

---

61. See for example, Ronald Vern Jackson, ed., *Mortality Schedule: Ohio, 1850* [counties H-W] (Bountiful, UT: Accelerated Indexing Systems, 1979), and Jeanne Britton Workman, *1880 Ohio Mortality Records: Counties Adams through Geauga* (North Olmsted, OH: S&J Workman, 1991), as two examples. Some Ohio mortality schedules have also been published in periodicals.

62. William B. Saxbe, Jr., "Nonpopulation Census Schedules, 1850-1880," *The Report* 24 (Spring 1984): 1-2.

63. Ann S. Lainhart, *State Census Records* (Baltimore: Genealogical Publishing Co., 1992). See also Ronald Vern Jackson, et al., eds., *Early Ohio Census Records* (Bountiful, UT: Accelerated Indexing, 1974), an introduction by K. Haybron Adams; and Ronald Vern Jackson, et al., eds., *Ohio Early Census Index*, 2 vols. (Salt Lake City: A.G.E.S., 1974-80). For a discussion of quadrennial enumerations see *Ohio Laws* 25 v 16 (1827) and Kenneth J. Winkle, *The Politics of Community: Migration and Politics in Antebellum Ohio* (Cambridge: Cambridge University Press, 1988), p. 189.

Valuable census substitutes do exist, principally tax records and tax duplicates, city directories (especially for large cities), school records, and land records. *The 1812 Census of Ohio: A Statewide Index of Taxpayers* serves as a statewide finding aid for Ohio for this time period.[64] Pre-1850 school records are particularly valuable as a genealogical source in Ohio. Most of these records give the name of the head of the family, and the names, ages, and sex of school-aged children.[65] School enumeration records are housed in public and other local libraries, as well as historical societies throughout the state; some are on microfilm at the FamilySearch Library. Random school records have been transcribed and published. School attendance books may also be helpful in locating names of ancestors. City and county directories also help locate people in large cities and may be useful as census substitutes.

---

64. *The 1812 Census of Ohio: A Statewide Index of Taxpayers* (Miami Beach, Florida: T.L C. Genealogy, 1992).

65. School records have been beneficial for the author in compiling Ohio genealogies. See, for example, Kip Sperry, "The Harrison Family: Manx Immigrants to the Western Reserve in Ohio," The Genealogist 5 (Fall I 984): 240-55.

Useful Ohio and U.S. census websites include the following:

Ancestry.com, Ohio Census, 1820-1950:
https://www.ancestry.com

Census Images-Ohio (USGenWeb Archives):
http://www.usgwarchives.net/census/cen_o.htm

Census Links (Ohio):
https://www.census-online.com/links/OH/

Cyndi's List: U.S. Census:
https://www.cyndislist.com/us/census/

Genealogy.com:
https://www.genealogy.com

HeritageQuest Online
https://www.heritagequest.com

RootsWeb:
https://www.rootsweb.com

U.S. Census Bureau Quick Facts:
https://www.census.gov/quickfacts/fact/table/US/PST045221

Church Records

Ohio's religious heritage is rich and panoramic. Major denominations in the state before 1900 included Baptist, Congregational, Episcopal, Lutheran, Methodist, Presbyterian, Roman Catholic, and others. Other religious groups in the state are African Methodist Episcopal, Amish, Brethren in Christ, Church of God, Church of the Brethren, Church of Christ Scientist, Disciples of Christ, The Church of Jesus Christ of Latter-day Saints (Mormon), Evangelical, Mennonite, Moravian, Quaker (Society of Friends), Reformed, Seventh-day Adventist, Seventh-day Baptist, Shakers, Unitarian, United Brethren, United Church of Christ (UCC), among others.[66] Jewish congregations in Ohio began to increase during the nineteenth century.

Church inventories exist, particularly those compiled by the Work Projects Administration, which describe many surviving church records in the state. Of the WPA titles, one of the most significant is *Inventory of the Church Archives of Ohio Presbyterian Churches.*[67] This inventory is available at the Presbyterian Historical Society in Philadelphia, Ohio History Connection in Columbus, and FamilySearch Library in Salt Lake City.

Church records are among the most useful of primary sources available for genealogical research in Ohio—although it must be remembered that not all Ohioans regularly attended church. The records created by the various denominations can substitute for nonexistent civil vital records, and in some cases they provide even better information than civil vital records.

---

66. *Churches in the Buckeye Country* (Religious Participation Committee, Ohio Sesquicentennial Commission, 1953).

67. Work Projects Administration, *Inventory of the Church Archives of Ohio Presbyterian Churches*, T.W. Marshall, comp. (Columbus: Ohio Historical Records Survey, 1940).

Church records usually contain minutes of church meetings and records of births, baptisms, marriages, deaths or burials, and other events. A place of previous residence is sometimes given; therefore, church records are useful in tracing migration of individuals and families to Ohio and within the state. The breadth and genealogical value of such records vary widely; some denominations or congregations kept better records than others, and some records have been preserved better than others.

Although church records are sometimes difficult to locate, a number of Ohio church records have been microfilmed, and many have been transcribed or published in books or periodicals. Many records may be found online. Good collections of church records are available at the Western Reserve Historical Society Library, regional centers in Ohio, and other libraries in Ohio. Many church records are online at FamilySearch,org, Ancestry.com, MyHeritage.com and others. Local churches may still have custody of original records, or they may be housed in denominational archives. For example, many Presbyterian Church records are available at the Presbyterian Historical Society in Philadelphia. Early Mennonite records are located at Bluffton College in Bluffton, Ohio.

Some Ohio church records have been published, most notably those of the Society of Friends (Quakers), which appear in Hinshaw's *Encyclopedia of American Quaker Genealogy*.[68] Many early records for Quaker meetings appear online at Ancestry.com. Church histories are also available for some congregations; they contain historical background as well as information on early church members and leaders.

---

68. William Wade Hinshaw, *Ohio Quaker Genealogical Records,* vols. 4-5 of *Encyclopedia of American Quaker Genealogy,* 6 vols. (Ann Arbor, MI: Edwards Brothers, 1946). These volumes are indexed. Consult also Willard Heiss, "Migrations of Quakers in the Late 18th Century," *National Genealogical Society Quarterly* 65 (March 1977): 35-44, which discusses Quaker migrations to the Old Northwest; and Corinne Hanna Diller, "Quaker Migrations," *The Report* 23 (Winter 1983): 196-97.

A useful historical overview of church groups in Ohio is *Advent of Religious Groups into Ohio.*[69]

Many early Ohio church records, mostly christenings, baptisms, and marriages are at FamilySearch.org.

The Ohio Genealogical Society in Bellville, Ohio, has an ongoing church records survey project that identifies church records in the state; this survey is being expanded and revised. Researchers should contact OGS regarding the status of this project for their area of research interest.

See also Sunny Jane Morton and Harold A. Henderson's, *How to Find your Family History in U.S. Church Records: A Genealogist's Guide.*[70]

---

69. Ferne Reedy Lubbers and Margaret Dieringer, eds., *Advent of Religious Groups into Ohio* (Mansfield, OH: Clark County Chapter, Ohio Genealogical Society, 1978).

70. Sunny Jane Morton and Harold A. Henderson, *How to Find your Family History in U.S. Church Records: A Genealogist's Guide* (Baltimore: Genealogical Publishing Co., 2019).

Court Records

Court records contain an abundance of primary source materials of interest to genealogists and historians. Within Ohio, various judicial levels that need to be searched include Chancery Court (1802-1851), Circuit Court, Court of Common Pleas, District Court, Probate Court, Supreme Court, as well as other state and local courts. Court records commonly include record books, court dockets (a listing of cases held each term), bonds, petitions, minutes, journals, final records, case files (loose papers), adoption records, guardianships, appearance dockets, civil dockets, civil journals, Chancery records, criminal journals, execution dockets, jury books, ministers' license records, record of bonds, Sheriff's returns, Justice of the Peace dockets, trial lists, witness records, and related indexes. Ownership of land may suggest that a case was generated in Chancery records, and these records often provide names of family members, relationships, residence, and other valuable genealogical information. Occasionally, family information may be found in criminal and similar court records.

Ohio's court records may be found in county courthouses and in regional network centers in Ohio; many court records are on microfilm at the FamilySearch Library in Salt Lake City. Several Ohio counties have a county archives which house court and other local records (Cuyahoga and Geauga counties are two examples).

For adoption records prior to 1964, adults born and adopted in Ohio, and their lineal descendants, may access their records with proper identification. For the period of 1 January 1964 to 18 September 1996, adults can access their records. For adoptions on or after 18 September 1996, who have reached the age of 21, may access their records if their birth parents consented and consents are on file.

If the adopted person is between 18-21 years old, his or her adoptive parents may access the adoption records.[71] Records of some nineteenth-century adoptions are available in county courthouses.

Since the history of Ohio's court system is quite complex, researchers are advised to study David Levine's article in *The Report*[72] and Carrington Tanner Marshall's detailed study of the state's court system, *A History of the Courts and Lawyers of Ohio*.[73] *Baldwin's Ohio Revised Code: Annotated Ohio Administrative Code,* is a standard legal reference source that includes biographical sketches of many Ohio attorneys.[74] A useful Ohio court reference manual, though partially dated, is *A Digest of All Reported Decisions of the Courts of Ohio from the Earliest Period to Date*.[75] Transcriptions of early Ohio federal court records, 1803-1807, are published in *Ohio Federal Court Orders, 1809-1807*.[76] Also useful is the Ohio Revised Code for specific statues involving the open records laws.[77]

---

[71]. https://www.adopteerightslaw.com/ohio-obc/

[72]. David Levine, "Ohio's Court System," *The Report* 20 (Winter 1980): 171-74. See also, Diane VanSkiver Gagel, *Ohio Courthouse Records,* Ohio Genealogical Society Research Guide No. 1 (Mansfield, OH: The Society, 1997); Christine Rose, *Courthouse Research for Family Historians: Your Guide to Genealogical Treasurers,* 2nd ed. (San Jose, CA; CR Publications, 2020); and Christine Rose, *Courthouse Indexes Illustrated* (San Jose, CA: CR Publications, 2006).

[73]. Carrington Tanner Marshall, ed., *A History of the Courts and Lawyers of Ohio,* 4 vols. (New York: American Historical Society, 1934). This work includes many detailed biographies. See also Henry R. Timman, "Undiscovered Treasures in Ohio Court Houses," *The Report* 18 (Fall 1978): 93-98; Edward N. McConnell, "Ohio County Court Records: A Genealogical Research Tool," *Genealogy* 37 (May 1978): 1-5; and Frank R. Levstik, "A Guide to Ohio County Records for Genealogical Research," *Genealogy* 55 (August 1980): 6-7.

[74]. *Baldwin's Ohio Revised Code: Annotated Ohio Administrative Code* (Banks-Baldwin Law Publishing Co., 1996).

[75]. *A Digest of All Reported Decisions of the Courts of Ohio from the Earliest Period to Date* (Cincinnati: W.H. Anderson Co., 1952).

[76]. TLC Genealogy, *Ohio Federal Court Orders, 1803-1807* (Miami Beach, FL: TLC Genealogy, 1998).

[77]. Ohio Revised Code: **https://www.codes.ohio.gov/ohio-revised-code**

Directories

City directories and rural directories are useful in identifying an individual's residence. City directories are especially useful in locating people in large cities. They can be used along with and as a substitute for census schedules and other genealogical sources. They may be used for studying migration patterns of rural and urban people. City and rural directories are alphabetically arranged by surname and are published chronologically by years. Directories begin in the early nineteenth century and continue to present time. The volume and quality of directories after the 1860s improves dramatically.

In addition to the person's name (usually the head of the family), an address and occupation are shown (business and residence addresses are shown for individuals). Occasionally a wife's given name is shown and if she is a widow. Often a deceased husband's given name is shown for widows. Clues to when a person died or moved from an area may be found, and sometimes even a date of death. Civic information includes names and addresses of churches, schools, business firms, and others. The preface to city and rural directories may provide a great deal of local information, including a brief local history.

City and rural directories are available at public and university libraries; local historical societies; State Library of Ohio; Ohio History Connection; Ohio Genealogical Society, Bellville; Library of Congress, Washington, DC; Allen County Public Library, Fort Wayne, Indiana; and the FamilySearch Library, Salt Lake City. Major libraries within Ohio may have city directories for their locale.

County and rural directories are available for many areas of Ohio and show the name of person, residence (usually road or township), and other information. Researchers will also find locations of cemeteries, churches, children's homes, schools, funeral homes, and other businesses.

If no county or rural directory is available, check for local telephone books for addresses of people, schools, churches, and businesses.

"Blue Books," such as *The Cleveland Blue Book*, lists names of prominent residents, their address, and sometimes names of clubs they belong to and college degrees received. Club membership rosters may be included. A list of maiden names of females may also be included in "Blue Books."

Research Publications of Connecticut has made thousands of city and local directories available on microfiche and microfilm in a collection titled *City Directories of the United States*, which may be found in larger research libraries throughout America.

Representative titles of interest for this subject are:

City Directories: Southern Midwest, 1882-1898 (selected Ohio cities and years). **https://www.ancestry.com**

Ohio Museums Association. *Ohio Cultural Directory.* Columbus: OH Museums Association, 1998.
> Identifies historical societies, church archives, museums, genealogical societies, cemeteries, and similar organizations.

Ohio Physician and Dentist Directory, 1905
https://www.ancestry.com

Reilly, W.W. & Co., *W.W. Reilly & Co's Ohio State Business Directory for 1853-54.* Cincinnati: Morgan & Overend, 1853.
> List of post offices in Ohio, 1853-1854, and lists of businesses (such as newspapers); arranged by county.

Williams & Company, comp. *Ohio State Directory.* Cincinnati: Williams & Co., 1868-82.

Divorce Records

Jurisdiction for granting divorce in early Ohio was conferred by statute upon the State Supreme Court and the Court of Common Pleas in each respective county. Divorces may be found in records of Supreme Court, Chancery, Common Pleas, District Court, and elsewhere. Records of marriage dissolution are maintained by the Court of Common Pleas in each county. Contact the appropriate clerk of Court of Common Pleas in the county where the divorce was granted.

The State Supreme Court had jurisdiction over divorces during early statehood, but petitions were filed in the county court. Divorce records prior to 1851 may be found in State Supreme Court, County Supreme Court, County Chancery Court, or County Common Pleas Court records. Divorce appeals may have been made to Ohio's state legislature. Divorce records after 1913 are available in a division of the County Court of Common Pleas known as Domestic Relations Court.

A record of a divorce granted prior to 7 September 1949 may be recorded the County Clerk of Courts office of the county where the divorce was granted. Divorce abstracts from 7 September 1949 to the present are recorded at the Ohio Department of Health (Vital Statistics Office) in Columbus (an abstract is not a divorce decree). Certified copies of divorce records after 1949 are not available from the Ohio Department of Health. Certified copies of earlier divorce records may be available from the Court of Common Pleas where the divorce was granted. The address of the Ohio Department of Health is:

Ohio Department of Health
Vital Statistics
P.O. Box 15098
Columbus, OH 43215

Early Ohio divorce records are discussed by David G. Null in a useful article in the *National Genealogical Society Quarterly*, which includes a list of persons granted legislative divorce in Ohio between 1795 and 1852.[78] Mary L. Bowman compiled many abstracts and extracts of Ohio legislative acts and resolutions in *Abstracts and Extracts of the Legislative Acts and Resolutions of the State of Ohio, 1803-1821*, and continued for the period 1821-1831.[79]

A major guide to early Ohio divorce records is Carol Willsey Bell's *Ohio Divorces: The Early Years*.[80] An early discussion of divorce laws in Ohio is Henry Folsom Page's *A View of the Law Relative to the Subject of Divorce in Ohio, Indiana, and Michigan*.[81]

---

78. David G. Null, "Ohio Divorces, 1803-1852," *National Genealogical Society Quarterly 69* (March 1981): 109-14.

79. Mary L. Bowman, *Abstracts and Extracts of the Legislative Acts and Resolutions of the State of Ohio, 1803-1821* (Mansfield, OH: Ohio Genealogical Society, 1994. Continued with volumes 20 to 29, 1821-1831 (OGS, 1996).). This work is useful for locating laws relating to marriage and divorce, inheritance, and related topics.

80. Carol Willsey Bell, *Ohio Divorces: The Early Years* (Boardman, OH: Bell Books, 1994). See especially the introduction to this book for a discussion of divorce records in Ohio.

81. Henry Folsom Page, *A View of the Law Relative to the Subject of Divorce in Ohio, Indiana, and Michigan* (Columbus: J.H. Riley & Co., 1850). Discusses the early divorce laws of Ohio, Indiana, and Michigan.

Ethnic Records

Ohio is a state where many immigrants with different ethnic origins settle, especially in larger cities and industrial centers. Most early immigrants to America came from England, Ireland, and Germany. Ethnic groups to Ohio beginning in mid- to late nineteenth century and continuing into early twentieth century included African Americans, Asian (especially Chinese and Japanese), Croatians, Czechs, Germans, Greek, Hungarians, Irish, Italians; Jewish, Polish, Russians, Scots, Slovaks, Slovenians, (and immigrants from other Slovak countries) Hispanic (including Mexico, South America, and Spain); Native Americans; Norway, Welsh, and other immigrant groups, especially from Western Europe and later Eastern Europe countries as well.[82] Canadians also settled in Ohio beginning in the nineteenth century.

Many ethnic records are housed at the Ohio History Connection in Columbus, as well as university and public libraries and historical societies in the state. African American heritage is traceable in Ohio through various resources. An African American Archives, Cleveland Jewish Archives, Irish American Archives, newspaper and photograph archives, are housed at the Western Reserve Historical Society in Cleveland, along with similar archives for Acadians (French Canadians) and others. See especially WRHS Genealogy Index. Other repositories of ethnic resources include Ohio State University in Columbus, Cleveland State University in Cleveland, historical societies, and public libraries.

---

82. United States Census Bureau, "QuickFacts Ohio" **https://www.census.gov/quickfacts/OH**. See also Sharon DeBartolo Carmack, *A Genealogist's Guide to Discovering Your Immigrant & Ethnic Ancestors* (Cincinnati: Betterway Books, 2000); and Lubomyr Roman Wynar, *Ethnic Groups in Ohio, with Special Emphasis on Cleveland* (Cleveland: Cleveland State University, 1976).

Once an ancestor's name is known, the next step is to search for genealogical and historical records. Be sure to first search for records and documents in family and home sources. Records of value for research into Ohio ethnic groups include federal population census schedules since 1820, biographies, church records, immigration papers, gravestones and cemetery records, military records, ethnic and other newspaper, obituaries, civil registration (vital records), citizenship and naturalization records, passenger lists, photographs, and other records. Also valuable are records of social and cultural organizations and oral history interviews.

Regarding African American records, researchers should study David A. Gerber's scholarly work, *Black Ohio and the Color Line 1860-1915*.[83] Sara Fuller's *The Oho Black History Guide* is a useful bibliography of both published and unpublished works for this subject.[84] A representative title from the ranks of published source records in this field is Joan Turpin's *Register of Black, Mulatto, and Poor Persons in Four Ohio Counties, 1791-1861.*[85] Paul E. Nitchman's *Blacks in Ohio, 1880*, arranged by counties, identifies Africa Americans in the Ohio 1880 U.S. Census.[86] A general guidebooks is *African American Genealogical Sourcebook*, edited by Paula K. Byers.[87]

---

83. David A. Gerber, *Black Ohio and the Color Line, 1860-1915* (Urbana, IL: University of Illinois Press, 1976).

84. Sara S. Fuller, et al., eds., *The Ohio Black History Guide* (Columbus: Ohio Historical Society, 1975). A guide to printed materials, dissertations and theses, manuscripts, government records, and audiovisual materials for Ohio African Americans.

85. Joan Turpin, *Register of Black, Mulatto, and Poor Persons in Four Ohio Counties, 1791-1861* (Bowie, MD: Heritage Books, 1985); also, David Meyers, *Historic Black Settlements of Ohio* (Charleston, SC: History Press, 2020).

86. Paul E. Nitchman, *Blacks in Ohio, 1880*, 10 vols. (Decorah, IA: Anundsen Publishing, 1985-87. This is a useful reference for African American research in Ohio. See also "Blacks in Ohio in 1870 Who Were Born in Ohio,"*The Report* (Spring 2001): 4-10, and other issues of *The Report* (now *Ohio Genealogical Society Quarterly)*.

87. Paula K. Byers, ed., *African American Genealogical Sourcebook* (Detroit: Gale Research, 1995).

Other African American titles of interest to Ohio researchers include *African American Genealogy: A Bibliography and Guide to Sources and Bibliography of Sources for Black Family History in the Allen County Public Library Genealogy Department*, by Curt Bryan Witcher: *Black Genealogy*, by Charles L. Blockson; *Blacks Immigrating to Ohio, 1861-1863*, Special Enumeration, by the Auditor of State, Ohio Historical Society; *The Blacks of Pickaway County Ohio in the Nineteenth Century*, by James Buchanan; *Guernsey County's Black Pioneers, Patriots, and Persons*, by Wayne L. Snider; and *History of Black People in Dayton and Montgomery County, 1802-1887*, by Charles Mosley Austin. Ohio History Connection maintains an online digital collection of historical documents, titled *African America Experience in Ohio*, that focuses on the years 1850-1920 **https://ohiomemor.org/digital/collection/p16007coll98**.

Native American tribes in Ohio included, among others, the Delaware, Erie, Miami (the dominant group for much of Ohio), Ottawa, Seneca, Shawnee, Tuscarora, and Wyandot.[88] It is estimated that the original Native American population in Ohio did not exceed 45,000 people; by 1817 the Native American population had decreased drastically.

Bibliographies and reference sources for Ohio ethnic groups are available. See the "Ethnic Sources" bibliography later in this volume. Consult also "African American Resources for Ohio" (FamilySearch Research Wiki), Genealogy Bank, WikiTree, and others. See also "African American Heritage" online at the National Archives **https://www.archives.gov/research/african-americans**.

---

88. Randall L. Buchman, *The Confluence "The Site of Fort Defiance"* (Defiance, OH: Defiance College Press, 1994).

Family and Home Sources

The first place to begin your family history research is with personal knowledge about you and your family, then work back through the generations. Contact family members, such as parents grandparents, older siblings, or cousins, to determine what family history information they may have.

Family and home sources may include family Bibles, certificates (such as birth, marriage, and death), diaries, photographs, letters and postcards, church records, compiled genealogies, newspaper clippings, obituaries, funeral notices, scrapbooks, military records, naturalization papers, school records, legal papers, baby books, and similar records. Remember, Ohio family records, such as family Bibles, scrapbooks, and photo albums, may be kept with older family members. Records may have been taken to other states, such as when a couple retires to Arizona, California, Florida, or some other locality.

Record your information on pedigree charts and family group sheets—blank forms are readily available online and at stores that sell genealogical supplies. Many people use genealogy software programs, which also print charts and forms, and many people keep their records in three-ring binders or in file folders.

As you interview older family members, such as parents and grandparents, you might consider recording and then transcribing their oral history experience. In addition to asking specific questions about their life, be sure to ask "open-ended" questions, such as, "Tell me what it was like to experience the Great Depression when you lived in Cincinnati."

In summary, be aware of family traditions, but use them cautiously—work from known family information to the unknown, search family records and interview relatives, work on one or two generations at a time, be aware of possible spelling variations when doing research (especially surname variations), use a good note-keeping system, and cite your sources accurately and completely. You should share your family history information, copies of photos, and oral history transcriptions with other family members, and perhaps even with local libraries and historical societies. You may wish to place your compiled genealogy on your own website (but do not place names of living people online without their permission). Be sure to include notes and source references.

Websites such as Ancestry.com and FamilySearch.org have locations to build an online family tree. While clues may be given at these sites, be sure to verify each bit of information.

Libraries housing Ohio family history and local history sources may be interested in having a copy of your compiled genealogy, especially if it includes a title page, documentation is included with notes and sources, and it is indexed. In addition to your local public library, local genealogical society, and FamilySearch Centers, you might consider donating a copy of your compiled genealogy to one or more of the following libraries (this is a selected list; addresses are listed near the end of this volume):

  Allen County Public Library, Fort Wayne, IN
  Brigham Young University, Harold B. Lee Library, Provo, UT
  Cleveland Public Library, Cleveland, OH
  Columbus Metropolitan Library, Columbus, OH
  DAR Library, Washington, DC
  FamilySearch Library, Salt Lake City, UT
  Midwest Genealogy Center, Independence, MO
  Newberry Library, Chicago, IL
  New England Historic Genealogical Society, Boston, MA
  Ohio Genealogical Society, Bellville, OH
  Ohio History Connection, Columbus, OH
  Public Library of Cincinnati and Hamilton County, History and Genealogy Department, Cincinnati, OH
  St. Louis County Library, St. Louis, MO
  State Library of Ohio, Columbus, OH
  Toledo-Lucas County Public Library, Toledo, OH
  Western Reserve Historical Society, Cleveland, OH

Institutional Records and Lodges

Various public institutions-such as jails, penitentiaries, and county children's homes-have kept records of genealogical value.[89] These include inmate records, journals, applications, admission books, case records, and registers, among other catagories.. Many of these records are housed at the Ohio History Center and in county courthouses, Ohio regional centers, and some on microfilm at the FamilySearch Library. Occasionally, institutional records are published in the *Ohio Genealogical Society Quarterly* (formerly *The Report*) and in other Ohio genealogical and historical periodicals.

Institutional records may also include those living in a convent or seminary. To find a listing of those individuals at ten year increments, check the U.S. Federal Population Schedule for Ohio. From these clues, church records should be utilized.

Other institutional records, such as records of asylums, may also be useful to Ohio researchers, including those of such fraternal organizations as the Masons.[90] A history of Ohio Freemasonry and the Masons in the state was written by Allen E. Roberts, *Frontier Cornerstone: The Story of Freemasonry in Ohio, 1790-1980*.[91] A partial list of inmates at the Ohio State Penitentiary in Columbus is available online at:
https://www.ohiohistory.libguides.com/c.php?g=1110058&p=8092325

---

89. Carol Bell, "Little-Used Ohio Sources," *Genealogical Journal* 10 (March 1981): 13-24.

90. William B. Saxbe, Jr., "Masonic Records as Genealogical Sources," *The Report* 23 (Winter 1983): 195-96. Articles discussing similar organizations are frequently published in *The Report* (quarterly of the Ohio Genealogical Society, Bellville, OH), now *Ohio Genealogical Society Quarterly*.

91. Allen E. Roberts, *Frontier Cornerstone: The Story of Freemasonry in Ohio, 1790-1980* (n.p., Grand Lodge of Free and Accepted Masons of Ohio, 1980). Includes a list of lodges and officers.

Internet Addresses

Libraries and Library Catalogs

Academic Library Association of Ohio
    https://www.alaoweb.org
Bowling Green State University, Center for Archival Collections, Jerome Library, Bowling Green, OH
    https://www.bgsu.edu/library/cac.html
Cincinnati Historical Society Library
    https://www.cincymuseum.org/research/cincinnati_library.asp
Cleveland Public Library https://www.cpl.org
Columbus Metropolitan Library https:www.cml.lib.oh.us;
    https://www.columbuslibrary.org
Cuyahoga County Public Library, Fairview Park Regional Library
    https://www.cuyahogalibrary.org/branches/fairview-park
Find an Ohio Public Library https://www.library.ohio.gov/using-the-library/find-an-ohio-library/
German-American Collection, University of Cincinnati
    https://www.libraries.uc.edu/libraries/arb/collections/german-americana.html
Mennonite Historical Library, Bluffton, OH
    https://www.libguides.bluffton.edu/asc/mhc
National Archives-Great Lakes Region (Chicago)
    https://www.archives.gov/chicago
Oberlin College Library, Oberlin, OH
    https://www.oberlin.edu/libraries
OCLC First Search
    A combined catalog of holdings of thousands of libraries
    https://www.firstsearch.oclc.org
Ohio Genealogical Society
    https://www.ogs.org
Ohioana Library Association
    https://www.ohioana.org

Ohio History Connection, Columbus
    https:www/ohiohistory.org
Ohio History Connection, Archives/Library, Columbus
    https://www.ohiohistory.org/research/archives-library/
Ohio History Connection Resources, Columbus
    https://www.ohiohistory.org/research/archives-library
Ohio Libraries and Genealogical Societies
    https://wiki.rootsweb.com/wiki/index.php/Ohio_Archives,_Libraries-and-Societies
Ohio Library Council
    https://www.olc.org
OhioLINK: Ohio Library and Information Network
    Combined catalog of over 50 Ohio university and college libraries, including the State Library of Ohio
    https://www.ohiolink.edu
OhioLINK Central Catalog
    https://www.ohiolink.edu (Resources and services tab)
OHIONET
    https://www.ohionet.org
OHIONET, Reference Databases and Services
    https://www.ohionet.org/eresources
Ohio Network of American History Research Centers
    https://www.ohiohistory.org/research/local-government-records-program/
    https://homepages.rootsweb.com/~maggieoh/ohionet.html
    Note: Bowling Green State University and Ohio University are no longer a part of the research centers. However, they still retain local records.
Ohio Public Libraries
    https://www.publiclibraries.com/state/ohio
Ohio State University, William O. Thompson Memorial Library, Columbus
    https://www.library.ohio-state-edu/
Ohio University Archives, Athens
    https://www.ohio.edu/library
OPAL, Ohio Private Academic Libraries Catalog:
    https://www.opal-libraries.org/

OPLIN, Ohio Public Library Information Network:
    https://www.oplin.lib.oh.us
Ohio State University Libraries online catalog:
    https://www.library.osu.edu
Public Library of Cincinnati and Hamilton County, Cincinnati
    https://cincinnatilibrary.org
Society of Ohio Archivists
    https://www.ohioarchivists.org
Southeastern Ohio Regional Libraries
    https://www.serls.org
Stark County District Library, Genealogy Division, Canton
    https://www.starklibrary.org/home/genealogy
State Library of Ohio, Columbus
    https://library.ohio.gov
Toledo-Lucas County Public Library
    https://www.toldolibrary.org
University of Cincinnati Library, Cincinnati
    https://www.libraries.uc.edu
Western Reserve Historical Society, Cleveland
    https://www.wrhs.org
WorldCat
    https://www.worldcat.org
Wright State University, Dunbar Library, Dayton
    https://www.wright.edu
WWW Library Directory, Ohio
    https://www.librarytechnology.org/document/8659/
Youngstown Historical Center of Industry & Labor, Youngstown
    https://www.youngstownohiosteelmuseum.org/

Research Sources and Indexes

Along the Ohio Trail (download)
https://ohio.gov/government/resources/along-the-ohio-trails
Ancestry.com (Ohio census records and indexes; birth, marriage, and death records; biography and history, community and message boards; military records; reference and finding aids; and others
https://ancestry.com
Biographical Encyclopaedia of Ohio of the Nineteenth Century
https://ancestry.com
https://archive.org/details/biographicalency01robs_0
BLM Land Patents/OH GenWeb:
http://www.usgwarchives.net/oh/oh_blm.htm
BLM Land Records
https://www.ancestry.com
Bureau of Land Management
https://www.glorecords.blm.gov
Census Online, Ohio www.census-online.com/links/OH
Civil War, Ohio in the http://www.ohiocivilwar.com
Cleveland Necrology File http://www.cpl.org
Cyndi's List of Genealogy Sites on the Internet, Ohio:
https://www.cyndislist.com/oh.htm
Discover Ohio Genealogy WebRing:
https://www.accessgenealogy.com
Footpaths Across Ohio, County Information Page
http://homepages.rootsweb.com/~maggieoh/mohcoun1.html
GeneaLinks, Ohio Genealogy www.genealinks.com/states/oh.htm
Genealogy Mailing Lists for Ohio:
https://sites.rootsweb.com/~jfuller/gen_mail_states-oh.html
HeritageQuest Online (ProQuest)-Genealogy and Local History Online
https://www.heritagequestonline.com
History of the Western Reserve:
http://homepages.rootsweb.com/~maggieoh/western.html

Maggie's World of Courthouse Dust & Genealogy Fever:
    https://homepages.rootsweb.com/~maggieoh/mindex.html
Miami Valley Genealogical Index (Computerized Heritage Assoc.):
    https://gen.pcdl.lib.oh.us/miami/miami.htm
The Official Ohio Lands Book
    https://ohioauditor.gov/publications.html
Ohio Cemeteries
    https://www.ohiograveston4es.org/cemeteries.php
Ohio Census
    https://www.ancestry.com/serch/collections/catalog/?keyword=hio&catagory=35&location=38_2
Ohio Clickable County Map
    https://www.ohgenweb.org/map.php
Ohio County Courthouse Project
    https://homepages.rootsweb.com/~maggieoh/Courthouses/county_courthouses.html
Ohio Death Certificate Index, 1913-1937
    http://resources.ohiohistory.org/death/
Ohio Deaths, 1908-1932, 1938-2018
    https://www.ancestry.com/search/collections/5763/
Ohio Department of Health, Columbus
    https://odh.ohio.gov/
Ohio Early Land Ownership Records
    https://www.ancestrly.com/search/collections/4642/
Ohio GenWeb Project
    https://www.ohgenweb.org/
Ohio Genealogy
    https://www.genealinks.com/states/oh.html
Ohio Genealogy Forum
    https://www.genealogy.com/forum/regional/states/topics/oh/
Ohio Mailing Lists
    https://lists.rootsweb.com/listindexes
Ohio Maps
    https://fermi.jhuapl.edu/states/oh_0.html

Ohio Marriages, 1803-1900
   https://www.ancestry.com/search/collections/5194/
Ohio Memory: An Online Scrapbook of Ohio History
   https://www.ohiomemory.org
Ohio Military Men, 1917-1918
   https://www.ancestry.com/search/collections/7895/
Ohio Municipalities
   https://en.wikipedia.org/wiki/List_of_municipalities_in_Ohio
Ohio Newspaper Index (list of newspapers at OHC)
   https://ohiohistory.libguides.com/newspapers
Ohio Obituary Links
   https://www.legacy.com/us/obituaries/ohio
Ohio Public Library Information Network (OPLIN)
   http://www.oplin.ohio.gov
Ohio Query Surname Index
   https://sites.rootsweb.com/~ohfrankl/Free/query007.htm
Ohio Records on the USGenWeb Project
   http://www.usgwarchives.net/oh/
Ohio Research Outline ("Research Helps")
   https://www.familysearch.org/en/wiki/Ohio,_United_States_Genealogy
Ohio River Valley Families
   https://www.freepages.rootsweb.com/~harringtonfamilies/history/orvf.htm
Ohio's Guide to Genealogy
   https://www.familytreemagazine.com/ohio-genealogy/
Random Acts of Genealogical Kindness, Ohio
   https://raogk.org/ohio/
Rutherford B. Hayes Presidential Center (Online Obituary Index)
   http://index.rbhayes.org
State Archives: Ohio History Connection
   https://www.ohiohistory.org/research/archives-library/state-archives/

Vital Records Agencies in Ohio
>http:www.vitalchek.com/region_overview.asp?region_id+44

Vital Records Information, Ohio Links
>http://www.vitalrec.com/ohlinks.html
>http://www.vitalrec.com/oh.html

War of 1812, Roster of Ohio Soldiers
>https://www.familysearch.org/library/books/records/item/212664-roster-of-ohio-soldiers-in-the-war-of-1812?offset=1

Welcome to Ohio Genealogy
>http://www.geocities.ws/ohgenealogy/Index-2.html

Land and Property Records

Land was Ohio's most coveted commodity during the nineteenth century—the formative years of the state's development. The history of Ohio's land divisions and surveys is more complex than that of most other states because of various types of land grants and surveys that were common. See Introduction of Ohio Land History at **https://en.wikipedia.org/wiki/Ohio_Lands**.

After the Northwest Ordinance of 1787 was passed, the new territory of Ohio was parceled out by Congress in many different (but major) divisions—the Seven Ranges, Ohio Company's First and Second Purchases, the Donation Tract, Congress Lands, the French Grant (near Gallipolis), Virginia Military District, Symmes Purchase, Michigan Survey, Virginia Military District, United States Military District, Refugee Tract, and the Connecticut Western Reserve, (the Fire Lands, also called Suffers' Land, set off by the Connecticut Western Reserve today comprising of Erie and Huron counties and parts of Ashland and Ottawa counties), plus other grants for specific purposes. Ohio used the new rectangular (federal) survey system for much of the state, with the notable exception of the Virginia Military District, where the land was surveyed and divided into tracts six miles square, known as townships. Each township was divided into thirty-six one mile square sections. Section 16 was reserved for the use of public schools. The Virginia Military District was surveyed by the metes and bounds (indiscriminate) survey system used in the colonies. For platting land using the metes and bounds system, see DeedMapper by Direct Line Software.
https://directlinesoftware.com/

An illustrated study of Ohio land records is George W. Knepper's *The Official Lands Book*, but also valuable is Christopher Elias Sherman's Original Ohio Land Subdivisions.[92] The small paperback booklet *Ohio Lands: A Short History* offers an indispensable overview of the original land subdivisions and federal land grants in Ohio; it includes a section giving the origins of Ohio's county names.[93]

A related and useful booklet, especially for those beginning their Ohio research, is *Along the Ohio Trail: A Short History of Ohio Lands*.[94] Every serious Ohio genealogist should own a copy of George W. Knepper's *The Official Ohio Lands Book* (paperback booklet) and *Along the Ohio Trail* (paperback booklet).

---

92. George W. Knepper. *The Official Ohio Lands Book* (Columbus: Auditor of State, 2002). Includes many valuable Ohio maps. It is available in Paperback and online at
https://www.ohioauditor.gov/publications/docs/OhioLandsBook.pdf,

93. Thomas Aquinas Burke. *Ohio Lands: A Short History*, 9th ed. (Columbus Auditor of State, 1997). This useful booklet, formerly titled *Ohio Land Grants*, includes valuable maps and illustrations of interest to Ohio genealogists. Also helpful is Thomas Aquinas Burke, "Digging Into Ohio's Early Land Records," *Ohio Historical Society's Preview* 4 (Spring 1995) :11-13; Ulysses S. Brandt, "Land Grants in Ohio" in *Ohio History Sketches*, Francis B. Pearson and J.D. Harbor, eds. (Columbus: Fred J. Heer, 1903); Edward N. McConnell, "The Genealogical Value of Ohio County Land Records," *Genealogy* 31 (August 1977): 1-5. See also the superb treatise by Malcolm J. Rohrbough, *The Land Office Business: The Settlement and Administration of American Public Lands, 1789-1837* (New York: Oxford University Press, 1968) which describes the public domain organization of the General Land Office, military bounty lands, and related topics. Rohrbough includes valuable maps showing land districts and offices in the Old Northwest and elsewhere. Additional useful references are James C. Barsi, *The Basic Researcher's Guide to Homesteads and Other Federal Land Records* (Fort McKavett, TX: Nuthatch Grove Press, 1994), E. Wade Hone, *Land & Property Research in the United States* (Salt Lake City: Ancestry, 1997), and Benjamin Hibbard, *A History of the Public Land Policies* (Madison, WI, 1965). See also, Patricia Law Hatcher, *Locating Your Roots: Discover your Ancestors Using Land Records* (Baltimore: Genealogical Publishing Co., 2014).

94. Tanya West Dean and W. David Speas, *Along the Ohio Trail: A Short History of Ohio Lands* (Columbus: Auditor of State, 2001). On-demand printing, or download
https://www.ohioauditor.gov/resources/studentcenter.html

A brief description of Ohio land grants and surveys is given in *Atlas of the State of Ohio*.[95] Also, Meredith Colket's article in the *National Genealogical Society Quarterly* puts the subject of the Old Northwest and federal lands into historical perspective.[96] William E. Peters, in his *Ohio Lands and their History*, gives a detailed and illustrated overview of Ohio lands, tracts, grants, and early settlements; it is an essential reference for a study of Ohio lands and migration in the Buckeye State.[97]

Deeds and other land records may help identify family members and their residences, and they often help determine relationships or trace family migrations. As an example, a deed recorded in Franklin County, Ohio, executed by John Eaton (grantor) and Paul Deerdorf (grantee), shows John Eaton's previous place of residence: "this Indenture made this Nineteenth day of August 1807 between John Eaton and Elizabeth his wife of the Town of Halifax in the State of North Carolina of the one part, and Paul Deerdorf, of Franklin County in the State of Ohio of the other part"...[98]

Although origin and relationships are not always directly stated in a single land document, they may sometimes be ascertained by the meticulous extracting and correlating of all land records executed by a particular family. Within Ohio, land records are kept at the Recorder's Office in each respective county courthouse. Land records may also be found at regional centers, the Ohio History Connection, and other repositories in the state. Local records commonly contain the transfers of property between individuals.

---

95. Walling, *Atlas of the State of Ohio*, pp. 2-3. See also William D. Pattison *Beginnings of the American Rectangular Land Survey System, 1784-1800* (Columbus: Ohio Historical Society, 1957) and *The Public Domain: Its History with Statistics* (Washington, DC: Government Printing Office, 1880).

96. Meredith B. Colket, Jr., Genealogical Research in the Old Northwest," *National Genealogical Society Quarterly* 65 (March 1977): 25-34.

97. William Edward Peters, *Ohio Lands and their History*, 3rd ed. (1930; Reprint, New York: Arno Press, 1979). This work includes maps showing land divisions. It is especially useful for Ohio migration studies.

98. Original deed, Franklin County, Ohio, D:96-97. FamilySearch Library microfilm no. 285,067.

Most Ohio deeds are indexed by the *grantee* (buyer) and the *grantor* (seller); most of these indexes have been microfilmed. The FamilySearch Library in Salt Lake City has a significant microfilm collection of Ohio deeds, mortgages, surveys, field notes, tract books, and related indexes to land records—see the FamilySearch Library Catalog under headings "Ohio—Land and property" and "Ohio, County—Land and property" under the county of interest.

The majority of the early Ohio land records formerly housed at the Auditor of State's Land Office in Columbus have been transferred to the Ohio History Connection in Columbus. These include copies of early federal land grants (public domain records), Virginia Military District (VMD) land records (land entry and survey books), WPA plat books of Ohio counties in the VMD, card index files to VMD records, tract and entry books, original land survey field notes, deeds issued by the state of Ohio, records of real property owned by Ohio, card indexes to federal land records, and other sources. This collection does not include records for the Western Reserve (Northeastern Ohio) counties. An article describing the records formerly at the state Land Office has been published in *The Report*.[99] The only land records the Office of the Auditor of State has retained are the actual deeds for state-owned land.

---

99. Stephen M. Heer, "A Description of Genealogical Records Located in the Land Office of the Auditor of State and Suggestions Regarding Their Use," *The Report* 13 (Spring 1973): 8-12. It is wise to search the State Auditor's land files now at the Ohio History Connection, particularly if patents cannot be found on the Bureau of Land Management website. See also Amy Johnson Crow, "The Virginia Military District: A Study in Contradictions, "*NGS Newsmagazine* 28 (July/August 2002): 208-209, 246, and Daphne S. Gentry, comp. *Virginia Land Office Inventory*, 3rd ed. Revised by John S. Salmon (Richmond, VA: Archives and Records Division, Virginia State Library, 1981).

A typical land record series at the Ohio History Connection shows name of land office, date the land was sold, purchaser's full name, residence (in Ohio or elsewhere), description of tract purchased (section, township, and range), number of acres, price per acre, and total amount of money (information varies, depending on records).[100] Land records are especially valuable as a resource for tracing migration, and sometimes give a person's previous place of residence in another county or state.

Land patents, survey plats, land entry case files, and federal land tract books for the public lands portion of the state of Ohio, as with other states whose original titles trace to the federal government, are available from the Eastern States Office, Bureau of Land Management (BLM), 5275 Leesburg Pike, Falls Church, VA 22041 or visit their website
https://www.glorecords.blm.gov/default.aspx.

An extensive card file, patents, and miscellaneous land records are also available at the BLM.[101] The original land entry files, final certificates, and other related records—which offer more personal data on those individuals who took out land—are housed at the National Archives and Records Administration and are available by correspondence or in person.[102]

---

100. Ohio History Connection, State Archives, Auditor of State, Account of Lands Record of Land Sales, BV 3030, Series 4340 (original land records at Ohio History Connection, Columbus, OH) is an example of early Ohio land records.

101. Public domain states include all except the original thirteen states, Hawaii, Kentucky, Maine, Tennessee, Texas, Vermont, and West Virginia. Researchers seeking patents issued in Ohio or any of the public-land states east of the Mississippi River (including all of Louisiana) should contact the Bureau of Land Management, Eastern States Office, 5275 Leesburg Pike, Falls Church, VA 22041.

102. When ordering land case files from the National Archives, the request should be addressed to the attention of Textual Reference Branch-Land (NNRI), National Archives and Records Administration, Washington, DC 20408.

The legal description of the land (range, township, and section) is needed to search federal land records that are not indexed. Federal land records are now located at the National Archives, Washington, DC 20408. Information from the BLM website will lead the researcher to original land records housed at the National Archives. Microfilm copies of tract books at the BLM, which will guide the researcher to the patent volumes and case files, are also on microfilm at the FamilySearch Library, Salt Lake City.

Bounty land warrant applications and other land records stemming from Virginia's grants within Ohio should be obtained from the Library of Virginia, 800 E. Broad St., Richmond, VA 23219. Check their website at **https://www.lva.virginia.gov/**. Land Office Military Certificates for the Virginia Military District in Ohio are available online from the Library of Virginia's website. Many of these land records have been microfilmed. For example, *Ohio Land Office, Records Relating to Virginia Military Lands, 1787-1851*.

Several genealogists have published compendia, indexes, and miscellaneous reference works that are indispensable to Ohio's land research. Carol Bell's *Ohio Lands: Steubenville Land Office, 1800-1820* contains records of federal sales from that land office and shows the names and residences of proprietors, dates of acquisition, certificate numbers, and location of lands.[103] However, many other early Ohio land office records have not yet been published.

Other standard Ohio references that assist in tracing migrations of early settlers are *Early Ohio Settlers*, compiled by Ellen T. and David A. Berry in three volumes.[104] *First Ownership of Ohio Lands*, by Albion Morris Dyer,[105] and Mayburt Riegel's *Early Ohioans' Residence from the Land Grant Records*.[106]

---

103. Carol Willsey Bell, comp., *Ohio Lands: Steubenville Land Office 1800-1820*. (Youngstown, OH: The author, 1983).

104. Ellen T. and David A. Berry, comps., *Early Ohio Settlers: Purchasers of Land in Southeastern, Ohio, 1800-1840* (Baltimore: Genealogical Publishing Co., 1984) and *Early Ohio Settlers: Purchasers of Land in East and East Central Ohio, 1800-1840* (Baltimore, Genealogical Publishing Co., 1989).

105. Albion Morris Dyer, *First Ownershp of Ohio Lands* (1911; reprint, Baltimore: Genealogical Publishing Co., 1982). Online Ancestry.com

106. Mayburt Stephenson Riegel, comp. *Early Ohioans' Residences from the Land Grant Records* (Mansfield, OH: Ohio Genealogical Society, 1976).

Also of interest is William T. Hutchinson's *The Bounty Lands of the American Revolution in Ohio*, which contains useful bibliographies and historical background on the subject.[107]

Similar guides exist for Ohio's federally dispensed lands. Genealogists researching federal land sales should consult Clifford Neal Smith's valuable published *Federal Land Series*, which has meticulous every-name indexes, historical background describing federal land records, and valuable Ohio maps; these volumes may be found in many large libraries.[108] The *American State Papers* (Public Land Series), readily indexed in *Grassroots of America*, may provide personal details not to be found elsewhere.[109]

For a monumental and detailed history of the rectangular survey system, consult C. Albert White's *A History of the Rectangular Survey System*.[110] This work includes maps and illustrations. A useful history of Ohio lands was written by William E. Peters, *Ohio Lands and their Subdivision*.[111] A verbatim copy of the entry book and records of John Cleves Symmes was compiled by Christ McHenry in his *Symmes Purchase Records*.[112]

---

107. William Thomas Hutchinson, *The Bounty Lands of the American Revolution in Ohio* (PhD. diss. University of Chicago, 1927: New York: Arno Press, 1979).

108. Clifford Neal Smith, *Federal Land Series*, 4 vols. (Chicago: American Library Association, 1972-1986). These volumes identify many land grants in the Virginia Military District of Ohio.

109. United States Congress, *American State Papers: Documents Legislative and Execcutive of the Congress of the United States* (Washington, DC: Gales & Seaton, 1832-1861), 7 vols. Public Land Series. Phillip W. McMullin, Ed., *Grassroots of America A Computerized Index to the American State Papers* (Salt Lake City: Genedex, 1972), indexes the volumes of land grants and claims and vol. 24 of *American State Papers* claims, but does not index the entire series.

110. C. Albert White, *A History of the Rectangular Survey System* (Washington, DC: U.S. Deparment of the Interior, Bureau of Land Management, 1983).

111. William E. Peters, *Ohio Lands and their Subdivision* 2nd ed. (Athens, OH: W.E. Peters, 1918).

112. Chris McHenry, comp., *Symmes Purchase Records* (Lawrenceburg, IN: The author, 1979). Transcript of land records kept by John Cleves Symmes, 1787-1800.

Early land records for Chillicothe, an important early Ohio land office, 1800-1829, have been compiled by Marie Taylor Clark, *Ohio Lands: Chillicothe Land Office*.[113] Early Virginia military surveys in Ohio have been abstracted by Alma Aicholtz Smith, *The Virginia Military Surveys of Clermont and Hamilton Counties, Ohio, 1787-1849*.[114]

Another useful source is the Governor's Deeds Card Index, 1833-1994 (microfilmed). For an introduction to land sales in Ohio, early land divisions, Land Ordinance of 1785, and related topics, consult Denise Kay Mahan Moore's *Land Sales of Ohio*.[115]

Two representative collections microfilmed at the State Auditor's Office in Columbus and available at the FamilySearch Library include (see FamilySearch Library Catalog, "Ohio—Land and property"):

Ohio. Auditor of State. *Tract Books and Index for U.S. Lands in Ohio*. Microfilm.

Ohio: Surveyor General. *Field Books to U.S. Lands in Ohio*. Microfilm.

---

113. Marie Taylor Clark, comp., *Ohio Lands: Chillicothe Land Office* (Chillicothe, OH: The Author, 1984). See also *Ohio Lands: South of the Indian Boundary Line* (Chillicothe, OH: The author, 1984).

114. Alma Aicholtz Smith, *The Virginia Military Surveys of Clermont and Hamilton Counties, Ohio, 1787-1849* (Cincinnati: Alma A. Smith, 1985).

115. Denise Kay Mahan Moore, *Land Sales of Ohio* (Gautier, MS: The author, 1997).

Local Histories and Biographies

Regional, county, city, and other local histories are available for most Ohio localities, and some counties have more than one history or biography. In addition to historical background for the locality, most contain biographical sketches—especially of prominent citizens; lists of early settlers and township officers; military rosters; and accounts of military activities, church history with names of ministers for each denomination, and school history. Previous residence and dates of arrival are often given for early settlers. Some local histories include a map of the locality and other genealogical aids. Similarly, county and local atlases provide historical background, and many include biographical sketches. Many county histories and atlases have been reprinted with every-name indexes, although most are only partially indexed.

For assistance in locating Ohio local histories, consult online library catalogs and P. William Filby's *A Bibliography of American County Histories*.[116] Research Publications in New Haven, Connecticut, has microfilmed many Ohio county histories, atlases, and biographies (as well as similar titles for other states). These microfilms are available at major libraries. See Research Publications, *Reel Index to the Microform Collection of County and Regional Histories of the "Old Northwest," Series II: Ohio,* a guide to Ohio county and regional histories and atlases on microfilm; many of these titles are now out of print.[117]

Biographical works, sometimes known as *mug books,* are available for most Ohio counties and contain biographical sketches of prominent pioneers and early settlers.

---

116. P. William Filby, comp., *A Bibliography of American County Histories* (Baltimore: Genealogical Publishing Co., 1985).

117. Research Publications, *Reel Index to the Microform Collection of County and Regional Histories of the "Old Northwest," Series II: Ohio* (New Haven, CT: Reseaerch Publications, 1975). Sources are arranged by author or title. Research Publications has microfilmed many county and regional histories and atlases for other states as well.

Similar to biographies that appear in county and local histories, these are compiled sources; the genealogical information in them needs to be verified through research into original records. Even so, biographies provide much genealogical and biographical information useful as research clues—dates and places of births and marriages; parents' names and their spouses, residences, names of children, and other family details; occupation; education; military service information; civic, social, political, and religious affiliation; and family migration. Sometimes portraits and sketches of family homes and farms are included. Mug books may provide valuable clues for further research. The *Ohio Biographies Project* (part of the U.S. Biographies Project) is online at **https://us-biographies.org/ohio/index.html**.

Two representative titles are *The Biographical Encyclopedia of Ohio of the Nineteenth Century* and *Biographical History of Northeastern Ohio*.[118] Similar material may be found in such works as *Memorial to the Pioneer Women of the Western Reserve*, which is a valuable source for this area but is certainly not error free;[119] Harriet Taylor Upton's *History of the Western Reserve*, which has extensive biographical sketches and many portraits;[120] and *History of Ohio*, which highlights prominent Ohio citizens.[121]

---

118. *The Biographical Encyclopedia of Ohio of the Nineteenth Century* (Cincinnati: Galaxy Publishing Co., 1876) also Ancestry.com and *Biographical History of Northeastern Ohio* (Chicago: Lewis publishing Co., 1893). See the bibliography at the end of this volume for more biographical, genealogical, and other titles.

119. Gertrude van Rensselaer Wickham, ed., *Memorial to the Pioneer Women of the Western Reserve* (1896; reprint 5 vols. In 2, Evansville, IN; Whipporwill Publications, 1982). This biographical work includes an index to early Western Reserve pioneers.

120. Harriet Taylor Upton, *History of the Western Reserve*, 3 vols. (Chicago: Lewis Publishing Co., 1910). This work is known to contain some biographical and genealogical errors; information should be verified by research into other sources.

121. Galbreath, *History of Ohio*. Separately indexed by Robertalee Lent.

A splendid example of a comprehensive history of an American city is *The Encyclopedia of Cleveland History,* which includes many biographical sketches of prominent Cleveland, Ohio, citizens.[122]

The Ohio County History Surname Index, sometimes known as the Ohio Surname Index, is a valuable statewide card file, although it is not a complete personal name index to all Ohio local histories. Housed at the Ohio History Connection, it indexes some 450,000 names in Ohio county histories, atlases, biographical records, some newspapers and periodicals, and other sources. This personal name finding aid should be searched when researching early Ohio pedigrees in order to determine if a biographical sketch is available for an ancestor. Cards show a person's name, full bibliographic data, and page numbers where the sketch appears. Entries are alphabetical by surname. Researchers are cautioned, however, that the sources this index covers are basically those issued between about 1880 and 1915, not current publications. In addition, not every Ohio local history is indexed here nor are all counties represented. This file was compiled by DAR members during the period 1928-1936. It has been microfilmed and is available at the FamilySearch Library and other libraries. Copies of microfilms are available to libraries through inter-library loan from the Interlibrary Loan Department at the Ohio Historical Society in Columbus.

Don H. Tolzmann's *Ohio Valley German Biographical Index* is an index to sketches found in selected German-American histories and biographical directories.[123] See *County and Family Histories: Ohio, 1780-1970.*

---

122. David D. Van Tassel and John J. Grabowski, eds., *The Encyclopedia of Cleveland History*, 2 vols., 2nd ed. (Bloomington, IN: Indiana University Press,1996). Online **http://ech.cwru.edu.**

123. Don Heinrich Tolzmann, *Ohio Valley German Biographical Index* (Bowie, MD: Heritage Books, 1992). Focus is on the Ohio Valley with emphasis on the tri-state region of Ohio, Indiana, and Kentucky.

Maps, Atlases, and Gazetteers

Identifying place-names (localities) where ancestors lived is one of the first steps in family history research. Maps, atlases, gazetteers, reference guides, and other resources are available to help researchers learn more about Ohio place-names. Computer programs are also available, such as Ani-Map (county boundary historical atlas). This program displays over 2,300 maps to show county boundary changes since colonial times. Check **https://goldbug.com/animap/**. An online tutorial, by Nicky Smith for Animap is found at **https://fh.lib.byu.edu/2020/10/13/animap-by-nicky-smith-23-mar-2016/**

One of the most useful Ohio locality finding aids is Julie Minot Overton's *Ohio Towns and Townships to 1900: A Location Guide*.[124] This monumental work is an alphabetical listing of hundreds of pre-1900 Ohio towns and township names, showing in which county they are located, year organized, and other information. Another valuable reference is John S. Gallagher and Alan H. Patera's *The Post Offices of Ohio*.[125] This reference guide shows the name of the post office, date established, the date if discontinued, and where the mail should be sent.

---

124. Julie Minot Overton, *Ohio Towns and Townships to 1900: A Location Guide,* edited by Kay Ballantyne Hudson and Sunda Anderson Peters (Mansfield, OH: Ohio Genealogical Society, 2000). For additions see Kay Ballantyne Hudson, comp., "Ohio Towns and Townships to 1900, Addendum 1," *The Report* 41 (Summer 2001): 87-90. See also "100 Largest Townships in Ohio According to the 2000 Census," *OGS Genealogy News* 34 (January/February 2003): 20. Also consult Carol Mehr Schiffman, "Geographic Tools: Maps, Atlases, and Gazetteers," in Kory L. Meyerink, ed., *Printed Sources: A Guide to Published Genealogical Records* (Salt Lake City: Ancestry, 1998), pp. 95-144.

125. John S. Gallagher and Alan H. Patera, *The Post Offices of Ohio* (Burtonsville, MD: The Depot, 1979).

Begun in 1996, the David Rumsey Map has a digitized collection of over 117,000 items online, with new additions added regularly. David has donated his entire physical map collection to Stanford University where it is housed at the David Rumsey Map Center in the Stanford University Library. The Rumsey Map Center is open to the public. His free website is **https://www.davidrumsey.com**

Ohio websites for geographical studies include the following:
Ohio Locations:
http://homepages.rootsweb.com/~maggieoh/Towns
Ohio State Gazetteer and Business Directory for 1860-61:
https://babel.hathitrust.org/cgi/pt?id=miun.aja 2907.0001.001&view=1up&seq=9&skin=2021
Sanborn Fire Insurance Maps, 1882-1962, Ohio (over 40,000 detailed maps showing streets, buildings, businesses, and other useful locality details):
https://www.sanborn.ohioweblibrary.org/?t=INFOhio

Marriage Records

The recording of civil marriages in Ohio generally began with each county's formation. Ohio marriage records are available from the Probate Court in the county where the marriage occurred. These records include marriage records, marriage returns, marriage consents of minors by parents, (and sometimes non-consent), and ministers' license records.

Marriage records give the names of the bride and groom, date of event, county in which the marriage occurred and sometimes the specific place of the ceremony, and officiating party, additional information may be shown in later records, such as age and residence of the bride and groom, or if is not a first marriage. Because marriage records began at such an early date in Ohio and are complete for most periods, they are considered one of Ohio's most valuable genealogical resources. Names of brides and grooms are indexed on a county basis by a general index to marriages.

Both transcribed and microfilmed versions of actual marriage records are available in a variety of repositories. Marriage records since 7 September 1949 for some counties are available at the Ohio History Connection in Columbus. The Ohio Department of Health (Vital Statistics Office) in Columbus has marriage abstracts for Ohio counties from 7 September 1949 to the present (an abstract is not a marriage license, rather it shows basic information found on an original marriage license). Marriage licenses are not available from the Ohio Department of Health in Columbus (contact the Probate Court in the county for a copy of a marriage license). The address of the Ohio Department of Health is:

Ohio Department of Health Vital Statistics
P.O. Box 15098
Columbus, OH 43215-0098

Jean Nathan served as chairperson of a monumental reference work compiled by the Ohio Genealogical Society, *Ohio Marriages Recorded n County Courts through 1820: An Index.*[126] Names of brides and grooms are alphabetically arranged by surname, with date married, name of county, book or volume number, and page number. This work identifies all known court-recorded marriages in Ohio before 1821.

Transcriptions of early marriages for Ohio counties have been compiled by members of the National Society Daughters of the American Revolution (DAR) and are available at the National Society Library in Washington, DC, as well as the State Library of Ohio in Columbus. Microfilm copies of both the transcriptions and the original marriage records are available at the FamilySearch Library, Ohio History Connection, the appropriate regional center, and other major libraries in Ohio. Ohio marriage records have also been published by some individuals and organizations. A useful reference source for early marriage records is *Ohio Marriages Extracted from the Old Northwest Genealogical Quarterly.*[127]

Ohio marriages taken from several different sources and selected counties are available on Ancestry's website for the years 1803-1900:

http://www.ancestry.com/search/rectype/inddbs/51 94a.htm

---

126. Ohio Genealogical Society, comp., *Ohio Marriages Recorded in County Courts through 1820: An index,* Jean Nathan, chair (Mansfield, OH: Ohio Genealogical Society, 1996). Updated by OGS, *Ohio Marriages, 1821-1830.*

127. Marjorie Smith, ed., *Ohio Marriages Extracted from the Old Northwest Genealogical Quarterly* (Baltimore: Genealogical Publishing Co., 1980). Marriages are arranged alphabetically. *The Old Northwest Genealogical Quarterly* published from 1898-1912 in fifteen volumes, is a valuable reference source for Ohio genealogists.

Migration and Immigration Records

Individuals and families migrated to Ohio for a variety of reasons. Among these include Ohio's rich land and opportunity to farm, land grants, economic reasons, employment, family, following a religious leader, as a reward for military service, politics, weather, and for other reasons. Maps showing population migration routes are available on some Internet sites and in some historical texts.

A useful Internet site that may provide additional clues for tracing migration to Ohio is *Pioneer Migration Routes through Ohio:* **http://homepages.rootsweb.com/~maggieoh/pioneer.html**.

Tracing the migration of individuals and families to and within Ohio, depends on the time period, place of settlement, religion, ethnic origin, or perhaps other factors. Early immigrants to Ohio came primarily from the New England and Mid-Atlantic states Virginia, Kentucky, and Indiana. Later, immigrants arrived (or returned) from Michigan, Indiana, Illinois, Iowa, and several other Midwestern states (this is sometimes known as "reverse migration"). Key foreign countries providing immigrants to Ohio included Germany, Ireland, England, France, Wales, Canada, Scotland, Switzerland.

The following sources may assist in tracing ancestors who migrated to Ohio or within the state (a listing of published migration sources to Ohio and migration sources within the state appears in the bibliography later in this volume):

- Bible records (births, marriages, and deaths)
- Biographical works and biographical encyclopedias
- Business records
- Cemetery and sexton records
- Census population schedules (especially after 1850)
- Church histories-histories of individual churches
- Church records: baptisms, christenings, confirmations, marriages, membership records, removals, lists of church members, burials, and similar church records
- Computer databases
- Correctional institution records and jail records
- Court records: dockets, minutes, orders, case files
- Directories—city and rural directories
- Divorce records
- Family and home sources, correspondence, family record books
- Fraternal organization records
- Funeral home records
- Genealogies and compiled family histories
- Gravestone and tombstone inscriptions
- Indexes, such as Ohio County History Surname Index
- Internet and genealogical computer databases
- Land and property records, deeds, land grants, mortgages
- Manuscript collections and unpublished records
- Military records, especially pension and service records
- Military regimental and unit histories (especially Civil War)
- Mortality schedules: 1850, 1860, 1870, 1880 (incomplete)
- Naturalization and citizenship records
- Newspapers, obituaries, marriage notices, biographies
- Passport applications, 1795 to ca. 1925
- Patriotic and lineage society applications and papers
- Periodicals containing genealogical and historical articles

- Photographs
- Probate records, wills, administrations, case files
- School records
- Scrapbooks
- Town and county histories
- Township records
- Vital records (civil births, marriages, and deaths)

Military Records

Military-related records may often be very valuable for genealogists—depending on the war, ancestor's involvement, and the organizations that created these records. Many soldiers from Ohio served in the military, creating a variety of service records, pension records, rosters, unit histories, and associated records. The major repository of federal military records for the United States is the National Archives and Records Administration in Washington, DC. Digital and microfilm copies of many of these records are available at the National Archives and their regional archives, FamilySearch.org, and at other libraries with genealogical holdings. Most of these records date from the 1780s to the twentieth century. Military history and lists of soldiers can also be found in records of state and local archives, (for example, cemetery records kept by the county), as well as in township, and other local histories.

Pension files and applications exist for U.S. military service between 1775 and 1916. Pension records and application files are often more genealogically valuable than service or other military records. Some pension applications contain supporting documents, affidavits, names of witnesses, discharge papers, marriage certificates or related testimony, indicating the date and place of the pensioner's marriage and identifying the officiating party. Some files contain birth or death records or pages from family Bibles submitted to prove relationships.

An essential reference work describing federal military records is the *Guide to Genealogical Research in the National Archives of the United States*.[128] The DAR Library in Washington, DC also has a large collection of copies of Revolutionary War records and related name indexes, typescripts of genealogical records, and published sources which are national in scope. See especially records online at Fold3.com and FamilySearch.org (e.g., Revolutionary War Pension Records and Bounty Land Warrants).

A valuable Ohio statewide military research aid is the Graves Registration Card File compiled by Ohio Adjutant General's Office and housed at Ohio History Connection, also known as Grave Registrations of Soldiers Buried in Ohio. It identifies names of soldiers buried in Ohio, from the Revolutionary War to World War II. Names of some Ohio soldiers buried outside the state are also included in this card file. In addition to the soldier's name, the contents of each card often include address, date and place of death, cause of death, date of burial, date and place of birth (sometimes a foreign country), name of cemetery and location of grave, next of kin, and service record (war served in, company, rank, and so forth). Grave registration cards are alphabetically arranged by surname and are digitized at FamilySearch.org, Grave Registrations of Soldiers, 1810-1955.
https://www.familysearch.org/search/collection/2155397

Often overlooked by genealogists are various military records kept in county courthouses (for Ohio, see especially records in the Recorder's Office), Ohio university libraries in the state, veteran's services offices, the Ohio History Connection in Columbus, Western Reserve Historical Society, and other record repositories in the state. On the county level, these often include soldiers' discharge records, burial records, enlistments, pay records, correspondence, and others.

---

128. *Guide to Genealogical Research in the National Archives of the United States*, 3rd ed., edited by Anne Bruner Eales and Robrt M. Kvrasnicka (Washington, DC: National Archives and Records Administration, 2000), and online microfilm catalog.

On the state level, the Governor's Office of Veterans Affairs in Columbus maintains some military records for servicemen, as well as a card file for every person known to have served Ohio in the military. Records at the Ohio History Connection include military rosters, muster in and muster out rolls, printed histories, manuscript collections, the 1890 Special Union Veterans Census (or their widows), and many other records. The 1890 special census is sometimes known as the Civil War Veterans Schedule. Consult the Ohio History Connection website for more details.

Extensive microfilming has been done by the Genealogical Society of Utah in the military records created by Ohioans at the federal, state, and county levels, which have now been digitized. Principal among these are the following collections: Graves Registration Card File; Index to Compiled Service Records of Volunteer Union Soldiers Who Served in Organizations from Ohio, 1861-1865; Official Roster of the Soldiers of the State of Ohio in the War of the Rebellion (original muster-in and muster-out rolls); World War I draft records; and a variety of other pension and service record collections. Found in many major libraries, Marilyn Deputy's *Register of Federal United States Military Records a Guide to Manuscript Sources available at the Genealogical Library in Salt Lake City and the National Archives in Washington, DC* provides a catalog of military records and indexes.

A variety of secondary publications relating to Ohio military records exist for genealogical study. *Annotated Bibliography of Ohio Patriots: Revolutionary War and War of 1812*, by W. Louis Phillips, catalogs principally published works, although a few unpublished sources are cited as well.[129] Full bibliographic data is offered in each entry, followed by a description of contents, making this a valuable reference for locating early Ohio military records.

---

129. W. Louis Phillips, *Annotated Bibliography of Ohio Patriots: Revolutionary War and War of 1812* (Bowie, MD: Heritage Books, 1985). Many of the sources cited in the annotated bibliography are not limited to Ohio but are national in scope.

Inez Waldenmaier's *Revolutionary War Pensioners Living in Ohio before 1834* gives name, age, residence in Ohio, and unit.[130] An older publication, *The Military History of Ohio,* includes rosters of soldiers arranged by counties.[131] The twelve-volume *Official Roster of the Soldiers of the State of Ohio in the War of the Rebellion, 1861-1866* is an important source for locating Ohioans who served in the Civil War, as well as the War with Mexico, 1846-1848.[132] Contents of these volumes include name, rank, age, date entered service, period of service, and remarks (date died, place died, whether killed or captured, date mustered out, service information, transfer to another military company, etc.). Many Ohio county and local histories have military sections with historical details and lists of soldiers.

Two official state publications, *The Official Roster of the Soldiers of the American Revolution Buried in the State of Ohio* and *Roster of Ohio Soldiers in the War of 1812,* should be consulted for the wars they cover.[133] Additionally, Union regimental and unit histories are available in major research libraries to help genealogists reconstruct the military activities of their ancestors and are fairly abundant for Ohio.

---

130. Inez Waldenmaier, *Revolutionary War Pensioners Living in Ohio before 1834* (Tulsa, OK: The author, 1983). See also Daughters of the American Revolution of Ohio, *The Official Roster of the Soldiers of the American Revolution Buried in the State of Ohio* (Columbus, OH, 1929).

131. A. Parsons Stevens, *The Military History of Ohio* (New York: H.H. Hardesty, 1885-1887). This work includes historical background, portraits, and lists of deceased soldiers.

132. Ohio, Adjutant General's Office, *Official Roster of the Soldiers of the State of Ohio in the War of the Rebellion, 1861-1866,* 12 vols. (Akron and Norwalk, OH [publisher varied], 1886-1895). FamilySearch.org. See also the separate index by Jana Sloan Broglin, *Official Roster of the Soldiers of the State of Ohio in the War with Mexico 1846-1848* (Mansfield, OH: Ohio Genealogical Society, 1991).

133. Adjutant General of Ohio, *The Official Roster of the Soldiers of the American Revolution Buried in the State of Ohio* (1929-59, reprint 2 vols. in 1; Mineral Ridge, OH: Trumbull County Chapter of the Ohio Genealogical Society, 1973), and Adjutant General of Ohio, *Roster of Ohio Soldiers in the War of 1812* (1916; reprinted, Baltimore: Genealogical Publishing Co., 1968). See also Ohio Society, United States Daughters of 1812, *Index to the Grave Records of Servicemen of the War of 1812, State of Ohio,* ed. by Phyllis Brown Miller (Huber Heights, OH: The Society, 1988).

Major military collections of published unit histories and similar sources are available at the Library of Congress, Ohio History Connection, FamilySearch Library, Western Reserve Historical Society Library, and other major libraries with genealogical collections.[134] The Ohio Genealogical Society in Bellville, Ohio, has published military indexes and rosters of soldiers for various wars.

Mary L. Bowman's *Some Ohio Civil War Manuscripts: A Finding Tool* describes many Ohio Civil War manuscript collections housed in seventeen repositories, most notably the Ohio History Connection.[135] This is a valuable reference tool for Civil War research. Some of the collections are described in great detail, and there is a name and subject index. The Ohio Genealogical Society publishes Civil War and other military articles in their quarterly, *Ohio Civil War Genealogy Journal*. This journal includes Civil War rosters, biographies, compiled genealogies, and similar material.

Depending on the war and time period, additional Ohio military records of interest include enlistment records, state veterans' and soldier's homes records (for example, Ohio Veterans Home, Sandusky, Ohio), genealogical patriotic or lineage society records (some county and regional societies exist in the state), Ohio state and local histories, gravestone inscriptions, cemetery records, and veterans' gravesites (for example, Ohio Western Reserve National Cemetery), veterans organizational records (VetFriends.com), records of the Daughters of the American Revolution, records of lineage and patriotic societies, soldier pension indexes, draft registration cards, muster rolls and lists,

---

134. Regimental histories provide details regarding the organization and details of military units and provide names of soldiers. See U.S. Civil War Regimental Histories in the Library of Congress **https://www.loc.gov/rr/main/uscivilwar**

135. Mary L. Bowman, comp., *Some Ohio Civil War Manuscripts: A Finding Tool* (Mansfield, OH: Ohio Genealogical Society, 1997). See also Library of Congress, *National Union Catalog of Manuscript Collections* (Washington, DC: Library of Congress, 1959-).

bounty land records, personnel records, photographs, oral histories, medical records, prison records (especially for the Civil War), newspapers, maps, payment vouchers, guardianship records, correspondence, personal records, diaries and memoirs, and other records of genealogical value.[136]

Many Ohio residents are members of patriotic and lineage societies, or they are eligible to join. Many societies have chapters, lineage books, and publish periodicals with genealogical data on their members. Examples include:

Daughters of the American Revolution (DAR)
   https://www.dar.org
National Society of the Colonial Dames of America in the State of Ohio (See also National Society Colonial Dames of the XVII Century)
   https://nscda-oh.org/
National Society of the Sons of the American Revolution (SAR)[137]
   https://www.sar.org
Ohio Genealogical Society: Society of Civil War Families of Ohio, also Military Order of the Daughters and Sons of Ohio
   https://www.ogs.org/about/lineage/
Order of the Founders and Patriots of America
   https://ofpa.org
Society of Colonial Wars in the State of Ohio
   https://www.colonialwarsoh.org/
Society of Mayflower Descendants in the State of Ohio
   https://ohiomayflower.org/cleveland/

---

   136. Military veterans could have been buried in private, church, hospital, public (for example, township, national, military post, prison, another cemetery, or on a battlefield).

   137. See for example, Sons of the American Revolution, *Western Reserve Society, Sons of the American Revolution, Cleveland, Ohio Centennial Register, 1892-1992* (Cleveland: Burton Printz, 1992).

Military Records Repositories

Major repositories of military records for Ohio include county courthouses (county clerk, auditor, or recorder), county archives or record centers, private libraries, public libraries, historical societies, university libraries, and the Columbus Metropolitan Library. Search individual library catalogs for references to Ohio military records, abstracts, and personal name and subject indexes.

The State Library of Ohio houses military rosters for Ohio soldiers and sailors, and includes rosters for the Revolutionary War, War of 1812, Civil War (Union), Spanish-American War, World War I, Ohio regimental histories, and pension indexes. The State Library has online resources that can be accessed on site, including the library versions of Ancestry.com, Fold3.com, and HeritageQuest.com.

The Allen County Public Library Genealogy Center in Fort Wayne, Indiana, has many company, regimental, and division histories, state adjutant general reports, and online military databases. The Center also has its own collection of military records, "Our Military Heritage" (search "Keywords") **https://www.genealogycenter.info/military/**.

For online military records, consult especially Fold3.com (by Ancestry), FamilySearch.org, Findmypast.com, Linkpendium Ohio.com, HeritageQuest Online.com (from ProQuest), the Library of Congress, MyHeritage.com, WorldCat, and other online databases. Major military collections include the following:

Revolutionary War Pension Records: pension and bounty-land warrant application files

War of 1812, Soldiers who Served in Volunteer Organizations

Civil War Pension Index, General Index to Pension Files, 1861-1934

Union Soldiers Compiled Service Records, 1861-1865

Civil War Prisoner of War Records, 1861-1865

Civil War Soldiers, 1861-1865: names of soldiers who served in the Union and Confederate armies

Compiled Military Service Records (information about soldiers abstracted various National Archives military sources, such as enlistment papers), and pension records. See especially records at FamilySearch.org and Fold3.com.

General Index to Pension Files, 1861-1934 (Civil War and later pensions, for service between 1861 and 1916). See FamilySearch.org, Fold3.com, and **https://bit.ly/2vzIPea**

World War I Draft Registrations, 1917-1918 (records for over 24 million men), most records show name of person, date and place of birth, current residence, age, marital status, occupation, citizenship status, and other family details.

Military service records since 1917 are housed at the National Personnel Records Center, 1 Archives Drive, St. Louis, MO 63138. (Note that many records were destroyed by fire in 1973.) Older military personnel records (mostly prior to 1917) are available at Textual Archives Services Division.

World War II Army Enlistment, name, serial number, residence, and other details.

World War II Draft Registration Cards: there were several registrations.

Several U.S. federal census schedules are helpful in identifying military service—1840, 1910, 1930, and 1890 Veterans Schedule (Union veterans and widows available for some states).

Adjutant General Military Records, 1631-1976. Lists of military personnel.

Personal name index to pension files held at National Archives (mostly Union Civil War).

National Archives

National Archives and Records Administration, 700 Pennsylvania Avenue, NW, Washington, DC 20408, houses and preserves historical U.S. government documents, including military records.

The National Archives in Washington, DC, has the largest collection of federal military service records in the United States dating from the Revolutionary War to 1912, including the Civil War. Copies of many National Archives military records are available by mail (see How to Obtain Copies of Records).

Military service records from World War I to the present are held at the National Military Personnel Records Center in St. Louis, Missouri. Post-World War I regimental and unit records are available at the National Archives, 8601 Adelphi Road, College Park, MD 20740, and at many research libraries.

National Archives regional branches and facilities collect federal records for the areas they serve, including federal government records, court records, military records, and much more. The federal records centers covering Ohio are:

Chicago Federal Records Center, 7358 South Pulaski Road, Chicago, IL 60629
Dayton Federal Records Center, 3150 Springboro Road, Moraine, OH 45439
Kingsridge Federal Records Center, 8801 Kingsridge Drive, Miamisburg, OH 45458

Bounty land warrant application files relate to claims between 1775 and 3 Mar 1855. See also the FamilySearch.org Land entry (land patent) files for transfer of public lands from the U.S. government to individuals.

Land Entry Case Files, Homestead Records, Military Bounty Land Warrants.[138]
https://www.archives.gov/researcj/land/land-records

Military Records
https://www.archives.gov/research/military

Resources for Genealogists
https://www.archives.gov/reseaerch/genealogy

National Archives Catalog
https://catalog.archives.gov

    The following databases have major collections of online military records—rosters, muster rolls, pension records, regimental histories, and many others. Search online catalogs under "Military Records" by locality—for example, United States, Ohio, county, and other local jurisdictions. Also search for abstracts, indexes, related categories, and keywords. See also military records for individual states.

The Ancestor Hunt
https://theancestorhunt.com/blog/categor/military-records

Ancestry.com
https://www.ancestry.com
See especially digitized and indexed records from the National Archives.

Ancestry.com U.S. Military Collection
https://www.ancestry.com/search/categories/39

The Ancestor Hunt
https://theancestorhunt.com/blog/categor/military-records

---

    138. Kenneth Hawkins, comp., *Research in the Land Entry Files of the General Land Office, Record Group 49*. Reference Information Paper 114 (Washington, DC: National Archives and Records Administration, 2009).

Ancestry.com
https://www.ancestry.com
See especially digitized and indexed records from the National Archives.

Ancestry.com U.S. Military Collection
https://www.ancestry.com/search/categories/39

FamilySearch.org (see especially FamilySearch Research Wiki)
https://www.familysearch.org/search/catalog

Fold3.com (by Ancestry)
https://www.fold3.com/
A major online website for locating genealogical and historical military records. See especially online Revolutionary War Collection.

Genealogy Bank
https://www.genealogybank.com

Library of Congress, Washington, D.C.
https://catalog2.loc.gov/
See the Library of Congress online catalog under military records, especially Keyword Search.

MyHeritage.com
https://www.myheritage.com
Search Historical Records, Research, Selection Catalog, Military

Ohio Genealogical Society Library
https://www.ogs.org
Located in Bellville, Ohio, OGS has state and local military records, abstracts, indexes, especially Civil War Union records (see Ohio Civil War Genealogy Center at OGS), digitized books, manuscripts, pension records, photographs, rosters, rolls of honor, and others. OGS published the *Ohio Civil War Genealogy Journal* between 1997 and 2012 (see also *Ohio Genealogy News* and *Ohio Genealogical Society Quarterly*), which included collections of Ohio military records. OGS has a lineage society devoted to the Civil War, Society of Civil War Families of Ohio. See the OGS online catalog under the heading military records, especially for county and local records.

Ohio History Connection in Columbus houses a major collection of military records.
https://www.ohiohistory.org

Military Records at the Archives & Library of the Ohio History Connection
https://ohiohistory.libguides.com/military/

Search Ohio History Connection's Online Collections Catalog, by name of war, regiment, or record type (for example, biographies, military rosters, muster rolls, regimental histories).
- Ohio History Connection—Research
  https://www.ohiohistory.org/research/
- Ohio History Connection Library Catalog
  https//www.ohiohistory.on.worldcat.org/discovery
- Ohio Memory—free digital library containing over one million full-text searchable digital images representing every Ohio county.[139] Search "Ohio Military"
  https://www.ohiomemory.org/

---

139. Ohio Memory is a collaborative project of Ohio History Connection and the State Library of Ohio to digitize current and historical Ohio records.

The Western Reserve Historical Society, in Cleveland has a large collection of Ohio military records, Civil War records, photographs, and many other genealogical and historical records. See Online Collections Catalog (Library Collections Search) for unit histories, rosters, and other military records.
https://catalog.wrhs.org/collections/search

Western Reserve Historical Society Library (see American Civil War and Genealogy Index)
https://www.wrhs.org/research/library

A selected list of Internet sites relating to the subject of Ohio military records:

Civil War Soldiers, 1861-1865
https://www.myheritage.com/

Civil War Soldiers and Sailors System (National Park Service)[140]
https://www.nps.gov/civilwar/soldiers-and-sailors-database.htm

Cyndi's List—Military
https://www.cyndislist.com/us/military

LDS Genealogy: Ohio Military Records
https://ldsgenealogy.com/OH/Military-Records.htm

Ohio, Grave Registrations of Soldiers, 1810-1955
https://www.familysearch.org/search/colletion/2155397

Ohio in the Civil War
https://ohiocivilwar.com

Ohio Memory—Military
https://ohiomemory.ohiohistory.org/military

Ohio Military Records—FamilySearch Research Wiki
https://www.familysearch.org/en/wiki/Ohio_Military_Records

Ohio, Veterans Home Deaths and Burials, 1889-1930
https://www.familysearch.org/search/collection/2205726

RootsWeb/Ancestry.com
https://home.rootsweb.com

---

140. The Civil War Soldiers and Sailors System is an online database with information about soldiers who served in the Union and Confederate armies during the Civil War and includes histories of regiments, links to battles, cemetery records, and other Civil War records.

Roster of Ohio Soldiers in the War of 1812
https://www.ancestry.com/search/collectios/20073

Society of the War of 1812 in the State of Ohio
https://ohiosociety1812.wordpress.com

War of 1812 Index to Pension Application Files, 1812-1910[141]
https://www.familysearch.org/search/collection/1834325

U.S.Veterans Burial Sites, 1775-2013
https://www.myheritage.com

World War I Draft Registrations, 1917-1918
Draft registration cards of men age 18-45
https://www.myheritage.com/

World War II Army Enlistment
https://www.myheritage.com/

World War II Draft Registration Cards for Ohio, 1940-1946 (U.S Selective Service System)
https://www.familysearch.org

---

141. See also "Preserve the Pensions" project for 1812," ancestry.com, familysearch.org, Fold3.com, and the National Genealogical Society https://www.ngsgenealogy.org/preserve-the-pensions/.

Military References

Bowman, Mary L., comp. *Some Ohio Civil War Manuscripts: A Finding Tool*. Mansfield, OH: Ohio Genealogical Society, 1997.

Harper, Robert S., et al. *Ohio Handbook of the Civil War*. Columbus: Ohio Historical Society, 1961.

Keifer, Joseph Warren. *Civil War Regiments from Ohio*. Pensacola, FL: The author, 2004.

Mangus, Michael. *Ohio: A Military History: The Seventeenth State of the Union*. Yardley, PA: Westholme Publishing, 2016.

The Military History of Ohio. New York: H.H. Hardesty, 1886.

Neagles, James C. *U.S. Military Records: A Guide to Federal & State Sources, Colonial America to the Present*. Orem, UT: Ancestry Publishing, 1994.

Nudd, Jean. "Using Revolutionary War Pension Files to Find Family Information." *Prologue Magazine* (Summer 2015): 47, no. 2.

Ohio and Jane Dowd Dailey. *The Official Roster of the Soldiers of the American Revolution Buried in the State of Ohio*. Kokomo, IN: Selby Publishing & Printing, 1988.

Ohio. Adjutant General's Department. *Roster of Ohio Soldiers in the War of 1812*. Baltimore: Genealogical Publishing Co., 1968.

Ohio. Adjutant General's Department. *The Official Roster of Ohio Soldiers, Sailors, and Marines in the World War, 1917-1918*. 23 vols. Columbus: F.J. Heer Printing, 1926-29.

Ohio. Adjutant General's Office. *Official Roster of the Soldiers of the State of Ohio in the War of the Rebellion, 1861-1866.* 12 vols. Akron, OH: Werner, Co., 1886-1895.

"Ohio Military Records." FamilySearch Research Wiki. **https://www.familysearch.org/en/wiki/ Ohio_Military_Records**

Phillips, W. Louis. *Annotated Bibliography of Ohio Patriots: Revolutionary War & War of 1812.* Bowie, MD: Heritage Books, 1985.

———. *Index to Ohio Pensioners of 1883.* Bowie, MD: Heritage Books, 1987.

Plante, Trevor K. "An Overview of Records at the National Archives Relating to Military Service," *Prologue Magazine* (Fall 2002): 34, no. 3.

Poland, Charles A. *Army Register of Ohio Volunteers in the Service of the United States.* Columbus: Ohio State Journal Printing Co., 1862.

Rose, Christine. *Military Bounty Land, 1776-1855.* San Jose, CA: CR Publications, 2011.

Scott, Craig R. *Genealogy at a Glance: Revolutionary War Genealogy Research.* Baltimore: Genealogical Publishing Co., 2011.

United States. Adjutant General's Office. *Index to Compiled Service Records of Volunteer Union Soldiers in Organizations from the State of Ohio.* Washington, DC: National Archives, 1964.

United States. War Department. *The War of the Rebellion: A Compilation of the Official Records of the Union and Confederate Armies.* 70 vols. Washington, DC: Government Printing Office, 1880-1901.

Naturalization Records

Ohio's naturalization records contain important information for locating immigrants, such as date of arrival in the United States. Later records show port of arrival and other valuable genealogical information. The declaration of intention and the petition for naturalization provide much of the information of interest to genealogists, although other naturalization records do exist, such as depositions and naturalization stubs. Before 1851, the Court of Common Pleas had jurisdiction over the naturalization process in the state.

Naturalization records dating after 1851 are available in the Probate Court in each county to 1906; federal District Court; regional network centers in Ohio; and the National Archives and Records Administration-Great Lakes Region, Chicago, Illinois; as well as in other repositories.[142] A useful but dated guide to naturalization records, with a section outlining Ohio's records, is James and Lila Neagle's *Locating Your Immigrant Ancestor*.[143]

---

142. For a descriptive article, consult Peter Bunce, "National Archives-Chicago Branch," *National Genealogical Society Newsletter* 12 (July-August 1986): 85-87, which summarizes the holdings of this regional archives. Naturalization indexes are also available in this archives, along with other valuable genealogical and historical records. The holdings of other National Archives branches are described in various issues of the *National Genealogical Society Newsletter* (now *NGS Newsmagazine),* Loretto Dennis Szucs and Sandra Hargreaves Luebking, *The Archives: A Guide to the National Archives Field Branches* (Salt Lake City: Ancestry Publishing, 1988), and *Prologue: The Journal of the National Archives*. In addition to the National Archives Web site (www.archives.gov), also useful is National Archives and Records Administration, *Guide to Records in the National Archives-Great Lakes Region,* comp. by Glenn Longacre and Nancy Malan (Chicago: National Archives and Records Administration, 1996). Numerous naturalization and related immigration records and indexes are on microfilm at the FamilySearch Library.

143. James C. and Lila Lee Neagles, *Locating Your Immigrant Ancestor: A Guide to Naturalization Records,* rev. ed. (Logan, UT: Everton Publishers, 1986).

Also helpful is John J. Newman's *American Naturalization Records, 1790-1990: What They Are and How to Use Them,* an illustrated guidebook useful to all American genealogists working with naturalization records.[144]

The largest collection of federal and local naturalization records and immigration records in the United States is available at the FamilySearch Library in Salt Lake City. Ohio records include those from the United States District Court naturalization records and indexes (northern and southern districts), county Probate Court naturalization records and indexes, Court of Common Pleas records, Board of Election records, and records from other local courts.

Passport applications created by the United States Immigration and Naturalization Service are another valuable source for locating Ohioans and other Americans. Typically they show the name of the person, birth date and birthplace, county of residence in Ohio (or elsewhere), occupation, physical description of applicant, and sometimes other data (more information is included in later records, such as photographs). Passport applications and related indexes are available at the National Archives in Washington, DC; they are online at FamilySearch.org from 1795 to about 1925. Passport indexes may serve as useful genealogical finding aids for those individuals who may have traveled to Europe or other foreign countries.

---

144. John J. Newman, *American Naturalization Records, 1790-1990. What They Are and How to Use Them* (Bountiful, UT: Heritage Quest, 1998).

Newspapers

Newspapers provide valuable genealogical and historical information—birth announcements and notices, marriage license applications and notices, divorce notices, death notices, obituaries, local news items, probate matters, accounts of church services and activities, court notices, court actions, and other local events and activities. Online research databases may include military records and activities, historical events, especially during the American Civil War period. Biographical and family information, especially regarding local residents, can be found in obituaries and historical sketches. Newspapers are especially valuable to fill in data and as vital record substitutes for census records, civil vital records, church records, gravestones, military service, wills and probate records, and other records of genealogical value. Photographs are often available, for example in obituaries, pioneer sketches, and of American Civil War soldiers. Additional information sometimes found in newspapers include advertisements, weddings and other anniversaries, appointment of guardians, lists of county and local officials, lists of passenger arrivals, names of school members and graduates, names of people listed in unclaimed mail at the local Post Office, naturalizations, real estate transactions, location of property, and many others. Some newspaper articles publish family history, including sometimes family trees in dedicated, genealogy columns.

Small town newspapers published in counties and rural localities are often a good source for locating biographical sketches, church membership and church events, coroner's inquest, marriage engagements, family reunions, funeral notices, interment information, maiden name of women, membership in associations and lodges, names and residences of family members, occupation, personal notices, school activities, and other local news activities and events regarding the everyday life and culture of early Ohio families. Newspapers were frequently printed soon after a town was established and chronicled local historical events. Religious and denominational newspapers are also available, especially for smaller localities, and detail American religion and life. Large city newspapers can also be useful, mostly for national and regional news, for example, *The New York Times*. English and foreign language newspapers are available for some Ohio localities. Ethnic newspapers are also available, for example, that yield information regarding new immigrants to America, African Americans, American Indians, Hispanic, Jews, and various ethnic groups.

Newspaper obituaries are especially valuable for genealogical research, especially those published since the middle and late nineteenth century. Information in obituaries varies from short death notices to more detailed family information, depending on the time period and locality of the death. In addition to name and age of the deceased, they may show birth date and place, death date and place, cause of death, address and residence of the deceased, religious affiliation, occupation, name of spouse, date and place married, names of survivors and sometimes their residence, names of parents, military information, membership in organizations, political affiliation, probate notices, school attendance, name of funeral home handling the funeral arrangements, place of funeral or if a graveside service, and sometimes more family details, including hobbies of the deceased. Obituaries were written by members of the family or the newspaper staff. In addition to information in obituaries, other sources to consider include death certificates, church records, family Bibles, military records, probate records, and other genealogical records. For online obituaries see the following:

- Legacy.com (Ohio Obituaries):
  https://www.legacy.com/us/obituaries/ohio
- NewspaperObituaries.net (Ohio):
  https://www.newspaperobituaries.net
- USGenWeb Archives: OhioUSGenWeb Obituary Project:
  http://www.usgwarchives.net/obits/oh/obitsoh.htm
- Ancestry.com, GenealogyBank.com, and other major websites cited in this book.

The earliest newspaper in the Northwest Territory was published in Cincinnati 1793-1796, the *Centinel of the North-Western Territory*, before Ohio was admitted as a state. Soon, thereafter, these other newspapers were published in Ohio: *Freeman's Journal* (1796-99); *Scioto Gazette and Chillicothe Advertiser* (Chillicothe, 1800-1810); *Chillicothe Supporter; Chillicothe Fredonian;* the *Western Spy and Hamilton Gazette*, often cited as *Western Spy* (Cincinnati, 1799-1810); *Cincinnati Liberty Hall; Zanesville Muskingum Messenger; Zanesville Express and Republican Standard; St. Clairsville Ohio Federalist; American Friend and Marietta Gazette; Chillicothe Independent Republican; Chillicothe Ohio Herald; Marietta Western Spectator;* and the *Ohio Gazette and Virginia Herald* (Marietta, Ohio, 1801), to name a few.[145]

Although some Ohio newspapers have been published continuously for several years, others frequently changed names throughout their years of publication and many were published for only a short period of time. Some newspapers have a political bias—sometimes found in newspaper obituaries if the deceased was not of the same political party as the newspaper editor or publisher. Newspapers on microfilm are frequently available for sale from historical societies, libraries, newspaper offices, or from other agencies.

Finding aids exist which help locate both original, microfilm, and digitized copies of newspapers. Of special interest is Stephen Gutgesell's *Guide to Ohio Newspapers, 1793-1973*, a union list of newspapers available in Ohio libraries.[146]

---

145. Andrew R. L. Cayton, *The Frontier Republic: Ideology and Politics in the Ohio Country, 1780-1825* (Kent, OH: Kent State University Press, 1986).

146. Stephen Gutgesell, ed., *Guide to Ohio Newspapers, 1793-1973: Union Bibliography of Ohio Newspapers Available in Ohio Libraries* (Columbus: Ohio Historical Society, 1974). Although partially outdated, this valuable reference guide and union bibliography is a major resource for locating Ohio newspapers. Entries are arranged by locality and show name of newspaper, title changes, dates available, library holdings, and other information. Newspaper titles, place published, political affiliation, and years published varies. See also Gary Arnold's "Newspapers and Newspaper Indexes Available at Ohio Historical Society Archives-Library," *The Report* 26 (Spring 1986): 33, and articles regarding abstracts from local newspapers.

Newspaper holdings of major Ohio libraries are identified in regional guides. For example, Marilyn Levinson, ed., *Guide to Newspaper Holdings at the Center for Archival Collections*.[147] Levinson's guide identifies Northwest Ohio newspapers housed at Bowling Green State University, Bowling Green, Ohio. This center has been collecting and microfilming newspapers in nineteen Northwest Ohio counties. An historical overview of Ohio's newspapers is Osman Hooper's *History of Ohio Journalism, 1793-1933*.[148] Hooper details the history of journalism in each Ohio county. The *Gale Directory of Publications and Broadcast Media* identifies names and addresses of current newspapers in Ohio and elsewhere.[149]

Karen Mauer Green's *Pioneer Ohio Newspapers* contains genealogical and historical abstracts from some of the earliest newspapers published in the state.[150] These abstracts chronicle the development of the Ohio country from frontier settlement into statehood.

---

147. Marilyn Levinson, ed., *Guide to Newspaper Holdings at the Center for Archival Collections*, 2nd ed. (Bowling Green, OH: Center for Archival Collections, Bowling Green State University, 1987).

148. Osman Castle Hooper, *History of Ohio Journalism, 1793-1933* (Columbus: Spahr & Glenn Co., 1933).

149. *Gale Directory of Publications and Broadcast Media*, 155th ed. (Farmington Hills, MI: Gale, 2019). See for a list of current Ohio newspapers. See also *Ohio News Media Directory* (Mount Dora, FL: News Media Directories, 1980), and N.W. Ayer & Sons, *Directory of Newspapers and Periodicals* (Philadelphia: N.W. Ayer, 1930-71).

150. Karen Mauer Green *Pioneer Ohio Newspapers, 1793-1810: Genealogical and Historical Abstracts* (Galveston, TX: Frontier Press, 1986), and *Pioneer Ohio Newspapers, 1802-1818: Genealogical and Historical Abstracts* (Galveston, TX: Frontier Press, 1988). Entries show local historical events, military news, obituaries and death notices, personal accounts, and much more. See especially the Preface to Green's books for the history of early Ohio newspapers and changes of newspaper titles. Consult also, Michael Barren Clegg, *Newspaper Obituary Extracts* (Fort Wayne, IN: M. B. Clegg, 1981-87), which covers Mahoning, Ottawa, Portage, Trumbull, and several other Ohio counties for the years ca. 1812-70.

Annals of Cleveland are abstracts from early Cleveland newspapers (1818-1935) available at the Ohio Genealogical Society, Ohio History Connection, the FamilySearch Library in Salt Lake City; these abstracts are indexed.[151] The Cleveland Necrology File contains local cemetery records and newspaper death notices (ca. 1833-1975). It does not have full text, although searching is online **https://cpl.org/research-learning/genealogy**. See also *Cleveland News Index* for local news stories.

Newspaper genealogy columns usually include articles on resources and repositories, news of recent publications, local genealogical news, how to do research (methodology), and queries. An example of an Ohio genealogical newspaper column is Joy Wade Moulton's "Find Your Ancestors," published in *The Columbus Dispatch*, Columbus, Ohio, which began in February 1975, but has now been discontinued. Newspapers in large and small Ohio cities and towns are being digitized, many through cooperation with the United States Newspaper Program: **https://www.neh.gov/us-newspaper-program**.

---

151. *Annals of Cleveland* (Michael Schwartz Library, Cleveland State University; Cleveland Public Library; Cleveland Memory). A depression-era project of the WPA.

Newspaper Repositories

Major repositories of Ohio newspapers include Akron-Summit County Public Library, Akron; Cincinnati and Hamilton County Public Library, Cincinnati; Columbus Metropolitan Library, Columbus; Toledo Public Library, Toledo; as well as public libraries, historical societies, and local newspaper offices. Some Ohio libraries and historical societies have digitized their own newspaper collections and have published abstracts, newspaper finding aids, subject indexes, and personal name indexes. College and university libraries in Ohio and elsewhere have current and historical newspapers and digital newspaper databases. Search individual library catalogs for references to Ohio newspapers, abstracts, death notices, obituaries, personal names, and subject indexes. See OPLIN Find a Library [public library in Ohio]: **https://oplin.org/fal/**.

The Ohio State University Library in Columbus houses current and historical newspapers in print, electronically, and on microform. OSU no longer has physical copies of newspapers in its Thompson Library. See guide to finding newspapers at OSU: **https://guides.osu.edu/newspapers/home**.

American Ancestors (New England Historic Genealogical Society) has a 19th century U.S. Newspapers database with approximately 1.7 million pages of primary-source newspaper content with full-text and images from hundreds of U.S. newspapers with genealogical sources, including birth, marriage, and death notices. Also available is Early American Newspapers, Series 1, 1690-1876, and American Indian Newspapers: **https://www.americanancestors.org**.

Ancestry.com has a major collection of online newspapers. Search Ancestry's Catalog by title or locality of interest and the keyword "Newspapers."
https://www.ancestry.com/search/categories/histnews/

See also Fold3.com and Newspapers.com.

- Ancestry.com: Historical Newspapers Collection
https://www.ancestry.com/search/categories/histnews/
- Ancestry.com: Ohio Newspapers & Periodicals
https://www.ancestry.com
- Ancestry.com: Ohio, U.S., Rutherford B. Hayes Presidential Center Obituary Index, 1810x-2016
https://www.ancestry.com/search/collections/1671/
- Ancestry.com: U.S., Newspapers.com Marriage Index, 1800s-current
https://www.ancestry.com/search/collections/62116
- Ancestry.com: Web: Ohio, U.S., MOLO Obituary Index, 1865-2012
https://www.ancestry.com/seaerch/collections/70643

Bowling Green State University houses a major collection of Ohio newspapers and newspaper indexes, especially for Northwest Ohio counties. See Center for Archival Collections and OhioLINK Library Catalog for newspaper references.
https://www.bgsu.edu/library/cac/collections/newspapers.html

FamilySearch.org has many references to newspapers. See FamilySearch Catalog for "Newspapers" by locality, abstracts, indexes, related categories, and keyword; for example try "Ohio Newspapers," "Ohio Newspaper Indexes," and subject, "United States, Ohio, County-Newspapers."
https://www.familysearch.org/search/catalog
See also FamilySearch Wiki—United States—Newspapers
https://www.familysearch.org/en/wiki/United States_Newspapers

Chronicling America Historic American Newspapers.[152] See "Digitized Newspapers: Ohio."
https://chroniclingamerica.loc.gov/

U.S. Newspaper Collections at the Library of Congress (Historical Newspapers)
https://guides.loc.gov/united-states-newspaper/historical-newspapers

U.S. Newspaper Directory, 1690-Present[153]
https://chroniclingamerica.loc.gov/search/titles/

MyHeritage.com has a major online historical newspaper collection. MyHeritage also has a large Newspaper Name Index for the USA and Canada. See Ohio Newspapers, 1793-2009, a compendium of newspapers published in various Ohio cities. Coverage varies by newspaper title.
https://www.myheritage.com

---

152. Chronicling America "is a Website providing access to information about historic newspapers and select digitized newspaper pages…it is a long-term effort to develop an Internet-based, searchable database of U.S. newspapers with descriptive information and select digitization of historic pages." Chronicling America is sponsored jointly by the National Endowment for the Humanities and the Library of Congress.

153. "U.S. Newspaper Directory" lists information regarding American newspapers published from 1690 to the present where users can browse the directory by newspaper title for online digital copies.

Ohio History Connection (OHC) in Columbus houses the state's largest collection of newspapers and indexes to Ohio newspapers (**http://www.ohiohistory.org**). They have over one million full-text searchable pages of Ohio newspapers. OHC also has newspaper finding aids, abstracts, and printed indexes to Ohio newspapers, which vary according to regarding county and time period.[154] Microfilm copies of newspapers are available through interlibrary loan from local libraries. Newspapers on microfilm can be purchased from Ohio History Connection.[155]

- Ohio History Connection Digital Newspaper Collections are listed in Chronicling America (Library of Congress—Historic American Newspapers)
  https://chroniclingamerica.loc.gov/
- Ohio History Connection—Research
  https://www.ohiohistory.org/research/
- Ohio History Connection Library Catalog
  https://ohiohistory.on.worldcat.org/discovery
- Ohio Memory—Free digital library containing over one million full-text searchable digital images representing every Ohio county. Keyword searchable from 1832 to 2011.[156]
  https://www.ohiomemory.org/
  https://ohiomemory.ohiohistory.org/newspapers
- National Digital Newspaper Program in Ohio
  https://ndnpohio.hiohistory.org/newspapers
- Newspapers at the Archives & Library of the Ohio History Connection
  https://ohiohistory.libguides.com/newspapers

---

154. Appreciation to Jenni Salamon, Manager, Digital Services, Ohio History Connection, for her reference assistance.

155. See Ohio History Connection online collections catalog for specific newspaper titles.

156. Ohio Memory is a collaborative project of Ohio History Connection and the State Library of Ohio to digitize current and historical Ohio newspapers. Consult also National Endowment for the Humanities National Digital Newspaper Program for more information.

Beginning in 1850 county auditors in all Ohio counties were required to collect leading newspapers for each political party in their county. That law was repealed in 1967 (Stephen Gutgesell, ed., *Guide to Ohio Newspapers, 1793-1973: Union Bibliography of Ohio Newspapers Available in Ohio Libraries,* Columbus: Ohio Historical Society, 1974, Introduction). These newspapers, along with numerous files from the Ohio State University, the entire newspaper collection of the State Library of Ohio, and a statewide newspaper collection sponsored by WPA, were transferred to the Ohio Historical Society (now Ohio History Connection in Columbus). Today, the State Library of Ohio has some newspapers on microfilm as well as access to some online newspaper databases.[157] In summary, the Ohio History Connection is the major resource for Ohio newspapers.

Rutherford B. Hayes Presidential Library in Fremont, Ohio, has a valuable online Ohio Obituary Index to over 3,700,000 newspaper obituaries, death notices, marriage notices, and other items from Ohio newspapers from the 1810s to the present (biographies, funeral home records, mortality schedules, probate records, scrapbooks, etc.). It is cross-indexed by maiden names and previous married names listed in the obituary and is searchable by several methods. Copies of obituaries may be requested from over 65 partner libraries. Hayes Library provides online ordering.
https://www.rbhayes.org/main/ohio-obituary-index

Western Reserve Historical Society (WRHS) in Cleveland has a large collection of Ohio newspapers, especially for Northeastern Ohio counties. Some newspapers in their collection have been digitized. See WRHS Online Collections Catalog for newspaper titles and indexes. The online catalog identifies newspapers by category and format (over 14,000 references to periodicals and newspapers). For newspapers, search by county, town, or village. Search also for title and "Ohio Newspapers."
https://catalog.wrhs.org/collections/search

---

157. Appreciation to Nicole Merriman, Head, Research & Catalog Services, State Library of Ohio, for her reference assistance.

Digitized newspaper images are appearing more frequently on the Internet and many websites include Ohio newspapers and related abstracts and indexes. Major genealogical websites cited in this book have references to Ohio newspapers, including the following: African American Newspapers,[158] AmericanAncestors.org (New England Historic Genealogical Society), Ancestry.com Library Edition, FamilySearch.org, Findmypast.com, Fold3.com, Linkpendium Ohio.com, HeritageQuest Online.com (ProQuest), the Library of Congress, MyHeritage.com (Historical Newspaper Collection), ProQuest Historical Newspapers, WorldCat, and other online databases. In addition, consult public and academic libraries, university libraries, private libraries, and others. Search for newspapers by name and locality, abstracts, indexes, obituaries, and so forth. A selected list of online newspaper websites and references to Ohio newspapers includes the following:

- Accessible Archives.com
  https://www.accessible-archives.com
- America's Historical Newspapers, 1690-1922 (Readex—NewsBank)
  https://www.readex.com
- Ancestor Hunt.com (Newspaper Links)
  https://theancestorhunt.com/newspaper-research-links.html
- Ancestor Hunt.com (Obituaries)
  https://theancestorhunt.com/obituaries.html
- Chronicling America (Historic American Newspapers—Library of Congress)
  https://chroniclingamerica.loc.gov
- Cleveland Public Library
  https://www.cpl.org

---

158. Consult "Historical African American Newspapers Available Online" https://libguides.marist.edu/AfricanAmericanNews

- Cleveland State University, Michael Schwartz Library
  https://library.csuohio.edu/
- Cyndi's List—Newspapers
  https://www.cyndislist.com/newspapers
- Elephind.com
  https://elephind.com
- Findmypast.com
  https://findmypast.com
- Fold3.com (by Ancestry)
  https://fold3.com
- GenealogyBank.com (Ohio Newspaper Archives, 1795-2007
  https://www.genealogybank.com/
- Google News Archive
  https://news.google.com/newspapers
- Historical Newspapers
  https://historynews.chadwyck.com/home/home.cgi?source=config2.cfg
- Internet Public Library (Newspapers & Magazines)
  https://www.ipl.org
- LDS Genealogy: Ohio Newspapers and Obituaries
  https://ldsgenealogy.com/OH/Newspapers-and-Obituaries.htm
- Legacy.com
  https://www.legacy.com
- NewsBank.com[159]
  https://www.newsbank.com
- NewsLibrary.com
  https://www.genealogybank.com/
- Newspaper and Current Periodical: U.S. Newspaper Indexes—Ohio
  https://www.loc.gov.rr/news/ind/oh.html

---

159. America's Obituaries and Death Notices [NewsBank]. Covers recent U.S. deaths in newspapers nationwide. Available in large public and other libraries

- NewspaperArchive.com
  https://newspaperarchive.com
- Newspapers.com (by Ancestry)
  https://www.newspapers.com
- Nineteenth-Century U.S. Newspapers
  https://www.gale.com/c/nineteenth-century-us-newspapers
- ObitsArchive.com
  https://www.obitsarchive.com/
- Ohio Memory—Newspapers
  https://ohiomemory.ohiohistory.org/newspapers
- Ohio Newspapers—FamilySearch Research Wiki
  https://www.familysearch.org/en/wiki/Ohio_Newspapers
- Ohio Obituary Index
  https://www.rbhayes.org/main/ohio-obituary-index/
- Onlinenewspapers.com
  https://www.onlinenewspapers.com/index.shtml
- ProQuest Historical Newspapers
  https://about.proquest.com/en/products-services/pq-hist-news/
- RootsWeb/Ancestry.com
  https://home.rootsweb.com

Newspaper References

Beidler, James M. *The Family Tree Historical Newspapers Guide: How to Find Your Ancestors in Archived Newspapers*. Cincinnati: Family Tree Books, 2018.

Breland, Claudia C. *Searching for Your Ancestors in Historic Newspapers*. Gig Harbor, WA: Claudia C. Breland, 2014.

Cooke, Lisa Louise. *How to Find Your Family History in Newspapers*. [Rhome, TX]: Genealogy Gems Publications, 2012.

Danky, James Philip, et al. *Native American Periodicals and Newspapers, 1828-1982*. Westport, CT: Greenwood Press, 1984.

Green, Karen Mauer. *Pioneer Ohio Newspapers, 1793-1810: Genealogical and Historical Abstracts*. Galveston, TX: Frontier Press, 1986.

———. *Pioneer Ohio Newspapers, 1802-1818: Genealogical and Historical Abstracts*. Galveston, TX: Frontier Press, 1988.

Gutgesell, Stephen, ed. *Guide to Ohio Newspapers, 1793-1973: Union Bibliography of Ohio Newspapers Available in Ohio Libraries*. Columbus: Ohio Historical Society, 1974.

Kemp, Thomas Jay. *Newspapers for Genealogy: Research Tips & Tools for Discovering Your Ancestors' Lives*. Naples, FL: NewsBank, GenealogyBank, 2013.

Levinson, Marilyn I., ed., *Guide to Newspaper Holdings at the Center for Archival Collections*, 4th rev. ed. Bowling Green, OH: Center for Archival Collections, Bowling Green State University, 1995.

Mink, Arthur De Witt. *Union List of Ohio Newspapers Available in Ohio*. Columbus: Ohio Historical Society Library, 1946.

"Ohio Newspapers." FamilySearch Research Wiki. **https://www.familysearch.org/en/wiki/Ohio_Newspapers**

Philibert-Ortega, Gena. *A Genealogist's Guide to Newspaper Research*. Ajax, ON: Moorshead Magazines Ltd., 2020.

Pinnick, Tim. *Finding and Using African American Newspapers*. Wyandotte, OK: Grebarth Publishing, 2008.

Thode, Ernest. *Historic German Newspapers Online*. Baltimore: Genealogical Publishing, 2018.

Wheeler, Robert Cordell, comp. *Ohio Newspapers: A Living Record*. Columbus: Ohio Historical Press, 1950.

Periodicals

A wealth of genealogical information can be found in genealogical and historical journals, magazines newsletters, and periodicals. Articles often include compiled genealogies and family histories, biographies, cemetery records and gravestones, census schedules and indexes, church records, compiled genealogies, divorce records, family Bible records, DNA articles, indexes to records, land and property records, legal notices, local history and historical articles, migration articles, military records, newspaper abstracts and obituaries, pedigrees, genealogical research methodology, maps, queries, tax records, typescripts of genealogical records, vital records (births, marriages, deaths), will abstracts and other probate records, book notices and reviews, and other similar articles. Some periodicals include names of letters left in the local Post Office, names of licensed tavern keepers, and many others.

The state's premier genealogical periodical, *Ohio Genealogical Society Quarterly* (OGSQ), is published quarterly by the Ohio Genealogical Society in Bellville, Ohio. Published in this periodical are transcriptions of many Ohio source records, abstracts from the Draper Manuscripts, ancestor charts, biographies, book notices, compiled genealogies and family history articles, family Bible records, family and other photographs, migration articles, military records (especially Revolutionary War and Civil War), names of Ohioans who resided in other states, OGS library news, philatelic genealogy articles (post cards), research methodology, vital records, and other articles of interest to Ohio researchers. OGSQ publishes an annual surname index in the last issue of the year.

OGS also publishes the quarterly *Ohio Genealogy News* (OGN) which includes OGS news and chapter activities, events calendar, publication notices, information on seminars and workshops, research techniques, computer news, descriptions of records from the OGS library and archives, recent OGS library acquisitions, lineage society information, queries, advertisements, book notices and reviews, DNA articles, OGS awards, and other news items of interest to Ohio genealogists.

Archived periodicals previously published by OGS have been digitized and are online at the OGS website:

Ohio Civil War Genealogy Journal (OCWGJ) (1997-2012) includes many Civil War-related articles for the state.
Ohio Genealogical Society Report (OGSR) (1961-2002) renamed the *Ohio Genealogical Society Quarterly* (OGSQ).
Ohio Records and Pioneer Families (ORPF) (1960-2012)

Researchers can search all OGS online archived periodicals under "Search Periodical Article Titles" on the OGS website. Standard search terms are names of people, places (localities), or titles. OGS members can view articles of interest.
https://www.org.org/periodical-search

Other Genealogical Titles

Other periodicals of interest include publications from the Ohio Genealogical Society such as *OGS Genealogy News* (titles vary). *Ohio Genealogy News* published since 1970, has articles regarding research techniques, repositories, OGS chapters, Ohio genealogical news, and other material for the state.

Ohio, The Cross Road of Our Nation, Records and Pioneer Families (Mansfield, OH: Ohio Genealogical Society, 1960-). Also known as *Ohio Records and Pioneer Families* (Akron, OH: Esther Weygandt Powell, 1960-), this periodical publishes many genealogical records regarding Ohio families.[160]

The "Old Northwest" Genealogical Quarterly, published by the "Old Northwest" Genealogical Society in Columbus, Ohio, beginning in January 1898 was published in 15 volumes. It published Ohio cemetery records, church records, court records, genealogies, and vital records. Even though selected abstracts from this periodical have been published in book form, there remain many significant articles that have not been reprinted. It ceased publication with volume 15, whole number 60, October 1912. Two publications are available from this periodical:

- *Ohio Marriages Extracted from the Old Northwest Genealogical Quarterly,*" edited by Marjorie Smith and published by Genealogical Publishing Company in Baltimore, Maryland, 1980. Marriages from the 15-volume set are printed in this work—each bride and groom has two entries, one for the groom's surname and one for the bride's maiden name. Some marriages in church records are included. Marriages are alphabetically arranged by surname.

---

160. Esther Weygandt Powell, *Ohio Records and Pioneer Families* (Akron, OH and Mansfield, OH: Ohio Genealogical Society, 1960-1974).

- *Ohio Cemetery Records Extracted from the "Old Northwest" Genealogical Quarterly*, indexed by Elizabeth P. Bentley and published by Genealogical Publishing Company in Baltimore, Maryland, 1984. It includes tombstone inscriptions from cemeteries mostly from sixteen Ohio counties in Central and Northeastern Ohio (and including the city of Columbus). It includes cemeteries in churches and on private farms. Also included are cemeteries in East Haddam, Connecticut, and Rutland, Massachusetts. This work concludes with a personal name index to approximately 20,000 individuals.

The *Ohio Genealogical Quarterly* began publication by the Columbus Genealogical Society in 1937 and was discontinued in April 1944. Its emphasis was on genealogical articles covering Columbus, surrounding Franklin County, and on occasion other Ohio counties. Included are articles relating to early Ohio settlements, cemetery records, church records, compiled genealogies, family Bible records, local history and historical notes, newspaper abstracts and legal notices, military records, obituaries, vital records, will abstracts and settlements of estates, and the 1810 tax list for nineteen Ohio counties (pages 101-159) accompanied by an 1810 map of the state. *Ohio Source Records from the Ohio Genealogical Quarterly* which consolidates much of this content, was published by Genealogical Publishing Company and includes a comprehensive personal name index.[161]

---

161. *Ohio Source Records from the Ohio Genealogical Quarterly* (Baltimore: Genealogical Publishing Co., 1986).

Other periodicals have been published throughout the state. *Ohio Records and Pioneer Families* (ORPF), a valuable companion to *The Report,* was begun in 1960 to 2012 as a private publication and was later published quarterly by OGS. This periodical includes source material for many Ohio counties, information on pioneer families, Ohio vital records (births, marriages, and deaths), gravestone inscriptions, military records, deed abstracts, biographies, newspaper abstracts, register of physicians, prison records, lists of Ohioans in other states, tax lists, mortality schedules (1850-80), court records, family Bible records, queries, and much more. Each volume has an annual surname index, and there are published cumulative indexes.

The Firelands Pioneer, begun in 1858 and published by the Firelands Historical Society in Norwalk, Ohio, is invaluable for north central Ohio counties. Publication years vary. Includes biographies, early settlers and pioneer sketches, family histories and genealogies, personal memoirs, lists of members of the Firelands Historical Society, and other local history and records for the Firelands (also known as the "Sufferers' Lands") in the Western Reserve, which covers nearly all of Huron and Erie counties, Ohio.[162] See Firelands Historical Society Museum and Library: **https://www.firelandsmuseum.com/**

Gateway to the West, compiled by Ruth Bowers and Anita Short, 2 vols. (Baltimore: Genealogical Publishing Co., 1989), with articles reprinted and excerpted from the original eleven volumes and consolidated in two volumes. The two reprint volumes are arranged by counties and include new every-name comprehensive indexes. The periodical was originally published quarterly from September 1967 to 1978 and is a significant source for Ohio research. Reprinted in two volumes with selected articles from the original publication the reprint includes church records, cemetery records, court records, deed abstracts, guardianships, naturalizations, newspaper notices, township records, vital records, wills, and other genealogical source material.

---

162. Huron County Chapter of Ohio Genealogical Society is now known as Firelands Genealogical Society and publishes a quarterly newsletter, the *Kinologist*.

Ohio History began publication in June 1887 as *Ohio Archaeological and Historical Quarterly,* publishing Ohio history articles and book reviews regarding the social, economic, military, and cultural history of Ohio and the Midwest. *Ohio History* was originally published by the Ohio Historical Society (now Ohio History Connection) which provides a free and fully searchable online archives of *Ohio History* issues from 1887 through 2004. The *Ohio History Journal* has been published by Kent State University Press since 2007. The Ohio History Connection publishes *Echoes Magazine* and an online eNewsletter regarding activities and events. Back issues of the Ohio History Connection's *Timeline* are available. Ohio Local History Alliance publishes *The Local Historian.*

Ohio Queries, edited by Shirley Elizabeth Penna-Oakes, contains genealogical material and family names of interest to Ohio researchers along with a directory of individuals researching surnames connected to Ohio.[163] Some Ohio counties include queries in their publications. For example, *Wood County Ohio Queries* are published in the *Newsletter of the Wood County Chapter of the Ohio Genealogical Society,* with an every-name index and chapter membership list.

County and local genealogical organizations, especially OGS chapters and local historical societies, publish a wealth of information in their newsletters and periodicals and as separate publications. Newsletters and other local publications have been published by OGS genealogy chapters, local historical societies, and other Ohio organizations. In addition to news items relating to their organization, they often publish family histories, newspaper abstracts, cemetery records, church records, vital records, and much more. An example is *Newsletter Northwestern Ohio Genealogical Society* (Toledo, OH), 1982-1992.

---

163. Shirley Elizabeth Penna-Oakes, ed., *Ohio Queries* (Elk, WA: Pioneer Publications, 1986-1994).

Other genealogical periodicals published outside the state occasionally include valuable source materials and compiled genealogies of Ohio records and families, principally *The American Genealogist, The Detroit Society for Genealogical Research Magazine,* and the *National Genealogical Society Quarterly,* among others.

Newsletters and periodicals published by the OGS chapters often publish methodology ("how-to") articles for their locality, family genealogies, military records (especially for the Civil War), family Bible records, local Ohio records, ancestor charts, and more.

Periodical Source Index
https://www.genealogycenter.info/persi/

Periodical Source Index, also known as PERSI, is a subject and locality index to genealogy and local history articles published in periodicals and newsletters. Emphasis is on United States publications, but it includes titles from several other countries. It is arranged by surnames, localities, and subject headings. Researchers may discover biographical sketches and transcriptions of local records. It is not an index to every personal name in periodical articles and page numbers of articles are not included.

PERSI is available online for free and is produced by staff of the Allen County Public Library Genealogy Center (ACPL) (900 Library Plaza, Fort Wayne, IN 46802). With over 10,000 titles, the Genealogy Center houses one of the largest English-language genealogy and local history periodical collections in the world.

PERSI has over three million citations and is arranged by:
- Surname Search
- Location Search (example, US State—Ohio—county)
- Research Technique Articles (record type examples, biography, cemeteries, census records, church records, obituaries, vital records, and other keywords)
- Article Title Search (keywords)

An "Article Order Form" is available from ACPL where researchers can order copies of articles found in PERSI from ACPL. Send the order form citing the article(s) of interest to be copied, provide the full article title from PERSI, name of the publication, and other information requested on the order form. Request only six separate articles at a time. A small fee is charged with each order form. Requests are not accepted by phone. Copies of articles found in PERSI may also be available from other libraries housing the publication of interest, such as a public library, historical society, university library, the article publisher, or they may be available through Interlibrary Loan.

Other Periodical Indexes

Some journals, newsletters, and periodicals have their own personal name and locality indexes. Some personal names indexes are published annually and some have been digitized online, including subject and locality indexes. *Ohio Genealogical Society Quarterly* publishes an annual surname index in the year's final issue. Here are some others.

The Ohio Genealogical Society Periodicals Index: Topical by Location, 1960-2000: Ohio Civil War Genealogy Journal, compiled by Susan Dunlap Lee, (Mansfield, OH: Ohio Genealogical Society, 2002), is a subject index to genealogical periodicals published by OGS.[164] It is arranged by localities and surnames, such as family names and names of pensioners. The preface includes a brief history of OGS periodical publications. The volume concludes with an every-name index to this valuable reference book.

Susan Lee and Jana Sloan Broglin, *Ohio Records & Pioneer Families, Ten Year Surname Index, 1985-1994* (Mansfield, OH: Ohio Genealogical Society, 1996).

Ohio Records and Pioneer Families: Topical Index by County, Volumes I-XXV, by Susan Lee (Mansfield, OH: Ohio Genealogical Society, 1985).

Many of the articles in the major periodicals and newsletters that publish Ohio articles are indexed in Carol Bell's *Ohio Genealogical Periodical Index: A County Guide,* which is expanded further by Periodical Source Index (PERSI).[165] Bell's guide is useful for a county-by-county listing of subject headings and citations to sources. Consult also Carol Willsey Bell, *Ohio Guide to Genealogical Sources*.[166]

---

164. Ohio Genealogical Society, *The Ohio Genealogical Society Periodicals Index: Topical by Location, 1960-2000: Ohio Civil War Genealogy Journal,* comp. by Susan Dunlap Lee (Mansfield, OH: The Society, 2002). Consult also Susan Dunlap Lee, *Ohio Records & Pioneer Families Ten Year Surname Index, 1985-1994* and *1960-1984* (Mansfield, OH: The Society).

165. Carol Willsey Bell, *Ohio Genealogical Periodical Index: A County Guide.* 6th ed. (Youngstown, OH: Bell Books, 1987).

166. Carol Willsey Bell, *Ohio Guide to Genealogical Sources* (Baltimore: Genealogical Publishing Co., 1988).

Photographs

Photographs of individuals and localities are a valuable resource for family history. Photographs of current and former Ohio residents have been published in *Ohio Genealogical Society Quarterly, Ohio Genealogy News*, Ohio county genealogical newsletters and periodicals (OGS chapters), and also other publications (including online archived OGS periodicals). Guidebooks are available which offer tips and suggestions for understanding and evaluating photos, and photo restoration, especially older historical photos.[167] Diane VanSkiver Gagel has written a valuable history and guidebook regarding early Ohio photographers.[168]

Many historical photographs and family portraits have been digitized and many are online. It is important to search family and home sources for photographs, scrapbooks, postcards and other family documents.[169]

A selected list of websites for finding family photographs include the following:

FamilySearch.org: FamilyTree profiles, albums, photos memories and others.

Ancestry.com: Public Member Photos and Scanned Documents attached to family trees, U.S. school yearbooks, historical postcards, among others.

---

167. Maureen Alice Taylor. *Family Photo Detective; Learn How to Find Genealogy Clues in Old Photos and Solve Family Photo Mysteries* (Cincinnati: Family Tree Books, 20133); Maureen Alice Taylor, *Capturing Memories: Your Family Story in Photographs* (Provo, UT: Ancestry Publishing, 2007); Maureen Alice Taylor, *Preserving Your Family Photographs* (Picture Perfect Press, 2010); Maureen Alice Taylor, *Searching for Family History Photos: How to Get Them Now!* (Picture Perfect Press, 2014); Maureen Alice Taylor, *Uncovering Your Ancestry through Family Photographs* (Cincinnati: Family Tree Books, 2005); Maureen Alice Taylor, *Dating Old Photographs, 1840-1929*, 2nd ed. (Toronto, ON: Family Chronicle, 2004).

168. Diane VanSkiver Gagel, *Ohio Photographers, 1839-1900*, 2nd ed. (Baltimore: Clearfield, 2013). See also Diane VanSkiver Gagel, *Directory of Photographers in the United States, 1888 & 1889, and Canada, 1889* (Bowie, MD: Heritage Books, 2002).

169. H. Roger Grant, *Ohio in Historic Postcards: Self-Portrait of a State*, (Kent, OH: Kent State University Press, 1997).

Ohio History Connection: photos and family portraits digitized from their collection are available at:
Ohio Memory **https://ohiomemory.org/**
OhioPix **https://ohiopix.org/**

MyHeritage.com: family trees, family photos (and animations), colorizing black and white photos, color restored photos, MyHeritage in Color, and AI Time Machine™ where users may transform themselves into historical figures throughout the ages using everyday photos. **https://www.myheritage.com/ai-time-machine?tr_date=20221204**

DeadFred: free genealogy photo archive site with a searchable database. Thousands of photographs have been identified, while many are unknown. It is possible for the individual to post photographs to DeadFred. See the website for more. **https://www.deadfred.com/**

Digital Public Library of America: digital materials from American archives, libraries, and museums, including photos.

Other resources for finding family photographs include benevolent and social unions, biographies (county and local biographies of prominent residents and others), church histories and collections, college and university portraits, county and local histories, county atlases (may have etchings of prominent people, farms, and homes), family histories (compiled genealogies), Find A Grave.com, genealogical societies, historical societies, military records (individual and group portraits), museums, newspapers and obituaries, postcards (people, homes, villages and towns), public libraries, school class portraits, school yearbooks, university libraries (some have a photograph archives); Cleveland Public Library Digital Gallery, Cleveland; Ohio University, Athens; Ohio Genealogical Society Library, Bellville, Ohio; Western Reserve Historical Society, Cleveland; and others. Many of these collections include photos of African Americans and other ethnic groups.

Probate Records

Ohio's county level Probate Court, created in 1852, took the responsibility of probate matters from the Common Pleas Court. Here the genealogist will find records relating to the estates of deceased individuals, wills, administrations, and guardianships of minors and other dependents. All such probate records are valuable for determining names of family members, relationships, residences, dates of deaths, and other genealogical information; most records date from the origin each county was created.

Although some genealogists are prone to look only for a will copied in a will book, it is always advisable to locate the estate file (sometimes known as the probate packet or case file), carefully studying all documents created by or for the deceased ancestor. Probate files include not only original wills, but also other original probate documents, settlement papers, inventories, receipts, correspondence, newspaper clippings, and other similar records. Auxiliary probate documents may be useful in learning more about an ancestor and in providing background information for writing a family history. Equally important is the possibility that relationships that cannot be gleaned from a will may be stated or implied in these probate papers, and such documents normally exist whether or not a will was ever drafted. Guardianship records likewise may identify names of minors, and other family members and may be included with probate documents.

Wills and related probate records, guardianship records, and probate indexes may be found in the Probate Court office or record room within each county courthouse, or in the appropriate Ohio Network of Research Centers. Many probate records are on microfilm at the Ohio History Connection and the FamilySearch Library in Salt Lake City, Utah. These records include will record books, administrations, inventories, dockets, probate journals, and indexes to probate records. (Check FamilySearch.org and Ancestry.com for probate records). For most Ohio counties, probate estate files (probate packets) have not been microfilmed but are generally available for researchers to use in local repositories, such as the county courthouse or a courthouse annex.

Two indispensable guides exist for using Probate Court records in the state. Carol Willsey Bell's overview of research in probate records is found in an article in *The Report*.[170] Carol Willsey Bell's *Ohio Wills and Estates to 1850: An Index* is a splendid compilation that should be available in major research libraries with a genealogical collection.[171] This probate index is one of the major pre-1850 genealogical research aids for the state and may assist in locating ancestors who died in Ohio or who left a probate record there. A valuable Ohio township and county outline map is included at the beginning of this volume. Many OGS volunteers assisted Carol Bell in indexing probate records in Ohio's eighty-eight counties.

---

170. Carol Willsey Bell, "What to Look for When Searching in the Courthouse: Probate Court," *The Report* 13 (Winter 1973): 170-174. Carol Bell has written several other useful articles in *The Report* describing Ohio genealogical sources.

171. Carol Willsey Bell, *Ohio Wills and Estates to 1850: An Index* (Youngstown, OH: Bell Books, 1981). This volume is the culmination of a ten-year project to provide a comprehensive index to Ohio probate records. A summary of genealogical sources used for each county is included. In addition, this work is useful in identifying which counties had courthouse fires (and the year of the courthouse fire) and which records were destroyed. *Ohio Wills and Estates to 1850: An Index* is a significant reference source for Ohio genealogists, historians, and reference librarians.

School Records

School records and enumeration returns of school-age children are available for some Ohio localities; some records begin during the early nineteenth century. Records show names of children in school, mostly from age six to twenty-one years of age, name of township and school district, age, sex, and sometimes name of parent or names of both parents. School records before 1850 are particularly useful since they may show names of children listed with their parent(s); if so, they can serve as a substitute for the lack of pre-1850 census data. Records have not been kept uniformly. Some school census records are also available. Records of less value genealogically, but important historically, include school board minutes, financial records, and attendance lists.

School records of genealogical value may be found at local public libraries, college and university libraries, historical societies, and some are on microfilm at the FamilySearch Library. Original school records are usually not indexed; however, some early records have been published. Records of colleges and universities are also valuable, such as published school histories, yearbooks, directories, biographies, and records of alumni associations and members.

The Ohio Genealogical Society has a large collection of school yearbooks.

A major reference source for school records is *The Ohio Municipal, Township, and School Board Roster.*[172] An early illustrated history of schools in Ohio, school records, and school statistics is *Historical Sketches of Public Schools in Cities, Villages, and Townships of the State of Ohio.*[173]

---

172. *The Ohio Municipal, Township, and School Board Roster* (Columbus: Ohio Secretary of State, 1994-95).

173. *Ohio, State Centennial Educational Committee, Historical Sketches of Public Schools in Cities, Villages, and Townships of the State of Ohio* (n.p., 1876).

Other schools in Ohio include the State of Ohio Boys' Industrial School and also the Girls' Industrial School records. The boys' school, located in Fairfield County, Ohio, has records from 1858-1918 while the girls' school in Delaware County, Ohio, has records from 1869-1911. Early records may contain information pertaining to the child's parentage, commitment, education, description, education, health, employment, and miscellaneous. These records may be found at FamilySearch.org.

The Ohio State School for the Blind, located in Columbus, was established in 1837 making it the nation's first public school for the visually impaired. The Ohio School for the Deaf was established in 1829, making it the fifth oldest residential school in the country.

Tax Records

Often known as tax duplicates, or Auditor's duplicate of tax assessments (tax inventory books), Ohio tax records begin as early as 1800. Used as a substitute census, they may help determine place of residence and dates of migration into and out of a specific locale. Used more expertly, they often provide clues to relationships, ages, and origins.

In general, tax records include resident and non-resident owners, delinquent tax properties, and personal property listings, inheritance tax duplicates, tax lists, incorporated companies, and others. Early records are usually arranged by township and then by the first letter of the surname, making them relatively easy to search. Many early Ohio tax records have been microfilmed.

Original pre-1850 (mostly pre-1838) tax records are available at county courthouses in the County Auditor's Office, the Ohio History Connection Library, regional network centers, and various other libraries in the state. The Ohio History Connection houses the Auditor of State's tax duplicates, 1800-1838.

Some tax records for early years have been abstracted (more or less completely) and published with indexes. Esther W. Powell's *Early Ohio Tax Records* is a transcription of many original tax lists found at the Ohio History Connection and covers the years 1800 to 1840.[174] Powell's work is a valuable reference for locating names of early Ohio residents.

---

174. Esther Weygandt Powell, comp., *Early Ohio Tax Records* (1971; reprint, Baltimore: Genealogical Publishing Co., 1985). This important Ohio reference source was reprinted with *The Index to Early Ohio Tax Records*, which is a surname index only. Unfortunately, this work does not contain a complete personal name index. See also the indexes to Ohio tax duplicates compiled by Gerald McKinney Petty for 1810, 1812, 1825, and 1835.

A large collection of Ohio tax records is also available on microfilm at the FamilySearch Library. City and county directories may also be useful in locating residents in a particular locality. Another useful reference and personal name finding aid is *The 1812 Census of Ohio: A Statewide Index of Taxpayers,* which shows a person's name and residence.[175] Gerald M. Petty compiled indexes to Ohio tax duplicates for the years 1810, 1812, 1825, and 1835.[176]

---

175. *The 1812 Census of Ohio: A Statewide index of Taxpayers* (Miami Beach, FL: T.L.C. Genealogy, 1992).

176. Gerald McKinney Petty (Columbus: Petty's Press, 1973,1976,1981, 1987). See also "An Act Levying a Tax on Land," *Laws of Ohio*, vol. 8, pp. 315-42, 19 Feb. 1810.

Township Records

Genealogists sometimes overlook township records in their Ohio research. These records may prove valuable, especially with difficult pre-1850 Ohio pedigree problems. A variety of records are found therein-minutes of meetings, lists of early township residents; names of trustees and officers; descriptions of property; and sometimes cemetery records, records of deaths, clues to relationships, ages, previous place of residence, and other information. Township records may have been created prior to the county's founding. Therefore, research should also be done in the parent county of the township.

As with many New England town records, the researcher may find *warnings out* recorded in some Ohio township records.[177] The author of this book has solved several difficult early Ohio pedigree problems by using township records.[178] Several articles in *The Report* have noted the merits of using township records in Ohio research.[179]

Township records may be found in the custody of township trustees, Ohio regional network centers, public and other local libraries, and local historical societies. Some tax records are on microfilm at the FamilySearch Library in Salt Lake City. Check also FamilySearch.org and Ancestry.com for tax records.

---

177. Warnings out is a custom from colonial New England. "Warnings out" occurred when indigent persons or families arriving in a region, had no means of support, and promised to become an economic burden upon the community. Suspected individuals or families would be brought to the attention of the town or township authorities; if the community's concern appeared justified, the governing body would rule that the unwelcome family had to move out of its jurisdiction by a specified date or face the penalties prescribed by law. Thus they were "warned out" of the Ohio township. A useful reference is Josiah Henry Benton, *Warning Out in New England, 1656-1817* (1911; reprint. Freeport, NY: Books for Libraries Press, 1970).

178. See, for example, Kip Sperry, ""The Morse Family of the Western Reserve in Ohio," *The American Genealogist* 60 (Oct 1984): 205-212. Ohio sources for genealogists are described in Kip Sperry, "Finding Tools for Ohio Research," *Genealogical Journal* 1 (December 1972): 122-25; and "Genealogical Research in Ohio," *National Genealogical Society Quarterly* 75 (June 1987): 81-104.

179. Diane V. Gagel, "Township Records," *The Report* 25 (Summer 1985): 83, is an example.

Vital Records

Vital record information (births, marriages, and deaths) may be found in civil government records (often known as vital statistics or civil vital records), church records, military records (service and pension files), Daughters of the American Revolution (DAR) transcriptions, family Bibles, home sources, and elsewhere. Most Ohio vital records begin at various times during the nineteenth century. Birth and death records, divorce records, and marriage records are described in greater detail in separate sections earlier in this book. Be sure to contact the county where the event occurred for the full record.

Recording of civil birth records in Ohio began in the counties in 1867, but births in some counties were recorded earlier during the period 1856-1857. Prior to 20 December 1908, births are available from the Probate Court of the county where the birth occurred. The Ohio Department of Health (Vital Statistics Office) in Columbus has birth records of people born in Ohio since 20 December 1908 to the present, records for deaths that occurred in Ohio from 1971 to the present, and marriage abstracts since 7 September 1949 to the present. Births after 20 December 1908 are also recorded with the Local Registrar of Vital Statistics or County Health Department where the birth occurred. Most government offices respond to mail requests for vital records.

Recording of civil death records in Ohio began in the counties in 1867, but a few were recorded earlier during the period 1856-57. Deaths prior to 20 December 1908 are recorded in the Probate Court of the county where the death occurred. Death records from 20 December 1908-1971 are available at the Ohio History Connection in Columbus and the Local Registrar in each county.

As of 1 Nov 2021, all records for deaths before 1971 have been transferred to the custody of the Ohio History Connection. Customers may obtain certified copies of pre-1971 death records by contacting the local county health where the death occurred.[180]

See especially the Ohio History Connection database, Ohio Death Certificate Index, 1913-1944, 1954-1970; the Ohio Department of Health Stillborn Death Certificates 1913-1935, 1942-1953, as well as the Columbus Board of Health Death Certificates, 1904-1908. **http://resources.ohiohistory.org/death/**. Death records from January 1972 to the present are available from the Ohio Department of Health (Vital Statistics Office) in Columbus for people who died in Ohio.

Ohio death indexes and death records for recent years are on microfilm at the FamilySearch Library in Salt Lake City. See the FamilySearch Library Catalog under the heading "Ohio-Vital records" and "Ohio-Vital records-Indexes."

Although recording of early marriages in the Buckeye State began with the origin of each county, the Ohio Department of Health in Columbus has Ohio marriage records and divorce records since 7 September 1949. They do not issue certified copies of these records, however. To obtain a certified copy of a marriage record, researchers should write to the Probate Court of the county where the marriage license was issued, or the Court of Common Pleas where the divorce was granted. The address of the Ohio Department of Health is:

Ohio Department of Health Vital Statistics
P.O. Box 15098
Columbus, OH 43215-0098

Sometimes vital record data may be difficult to locate because records have been destroyed, information may be missing in the records, or data may be difficult to read because of the handwriting, an ink spot, destruction of or damage to a record, or for other reasons.

---

180. The Ohio Department of Health has updated their website to indicate the transfer of the death records to the Ohio History Connection, Columbus. https://odh.ohio.gov/know-our-programs/vital-statistics/how-to-order-certificates

Substitute records for missing or incomplete Ohio civil vital records (births, marriages, and deaths) may include some of the sources on the list at the end of this section. Information in these records varies, and the reliability of the records vary since some are compiled sources while others are original records. Original records are always the best source to use for genealogical and historical research.

The records listed in the next section may be available in county courthouses, regional network centers in Ohio, genealogical and historical societies, public and university libraries, county archives, and so forth. Many of the sources described in this list are housed at the Ohio History Connection, State Library of Ohio; many are on microfilm at the FamilySearch Library in Salt Lake City, Utah; and they may be found at other libraries or archives housing Ohio records. A vital records register (list of call numbers) is available at the FamilySearch Library, as well as online at FamilySearch.org, which gives FamilySearch microfilm and microfiche numbers.[181]

---

181. U.S./Canada Staff, *Register of Vital Records at the FSL & Other Repositories: U.S./Canada* (Salt Lake City: FamilySearch, 2001). Thomas Jay Kemp's *International Vital Records Handbook*, 4th ed. (Baltimore: Genealogical Publishing Co., 2000) includes vital record application forms that may be useful in obtaining copies of civil vital records.

Substitutes for Missing or Incomplete Civil Vital Records Information in Ohio

Ancestor Card File (Ohio Genealogical Society card file)
Ancestral Charts (Ohio Genealogical Society)
Ancestral File (FamilySearch) **https://www.familysearch.org**
Bibles (family Bibles and family records found in family and home
    sources, genealogical libraries, historical societies, etc.)
Bible records (Ohio Genealogical Society)
Biographies (biographical sketches, compiled biographies)
Biographical encyclopedias
Bounty land applications (federal land records)
Bureau of Land Management records
    https://www.glorecords.blm.gov Business records
    (employment and social/commercial records) Canadian
    Border Crossings, 1895-1924
Cemetery records, burial records, gravestones
Census records (federal population census schedules): 1850, 1860,
    1870, 1880, 1900, 1910, 1920, 1930, 1940, 1950
    (microfilm and Internet)
Century home records (biographical sketches of homeowners
    maintained at some local historical societies)
Church histories (histories of individual congregations)
Church newspaper notices (births, marriages, deaths) and
    biographical sketches in newspapers
Church records (baptisms or christenings, marriages, and deaths or
    burials; membership records; and other church records)
Computer databases (Internet and compact discs). For example:
    County and Family Histories: Ohio, 1780-1970
    Early Ohio Settlers, 1700s-1900s
    Marriage Index: Ohio, 1789-1850
Coroner's records, coroner's docket
Correspondence, family letters, manuscript genealogies
Court records (civil cases, divorce, Chancery, name changes, others)

Daughters of the American Revolution (DAR) transcriptions-family Bible records, vital records, genealogies, cemetery records, probate abstracts, newspaper clippings, and other records
Delayed and corrected registration of births
Diaries and journals (autobiographies)
Directories: city directories for large cities, and rural directories
Divorce records and divorce case files
    (see especially, Carol Bell, *Ohio Divorces: The Early Years)*
Drivers licenses Employment records
Family Group Records Collection (FamilySearch Library)
Family records and home sources, personal papers, scrap books, baby books, and similar family records described in this volume
Fraternal society records (association, lodge, membership records)
Funeral home records and mortuary records
Genealogies (compiled family histories)
Grave Registrations of Soldiers Buried in Ohio (Ohio History Connection)
Gravestones (tombstone inscriptions)
Guardianship records
Hospital records
Immigration records (passenger arrival lists)
Institutional records (correctional, prison, or jail records) Insurance records
International Genealogical Index-IGI. FamilySearch, **https://www.familysearch.org**
Internet sites containing vital records, Ohio genealogical indexes, compiled genealogies, and other genealogical sources
Land records (bounty land records, homestead records and other federal land records, state and local land records)
Local histories (especially biographical sketches in county histories)
Manuscript collections (genealogical collections, pedigree charts, family group records, correspondence, journals, account books, others)
Marriage banns or intentions to marry
Marriage certificates
Marriage consents of minors by parents

Marriage license applications
Marriage returns and marriage registers
Medical certificates
Military Index-Vietnam and Korean conflicts (FamilySearch.org)
Military records (service records, compiled service records, pension applications and records, military draft registrations, and others)
Military rosters, unit histories, regimental histories, published military pension lists, descriptive rolls, muster-in rolls, and others
Ministers' license records of marriages
Minority records, ethnic archives, histories, ethnic newspapers
Mortality schedules (lists of deaths): 1850, Ohio counties H- W; 1860 (all Ohio counties); 1870 (incomplete); 1880 (counties Adams through Geauga, Ohio)
Mortuary files
Naturalization and citizenship records: applications, petitions, oaths, declaration of intention for citizenship, naturalization journals, certificate of arrival, final papers
Newspapers (birth, marriage, death, and divorce notices; obituaries; biographies; local history sketches; pioneer sketches)
Ohio Death Certificate Index, 1913-37
   https://www.ohiohistory.org/dindex
Ohio Genealogical Society Lineage Societies
Ohio History Connection Surname Index (card index on microfilm)
Ohio Marriages, 1803-1900 **https://www.ancestry.com**
Ohio Veteran's Home death records
Passport applications (available at the National Archives and on microfilm at FamilySearch Library; indexed), 1795 to ca. 1925
Patriotic and lineage society records (application papers and published biographies); hereditary society records
Pedigree Resource File (PRF), index at **https://www.familysearch.org**; many submissions include notes and sources
Periodicals and journal articles (genealogical and historical serials) See *Periodical Source Index* (PERSI) and *Genealogical Periodical Annual Index* (GPAI) for periodical indexes.

Police records
Prisoner of war records (such as the Civil War, and other wars)
Probate records (wills, letters of administration, distribution and
 settlement of estates, probate estate files)
Railroad retirement records
Revolutionary War Pension/Bounty Land Warrant Application Files
School records (school and college records)
Sextons' records
Social Security Death Index
https://www.familysearch.org,
https://www.ancestry.com other Internet sites
Social Security Administration records
Society of Civil War Families of Ohio application files
Soldiers' home records
Veterans' records and grave reports, records of veterans'
 organizations
Vital records (state, county, and city or town vital records)
World War I Draft Registration Cards, 1917-1918

Ohio Counties

County	Year Established	County Seat	Regional Center
Adams	1797	West Union	UC
Allen	1820	Lima	BGSU*
Ashland	1846	Ashland	UA
Ashtabula	1808	Jefferson	WRHS
Athens	1805	Athens	OU**
Auglaize	1848	Wapakoneta	WSU
Belmont	1801	St. Clairsville	OU**
Brown	1818	Georgetown	UC
Butler	1803	Hamilton	UC
Carroll	1833	Carrollton	Y
Champaign	1805	Urbana	WSU
Clark	1818	Springfield	WSU
Clermont	1800	Batavia	UC
Clinton	1810	Wilmington	UC
Columbiana	1803	Lisbon	Y
Coshocton	1810	Coshocton	UA
Crawford	1820	Bucyrus	BGSU*
Cuyahoga	1808	Cleveland	WRHS
Darke	1809	Greenville	WSU

County	Year Established	County Seat	Regional Center
Defiance	1845	Defiance	BGSU*
Delaware	1808	Delaware	OHC
Erie	1838	Sandusky	BGSU*
Fairfield	1800	Lancaster	OHC
Fayette	1810	Washington CH	OHC
Franklin	1803	Columbus	OHC
Fulton	1850	Wauseon	BGSU*
Gallia	1803	Gallipolis	OU**
Geauga	1806	Chardon	WRHS
Greene	1803	Xenia	WSU
Guernsey	1810	Cambridge	OU**
Hamilton	1790	Cincinnati	UC
Hancock	1820	Findlay	BGSU*
Hardin	1820	Kenton	BGSU*
Harrison	1813	Cadiz	Y
Henry	1820	Napoleon	BGSU*
Highland	1805	Hillsboro	UC
Hocking	1818	Logan	OU**
Holmes	1824	Millersburg	UA
Huron	1809	Norwalk	BGSU*
Jackson	1816	Jackson	OU**
Jefferson	1797	Steubenville	Y

County	Year Established	County Seat	Regional Center
Knox	1808	Mt. Vernon	OHC
Lake	1840	Painesville	WRHS
Lawrence	1815	Ironton	OU**
Licking	1808	Newark	OHC
Logan	1818	Bellefontaine	WSU
Lorain	1822	Elyria	WRHS
Lucas	1835	Toledo	BGSU*
Madison	1810	London	OHC
Mahoning	1846	Youngstown	Y
Marion	1820	Marion	OHC
Medina	1812	Medina	WRHS
Meigs	1819	Pomeroy	OU**
Mercer	1820	Celina	WSU
Miami	1807	Troy	WSU
Monroe	1813	Woodsfield	OU**
Montgomery	1803	Dayton	WSU
Morgan	1817	McConnelsville	OU**
Morrow	1848	Mt. Gilead	OHC
Muskingum	1804	Zanesville	OU**
Noble	1851	Caldwell	OU**
Ottawa	1840	Port Clinton	BGSU*
Paulding	1820	Paulding	BGSU*

County	Year Established	County Seat	Regional Center
Perry	1818	New Lexington	OU**
Pickaway	1810	Circleville	OHC
Pike	1815	Waverly	OU**
Portage	1808	Ravenna	UA
Preble	1808	Eaton	WSU
Putnam	1820	Ottawa	BGSU*
Richland	1808	Mansfield	UA
Ross	1798	Chillicothe	OU**
Sandusky	1820	Fremont	BGSU*
Scioto	1803	Portsmouth	OU**
Seneca	1820	Tiffin	BGSU*
Shelby	1819	Sidney	WSU
Stark	1808	Canton	UA
Summit	184	Akron	UA
Trumbull	1800	Warren	Y
Tuscarawas	1808	New Philadelphia	UA
Union	1820	Marysville	OHC
Van Wert	1820	Van Wert	BGSU*
Vinton	1850	McArthur	OU**
Warren	1803	Lebanon	UC
Washington	1788	Marietta	OU**
Wayne	1808	Wooster	UA

County	Year Established	County Seat	Regional Center
Williams	1820	Bryan	BGSU*
Wood	1820	Bowling Green	BGSU*
Wyandot	1845	Upper Sandusky	BGSU*

Ohio Regional Network Centers
Abbreviations Used

BGSU* Bowling Green State University, Bowling Green
OHC   Ohio History Connection, Columbus
OU**   Ohio University, Athens
UA   University of Akron, Akron
UC   University of Cincinnati, Cincinnati
WRHS   Western Reserve Historical Society, Cleveland
WSU   Wright State University, Dayton
Y   Youngstown Historical Center, Youngstown

BGSU* and OU** are no longer a part of the network. BGSU does retain local records while OU has dispersed some of their local records. It is helpful to contact both universities before visiting.

The date for each county in the above chart is the date it was established, which may differ from the year actually organized. Some useful references are:

Auditor of State **https//www.auditor.state.oh.us**
Ohio Lands: A Short History. 9th ed. Columbus: Auditor of State, 1997.
   https://freepages.rootsweb.com/~maggie/history/ohio-lands/ohl7.html
Along the Ohio Trail (download)
   https://ohio.gov/government/resources/along-the-ohio-trails
The Official Ohio Lands Book. Columbus: Auditor of State, 2002.
   https://www.auditor.state.oh.us

Ohio County Records

County	B	M	D	Land	Prob	Court
Adams	1888	1881	1888	1797	1849	1797
Allen	1867	1831	1867	1831	1831	1831
Ashland	1867	1846	1867	1846	1846	1846
Ashtabula	1867	1811	1867	1798	1811	1811
Athens	1867	1817	1867	1792	1800	1806
Auglaize	1867	1848	1867	1824	1848	1848
Belmont	1867	1803	1867	1800	1804	1801
Brown	1867	1818	1867	1818	1817	1818
Butler	1856	1803	1856	1803	1851	1803
Carroll	1867	1833	1867	1831	1833	1833
Champaign	1867	1805	1867	1805	1804	1805
Clark	1867	1818	1867	1818	1818	1818
Clermont	1856	1801	1856	1797	1800	1801
Clinton	1867	1810	1867	1806	1810	1810
Columbiana	1867	1803	1867	1795	1803	1803
Coshocton	1867	1811	1867	1800	1811	1811
Crawford	1866	1831	1866	1816	1826	1831
Cuyahoga	1867	1810	1868	1810	1811	1823
Darke	1867	1817	1867	1817	1818	1817

County	B	M	D	Land	Prob	Court
Defiance	1866	1845	1866	1823	1845	1845
Delaware	1867	1835	1867	1805	1812	1818
Erie	1856	1838	1856	1837	1838	1838
Fairfield	1867	1803	1867	1801	1803	1801
Fayette	1867	1810	1868	1810	1810	1828
Franklin	1867	1803	1867	1804	1805	1803
Fulton	1867	1864	1867	1835	1863	1850
Gallia	1864	1803	1867	1803	1803	1811
Geauga	1867	1806	1867	1795	1806	1806
Greene	1869	1803	1870	1798	1803	1803
Guernsey	1867	1810	1867	1802	1812	1810
Hamilton	1846	1808	1881	1787	1791	1844
Hancock	1867	1828	1867	1820	1828	1828
Hardin	1867	1833	1867	1826	1830	1833
Harrison	1867	1813	1867	1800	1813	1814
Henry	1867	1847	1867	1846	1847	1847
Highland	1867	1805	1867	1804	1809	1805
Hocking	1867	1818	1867	1818	1819	1818
Holmes	1867	1821	1867	1808	1824	1825
Huron	1867	1818	1867	1809	1815	1818
Jackson	1867	1816	1867	1816	1819	1816
Jefferson	1867	1803	1867	1795	1798	1804

County	B	M	D	Land	Prob	Court
Knox	1867	1808	1867	1808	1808	1808
Lake	1867	1840	1867	1840	1840	1840
Lawrence	1867	1817	1867	1816	1847	1817
Licking	1875	1808	1875	1800	1875	1809
Logan	1867	1818	1867	1810	1851	1818
Lorain	1867	1824	1867	1822	1840	1825
Lucas	1867	1835	1856	1808	1835	1835
Madison	1867	1810	1867	1810	1810	1810
Mahoning	1864	1846	1864	1795	1846	1847
Marion	1867	1824	1867	1821	1825	1824
Medina	1867	1818	1867	1818	1819	1818
Meigs	1867	1819	1867	1820	1822	1819
Mercer	1867	1828	1867	1823	1824	1824
Miami	1853	1807	1867	1807	1807	1807
Monroe	1867	1866	1867	1836	1867	1818
Montgomery	1866	1803	1866	1805	1803	1803
Morgan	1867	1819	1867	1793	1818	1819
Morrow	1867	1848	1867	1848	1848	1848
Muskingum	1867	1804	1867	1800	1804	1804
Noble	1867	1851	1867	1851	1851	1851
Ottawa	1867	1840	1869	1820	1840	1840
Paulding	1867	1839	1867	1835	1842	1839

County	B	M	D	Land	Prob	Court
Perry	1867	1818	1867	1818	1817	1818
Pickaway	1867	1810	1867	1810	1810	1810
Pike	1867	1815	1867	1799	1817	1815
Portage	1867	1808	1867	1795	1808	1809
Preble	1867	1808	1867	1805	1808	1808
Putnam	1854	1834	1867	1830	1835	1834
Richland	1856	1813	1856	1814	1813	1820
Ross	1867	1798	1867	1797	1798	1798
Sandusky	1867	1820	1867	1822	1820	1820
Scioto	1856	1804	1856	1803	1810	1809
Seneca	1867	1841	1867	1822	1828	1824
Shelby	1867	1824	1867	1819	1825	1818
Stark	1867	1809	1867	1809	1811	1809
Summit	1866	1840	1870	1840	1839	1840
Trumbull	1867	1803	1867	1795	1803	1807
Tuscarawas	1867	1808	1867	1808	1810	1808
Union	1867	1820	1867	1811	1820	1820
Van Wert	1867	1840	1867	1824	1839	1834
Vinton	1867	1850	1867	1850	1852	1850
Warren	1867	1803	1867	1795	1803	1803
Washington	1867	1789	1867	1788	1788	1790
Wayne	1867	1813	1867	1813	1816	1812

County	B	M	D	Land	Prob	Court
Williams	1867	1824	1867	1823	1825	1824
Wood	1867	1820	1867	1817	1820	1823
Wyandot	1867	1845	1867	1826	1845	1845

Key:
B   beginning date of county civil birth records (some county civil birth an death records began as early as 1856-1857)
M   beginning date of county civil marriage records
D   beginning date of county civil death records
Land   beginning date of county land records, such as deeds, etc.
Prob   beginning date of county wills or other probate records
Court   beginning date of county court records

Addresses - Ohio

Ada: Ohio Northern University, Heterick Memorial Library, 525 S. Main St., Ada, OH 45810
Ada Exempted Village Schools, 725 W. North Ave., Ada, OH 45810
Ada Public Library, 320 N. Main St., Ada, OH 45810
Adams County Public Library, 157 High Street, Peebles, OH 45660
Akron: Hower House, University of Akron, 60 Fir Hill St., Akron, OH 44325
Akron: Portage Lakes Historical Society, 95 Parisette Ln., Akron, OH 44319
Akron: Summit County Historical Society, 550 Copley Rd., Akron, OH 44320
Akron: University of Akron, University Libraries, 302 Buchtel Mall, Akron, OH 44325
Akron: University of Akron, Archival Services, Polsky Building, Akron, OH 44325
Akron-Summit County Public Library, 60 S. High St., Akron, OH 44326
Alexandria Public Library, 10 Maple Dr. Alexandria, OH 43001
Alger Public Library, 100 W. Wagner St., Alger, OH 45812
Alliance: Mount Union College Library, 1972 Clark Ave., Alliance, OH 44601
Alliance: Rodman Public Library, Alliance Room, 215 E. Broadway St., Alliance, OH 44601
Alliance Historical Society, 1042 Parkside Dr., P.O. Box 2044, Alliance, OH 44601
Amherst Historical Society, 113 S. Lake St., Amherst, OH 44001
Amherst Public Library, 221 Spring St., Amherst, OH 44001
Andover Public Library, 142 W. Main St., Andover, OH 44003
Arcanum Public Library, 101 North St., Arcanum, OH 45304
Archbold Community Library, 205 Stryker St., Archbold, OH 43502
Ashland County Historical Society & Museum, 420 Center St., Ashland, OH 44805
Ashland Public Library, 224 Claremont Ave., Ashland, OH 44805

Ashland University Library, 509 College Ave., Ashland, OH 44805
Ashley: Warnstaff Memorial Public Library, 302 E. High, Ashley, OH 43003
Ashtabula: Harbor-Topky Memorial Library, 1633 Walnut Blvd., Ashtabula, OH 44004
Ashtabula County District Library, 4335 Park Ave., Ashtabula, OH 44004
Athens: Ohio University, Archives and Special Collections, Vernon R. Alden Library, 30 Park Pl., Athens, OH 45701
Athens County Historical Society & Museum, 65 N. Court St., Athens, OH 45701
Athens County Public Libraries, 95 W. Washington, Nelsonville, OH 45764
Attica: Seneca East Public Library, 14 N. Main St., P.O. Box 572, Attica, OH 44807
Attica Area Historical Society, c/o Seneca East Public Library P.O. Box 572, Attica, OH 44807
Auditor of State. *See* Columbus: Auditor of State
Auglaize County Libraries, 203 S. Perry St., Wapakoneta, OH 45895
Aurora Historical Society, 115 East Pioneer Tr., Aurora, OH 44202
Austintown Historical Society, 1181 S. Raccoon Rd., Austintown, OH 44515
Avon Historical Society, 35748 Detroit Ave., Avon, OH 44011
Avon Lake Historical Society, 35770 Lake Rd., Avon Lake, OH 44012
Avon Lake Public Library, 32649 Electric Blvd., Avon Lake, OH 44012
Barberton Public Library, 602 West Park Ave., Barberton, OH 44203
Barnesville Hutton Memorial Library, 308 E. Main St., Barnesville, OH 43713
Batavia: Clermont County Genealogical Society, 326 Broadway St., P.O. Box 394, Batavia, OH 45103
Batavia: Clermont County Public Library, 180 S. Third St., Batavia, OH 45103
Bay Village Historical Society, 27715 Lake Rd., Bay Village, OH 44140

Beachwood: Jewish Genealogical Society of Cleveland, 27100 Cedar Rd., Beachwood, OH 44122
Beavercreek Community Library, 3618 Dayton-Xenia Rd., Beavercreek, OH 45432
Bedford Historical Society and Library, 30 S. Park St., Bedford, OH 44146
Bellaire Public Library, 330 32nd St., Bellaire, OH 43906
Bellbrook: Winters-Bellbrook Community Library, 57 Franklin St., Bellbrook, OH 45305
Belle Center Free Public Library, 103 S. Elizabeth St., Belle Center, OH; 43310
Bellefontaine: Logan County District Library, 220 N. Main St., Bellefontaine, OH 43311
Bellefontaine: Logan County Genealogical Society, 521 E. Columbus Ave., P.O. Box 36, Bellefontaine, OH 43311
Bellefontaine: Logan County Historical Society, 521 E. Columbus Ave., Bellefontaine, OH 43311
Bellevue Public Library, 224 E. Main St., Bellevue, OH 44811
Bellville: Ohio Genealogical Society, 611 SR 97, Bellville, OH 44813
Belmont County District Library, 20 James Wright Pl. Martins Ferry, OH 43935
Berea: Baldwin-Wallace College, Ritter Library, 57 E. Bagley Rd., Berea, OH 44017
Berea Area Historical Society, 118 E. Bridge St., P.O. Box 173, Berea, OH 44017
Berlin Center Historical Society, P.O. Box 112, Berlin Center, OH 44401
Berlin Heights Historical Society, 18 Main St., Berlin Heights, OH 44814
Bettsville Public Library, 233 State St., Bettsville, OH 44815
Bexley Historical Society, 2242 E. Main St., Bexley, OH 43209
Bexley Public Library, 2411 E. Main St., Bexley OH 43209
Bexley: Capital University, Blackmore Library, 661 College Ave., Bexley, OH 43209
Birchard Public Library of Sandusky County, 423 Croghan St., Fremont, OH 43420

Blanchester Area Historical Society, 103 E. Center St., Blanchester, OH 45107

Blanchester Public Library, 110 N. Broadway, Blanchester, OH 45107

Bloomville: Bliss Memorial Public Library, 20 S. Marion St., Bloomville, OH 44818

Bluffton College, Musselman Library, 1 University Dr., Bluffton, OH 45817

BlufftonPublic Library, 145 S. Main St., Bluffton, OH 45817

Bluffton: Mennonite Historical Library, 280 W. College Ave., Bluffton, OH 45817

Bluffton: Swiss Community Historical Society, 8350 Bixel Rd, Bluffton, OH 45817

Bowerston Public Library, 200 Main St., P.O. Box 205, Bowerston, OH 44695

Bowling Green: Wood County District Public Library, 251 N. Main St., Bowling Green, OH 43402

Bowling Green: Wood County Historical Society, 13660 County Home Rd., Bowling Green, OH 43402

Bowling Green State University, Center for Archival Collections, Jerome Library, Bowling Green University, Bowling Green, OH 43403

Bradford Public Library, 138 E. Main St., Bradford, OH 45308

Bratenahl Historical Society, 10300 Brighton Rd., Bratenahl, OH 44108

Bristol: Public Library, 1855 Greenville Rd., Bristolville, OH 44402

Bristolville: Bristol Historical Society, P.O. Box 254, Bristolville, OH 44402

Bristolville: Girard Historical Society, 1011 N. State S., Girard, OH 44402

Brooklyn Historical Society, 4442 Ridge Rd., Brooklyn, OH 44144

Brookville Historical Society Library, P.O. Box 82, Brookville, OH 45309

Bryan: Williams County Genealogical Society, 211 W. High St., Bryan, OH 43506

Bryan: Williams County Public Library, 107 East High Street, Bryan, OH 43506
Bucyrus Public Library, 200 East Mansfield St., Bucyrus, OH 44820
Burton: Geauga County Historical Society Library, 14653 East Park St., Burton, OH 44021
Burton: Geauga County Historical Society, 14653 East Park St., P.O. Box 153, Burton, OH 44021
Burton Public Library, 14588 West Park St., P.O. Box 427, Burton OH 44021
Butler-Clearfork Valley Historical Society, 43 Elm St., Butler, OH 44822
Cadiz: Harrison County Genealogical Chapter Library, 45507 Unionvale Rd., Cadiz, OH 43907
Cadiz: Puskarich Public Library, 200 E. Market St., Cadiz, OH 43907
Caldwell Public Library, 517 Spruce St., Box 230, Caldwell OH 43724
Cambridge: Guernsey County District Public Library, 800 Steuben-ville Ave., Cambridge, OH 43725
Cambridge: Guernsey County Law Library, Guernsey County Court House, Cambridge, OH 43725
Campbell Historical Society, 211 Struthers-Liberty Rd., Campbell, OH 44405
Canal Fulton Heritage Society, 116 S. Canal St., Unit 1,Canal Fulton, OH 44614
Canal Fulton Public Library, 154 Market St. N.E., Canal Fulton, OH 44614
Canal Society of Ohio, 550 Copley Rd., Akron, OH 44320
Canal Winchester Area Historical Society, P.O. Box 15, Canal Winchester, OH 43110
Canton: Hoover Historical Center, 2020 E. Maple St., Canton, OH 44720
Canton: Jackson Township Historical Society, 7756 Fulton Dr. NW, Massillon, OH 44646
Canton: Malone College, Everett L. Cattell Library, 515 25th St. NW, Canton, OH 44709

Canton: Stark County District Library, 715 Market Ave. North, Canton, OH 44702
Canton: Stark County District Library, Genealogy Division, 715 Market Avenue North, Canton, OH 44702
Canton: Stark County Historical Society and McKinley Museum, 800 McKinley Monument Dr. NW, Canton, OH 44708
Canton: Stark County Historical Society, P.O. Box 20070, Canton, OH 44701
Cardington-Lincoln Public Library, 128 E. Main St., P.O. Box 38, Cardington, OH 43315
Carey: Dorcas Carey Public Library, 300 E. Findlay St., Carey, OH 43316
Carroll County District Library, 70 Second St. NE, Carrollton, OH 44615
Cedarville Community Library, 20 S. Miller St., Cedarville, OH 45314
Cedarville University Library, 251 N. Main St., Cedarville, OH 45314
Celina: Mercer County District Library, 303 N. Main St., Celina, OH 45822
Celina: Mercer County Historical Society, 130 E. Market St., Celina, OH 45822
Celina: Mercer County Law Library Association, 321 Main St., Court House, Celina, OH 45822
Centerburg Public Library, 49 E. Main St., Centerburg, OH 43011
Centerville Historical Society, 78 N. Main St., Springboro, OH 45066
Centerville: Washington-Centerville Public Library, 111 W. Spring Valley Rd., Centerville, OH 45458
Chagrin Falls Historical Society, 87 E. Washington St., Chagrin Falls, OH 44022
Champaign County Library, 1060 Scioto St., Urbana, OH 43078
Chardon: Geauga County Public Library, 110 E. Park St., Chardon OH 44024
Chesterland: Geauga West Library, 13455 Chillicothe Rd., Chesterland, OH 44026

Chesterville: Selover Public Library, 31 E. Sandusky St.,
Chesterville, OH 43317
Chillicothe & Ross County Public Library, 140-146 S. Paint St.,
P.O. Box 185, Chillicothe, OH 45601
Chillicothe: Ross County Genealogical Society, 303 N. Paint St.,
Chillicothe, OH 45601
Chillicothe: Ross County Genealogical Society Library, 270 S.
Paint St., Chillicothe, OH 45601
Chillicothe: Ross County Historical Society, 45 W. 5th St.,
Chillicothe, OH 45601
Cincinnati: American Jewish Archives, 3101 Clifton Ave.,
Cincinnati, OH 45220
Cincinnati: Anderson Township Historical Society, 6550 Clough
Pk., P.O. Box 30174, Cincinnati, OH 45244
Cincinnati: Blue Ash Historical Society, 7 Trailbridge Dr.,
Cincinnati, OH 45241
Cincinnati: Coleraine Historical Society, P.O. Box 39726,
Cincinnati, OH 45239
Cincinnati: College Hill Historical Society, 6061 Dunlap Rd.,
Cincinnati, OH 45224
Cincinnati: Delhi Historical Society, 468 Anderson Ferry Rd.,
Cincinnati, OH 45238
Cincinnati: Eugene H. Maly Memorial Library, 6616 Beechmont
Ave., Cincinnati, OH 45230
Cincinnati: Green Township Historical Association, 3973 Grave
Ave., Cincinnati, OH 45211
Cincinnati: Hebrew Union College-Jewish Institute of Religion,
Klau Library, 3101 Clifton Ave., Cincinnati, OH 45220
Cincinnati Historical Society Library, 1301 Western Ave.,
Cincinnati, OH 45203
Cincinnati: Indian Hill Historical Society, 8100 Given Rd.,
Cincinnati, OH 45243
Cincinnati Law Library Association, Court House, Cincinnati,
OH 45202
Cincinnati: Lloyd Library and Museum, 917 Plum St.,
Cincinnati, OH 45202
Cincinnati: Mariemont Preservation Foundation, 3919 Plainville
Rd., Cincinnati, OH 45227

Cincinnati: Montgomery Historical Society, 7650 Cooper Rd., Cincinnati, OH 45242
Cincinnati: Price Hill Historical Society, 4434 Glenway Ave., P.O. Box 7020, Cincinnati, OH 45205
Cincinnati: Public Library of Cincinnati and Hamilton County, History and Genealogy Department 800 Vine St., Cincinnati, OH 45202
Cincinnati: University of Cincinnati, Archives Department, Carl Blegen Library, P.O. Box 210033, Cincinnati, OH 45221-0033 (Mail: Archives and Rare Books, Blegen Library, University of Cincinnati, Cincinnati OH 45221)
Cincinnati: University of Cincinnati, College of Law, Robert S. Marx Law Library, 2540 Clifton Ave., Cincinnati, OH 45221
Cincinnati: University of Cincinnati, Raymond Walters College Library, Cincinnati, OH 45221
Cincinnati: Wyoming Historical Society, 800 Oak St., Wyoming, OH 45215
Cincinnati: Xavier University, McDonald Memorial Library, 3800 Victory Pkwy., Cincinnati, OH 45207
Circleville: Pickaway County Historical/Genealogical Society, 210 N. Court St., Circleville, OH 43113
Circleville: Pickaway County District Public Library, 1160 N. Court St., Circleville, OH 43113
Cleveland: Afro-American Historical and Genealogical Society, P.O. Box 201476, Cleveland, OH 44120
Cleveland: Case Western Reserve University, 10900 Euclid Ave., Cleveland, OH 44106
Cleveland: Cuyahoga Community College Library, 700 Carnegie Ave., Cleveland, OH 44115
Cleveland: Cuyahoga County Archives, 2905 Franklin Blvd., Cleveland, OH 44113
Cleveland: Cuyahoga County Public Library, Fairview Park Regional Library, 21255 Lorain Rd., Fairview Park, OH 44126
Cleveland Heights-University Heights Public Library, 2345 Lee Rd., Cleveland, OH 44118

Cleveland Law Library Association, 1 West Lakeside Ave. FL 4, Cleveland, OH 44113
Cleveland: Mayfield Township Historical Society, 606 Som Center Rd., Cleveland, OH 44143
Cleveland Police Historical Society, 1300 Ontario St., Cleveland, OH 44113
Cleveland Public Library, 325 Superior Ave. NE, Cleveland, OH 44114
Cleveland State University, University Library, 2121 Euclid Ave., Cleveland, OH 44115
Cleveland: Ukranian Museum/Archives, 1202 Kenilworth Ave., Cleveland, OH 44113
Cleveland: Western Reserve Historical Society Library, 10825 East Blvd., Cleveland, OH 44106
Clyde Heritage League, P.O. Box 97, Clyde, OH 43410
Clyde Public Library, 222 W. Buckeye St., Clyde, OH 43410
Coldwater Public Library, 305 W. Main St., Coldwater, OH 45828
Columbiana-Fairfield Township Historical Society, 410 E. Park Ave., Columbiana, OH 44408
Columbiana Public Library, 332 N. Middle St., Columbiana, OH 44408
Columbus: Adjutant General's Department Library, 2825 W. Dublin Granville Rd., Columbus, OH 43235
Columbus: Auditor of State, State Land Office, 88 E. Broad St., P.O. Box 1140, Columbus, OH 43216
Columbus: Division of Veterans' Affairs, 30 E. Broad St., Columbus, OH 43266
Columbus: Franklin County Genealogical Society, 96 S. Grand Ave., Columbus, OH 43215
Columbus: Franklin County Genealogical Society Library, 570 W. Broad St., P.O. Box 2406, Columbus, OH 43216
Columbus: Governor's Office of Veterans Affairs, 77 S. High St., Columbus, OH 43215
Columbus: Hilltop Historical Society, 2300 W. Broad St., Columbus, OH 43204
Columbus Jewish Historical Society, 1175 College Ave., Columbus, OH 43209

Columbus Law Library Association, 369 High St., 10th Floor, Columbus, OH 43215
Columbus Metropolitan Library, 96 S. Grant Ave., Columbus, OH 43215
Columbus: Ohio Attorney General, Law Library, 30 E. Broad St., 17th Floor, Columbus, OH 43266
Columbus: Ohio Department of Health, Vital Statistics, 35 E. Chestnut, Columbus, OH 43215
Columbus: Ohio Division of Travel and Tourism, P.O. Box 1001, Columbus, OH 43216
Columbus: Ohio History Connection, Archives/Library Division, 800 E. 17th Ave., Columbus, OH 43211
Columbus: Ohio Humanities Council, 541 W. Rich St., Columbus, OH 43215
Columbus: Ohio Memory Project, 717 W. Town St., Columbus, OH 43222
Columbus: Ohio State University, College of Law Library, Drinko Hall, 55 West 12th Avenue, Columbus, OH 43210
Columbus: Ohio State University, William Oxley Thompson Memorial Library, 1858 Neil Avenue Mall, Columbus, OH 43210
Columbus: Ohioana Library, 274 E. First Ave., Columbus, OH 43201
Columbus: Palatines to America Library, 611 E. Weber Rd., Columbus, OH 43211
Columbus: Pontifical College Josephinum, A.T. Wehrle Memorial Library, 7625 North High Street, Columbus, OH 43235
Columbus: Sons of the American Revolution, 545 E. Weisheimer Rd., Columbus OH 43214
Columbus State Community College Library, 550 E. Spring St., Columbus, OH 43215
Columbus: State Library of Ohio, 274 E. First Ave., Columbus, OH 43201
Columbus: Supreme Court of Ohio, Law Library, 65 S. Front St., Columbus, OH 43215
Columbus: Trinity Lutheran Seminary, Hamma Library, 2199 E. Maine St., Columbus, OH 43209

Columbus: University District Organization, 2231 N. High St., Room 200, Columbus, OH 43201
Conneaut Carnegie Library, 282 State Street, Conneaut, OH 44030
Cortland: Bazetta Cortland Historical Society, P.O. Box 411, Cortland, OH 44410
Coshocton: Roscoe Village Foundation, 381 Hill St., Coshocton, OH 43812
Coshocton Public Library, 655 Main St., Coshocton, OH 43812
Covington: J.R. Clarke Public Library, 102 Spring St., Covington, OH 45318
Creston Historical Society, 116 S. Main St., Creston, OH 44217
Crestline Public Library, 324 North Thomas St., Crestline, OH 44827
Cridersville Historical Society, P.O. Box 2444, Cridersville, OH 45806
Cuyahoga County Public Library, Fairview Park Regional Library, 21255 Lorain Road, Fairview Park, OH 44126
Cuyahoga Falls: Taylor Memorial Public Library, Cuyahoga Falls Public Library, 2015 Third St., Cuyahoga Falls, OH 44221
Cuyahoga Falls Historical Society 2083 Cook St., Cuyahoga Falls, OH 44221
Dayton Metro Library, 215 E. Third St., Dayton, OH 45402
Dayton: Jewish Genealogical Society of Dayton, 4624 Fayette Ct., Dayton, OH 45415
Dayton: Montgomery County Genealogical Society, P.O. Box 1584, Dayton, OH 45401
Dayton: Oakwood Historical Society Library, 1947 Far Hills Ave., Dayton, OH 45419
Dayton: Sinclair Community College Library, 444 W. Third St., Dayton, OH 45402
Dayton: United Theological Seminary Library, 45001 Denlinger Rd., Dayton, OH 45426
Dayton: University of Dayton Libraries, Roesch Library, 300 College Park, Dayton, OH 45469
Dayton: Wright Memorial Public Library, 1776 Far Hills Ave.,

Dayton (Oakwood), OH 45419
Dayton: Wright State University, Archives and Special
    Collections, Paul Laurence Dunbar Library, 3640
    Colonel Glenn Hwy., Dayton, OH 45435
Deerfield Historical Society, 2071 Bonner Rd., Deerfield, OH
    44411
Defiance College, Pilgrim Library, 201 College Pl., Defiance,
    OH 43512
Defiance County Historical Society, P.O. Box 801, Defiance, OH
    43512
Defiance Public Library, 320 Fort St., Defiance, OH 43512
Delaware: Methodist Theological School in Ohio, John W.
    Dickhaut Library, 3081 Columbus Pike, P.O. Box 8004,
    Delaware, OH 43015
Delaware: Ohio Wesleyan University, L.A. Beeghly Library, 43
    Rowland Ave., Delaware, OH 43015
Delaware: United Methodist Archives, Beeghly Library, 43
    Rowland Ave., Delaware, OH 43015
Delaware County District Library, 84 E. Winter St., Delaware,
    OH 43015
Delaware County Historical Society, 2690 Stratford Rd.,
    Delaware, OH 43015
Delphos Public Library, 309 W. Second St., Delphos, OH 45833
Delta Public Library, 402 Main St., Delta, OH 43515
Dennison: Tuscarawas County Genealogical Society, 307 Center
    St., Dennison, OH 44621
Deshler: Henry County Genealogical Society, 208 N. East Ave.,
    P.O. Box 231, Deshler, OH 42516
Deshler: Patrick Henry School District Public Library, 208 N.
    East Ave., Deshler, OH 43516
Dover Public Library, 525 N. Walnut St., Dover, OH 44622
Doylestown: Chippewa-Rogues' Hollow Historical
    Society, 17500 Gale House Rd., P.O. Box 283,
Doylestown, OH 44230
Dublin Historical Society, 6659 Coffman Rd,. P.O. Box 2,
    Dublin, OH 43017
Dunkirk: Hardin Northern Public Library, 153 N. Main St.,
    Dunkirk, OH 45836

East Cleveland Public Library, 14101 Euclid Ave., East Cleveland, OH 44112
East Liverpool: Carnegie Public Library, 219 E. Fourth St., East Liverpool, OH 43920
East Palestine Memorial Public Library, 309 N. Market St., East Palestine, OH 44413
Eaton: Preble County District Library, 450 S. Barron St., Eaton, OH 45320
Elmore: Harris-Elmore Public Library, 328 Toledo St., P.O..Box 45, Elmore, OH 43416
Elmore Historical Society, 353 Ottawa St., Elmore, OH 43416
Elyria: Lorain County Community College Library, 1005 Abbe Rd. N., Elyria, OH 44035
Elyria: Lorain County Historical Society, Gerald Hicks Memorial Library, 509 Washington Ave., Elyria, OH 44035
Elyria: North Ridgeville Historical Society, 145 Stanford Ave., Elyria, OH 44035
Elyria Public Library, 320 Washington Ave., Elyria, OH 44035
Enon Community Historical Society, 45 Indian Dr., Enon, OH 45323
Euclid Historical Society, 21129 North St., Euclid, OH 44117
Euclid Public Library, 631 East 222nd St., Euclid, OH, 44123
Fairborn Community Library, 1 E. Main St., Fairborn, OH 45324
Fairport Harbor Public Library, 335 Vine St., Fairport Harbor, OH 44077
Fairview Park: Cuyahoga County Public Library, Fairview Park Regional Library, 21255 Lorain Rd., Fairview Park, OH 44126
Farmersville Historical Society, 57 California St., Farmersville, OH 45325
Fayette: Normal Memorial Library, 301 N. Eagle, Fayette, OH 43521
Findlay-Hancock County Public Library, 206 Broadway St., Findlay, OH 45840
Findlay: Hancock Historical Museum Association, 422 W. Sandusky St., Findlay, OH 45840
Findlay: University of Findlay, Shafer Library, 1000 N. Main St.,

Findlay, OH 45840
Firelands Council of Historical Societies. *See* Monroeville.
Forest-Jackson Public Library, 102 W. Lima St., Forest, OH 45843
Fort Loramie Historical Association, P.O. Box 276, Fort Loramie, OH 45845
Fort Recovery Historical Society, One Fort Site St., P.O. Box 533, Fort Recovery, OH 45846
Fort Recovery Public Library, 113 N. Wayne, Fort Recovery, OH 45846
Fostoria: Tri-County Lineage Research Society, Kaubisch Memorial Public Library, 205 Perry St., Fostoria, OH 44830
Fostoria Area Historical Society & Museum, 123 W. North St., Fostoria, OH 44830
Franklin County Genealogy Society, P.O. Box 44309, Columbus, OH 43204
Franklin Area Historical Society, Harding Museum, 302 Park Ave., Franklin, OH 45005
Franklin-Springboro Public Library, 400 Anderson St., Franklin, OH 45005
Fredericktown Area Historical Society, 11 E. Sandusky St., Fredericktown, OH 43019
Fremont: Birchard Public Library of Sandusky County, 423 Croghan St., Fremont, OH 43420
Fremont: Rutherford B. Hayes Library, Spiegel Grove, 1337 Hayes Ave., Fremont, OH 43420
Fremont: Sandusky County Historical Society, 514 Birchard Ave., Fremont, OH 43420
Fremont: Sandusky County Kin Hunters, 1337 Hayes Ave., Fremont, OH 43420
Fremont: Terra Community College Library, 2830 Napoleon Rd., Fremont, OH 43420
Galion Historical Society, P.O. Box 125, Galion, OH 44833
Galion Public Library Association, 123 N. Market St., Galion, OH 44833
Gallipolis: Dr. Samuel L. Bossard Memorial Library, 7 Spruce St., Gallipolis, OH 45631

Gallipolis: Gallia County Historical & Genealogical Society, 340 South Ave., Gallipolis, OH 45631
Gambier: Kenyon College, Olin-Chalmers Memorial Library, 103 College Dr., Gambier, OH 43022
Gambier Folklore Society, Kenyon College, Gambier, OH 43022
Garfield Heights Historical Society, 5404 Turney Rd., Garfield Heights, OH 44125
Garrettsville: James A. Garfield Historical Society, 8107 Main St., Garrettsville, OH 44231
Garrettsville: Portage County District Library, 10482 South St., Garrettsville, OH 44231
Gates Mills Historical Society, 7580 Old Mill Rd., P.O. Box 191, Gates Mills, OH 44040
Geneva: Ashtabula County Genealogical Society, 860 Sherman St., Geneva OH 44041
Geneva: Harpersfield Heritage Society, 125 Jobey Tr., Geneva, OH 44041
Georgetown: Brown County Genealogy Society, 200 E. Cherry St., Georgetown, OH 45121
Georgetown: Mary P. Shelton Library, 200 W. Grant Ave., Georgetown, OH 45121
Germantown: Historical Society of Germantown, 47 W. Center St., P.O. Box 144, Germantown, OH 45327
Germantown Public Library, 51 N. Plum St., Germantown, OH 45327
Girard Free Public Library, 105 E. Prospect St., Girard, OH 44420
Gnadenhutten Historical Society, 352 S. Cherry St., P.O. Box 396, Gnadenhutten, OH 44629
Gnadenhutten Public Library, 435 S. Cherry St., Gnadenhutten, OH 44629
Grafton-Midview Public Library, 983 Main St., Grafton, OH 44044
Grandview Heights Public Library, 1685 W. First St., Grandview Heights, OH 43212
Granville: Denison University, Doane Library, 100 W. College St., Granville, OH 43023

Granville: Robbins Hunter Museum/Avery Downer House, 221
    E. Broadway, P.O. Box 183, Granville, OH 43023
Granville Public Library, 217 E. Broadway, Granville, OH 43023
Gratis: Marion Lawrence Memorial Library, 15 E. Franklin St.,
    Gratis, OH 45330
Greenville: Carnegie Library, 520 Sycamore St., Greenville, OH
    45331
Greenville: Darke County Historical Society, 205 N. Broadway
    St., Greenville, OH 45331
Greenville: Garst Museum, Genealogical Library, 205 N.
    Broadway, Greenville, OH 45331
Greenville Public Library, 520 Sycamore St., Greenville, OH
    45331
Grove City: Southwest Public Libraries, Grove City Library, SPL
    Admin., 3959 Park St., Grove City, OH 43123
Groveport: Motts Military Museum, 5075 S. Hamilton Rd.,
    Groveport, OH 43125
Hamden: Vinton County Historical & Genealogical Society, 207
    S. Sugar St., McArthur, OH 45651
Hamilton: Butler County Historical Society, 327 N. Second St.,
    Hamilton, OH 45011
Hamilton: Lane Public Library, 300 N. Third St., Hamilton, OH
    45011
Harrison: Village Historical Society, 105 Marvin Rd. Harrison,
    OH 45030
Hartville: Marlboro Township Historical Society, P.O. Box 275,
    Hartville, OH 44632
Hebron Public Library, 934 W. Main St., Hebron, OH 43025
Hicksville Historical Society, P.O. Box 162, Hicksville, OH
    43526
Hilliard: Northwest Franklin County Historical Society, 4162
    Avery Rd., P.O. Box 413, Hilliard, OH 43026
Hillsboro: Highland County District Library, 10 Willettsville
    Pike, Hillsboro, OH 45133
Hillsboro: Southern Ohio Genealogical Society, 1487 N. High
    St., (North High Business Center), Hillsboro, OH 45133
Hillsboro: Southern State Community College Library, 100

Hobart Dr., Hillsboro, OH 45133
Hinckley Historical Society, 889 Center Rd., P.O. Box 471,
 Hinckley, OH 44233
Hiram College, Hiram College Library, 11694 Hayden St.,
 Hiram, OH 44234
Hiram Historical Society, P.O. Box 1775, Hiram, OH 44234
Holgate Community Library, 204 Railway Ave., Holgate, OH 43527
Homer Public Library, 385 South Street NW, Utica, OH 43080
Hubbard Public Library, 436 W. Liberty St..t, Hubbard, OH
 44425
Hubbard Historical Society, 396 Hager St., Hubbard, OH 44425
Hudson Library & Historical Society, 96 Liberty St., Hudson,
 OH 44236
Huron: Bowling Green State University, Firelands College
 Library, 1 University Dr., Huron, OH 44839
Huron Public Library, 333 Williams St., Huron, OH 44839
Ironton: Briggs Lawrence County Public Library, 321 S. Fourth
 St., Ironton, OH 45638
Ironton: Lawrence County Historical Society, 506 S. Sixth St.,
 Ironton, OH 45683
Italian American War Veterans, National Headquarters, 115 S
 Meridian Rd., Youngstown, OH 44509
Jackson City Library, 21 Broadway St., Jackson, OH 45640
Jamestown Community Library, 86 Seaman Dr., Jamestown, OH
 45335
Jefferson Branch, Carnegie Public Library, 22 S. Main St.,
 Jeffersonville, OH 43218
Jefferson: Henderson Memorial Public Library, 54 E. Jefferson
 St., Jefferson, OH 44047
Jefferson: Lenox Historical Society, 2520 State Route 46 South,
 Box 58, Jefferson, OH 44047
Johnston Public Library, 1 S. Main St., Johnstown, OH 43031
Kalida: Putnam County Historical Society, 201 E. Main St., P. O.
 Box 264, Kalida, OH 45853
Kent Free Library, 312 W. Main, Kent, OH 44240
Kent Historical Society, 237 E. Main St., Kent, OH 44240
Kent State University, Libraries & Media Services, 1125 Risman

Dr., Kent, OH 44242

Kenton: Hardin County Historical Museums, 223, N. Main St., Kenton, OH 43326

Kenton: Mary Lou Johnson Hardin County District Library, 325 E. Columbus St., Kenton, OH 43326

Kidron Community Historical Society, 13153 Emerson Rd., Apple Creek, OH 44606

Killbuck Valley Historical Society, P.O. Box 142, Killbuck, OH 44637

Kingsville Public Library, 6006 Academy St., Kingsville, OH 44048

Kinsman Free Public Library, 6420 Church St., P.O. Box 166 Kinsman, OH 44428

Kirtland Hills: Lake County Historical Society, 8610 Mentor Rd., Kirtland Hills, OH 44060

Kirtland Public Library, 9267 Chillicothe R.d, Kirtland, OH 44094

Kirtland: Lakeland Community College Library, 7700 Clocktower Dr., Kirtland, OH 44094

Lakewood Historical Society & Library, 14710 Lake Ave., Lakewood, OH 44107

Lakewood Public Library, 13314 Detroit Ave., Lakewood, OH 44107

Lancaster: Fairfield County District Library, 219 North Broad St., Lancaster, OH 43130

Lancaster: Fairfield Heritage Association, 105 E. Wheeling St., Lancaster, OH 43130

Lancaster: Ohio University-Lancaster Library, 1570 Granville Pike, Lancaster, OH 43130

Lebanon Public Library, 101 S. Broadway, Lebanon, OH 45036

Lebanon: Warren County Genealogical Resource Center, Warren County Courthouse, 406 Justice Dr., Lebanon, OH 45036

Lebanon: Warren County Historical Society, Museum & Library, 105 S. Broadway, P.O. Box 223, Lebanon, OH 45036

Leetonia Community Public Library, 181 Walnut St., Leetonia, OH 44431

LeRoy Heritage Association, 12941 Girdled Rd., LeRoy, OH

44077
Lewisburg: Brown Memorial Library, 101 S. Commerce, P.O. Box 640, Lewisburg, OH 45338
Liberty Center Public Library, 124 East St., P.O. Box 66, Liberty Center, OH 43532
Lima: Allen County Historical Society, Elizabeth M. MacDonell Memorial Library, 620 W. Market St., Lima, OH 45801
Lima Public Library, 650 W. Market St., Lima, OH 45801
Lisbon: Lepper Library, 303 E. Lincoln Way, Lisbon, OH 44432
Lithopolis: Wagnalls Memorial Library, 150 E. Columbus St., P.O. Box 217, Lithopolis, OH 43136
Logan-Hocking County District Library, 230 E. Main St., Logan, OH 43138
Logan County Genealogical Society, 521 E. Columbus Ave., Bellefontaine, OH 43311
London Public Library, 20 E First St., London, OH 43140
Lorain: Black River Historical Society, 309 Fifth St., Lorain, OH 44052
Lorain Public Library, 351 Sixth St., Lorain, OH 44052
Loudonville Public Library, 122 E. Main St., Loudonville, OH 44842
Louisville Area Historic Preservation Society, 523 E. Main St., Louisville, OH 44641
Louisville Public Library, 700 Lincoln Ave., Louisville, OH 44641
Loveland: Greater Loveland Historical Society & Museum, 201 Riverside Dr., Loveland, OH 45140
Luckey Library, 228 Main St., Luckey, OH 43443
Madison: Mackenzie Memorial Public Library, Madison Public Library, 6111 Middle Ridge Rd., Madison, OH 44057
Madison Historical Society, 126 W. Main St., Madison, OH 44057
Manchester: Manchester Public Library, 401 Pike St., Manchester, OH 45144
Mansfield: Richland County Historical Society, 310 Springmill St., Mansfield, OH 44903
Mansfield-Richland County Public Library, 43 W. Third St., Mansfield, OH 44902

Mantua Historical Society, 4196 Twinsburg Warren Rd., Mantua, OH 44255
Marietta: Campus Martius Museum Library, 601 Second St., Marietta, OH 45750
Marietta College, Dawes Memorial Library, 215 Fifth St., Marietta, OH 45750
Marietta: Washington County Historical Society346 Muskingum Dr. Marietta, OH 45750
Marietta: Washington County Public Library, 615 Fifth St., Marietta, OH 45750
Marietta: Washington State Community College, Learning Resource Center, 710 Colegate Dr., Marietta, OH 45750
Marion County Historical Society, 169 E. Church St., Marion, OH 43302
Marion Public Library, 445 E Church St., Marion, OH 43302
Martins Ferry Public Library, 20 James Wright Plaza., P.O. Box 130, Martins Ferry, OH 43935
Marysville Public Library, 231 S. Plum St., Marysville, OH 43040
Mason Historical Society, 207 W. Church St., Mason, OH 45040
Mason Public Library, 200 Reading Rd., Mason, OH 45040
Massillon Heritage Foundation, 210 Fourth St. NE, Massillon, OH 44646
Massillon Museum, 121 Lincoln Way E., Massillon, OH 44646
Massillon: Ohio Society of Military History, 316 Lincoln Way E., Massillon, OH 44646
Massillon Public Library, 208 Lincoln Way E., Massillon, OH 44646
Maumee Valley Historical Society, 1031 River Rd., Maumee, OH 43537
McArthur: Herbert Wescoat Memorial Library, 120 N. Market St., McArthur, OH 45651
McComb Public Library, 113 S. Todd St., McComb, OH 45858
McConnelville: Kate Love Simpson Library, 358 E. Main St., McConnelville, OH 43765
Mechanicsburg Public Library, 60 S. Main St., Mechanicsburg, OH 43044

Medina: Granger Library & Historical Society, 1261 Granger Rd., Medina, OH 44256

Medina Community Design Committee, 141 S. Prospect St., Medina, OH 44256

Medina County District Library, 210 S. Broadway St., Medina, OH 44256

Medina County Historical Society, 206 N. Elmwood St., Medina, OH 44256

Mentor: Lake County Historical Society Library, 8610 King Memorial Rd., Mentor, OH 44060

Mentor: Library of Henry J. Grund, 4897 Corduroy Rd., Mentor Headlands, Mentor, OH 44060

Mentor Public Library, 8215 Mentor Ave., Mentor, OH 44060

Metamora: Evergreen Community Library, 253 Maple St., Metamora, OH 43540

Miamisburg Historical Society, P.O. Box 774, Miamisburg, OH 45343

Miamitown: Miami Historical Society of Whitewater Township, P.O. Box 744, Miamitown, OH 45041

Middletown Public Library, 125 S. Broad St., Middletown, OH 45044

Milan-Berlin Township Public Library, 19 E. Church St., Milan, OH 44846

Milan Public Library, 19 E. Church St., Milan, OH 44846

Milford Area Historical Society, 906 Main St., Milford, OH 45150

Millersburg: Holmes County District Public Library, 3102 Glen Dr., P.O. Box 111, Millersburg, OH 44654-1397

Minerva Area Historical Society, 128 N. Market St., Minerva, OH 44657

Minerva Public Library, 677 Lynnwood Dr., Minerva, OH 44657

Minster: Fort Loramie Historical Association, 37 N. Main St., Box 276, Fort Loramie, OH 45845

Monroeville: Firelands Council of Historical Societies, P.O. Box 11, Monroeville, OH 44847

Monroeville Public Library, 34 Monroe St., P.O. Box 276, Monroeville, OH 44847

Montpelier: Williams County Historical Society, P.O. Box 415, Montpelier, OH 43543
Montpelier Public Library, 216 E. Main St., Montpelier, OH 43543
Morgan County Historical Society, 142 E. Main St., McConnelsville, OH 43756
Morrow: Salem Township Public Library, 535 West Pike St., Morrow, OH 45152
Mount Gilead Public Library, 41 E. High St., Mount Gilead, OH 43338
Mount Gilead: Perry Cook Memorial Public Library, 7406 County Road 22, Mount Gilead, OH 43338
Mount Orab: Brown County Public Library, 613 S. High St., Mount Orab, OH 45154
Mount Pleasant: Historical Society of Mount Pleasant 342 Union St. Mount Pleasant, OH 43939
Mount Sterling Public Library, 60 W. Columbus St., Mount Sterling, OH43143-1236
Mount Vernon: Knox County Historical Society, 875 Harcourt Rd., Mount Vernon, OH 43050
Mount Vernon Nazarene University, Thome Library, 800 Martins-burg Rd., Mount Vernon, OH 43050
Mount Vernon: Public Library of Mount Vernon & Knox County, 201 N. Mulberry St., Mount Vernon, OH 43050
Mount Victory: Ridgemont Public Library, 124 E. Taylor St., P.O. Box 318, Mount Victory, OH 43340
Napoleon Public Library, 310 W. Clinton St., Napoleon, OH 43545
Navarre-Bethlehem Township Historical Society, 123 High St., Navarre, OH 44662
Nelsonville: Hocking College Library, 3301 Hocking Pkwy, Nelsonville, OH 45764
Nelsonville Public Library, 95 W. Washington, Nelsonville, OH 45764
New Albany-Plain Township Historical Society, P.O. Box 219, New Albany, OH 43054
New Bremen Historic Association, 102 N. Main St., New

Bremen, OH 45869
New Carlisle Public Library, 111 E. Lake Ave., New Carlisle, OH 45344
New Concord: Muskingum College Library, 260 Stadium Dr., New Concord, OH 43762
New Lexington: Perry County District Library, 117 S. Jackson St., New Lexington, OH 4376
New London Public Library, 67 S. Main St., New London, OH 44851
New Madison Public Library, 142 S. Main St., P.O. Box 32, New Madison, OH 45346
New Matamoras: Matamoras Area Historical Society, 200 Main St., P.O. Box 1846, New Matamoras, OH 45767
New Philadelphia: Ragersville Historical Society, 8800 Crooked Run Rd., Sugarcreek, OH 44681
New Philadelphia: Tuscarawas County Public Library, 121 Fair NW, New Philadelphia, OH 44663
New Straitsville Public Library, 102 E. Main St., P.O. Box 8, New Straitsville, OH 43766
Newark: Emerson R. Miller Library, 990 W. Main St., Newark, OH 43055
Newark: Licking County Genealogical Society Library, 101 W. Main St., P.O. Box 4037, Newark, OH 43055
Newark: Licking County Historical Society, P.O. Box 785, Newark, OH 43055
Newark Public Library, 101 W. Main St., Newark, OH 43055
Newcomerstown Public Library, 123 N. Bridge St., Newcomerstown, OH 43832
Newton Falls Public Library, 204 S. Canal, Newton Falls, OH 44444
Niles: McKinley Memorial Library, 40 N. Main St., Niles, OH 44446
North Baltimore Public Library, 230 N. Main St., North Baltimore, OH 45872
North Canton Heritage Society, 185 Ream St., North Canton, OH 44720
North Canton Public Library, 185 N. Main St., North Canton, OH 44720

North Royalton Historical Society, 13759 Ridge Rd., Cleveland, OH 44133
Northfield: Historical Society of Olde Northfield, 9390 Olde Eight Rd., Northfield, OH 44067
Norwalk: Firelands Historical Society Laning-Young Research Library, 9 Case Ave.,P.O. Box 572, Norwalk, OH 44857
Norwalk: First Presbyterian Church Library, 21 Firelands Blvd., Norwalk, OH 44857
Norwalk Public Library, 46 W. Main St., Norwalk, OH 44857.
Norwood Public Library, 4325 Montgomery Rd., Norwood, OH 45212
Oak Harbor Public Library, 147 W. Main St., Oak Harbor, OH 43449
Oak Hill Public Library, 226 S. Front St., Oak Hill, OH 45656
Oak Hill: Welsh-American Heritage Museum, 412 E. Main St., Oak Hill, OH 45656
Oberlin College Library, 148 W. College St., Oberlin, OH 44074
Oberlin Public Library, 65 S. Main St., Oberlin, OH 44074
Ohio Department of Health. *See* Columbus: Ohio Department of Health
Ohio Genealogical Society. *See* Bellville: Ohio Genealogical Society
Ohio History Connection. *See* Columbus: Ohio History Connection
Ohio Society of Military History. *See* Massillon
Ohio State Library. *See* Columbus: State Library of Ohio
Orrville Historical Museum, 142 Depot St., Orrville, OH44667
Orrville Public Library, 230 N. Main St., Orrville, OH 44667
Orrville: University of Akron, Wayne College Library, 1901 Smucker Rd., Orrville, OH 44667
Orwell: Grand Valley Public Library, 1 N. School St, Orwell, OH 44076
Ottawa: Putnam County District Library, 525 N. Thomas St., P.O. Box 308, Ottawa, OH 43875.
Oxford: Miami University, 151 S. Campus Ave., Oxford, OH 45056
Oxford: Smith Library of Regional History, Lane Public Library, Oxford Branch, 441 S. Locust St.., Oxford, OH 45056
Painesville: Morley Library, 184 Phelps St., Painesville, OH 44077
Parma: Cuyahoga County Public Library, 6996 Powers Blvd., Parma, OH 44129

Pataskala Public Library, 101 S. Vine St., Pataskala, OH 43062
Paulding County Carnegie Public Library, 205 S. Main St., Paulding, OH 45879
Pemberville Public Library, 375 E. Front St., Pemberville, OH 43450
Peninsula Library & Historical Society, 6105 Riverview Road, P.O. Box 236, Peninsula, OH 44264
Pepper Pike: Ursuline College, Ralph M. Besse Library, 2550 Lander Rd., Pepper Pike, OH 44124
Perry Historical Society of Lake County, P.O. Box 216, Perry, OH 44081
Perry Public Library, 3753 Main St., Perry, OH 44081
Perrysburg: Historic Perrysburg, P.O. Box 703, Perrysburg, OH 43552
Perrysburg: Way Public Library, 101 E. Indiana Ave., Perrysburg, OH 43551
Pickaway County Historical and Genealogical Library, 210 N. Court St., Circleville, OH 43113
Pickerington Public Library, 201 Opportunity Way, Pickerington, OH 43147
Pickerington-Violet Township Historical Society, 15 E. Columbus St., Pickerington, OH 43147
Piqua Public Library, 116 W. High St., Piqua, OH 45356
Piqua: Edison Community College Library, 1973 Edison Drive, Piqua, OH 45356
Piqua: Flesh Public Library, 124 W. Greene St., Piqua, OH 45356
Piqua: Historical Society, 9845 N. Hardin Road, Piqua, OH 45351
Piqua: Rossville Museum & Cultural Center, 8280 McFarland Rd., P.O. Box 627, Piqua, OH 45356
Piqua: Rossville-Spring Creek Historical Society, 8280 McFarland Rd., Piqua, OH 45356
Plain City Public Library, 305 W. Main St., Plain City, OH 43064
Pleasant Hill: Oakes-Beitman Library & Newton Museum, 12 N. Main St., Pleasant Hill, OH 45359
Plymouth Area Historical Society, 7 E. Main St., Plymouth, OH 44865
Pomeroy: Meigs County District Public Library, 216 W. Main St., Pomeroy, OH 45769

Pomeroy: Meigs County Genealogical Society, 43119 Pomeroy Pike, Pomeroy, OH 45769
Pomeroy: Meigs County Pioneer & Historical Society, P.O. Box 145, Pomeroy, OH 45769
Port Clinton: Ida Rupp Public Library, 310 Madison St., Port Clinton, OH 43452
Port Clinton: Ottawa County Historical Society, P.O. Box 385, Port Clinton, OH 43452
Portsmouth Public Library, 1220 Gallia St., Portsmouth, OH 45662
Portsmouth: Shawnee State University, Clark Memorial Library, 940 Second St., Portsmouth, OH 45662
Preble County District Library, 450 S. Barron St., Eaton, OH 45320
Put-In-Bay: Perry's Victory & International Peace Memorial, 93 Delaware Ave., P.O. Box 549, Put-In-Bay, OH 43456
Ravenna: Portage County Historical Society & Library, 6549 N., Chestnut St., Ravenna, OH 44266
Ravenna: Reed Memorial Library, Ravenna Public Library, 167 E. Main St., Ravenna, OH 44266
Reynoldsburg-Truro Historical Society, 1399 Lancaster Ave., P.O. Box 144, Reynoldsburg, OH 43068
Richfield Historical Society, 3907 Broadview Rd., Richfield, OH 44286
Richwood North Union Public Library, Four E. Ottawa St., Richwood, OH 43344
Rio Grande: University of Rio Grande and Rio Grande Community College Library, 218 N. College Ave., Rio Grande, OH 45674
Ripley: Union Township Public Library, 27 Main St., Ripley, OH 45167
Rock Creek Public Library, Frederick A. Swan Memorial Bldg., 2988 High St., P.O. Box 297, Rock Creek, OH 44084
Rockford Carnegie Library, 162 S. Main St., P.O. Box 330, Rockford, OH 45882
Rocky River Public Library, 1600 Hampton Road, Rocky River, OH 44116
Rossford Public Library, 720 Dixie Hwy, Rossford, OH 43460
Sabina Public Library, 11 E. Elm St., Sabina, OH 45169

Saint Clairsville Public Library, 108 W. Main St., Saint Clairsville, OH 43950

Saint Martin: Chatfield College Library, 20918 State Route 251, Saint Martin, OH 45118

Saint Marys: Community Public Library, 140 S. Chestnut, Saint Marys, OH 45885

Saint Paris Public Library, 127 E. Main St., Saint Paris, OH 43072

Salem Public Library, 821 E. State St., Salem, OH 44460

Sandusky: Erie County Historical Society, 629 S. Market St., P.O. Box 944, Sandusky, OH 44870

Sandusky: Follet House Museum, c/o Sandusky Library Association, 404 Wayne St., Sandusky, OH 44870

Sandusky Library, 114 W. Adams St., Sandusky, OH 44870

Sardinia: Southern State Community College, Learning Resources Center, 12681 U.S. Route 62, Sardinia, OH 45171

Sebring RR Museum & Historical Society, 216 E. Penn Ave., Sebring, OH 44672

Shaker Heights Public Library, 16500 Van Aken Blvd., Shaker Heights, OH 44120

Sharon Center: Sharon Township Heritage Society, P.O. Box 154, Sharon Center, OH 44274

Sharonville: Society of Historic Sharonville, 10900 Reading Rd., Sharonville, OH 45241

Sheffield Lake: 103rd OVI Memorial Foundation, 5501 E. Lake Rd. 7, Sheffield Lake, OH 44054

Shelby County Genealogical Society, 201 N. Main St., Sidney, OH 45365

Shelby County Historical Society, 201 N. Main St., Sidney, OH 45365

Shelby: Marvin Memorial Library, 43 W. Main St., Shelby, OH 44875

Shelby Museum of History, 23 E. Main St., Shelby, OH 44875

Sidney: Amos Memorial Public Library, 230 E. North St., Sidney, OH 45365

Solon Historical Society, 33975 Bainbridge Rd., Solon, OH 44139

South Euclid: Notre Dame College of Ohio, Clara Fritzsche Library, 4545 College Rd., South Euclid, OH 44121

Southern Ohio Genealogical Society. *See* Hillsboro

Springboro Area Historical Society, 110 S. Main St., Springboro, OH 45066
Springfield: Clark County Genealogical Society, 117 S. Fountain Ave., Springfield, OH 45502
Springfield: Clark County Historical Society Library, 117 S. Fountain Ave., Springfield, OH 45502
Springfield: Clark County Public Library, 201 S. Fountain Ave., P.O. Box 1080, Springfield, OH 45501
Springfield: Clark State Community College Library, 570 E. Leffel Ln., Springfield, OH 45501
Springfield: Warder Public Library, 137 E. High St., Springfield, OH 45502
Springfield: Wittenberg University, Thomas Library, P.O. Box 7207, Springfield, OH 45501
State Library of Ohio. *See* Columbus: State Library of Ohio
Steubenville: Jefferson County Historical Association, 426 Franklin Ave., Steubenville, OH 43952
Steubenville: Jefferson County Historical Society Library, 426 Franklin Ave., Steubenville, OH 43952
Steubenville: Public Library of Steubenville & Jefferson County, 407 S. Fourth St., Steubenville, OH 43952
Steubenville: Schiappa Branch Library, 4141 Mall Dr., Steubenville, OH 43952
Stony Ridge Library, 5805 Fremont Pike, Stony Ridge, OH 43463
Stow-Munroe Falls Public Library, 3512 Darrow Rd., Stow, OH 44224
Strongsville Historical Society, 13305 Pearl Rd,. Strongsville, OH 44136
Struthers Historical Society, 50 Terrace St., Struthers, OH 44471
Sunbury Community Library, 44 Burrer Drive, Sunbury, OH 43074
Swanton Public Library, 305 Chestnut St., Swanton, OH 43558
Sycamore: Mohawk Community Library, 200 S. Sycamore Ave., Sycamore, OH 44882
Tallmadge Historical Society Library, 12 Tallmadge Cir., Tallmadge, OH 44278
Tiffin: Heidelberg College, Beeghly Library, 310 E. Market St., Tiffin, OH 44883

Tiffin: Seneca County Historical Society, 6741 S. State Route 100, Tiffin, OH 44883
Tiffin: Seneca County Museum Foundation, 28 Clay St., Tiffin, OH 44883
Tiffin-Seneca Public Library, 77 Jefferson St., Tiffin, OH 44883
Tipp City Public Library, 11 E. Main St., Tipp City, OH 45371
Tipp City: Studebaker Family National Association, 6555 S. State Route 202, Tipp City, OH 45371
Tipp City: Tippecanoe Historical Society, P.O. Box 42, Tipp City, OH 45371
Toledo Area Genealogical Society, P.O. Box 352258, Toledo, OH 43635
Toledo Firefighters' Museum, 918 W. Sylvania Ave., Toledo, OH 43612
Toledo Law Association Library, 905 Jackson St., Toledo, OH 43604
Toledo-Lucas County Public Library, 325 N. Michigan St., Toledo, OH 43624
Toledo: Owens Community College Library, P.O. Box 10,000, Toledo, OH 43699
Toledo Public Library, Local Historical and Genealogical Department, 325 Michigan St., Toledo, OH 43624
Toledo: University of Toledo, College of Law, LaValley Law Library, 1825 W. Rocket Dr., Toledo, OH 43606
Toledo: University of Toledo, William S. Carlson Library, 2801 W. Bancroft St., Toledo, OH 43606
Trenton Historical Society, 17-A E. State St., Trenton, OH 45067
Troy Historical Society, 301 W. Main St., Troy, OH 45373
Troy: Miami County Historical and Genealogical Society, P.O. Box 305, Troy, OH 45373
Troy-Miami County Public Library, 419 W. Main St., Troy, OH 45373
Twinsburg Public Library, 10050 Ravenna Rd., Twinsburg, OH 44087
Uhrichsville: Claymont Public Library, 215 E. Third St., Uhricsville, OH 44683
University Heights: John Carroll University, Grasselli Library, 20700 N. Park Blvd., University Heights, OH 44118

Upper Arlington Historical Society, 1670 Fishinger Rd., #220, Upper Arlington, OH 43221

Upper Arlington Public Library, 2800 Tremont Rd., Upper Arlington, OH 43221

Upper Sandusky Community Library, 301 N. Sandusky Ave., Upper Sandusky, OH 43351

Urbana: Champaign County Library, 1060 Scioto St., Urbana, OH 43078

Utica Historical Society, 45 N. Main St., P.O. Box 5, Utica, OH 43080

Utica: Hervey Memorial Library, 15 N. Main St., Utica, OH 43080

Van Wert: Brumback Library, Van Wert County Public Library, 215 W. Main St., Van Wert, OH 45891

Van Wert County Historical Society, 602 N. Washington St., Van Wert, OH 45891

Vermilion: Friends of Harbour Town, 5741 Liberty Ave., Vermilion, OH44089

Vermilion: Great Lakes Historical Society, Clarence S. Metcalf Research Library, 480 Main St., P.O. Box 435, Vermilion, OH 44089

Vermilion: Ritter Public Library, 5680 Liberty Ave., Vermilion, OH 44089

Versailles: Worch Memorial Public Library, 790 S. Center St., Versailles, OH 45380

Wadsworth: Ella M. Everhard Public Library, 132 Broad St., Wadsworth, OH 44281

Wapakoneta: Auglaize County Public District Library, 203 S. Perry St., Wapakoneta, OH 45895

Warren: Trumbull County Historical Society, 303 Monroe NW, Warren, OH 44483

Warren-Trumbull County Public Library, 444 Mahoning Ave. NW, Warren, OH 44483

Washington Court House: Carnegie Public Library, 127 S. North St., Washington Court House, OH 43160

Washington Court House: Fayette County Historical Society, 517 Columbus Ave., Washington Court House, OH 43160

Waterville Historical Society, 401 Farnsworth Rd., P. O. Box 263, Waterville, OH 43566

Wauseon: Fulton County Historical Society, 8848 State Hwy 108, Wauseon, OH 43567
Wauseon Public Library, 117 E. Elm St., Wauseon, OH 43567
Waverly: Gamet A. Wilson Public Library of Pike County, 207 N. Market St., Waverly, OH 45690
Waverly: Pike Heritage Foundation, 110 S. Market St., P.O. Box 663, Waverly, OH 45690
Wayne Public Library, 137 E. Main St., Wayne, OH 43466
Waynesville: Mary L. Cook Public Library, 381 Old Stage Rd., Waynesville, OH 45068
Wellington: Memorial Library, 101 Willard Memorial Square, Wellington, OH 44090
Wellston: Ohio Valley Area Libraries, 252 W. 13th St., Wellston, OH 45692
Wellston: Sylvester Memorial Wellston Public Library, 135 E. Second St., Wellston, OH 45692
Wellsville Carnegie Public Library, 115 Ninth St., Wellsville OH 43968
Wellsville Historical Society, P.O. Box 13, 1003 Riverside Ave., Wellsville, OH 43968
West Chester: MidPointe Library, 9363 Centre Pointe Dr., West Chester, OH 45069
Western Reserve Historical Society Library, 10825 East Blvd., Cleveland, OH 44106
Westerville: Otterbein College, Courtright Memorial Library, 138 W. Main St., Westerville, OH 43081
Westerville Public Library, 126 S. State St., Westerville, OH 43081
West Jefferson: Hurt-Battelle Memorial Library of West Jefferson, 270 Lily Chapel Rd., West Jefferson, OH 43162
Westlake: Porter Public Library, 27333 Center Ridge Rd., Westlake, OH 44145
West Milton: Milton-Union Public Library, 560 S. Main St., West Milton, OH 45383
West Union: Adams County Genealogical Society, 507 N. Cherry St., West Union, OH 45693
Westerville Historical Society, 160 W. Main St., Westerville, OH 43081

Westerville: Otterbein College, Courtright Memorial Library, 138 W. Main St., Westerville, OH 43081
Westerville Public Library, Local History Resource Center, 126 S. State St., Westerville, OH 43081
Westlake Historical Society, 1371 A. Clague Rd., Westlake, OH 44145
Weston Public Library, 13153 Main St., P.O. Box 345, Weston, OH 43569
Wickliffe Public Library, 1713 Lincoln Rd., Wickliffe, OH 44092
Wilberforce: Central State University, Hallie Q. Brown Memorial Library, 1400 Brush Row Rd., Wilberforce, OH 45384
Wilberforce: National Afro-American Museum and Cultural Center, P.O. Box 578, Wilberforce, OH 45384
Wilberforce University, Rembert E. Stokes Learning Resources Center Library, 1055 N. Bickett Rd., P.O. Box 1003, Wilberforce, OH 45384
Willard Area Historical Society, 707 Euclid St., Willard, OH 44890
Willard Memorial Library, Six W. Emerald St., Willard, OH 44890
Williamsburg: Grassy Run Historical/Arts Committee, P.O. Box 562, Williamsburg, OH 45162
Willoughby Historical Society, 1 Public Square, Willoughby, OH 44094
Willoughby: Little Red Schoolhouse Association, 38470 Bell Rd., Willoughby, OH 44094
Willowick-Eastlake Public Library, 263 E. 305th St., Willowick, OH 44095
Wilmington: Clinton County Genealogical Society, P.O. Box 529, Wilmington, OH 45177
Wilmington: Clinton County Historical Society & Museum, 149 E. Locust St., Wilmington, OH 45177
Wilmington College, Sheppard Arthur Watson Library, Pyle Box 1227, Wilmington, OH 45177
Wilmington Public Library of Clinton County, 268 N. South St., Wilmington, OH 45177
Windsor Historical Society, 6068 State Route 22, Windsor, OH 44099

Woodsfield: Monroe County District Library, 96 Home Ave., Woodsfield, OH 43793
Woodsfield: Monroe County Genealogical Society, P.O. Box 641, Woodsfield, OH 43793
Woodsfield: Monroe County Historical Society, 118 Home Ave., P.O. Box 538, Woodsfield, OH 43793
Woodsfield: Monroe County Park District, 96 Home Ave., Woodsfield, OH 43793
Wooster: College of Wooster, Andrews Library, 1140 Beall Ave., Wooster, OH 44691
Wooster: Wayne County Historical Society, 546 E. Bowman St., Wooster, OH 44691
Wooster: Wayne County Public Library, 304 N. Market St., Wooster, OH 44691
Worthington Historical Society Library, 50 W. New England Ave., Worthington, OH 43085
Worthington Public Library, 820 High St., Worthington, OH43085
Xenia Community Library, Greene County Room, 76 E. Market St., Xenia, OH 45385
Xenia: Greene County Historical Society, 74 W. Church St., Xenia, OH 45385
Xenia: Greene County Public Library, 76 E. Market St., P.O. Box 520, Xenia, OH 45385
Yellow Springs: Antioch College, Olive Kettering Library, 795 Livermore St., Yellow Springs, OH 45387
Yellow Springs Community Library, 415 Xenia Ave., Yellow Springs, OH 45387
Yellow Springs Historical Society, P.O. Box 501, Yellow Springs, OH 45387
Youngstown Historical Center of Industry and Labor, 151 W. Wood St., Youngstown, OH 44501
Youngstown: Public Library of Youngstown and Mahoning County, 305 Wick Ave., Youngstown, OH 44503
Youngstown State University, William F. Maag Jr. Library, One University Plaza, Youngstown, OH 44555
Zanesfield: Dr. Earl Sloan Library, 2817 Sandusky St., Zanesfield, OH 43360

Zanesville: Muskingum County Genealogical Society Library, 220 N. Fifth St., Zanesville, OH 43701
Zanesville: Muskingum County Library, 220 N. Fifth St., Zanesville, OH 43701
Zoar Community Association, P.O. Box 621, 221 E. Foltz, Zoar, OH 44697

Addresses – Outside Ohio

Allen County Public Library, 900 Library Plaza, Fort Wayne, IN 46802
Boston Public Library, 700 Boylston St., Boston, MA 02116
Brigham Young University, Harold B. Lee Library, P.O. Box 26800, Provo, UT 84602
Bureau of Land Management, Eastern States Office, 5275 Leesburg Pike, Falls Church, VA 22041
California State Library. *See* Sutro Library
Clayton Library Center for Genealogical Research, 5300 Caroline, Houston, TX 77004
Dallas Public Library, Genealogy Section, 1515 Young St., Dallas, TX 75201
Daughters of the American Revolution Library. *See* National Society Daughters of the American Revolution, DAR Library
Denver Public Library, Western History/Genealogy Department, 10 W. 14th Ave. Pkwy., Denver, CO 80204
Detroit Public Library, Burton Historical Collection, 5201 Woodward Avenue, Detroit, MI 48202
Family History Library, 35 North West Temple St., Salt Lake City, UT 84150
Genealogical Forum of Oregon, 2505 S.E. 11th Ave. Suite B-18, Portland, OR 972402
Heart of America Genealogical Society Library, c/o Kansas City Public Library, 311 E. 12th St., Kansas City, MO 64106
Kansas City Public Library, 14 W. 10th St., Kansas City, MO 64105
Library of Congress, Local History and Genealogy Division, 101 Independence Ave. SE, Washington, DC 20540
The Library of Virginia, 800 E.. Broad St., Richmond, VA 23219
Los Angeles Public Library, History and Genealogy Department, 630 W. Fifth St., Los Angeles, CA 90071
Midwest Genealogy Center, 3440 S. Lee's Summit Rd. Independence, MO 64055

National Archives and Records Administration, 8601 Adelphi Rd., College Park, MD 20740
National Archives and Records Administration-Great Lakes Region, 7358 S. Pulaski Rd., Chicago, IL 60629
National Genealogical Society, 6400 Arlington Blvd. Suite 810, Falls Church, VA 22042 (*See* also St. Louis County Library, St. Louis, MO)
National Personnel Records Center, Military Personnel Records, 1 Archives Dr., St. Louis, MO 63168
National Society Daughters of the American Revolution, DAR Library, 1776 D St. NW, Washington, DC 20006
Newberry Library, 60 W. Walton St., Chicago, IL 60610
New England Historic Genealogical Society Library, 99-101 Newbury Street, Boston, MA 02116
New York Public Library, Humanities and Social Sciences Library, 476 Fifth Ave. and 42nd St., New York, NY 10018
Orlando Public Library, 101 E. Central Blvd., Orlando, FL 32801
St. Louis County Library, 1640 S. Lindbergh Blvd., St. Louis, MO 63131
St. Louis Public Library, History and Genealogy Department, 1301 Olive St., St. Louis, MO 63103
Seattle Public Library, 1000 Fourth Ave., Seattle, WA 98104
Sutro Library, California State Library, 1630 Holloway Ave., San Francisco, CA 94132
Virginia State Library and Archives. *See* The Library of Virginia
Wisconsin Historical Society Library, 816 State St., Madison, WI 53706

Bibliography

Bibliographies, Guides, and Finding Aids

Adams, Marilyn L., comp. *Ohio Local and Family History Sources in Print*. Clarkston, GA: Heritage Research, 1984.

_____, comp. *Southeastern Ohio Local and Family History Sources in Print*. Atlanta: Heritage Research, 1979.

Adams, Marjorie E. And Martha S. Alt, comps. *Encyclopedia of Ohio Associations: A Guide to Statewide Organizations*. Rev. Ed. Columbus: OHIONET, 1988.
A comprehensive list of non-profit associations in Ohio which are statewide in scope or interest. May be partially outdated.

Beers, Henry Putney. *The French & British in the Old Northwest: A Bibliographical Guide to Archive and Manuscript Sources*. Detroit: Wayne State University Press, 1964.

Benson, Marjorie, comp. *Awesome Almanac: Ohio*. Walworth, WI: B&B Publishing, 1995.

Bentley, Elizabeth Petty. *County Courthouse Book*. 2nd ed. Baltimore: Genealogical Publishing, Co., 1995.

_____. *The Genealogist's Address Book*. 4th ed. Baltimore: Genealogical Publishing Co., 1998.

Biggs, Deb. *Guide to Local Government Records at the Center for Archival Collections*. Bowling Green, OH: Bowling Green State University, 1981.

Britton, J.D., comp. *Ohio History Resource Guide for Teachers*. Columbus: Ohio Historical Society, 1991.

Burke, Thomas Aquinas. *Ohio Lands: A Short History*. 9th ed. Columbus: Auditor of State, 1997.

Carson, Dina C., ed. *Directory of Genealogical and Historical Publications in the U.S. and Canada*. Niwot, CO: Iron Gate Publishing, 1992.

_____, ed. *Directory of Genealogical Societies in the U.S. and Canada*. Niwot, CO: Iron Gate Publishing, 1992.

Central Ohio Interlibrary Network. *Union List of Genealogy Material*. Bellville, OH: Central Ohio Interlibrary Network, 1975.

Christian, Donna. *Guide to Newspaper Holdings at the Center for Archival Collections*. Bowling Green, OH: Bowling Green State University, 1980.

City and County Directories at the Ohio Historical Society. Bowie, MD: Heritage Books, 1985

Clark, Donna K. *Ohio State Directory of Genealogical Records by TAD (The Ancestor Detective).* Arvada, CO: Ancestor Publishers, 1986.
    Lists of Ohio sources and bibliographic details.

Clements, John. *Ohio Facts: A Comprehensive Look at Ohio Today, County by County.* Dallas, TX: Clements Research II, 1988.
    A chronological history of Ohio, with a county-by-county summary of local information-the people, land, economy, etc. Partially out-dated.

Columbus Area Library and Information Council of Ohio. *CALICO Genealogical Resources.* n.p.: 1981.

Curtin, Michael F. *The Ohio Politics Almanac.* Kent, OH: Kent State University Press, 1996
    A guide to Ohio government and politics-both historical and contemporary. Shows details on each Ohio county.

Dean, Tanya West and W. David Speas. *Along the Ohio Trail: A Short History of Ohio Lands.* Edited by George W. Knepper. Columbus: Auditor of State, 2001.

Douthit, Ruth Long. *Ohio Resources for Genealogists, with Some References for Genealogical Searching in Ohio.* Rev. Ed. Detroit: Detroit Society for Genealogical Research, 1972.

Downes, Randolph C. *Evolution of Ohio County Boundaries.* 1927. Reprint. Columbus: Ohio Historical Society, 1970.

The Encyclopedia of Ohio, 1999. 2 vols. St. Clair Shores, MI: Somerset Publishers, 1999.
    Ohio history, chronology, dictionary of places, historic places, and other state information.

Filby, P. William, comp. *A Bibliography of American County Histories.* Baltimore: Genealogical Publishing Co., 1985.

Folck, Linda L., comp. *Local Government Records in the American History Research Center at the University of Akron.* Rev. Ed. n.p.: 1982.

Gagel, Diane VanSkiver. *Ohio Courthouse Records.* Ohio Genealogical Society Research Guide No. 1. Mansfield, OH: The Society, 1997.

_____. *Ohio Photographers, 1839-1900.* Nevada City, CA: Carl Mautz Publishing, 1998.

Genealogical Researcher's Manual: With Special References for Using the Ohio Historical Society Library. Columbus: Franklin County Chapter, Ohio Genealogical Society, 1982.

Gilkey, Elliot Howard. *The Ohio Hundred Year Book.* Columbus: Fred J. Heer, 1901.

Lists of members of the General Assembly, senators, representatives, and biographical sketches. This work is a revised and enlarged edition of *Taylor's Ohio Statesmen and Hundred Year Book* (1892).

The Golden Census Guide for the State of Ohio. Des Moines, IA: Golden Census Guide, 1991.

Goulder, Grace. *This is Ohio: Ohio's 88 Counties in Words and Pictures.* Rev. ed. Cleveland: World Publishing Co., 1965.

A brief histories of Ohio's counties and regions. Illustrated.

Gray, Judy Price. *Colorado Territorial Families from Ohio.* Denver: Colorado Chapter, Ohio Genealogical Society, n.d.

_____, comp. *County-by-County [Ohio] Research by Members.* Longmont, CO: Colorado Chapter, Ohio Genealogical Society, 1998.

Includes county, name of researcher, and surnames they are researching.

The Great 88: A Brief Guide to Each of Ohio's 88 Counties and their Beautiful Courthouses. Columbus: Ohio Department of Development, 1993.

Includes a brief history of each Ohio courthouse.

Green, Karen Mauer. *Pioneer Ohio Newspapers, 1793-1810: Genealogical and Historical Abstracts.* Galveston, TX: Frontier Press, 1986.

_____. *Pioneer Ohio Newspapers, 1802-1818: Genealogical and Historical Abstracts.* Galveston, TX: Frontier Press, 1988.

Gutgesell, Stephen, ed. *Guide to Ohio Newspapers, 1793-1973: A Union Bibliography of Ohio Newspapers Available in Ohio Libraries.* Columbus: Ohio Historical Society, 1976.

Hall, William K. *The Shane Manuscript Collection: A Genealogical Guide to the Kentucky and Ohio Papers.* Galveston, TX: Frontier Press, 1990.

Harfst, Linda L., ed. *Local History and Genealogy Resources Guide to Southeastern Ohio.* Wellston, OH: Ohio Valley Area Libraries, 1984.

Identifies genealogical and historical records found in libraries in Southeastern Ohio. See the work edited by Gail Zachariah listed later in this section.

Harter, Stuart. *Ohio Genealogy and Local History Sources Index.* Ft. Wayne, IN: CompuGen Systems, 1986.

Hehir, Donald M. *Ohio Families A Bibliography of Books about Ohio Families.* Bowie, MD: Heritage Books, 1993.
 An alphabetical listing by surname of genealogies that have some Ohio connection.

Historical Records Survey (Ohio). *American Imprints Inventory: Check List of Ohio Imprints, 1796-1820.* 1941. Reprint. New York: Kraus Reprint Corp., 1964.

_____. *Inventory of the County Archives of Ohio.* Columbus: 1940.

_____. *Inventory of the State Archives of Ohio.* Columbus: Ohio Historical Records Survey Project, 1940.
 Although dated, this inventory briefly describes records of the Secretary of State-house and senate journals, accounts, bonds, etc. Includes subject index.

Hutchinson, William Thomas. *The Bounty Lands of the American Revolution in Ohio.* 1927. Reprint. New York: Amo Press, 1979.

Kalette, Linda Elise. *The Papers of Thirteen Early Ohio Political Leaders: An Inventory of the 1976-77 Microfilm Editions.* Columbus: Ohio Historical Society, 1977.

Knepper, George W. *The Official Ohio Lands Book.* Columbus: Auditor of State, 2002. See **https:www.auditor.state.oh.us**.

League of Women Voters of Ohio. *Know Your Ohio Government.* 4th ed. Columbus: 1978.
 Describes the organization of Ohio state government-Court of Common Pleas, Court of Appeals, and other courts.

Lee, Susan Dunlap, comp. *The Ohio Genealogical Society Periodicals Index: Topical by Location, 1960-2000.* Mansfield, OH: Ohio Genealogical Society, 2002.
 Indexes topics in periodicals published by OGS; arranged by localities.

Leggett, Nancy G. and Dorothy E. Smith, comps. *A Guide to Local Government Records and Newspapers Preserved at the Department of Archives and Special Collections, Wright State University Library.* n.p.: 1987.

Levine, David, ed. *Ohio Municipal Records Manual,* comp. by George Bain, et al. Rev. ed. Columbus: Ohio Historical Society, 1986.
 Written to aid city and local officials in the retention and disposition of records in the state.

Levinson, Marilyn, ed. *Guide to Newspaper Holdings at the Center for Archival Collections.* 3rd ed. Bowling Green, Ohio: Center for Archival Collections, Libraries and Learning Resources, Bowling Green State University, 1991.

Linck, Bonnie J. and Suzanne Wolfe Mettle. *Bible Records: A Survey of Bibles and Related Books for Family and Historic Information in the Archives-Library Division of the Ohio Historical Society.* Columbus: Ohio Historical Society, 1994.
An inventory of many family Bibles housed at the Ohio Historical Society, Columbus.

Masley, Betty. *Ohio Books in Print: Genealogy Resources.* Indianapolis: Betty Masley, 1994.
A listing, though dated, of Ohio books in print, along with other Ohio reference aids.

Martz, Linda. *Ohio Records Finder: How to Use Public Documents to Uncover Information.* Mansfield, OH: The author, 1998.

Matusoff, Karen L., comp. *Central Ohio Local Government Records at the Ohio Historical Society.* Columbus: Ohio Historical Society, 1978.

Marzulli, Lawremce J., Ed.D, *The Development of Ohio's Counties and Their Historic Courthouses.* Fostoria, OH: Gray Printing Co., n.d.

McConnell, Edward N. and Theodore S. Foster. *Local Government Records at the Ohio University Library.* Columbus: 1979.

Mettle, Suzanne Wolfe, et al., comps. *Genealogical Researcher's Manual with Special References for Using the Ohio Historical Society Library.* Columbus: Franklin County Chapter, Ohio Genealogical Society, 1981.

Meyer, Mary Keysor, ed. *Meyer's Directory of Genealogical Societies in the U.S.A. and Canada.* 10th ed. Mt. Airy, MD: Libra Publications, 1994.

Morrison, Patricia, comp. *Southern California Library Survey of Books on Ohio.* Los Alamitos, CA: Southern California Chapter of the Ohio Genealogical Society, 1990.

Mullin, Patrick Joseph, comp. *Ohio Census Population Schedules in Ohio Libraries.* Columbus: Ohio Library Association, 1977.
A union list of Ohio census population schedules, 1800-1890, in eighty-three Ohio libraries.

North Central Library Cooperative. *Ohio Genealogy and Local History: A Resource Guide to the Holdings of Twenty-three Member Libraries.* Ed. by Michael G. Snyder. Bellville, Ohio: North Central Library Cooperative, 1984.

Northwest Library District. *Genealogical Resources Guide, Northwest Ohio Libraries.* Bowling Green, OH: NORWELD, 1996.
    Details genealogical holdings of libraries in northwest Ohio.
O'Bryant, Michael, ed. *The Ohio Almanac.* Wilmington, OH: Orange Frazer Press, 1997-98.
    An encyclopedia of Ohio facts, addresses, biographies, and many other details pertaining to the state.
The Ohio Almanac. 9th ed. Dayton, OH: Ohio Almanac, 1980.
    Includes a brief history of Ohio counties; illustrated.
The Ohio Almanac: An Encyclopedia of Indispensable Information About the Buckeye Universe. Michael O'Bryant, ed. Wilmington, OH: Orange Frazer Press, 1997.
Ohio. Department of Development. *Ohio's Museums and Mementos.* Columbus: Columbus Blank Book Co., 1967.
    Briefly describes Ohio museums and some historical societies.
_____. *1982 Ohio County Profiles.* Columbus: 1982.
Ohio Genealogical Society. *2003 Ohio Genealogical Society Chapter Directory & Publications List.* Mansfield, OH: The Society, 2003.
    Gives OGS chapter address and telephone number, meeting information, a list of publications, and other useful details.
_____. *Ohio Cemeteries.* Maxine Hartmann Smith, ed. Mansfield, OH: The Society, 1998.
    Identifies Ohio cemeteries. Arranged by counties and townships. Includes county maps. This title and the 1990 addendum were updated in 2003 as an OGS Bicentennial project (see below).
_____. *Ohio Cemeteries Addendum.* Baltimore: Gateway Press, 1990.
_____. Cemetery Committee, comp. *Ohio Cemeteries, 1803-2003.* Mansfield, OH: The Society, 2003.
Ohio Historical Society. *Abstract of Ohio County Records Inventory, 1803 through 1977.* Columbus: The Society, n.d.. Microfilm.
_____. *A Directory of Historical Organizations in Ohio.* 6th ed. Columbus: Ohio Historical Society, 1999.
    Arranged by locality, this essential Ohio reference gives address, telephone numbers, describes major programs, and other details regarding each institution listed.
_____. *Guide to Local Government Records at the Ohio University Library.* Athens, OH: Ohio University Library, 1992.

_____. *A Guide to Manuscripts at the Ohio Historical Society.*
Andrea D. Lentz and Sara S. Fuller, eds. Columbus: The
Society, 1972.
Describes private papers and manuscript collections housed at
the Ohio Historical Society. This guide is partially outdated.

_____. Local Government Records Program. *Guide to Local
Government Records at the Ohio University Library.* Rev. ed.
Athens, OH: Ohio University Library, 1992.
A county-by-county description of county and other local
records housed at the Ohio University Library, Athens.

_____. *OAHSM Lending Library Catalog and Local History
Bibliography.* Columbus: Ohio Historical Society, 1997.

_____. *Ohio County Records Manual.* Rev. ed. Columbus: The Society,
1983.
Arranged by county office, a brief description and duties of
each office, a description of the records of each office, and
retention schedule.

_____. *Ohio Newspaper Microfilm Catalog.* Columbus: The Society,
1991. Microfiche.

_____. *Union Bibliography of Ohio Printed State Documents, 1803-
1970.* Patricia Swanson, comp. et al. Columbus: Ohio
Historical Society, 1973.
A comprehensive union list of documents published by the
state of Ohio between 1803 and 1970. Arranged by agencies.

Ohio Legal Resources: An Annotated Bibliography and Guide. 3rd ed.
Columbus: Ohio Regional Association of Law Libraries and
Ohio Library Association, 1990.

Ohio Library Council. *Directory of Special Collections.* Columbus: The
Council, 1998.

Ohio Library Foundation. *Checklist: Publications of the State of
Ohio, 1803-1952.* Columbus: 1964.

Ohio Museums Association. *Ohio Cultural Directory.* Columbus:
Ohio Museums Association, 1998.
Identifies historical societies, church archives, museums,
genealogical societies, cemeteries, and similar organizations.

Ohio. Secretary of State. *Annual Report of the Secretary of State to the
Governor of the State of Ohio.* Columbus: Nevins & Myers,
1878.

Ohio State Library. *Checklist, Publications of the State of Ohio, 1803-
1952.* Columbus: Ohio Library Foundation, 1964.

Phillips, William Louis. *Annotated Bibliography of Ohio Patriots: Revolutionary War & War of 1812.* Bowie, MD: Heritage Books, 1985.

_____. *City and County Directories at the Ohio Historical Society.* n.p.: 1985.

_____. *Jurisdictional Histories for Ohio's Eighty-Eight Counties, 1788-1985.* Bowie, MD: Heritage Books, 1986.

_____. *Ohio City & County Directories: The Ohio Historical Society Collection.* Bowie, MD: Heritage Books, 1986.

Pike, Kermit J., comp. *A Guide to the Manuscripts and Archives of the Western Reserve Historical Society.* Cleveland: Western Reserve Historical Society, 1972.

_____. *A Guide to Shaker Manuscripts in the Library of the Western Reserve Historical Society.* Cleveland: Western Reserve Historical Society, 1974.

    An inventory of Shaker diaries, journals, sermons, and writings housed at the Western Reserve Historical Society.

_____, comp. *A Guide to Major Manuscript Collections Accessioned and Processed by the Library of the Western Reserve Historical Society Since 1970.* Cleveland: Western Reserve Historical Society, 1987.

Putnam, Melanie K. and Susan M. Schaefgen. *Ohio Legal Research Guide.* Buffalo, NY: William S. Hein & Co., 1997.

Research Publications. *Reel Index to the Microform Collection of County and Regional Histories of the "Old Northwest," Series II: Ohio.* New Haven: Research Publications, 1975.

    Identifies author, title, and imprint of Ohio local histories, atlases, and biographies filmed by Research Publications.

Rieger, Paul E., comp. *The Upper Ohio Valley: A Bibliography and Price Guide.* Baltimore: Gateway Press, 1983.

Rose, Albert H. *Ohio Government, State and Local.* 3rd ed. Dayton: University of Dayton Press, 1966.

    Describes growth of townships from Ohio land grants, Ohio municipalities, and state government.

Smith, Clifford Neal. *Federal Land Series.* Chicago: American Library Association, 1972-86.

Smith, Dorothy and Maggie Yax. *A Guide to Manuscripts, Special Collections and Archives, Paul Laurence Dunbar Library.* Dayton, OH: Wright State University Libraries, 1996.

Society of Ohio Archivists. *Guide to Manuscripts Collections & Institutional Records in Ohio.* David R. Larson, ed. Columbus: Society of Ohio Archivists, 1974.
Identifies church records, genealogical collections, account books, diaries, family papers, administrative records, and many other manuscript collections in Ohio.

State Library of Ohio. *County by County in Ohio Genealogy.* By Petta Khouw and Genealogy Staff. Rev. ed. Columbus: The Library, 1992.
A listing of Ohio county sources housed at the State Library of Ohio, Columbus-atlases, census and cemetery records, DAR records, and many others. A valuable reference, but it is updated by the State Library of Ohio's online catalog.

_____. *Directory of Ohio Libraries.* Columbus: State Library of Ohio, 1998.

Stebbins, Clair C. *Ohio's Court Houses.* Columbus: Ohio State Bar Association, 1980.

Stith, Bari, comp. *A Guide to Local Government Records in the Library of the Western Reserve Historical Society.* Cleveland: Western Reserve Historical Society, 1987.

Swanson, Hal. *The Ohio Township Helper.* n.p., n.d.

Thomson, Peter Gibson. *A Bibliography of the State of Ohio.* 2 vols. 1880-1890. Reprint. Ann Arbor, MI: University Microfilms, 1966; Salem, MA: Higginson Book Co., n.d.
An extensive bibliography of Ohio titles-histories, periodicals, directories, pamphlets, and many other titles.

Thrane, Susan W. *County Courthouses of Ohio.* Bloomington, IN: Indiana University Press, 2000.
Brief histories of Ohio's 88 county courthouses; illustrated.

United States Federal Writers Project (Ohio). *The Ohio Guide.* New York: Oxford University Press, 1940, 1956.
Historical background and chronology, tours of Ohio, maps, descriptions of cities, and photographs.

Vicory, Jacqueline, comp. *MILO: Union List of Genealogies in the Libraries of Champaign, Clark, Darke, Green, Miami, Montgomery, and Preble Counties, Ohio.* Dayton, OH: Miami Valley Library Organization, 1977.

Vonada, Damaine. *Amazing Ohio.* Wilmington, OH: Orange Frazer Press, 1989.

_____. *Matters of Fact.* Wilmington, OH: Orange Frazer Press, 1987.

_____, ed. *The Ohio Almanac.* Wilmington, OH: Orange Frazer Press, 1992.
   A listing of Ohio libraries, religious organizations, businesses, and similar information on each county.

Wagher, Victor S., ed. *Guide to Local Government Records at the Center for Archival Collections.* 2nd ed. Bowling Green, OH: The Center, 1988.

Weaver, Clarence L. and Helen M. Mills, comps. *County and Local Historical Material in the Ohio State Archaeological and Historical Society Library.* 2nd ed. Columbus: 1945.

Weaver, Polly Ann, comp. *Off the Ground and Into Your Family Tree.* Greenville, OH: Greenville Public Library, 1987.

Western Pennsylvania Genealogical Society. *Resources for Ohio Research in Pittsburgh, Pennsylvania.* Pittsburgh: The Society, 1978.

Western Reserve Historical Society, Genealogical Advisory Committee. *Ohio Genealogical Records.* Mrs. Carl Main, ed., Cleveland: The Society, 1968.

Wheeler, Robert C. *Ohio Newspapers: A Living Record.* Columbus: Ohio History Press, 1950.

Whitacre, Donald. *Ohio Firsts.* Lebanon, Ohio: Curious Facts Features, 1980.
   Firsts in Ohio, by Ohioans, and for Ohioans.

Work Projects Administration. *Inventory of Federal Archives in the States, Series II, The Federal Courts, No. 34, Ohio.* Columbus: Ohio Historical Records Survey Project, 1940.
   Though dated, this is an inventory of Ohio federal court records identified before 1940.

Wright, David K. *Ohio Handbook.* Emeryville, CA: Moon Publications, 1999.

Writers' Program (Ohio). *The Ohio Guide.* 1940. Reprint. St. Clair Shores, MI: Scholarly Press, 1979.
   State and city history, government, chronology, tours, and other valuable Ohio information; partially outdated.

W.W. Reilly & Company. *Ohio State Business Directory for 1853-54.* Cincinnati: Morgan & Overend, 1853.
   Arranged by type of business (such as plow manufacturers), county, name of person, and residence.

Wyllie, Stanley Clarke, Jr., comp. *A Guide to Genealogical Materials in the Dayton and Montgomery County Public Library.* Dayton, OH: 1987.

Yon, Paul D. *Guide to Ohio County and Municipal Records for Urban Research*. Columbus: Ohio Historical Society, 1973.
Arranged by counties and municipalities. Shows government record series, dates, size of collection, and location (courthouse, etc.).

Zachariah, Gail, ed. *Local History and Genealogy Resources Guide to Southeastern Ohio*. 2 vols. Wellston, OH: Ohio Valley Area Libraries, 1994.

Zacharias, Susan. "Ohio Public Libraries: Genealogical Collections." *OGS Genealogy News* 33 (May/June 2002): 90-93.

Biographies and Genealogies

Anderson-Burton, Robin J., ed. *Ohio Family Fann Heritage*. Marceline, MO: Walsworth Press, 1985.

Bell, Carol Willsey, comp. *Abstracts from Biographies in John Struthers Stewart's History of Northeastern Ohio*. Indianapolis: Ye Olde Genealogie Shoppe. 1983.

The Biographical Annals of Ohio: A Handbook of the Government and Institutions of the State of Ohio. 3 vols. Frank Edgar Scobey, comp., et al. Springfield, OH: State Printers, 1902-1908.
List of members of the General Assembly, Ohio House of Representatives, Ohio Senate; biographies, portraits, and population statistics. See also William A. Taylor, *Hundred-Year Book* (Columbus, 1891).

The Biographical Cyclopaedia and Portrait Gallery with An Historical Sketch of the State of Ohio. 6 vols. Cincinnati: Western Biographical Publishing Co., 1883-95.
A monumental six-volume biographical encyclopedia of the state, with detailed sketches and many portraits of major Ohio citizens. Index to biographies.

Biographical Directory, General Assembly, Ohio, 1929-1930. Columbus: F.J. Heer Printing Co., 1931.
List of members of the General Assembly, residence, term of service, biographies, portraits.

The Biographical Encyclopaedia of Ohio of the Nineteenth Century. Charles Robson, ed. Cincinnati: Galaxy Publishing Co., 1876.
Biographical sketches and portraits of many prominent Ohio citizens. Indexed. Online: **https://www.ancestry.com**.

Biographical History of Northeastern Ohio, Embracing the Counties of Ashtabula, Geauga, and Lake. Chicago: Lewis Publishing Co., 1893.
Index compiled by Joan A. Vaughn (1998).

Biographical History of Northeastern Ohio, Embracing the Counties of Ashtabula, Trumbull and Mahoning. Chicago: Lewis Publishing Co., 1893.

The Book of Ohio: Illustrating the Growth of Her Resources. 2 vols. Cincinnati: Queen City Publishing Co., 1910-12. Biographical sketches of prominent Ohioans; illustrated.

Boswell, Harry James. *American Blue Book: Attorneys of Ohio*. Minneapolis: n.p., 1924.

Bowers, Ruth and Anita Short, comps. *Gateway to the West.* 2 vols. 1967-78. Reprint. Baltimore: Genealogical Publishing Co., 1989.
    Reprint of articles from *Gateway to the West* published 1967-78. Indexed.

Brennan, Joseph Fletcher, ed. *A Biographical Cyclopaedia and Portrait Gallery of Distinguished Men, with an Historical Sketch of the State of Ohio.* 6 vols. Cincinnati: John C. Yorston & Co., 1879.
    Portraits and lengthy biographical sketches of prominent Ohio residents. A monumental biographical work.

_____, ed. *A Biographical Cyclopaedia and Portrait Gallery of Distinguished Men: With An Historical Sketch of the State of Ohio.* 2 vols. Cincinnati: Yorston, 1879.

Brien, Lindsay Metcalfe. *Miami Valley Genealogies.* 5 vols. n.p., n.d. Typescript.

_____, comp. *Miami Valley Records: Quaker Records.* N.p., 1935-.

Caccamo, James F. *Marriage Notices from the Ohio Observer Series, 1827-1855.* Apollo, PA: Closson Press, 1994.

Chataigne, J.H. *Photogravure Memories and B.P.O.E. Album of the Benevolent and Protective Order of Elks, Ohio Edition.* Columbus: New Franklin Printing Co., 1903.

Citizens Historical Association. "Ohio Biographical Sketches." 13 vols. Indianapolis: 1938-51.
    Sketches of Ohioans, with genealogical notes on their ancestry. Typescript at Ohio Historical Society.

Clark, Marie Taylor. *Ohio Lands: Chillicothe Land Office, 1800-1829.* Chillicothe, OH: The author, 1984.

_____. *Ohio Lands South of the Indian Boundary Line.* Chillicothe, OH: The author, 1984.

Cleave, Egbert. *Cleave's Biographical Cyclopaedia of the State of Ohio, Ashtabula, Geauga, Lake, Lorain, Lucas, Mahoning, and Trumbull Counties.* Philadelphia: J.B. Lippincott & Co., 1875.
    Volumes available for other Ohio major cities and counties.

Colonial Dames of America. Ohio. *Historic Counties and Court Houses of Ohio and the Prominent Men Associated with Them.* n.p., 1966.

Comley, W.J. and W. D'Eggville. *Ohio: The Future Great State.* Cincinnati: Comley Brothers Manufacturing, 1875.

Commemorative Biographical Record of the Upper Lake Region Containing Biographical Sketches of Prominent and Representative Citizens and Many of the Early Settled Families. Chicago: J.H. Beers & Co., 1905.

Commemorative Biographical Record of Northwestern Ohio, Including the Counties of Defiance, Henry, Williams, and Fulton. Chicago: J.H. Beers & Co., 1899.

Coyle, William, ed. *Ohio Authors and their Books: Biographical Data and Selective Bibliographies for Ohio Authors, Native and Resident, 1796-1950.* Cleveland: World Publishing Co., 1962. Brief biographical sketches and selective bibliographies of works written by Ohio authors, 1796-1950.

Crabb, W. Darwin. *Biographical Sketches of the State Officers and of the Members of the Sixtieth General Assembly of the State of Ohio.* Columbus: Ohio State Journal Book, 1872.

Cutler, Julia Perkins. *The Founders of Ohio: Brief Sketches of the Forty-eight Pioneers.* Cincinnati: Robert Clarke & Co., 1888.

Daughters of the American Revolution. *Ohio State History of the Daughters of the American Revolution,* Annie Jopling Lester, comp., n.d.

Downes, Randolph C. *History of Lake Shore, Ohio.* 3 vols. New York: Lewis Historical Publishing Co., 1952.
Volume 3 contains many biographical sketches.

Duff, William Alexander. *History of North Central Ohio, Embracing Richland, Ashland, Wayne, Medina, Lorain, Huron, and Knox Counties.* 3 vols. Topeka-Indianapolis: Historical Publishing Co., 1931.
Volumes 2 and 3 contain biographical sketches of prominent residents of the Ohio counties stated in the title to this work.

Eaton, S.J.M. *History of the Presbytery of Erie.* New York: Hurd and Houghton, 1868.

Encyclopedia of Ohio: A Volume of Encyclopedia of the United States. St. Clair Shores, MI: Somerset Publishers, 1982.

Fess, Simeon Davidson. *Ohio: A Four-Volume Reference Library on the History of A Great State.* 5 vols. Chicago: Lewis Publishing Co., 1937.
Volumes 4 and 5 contain biographical sketches.

Galbreath, Charles Burleigh. *History of Ohio.* 5 vols. Chicago: American Historical Society, 1925.
    Volumes 3-5 contain biographical sketches of prominent Ohio residents. See "Cross Index to Charles B. Galbreath's 1925, 5 Volume History of Ohio," compiled by Robertalee Lent Post Falls, ID: Genealogical Reference Builders, 1969.

Gardner, Frank W. *Central Ohio Genealogical Notes and Queries.* Columbus: n.p., n.d. Indexed.

Genealogical Data Relating to Women in the Western Reserve before 1840 (1850). Cleveland: Women's Department, Cleveland Centennial Commission, 1943.
    Genealogical information is arranged by counties.

Gilkey, Elliot Howard. *The Ohio Hundred Year Book.* Columbus: Fred J. Heer, 1901.
    Lists of members of the General Assembly, senators, representatives, and biographical sketches. This is a revised and enlarged edition of *Taylor's Ohio Statesmen and Hundred Year Book* (1892).

Goulder, Grace. *Ohio Scenes and Citizens.* 1964. Reprint. Dayton, OH: Landfall Press, 1973.
    Biographies of prominent Ohio citizens.

Grose, Parlee C., et al. *Biographical and Historical Sketches.* McComb, OH: General Publishing Co., 1947.

Hammond, Ernestine, ed. *Huguenot Ancestors of Some Ohioans.* Ohio Huguenot Society: 1996.

Hanna, Charles Augustus. *Ohio Valley Genealogies.* 1900. Reprint. Baltimore: Genealogical Publishing Co., 1989.
    Genealogies of families in Belmont, Harrison, and Jefferson counties, Ohio, and three Pennsylvania counties.

Harris, C.H. *The Harris History: A Collection of Tales of Long Ago of Southeastern Ohio and Adjoining Territories.* Athens, OH: Athens Messenger, 1957.

Haverstock, Mary Sayre, et al., comps. *Artists in Ohio, 1787-1900: A Biographical Dictionary.* Kent, OH: Kent State University Press, 2000.

Hawkins, CyriL *Sketches, Including Scenes and Incidents of Distinguished "Buckeyes" and Others.* n.p., n.d.

Hayden, Amos Sutton. *Early History of the Disciples in the Western Reserve, Ohio, with Biographical Sketches of the Principal Agents in their Religious Movement.* Cincinnati: Chase & Hall, 1875.

HeritageQuest Online (ProQuest).
    Online subscription available at large research libraries. Images of books and personal name index to some 25,000 family and local histories. Researchers may search by People (personal names), Places, and Publications. Also, census schedules and census indexes.

Hildreth, Samuel Prescott. *Biographical and Historical Memoirs of the Early Pioneer Settlers of Ohio, with Narratives of Incidents and Occurrences in 1775.* Cincinnati: H.W. Derby & Co., 1852.
    Biographical sketches of early Ohioans. 1854 edition has the title *Memoirs of the Early Pioneer Settlers of Ohio, with Narratives of Incidents and Occurrences in 1775* (Cincinnati: H.W. Derby & Co., 1854). See *Index* compiled by Marilyn Sims Vadakin (Marietta, OH: It's My Business, n.d.).

_____. *Pioneer History: Being An Account of the First Examinations of the Ohio Valley and the Early Settlement of the Northwest Territory.* Cincinnati: H.W. Derby & Co., 1848.

Hissong, Clyde. *Ohio Lives: The Buckeye State Biographical Record.* Hopkinsville, KY: Historical Record Association, 1968.
    Detailed sketches of prominent Ohioans, and some portraits.

History of Hocking Valley, Ohio. 1883. Reprint. Mt. Vernon, IN: Windmill Publications, 1991.

History of Lower Scioto Valley, Ohio. Chicago: Interstate Publishing Co., 1884.

History of the Upper Ohio Valley, with Family History and Biographical Skeiches. 2 vols. Madison, WI: Brant & Fuller, 1890. Includes many biographical sketches for this area.

Hood, Marilyn G., ed. *The First Ladies of Ohio.* Columbus: Ohio Historical Society, 1970.

Hooper, Osman Castle. *Ohio Journalism Hall of Fame.* Columbus: Ohio State University Press, 1929-32.

Houck, George Francis. *History of Catholicity in Northern Ohio and in the Diocese of Cleveland from 1749 to December 31, 1900.* 2 vols. Cleveland: Savage, 1903.
    Volume 1 historical background; volume 2 contains biographical sketches.

Howe, Henry. *Historical Collections of Ohio.* 2 vols. Cincinnati: State of Ohio, 1904. (Publisher varied).
    See "Index to Historical Collections of Ohio," index compiled by Fresno Genealogical Society, Fresno, CA. Typescript, WRHS, and "Index to Historical Collections of Ohio by Henry

Howe," typescript index compiled by Sandra Hudnall Day Steubenville, OH: Jefferson County Chapter, Ohio Genealogical Society, 1990.

Hutslar, Donald A. *Gunsmiths of Ohio, 18th & 19th Centuries.* Nancy Bagby, ed. York, PA: George Shumway, Publisher, 1973. Brief biographical sketches of gunsmiths alphabetically arranged by surname under each county name.

Izant, Grace Goulder. *Ohio Scenes and Citizens.* Cleveland: World Publishing Co., 1964.

Kennedy, William S. *The Plan of Union, or, A History of the Presbyterian and Congregational Churches of the Western Reserve with Biographical Sketches of the Early Missionaries.* Hudson, OH: Pentagon Steam Press, 1856.

Lake Shore & Michigan Southern Railway System and Representative Employees. Buffalo, NY: Biographical Publishing Co., 1900.

Leahy, Ethel Carter. *Who's Who on the Ohio River and Its Tributaries.* Cincinnati: E.C. Leahy Publishing Co., 1931.

Lester, Annie Jopling, comp. *Ohio State History of the Daughters of the American Revolution.* Greenfield, OH: Greenfield Printing & Publishing Co., 1928.

Lewis, Thomas William. *History of Southeastern Ohio and the Muskingum Valley, 1788-1928.* 3 vols. Chicago: S.J. Clarke Publishing Co., 1928.
Volume 3 contains biographical sketches and portraits.

Mansfield, E.D. *Personal Memories: Social, Political, and Literary, with Sketches of Many Noted People, 1803-1843.* Cincinnati: Robert Clarke & Co., 1879.

Marshall, Carrington Tanner, ed. *A History of the Courts and Lawyers of Ohio.* 4 vols. New York: American Historical Society, 1934.
Biographical sketches of prominent Ohio lawyers and judges; includes many portraits.

Memoirs of the Lower Ohio Valley: Personal and Genealogical with Portraits. 2 vols. Madison, WI: Federal Publishing Co., 1905. Evansville, IN: Unigraphic, 1971.
Portraits and biographical sketches of prominent Ohio citizens. See typescript index at FSL.

Memoirs of the Miami Valley, John C. Hover, ed. 3 vols. Chicago: R.O. Law Co., 1919.

Memorial Record of the Counties of Delaware, Union, and Morrow, Ohio. Chicago: Lewis Publishing Co., 1895.

Men of Ohio. Cleveland: Cleveland News and Cleveland Leader, ca. 1914.
> Intended as a newspaper office reference source. Portraits and brief biographical sketches of prominent Ohio citizens.

Men of Ohio in Nineteen Hundred. Cleveland: Benesch Art Publishing Co., 1901.
> A collection of portraits of 1,068 representative men of Ohio in 1900; shows their occupation.

Mercer, James Kazerta. Ohio *Legislative History, 1909-1913.* Columbus: Press of Edward T. Miller Co., n.d.

_____. *Representative Men of Ohio, 1884-1885.* Columbus: James K. Mercer, 1885.

_____ and C.N. Vallandigham. *Representative Men of Ohio, 1896-1897.* Columbus: Mercer & Vallandigham, 1896.

_____ and Edward K. Rige. *Representative Men of Ohio, 1900-1903.* Columbus: James K. Mercer, 1903.

_____. *Representative Men of Ohio, 1903-1908.* Columbus: Press of Fred J. Heer, 1908.

_____. *Representative Men of Ohio, 1904-1908.* Columbus: Press of Fred J. Heer, 1908.

Moore's Who Is Who in Ohio, 1961. Los Angeles, CA: Moore's Who Is Who Publications, 1961.

Neely, Ruth, ed. *Women of Ohio: A Record of their Achievements in the History of the State.* 3 vols. S.J. Clarke Publishing Co.: n.d.
> Biographical sketches and portraits of many prominent Ohio women.

Neff, William B., ed. *Bench and Bar of Northern Ohio: History and Biography.* Cleveland: Historical Publishing Co., 1921.
> Biographical sketches and portraits of attorneys in Northern Ohio.

Newton, Jim. *Our Most Famous Buckeyes.* Hamilton, OH: Fort Hamilton Press, 1963.

Ohio. Chicago: American Historical Society, 1925.
> Biographical sketches and portraits of prominent citizens.

Ohio Biographical Dictionary: People of All Times and All Places Who Have Been Important to the History and Life of the State. Wilmington, DE: American Historical Publications, 1986.
> Nineteenth and twentieth century biographical sketches of prominent Ohioans, alphabetically arranged by surname.

Ohio Biographical Dictionary. 2nd ed. 2 vols. St. Clair Shores, MI: Somerset Publishers, 1999.
> Includes biographical sketches of many prominent Ohioans.

Ohio Genealogical Society. *Ancestor Charts of Members of the Ohio Genealogical Society.* Mansfield, Ohio: The Society, 1987. Pedigree charts submitted to OGS by its members. This is a major reference source and finding aid for Ohio genealogists.

_____. *First Families of Ohio Roster, 1964-2000,* Sunda Anderson Peters and Kay Ballantyne Hudson, eds., Mansfield, OH: Ohio Genealogical Society, 2001.

_____. *First Families of Ohio.* Collection on microfilm, FSL.

Ohio. General Assembly. *Biographical Directory, General Assembly, Ohio, 1929-1930.* Columbus: F.J. Heer Printing Co., 1931.

_____. *Biographical Notices of State Officers and Members of the Fifty-ninth General Assembly of the State of Ohio.* Columbus: John Wallace, 1871.

_____. *Political Directory Containing Biographical Sketches of the State Officials of Ohio.* Columbus: L.G. Thrall & Co., 1879.

Ohio Obituaries and Biographical Sketches. 7 vols. Columbus: 1908. Bound newspaper clippings housed at the State Library of Ohio, Columbus.

Ohio Historical Society. *The Governors of Ohio.* Columbus: The Society, 1954.

Ohio's Progressive Sons, A History of the State: Sketches of Those Who have Helped to Build up the Commonwealth. Cincinnati: Queen City Publishing Co., 1905. Biographical sketches and portraits of prominent Ohioans.

Ohio Society, Colonial Dames XVII Century. *Our Ancestors' Families.* The Society, 1988. A monumental collection of family group records. Indexed.

Ohio Society, Sons of the American Revolution. *Centennial Register, 1889 to 1989.* Dayton, OH: The Society, 1988.

Ohio Women's Policy and Research Commission. *Women of the Ohio General Assembly, 1922-1996.* Columbus: The Commission, 1996.

Pearson, Francis Bail and J.D. Harlor. Ohio History Sketches. Columbus: Press of Fred J. Heer, 1903.

Portrait and Biographical Record of Auglaize, Logan, and Shelby Counties, Ohio. 1892. Reprint. Evansville, IN: Unigraphic, 1977.

Portrait and Biographical Record of Fayette, Pickaway, and Madison Counties, Ohio. Chicago: Chapman Bros., 1892.

Portrait and Biographical Record of Marion and Hardin Counties, Ohio. Chicago: Chapman Publishing Co., 1895.

A Portrait and Biographical Record of Mercer and Van Wert Counties, Ohio. 1896. Evansville, IN: Unigraphic, 1971.

A Portrait and Biographical Record of Portage and Summit Counties, Ohio. Logansport, IN: A.W. Bowen & Co., 1898.

Portrait and Biographical Record of the Scioto Valley, Ohio. Chicago: Lewis Publishing Co., 1894.

Progressive Men of Northern Ohio. Cleveland: Plain Dealer Publishing Co., 1906.
   Portraits and brief biographical sketches of prominent citizens of Northern Ohio; indexed.

Randall, Emilius Oviatt and Daniel J. Ryan. *History of Ohio: The Rise and Progress of An American State.* 6 vols. New York: Century History Co., 1912-15.
   Volume 6 includes biographical sketches.

Reed, George Irving, et al., eds. *Bench and Bar of Ohio: A Compendium of History and Biography.* 2 vols. Chicago: Century Publishing and Engraving Co., 1897.
   Detailed biographical sketches and many portraits of Ohio lawyers.

Reid, Whitelaw. *Ohio in the War: Her Statesmen, Her Generals, and Soldiers.* 2 vols. Cincinnati: Robert Clarke Co., 1895.
   History of Ohio regiments during the Civil War, rosters of soldiers, biographical sketches, and history of military organizations. Illustrated.

Reno, W.W. and Frank R. Whitzel, eds. *The Ohio Blue Book: Leaders in Ohio Politics for the Year 1898.* Montpelier, OH: Hann & Adair Printers, 1898.

Representative Men of Ohio, 1884-85. Columbus: James K. Mercer, 1885.

Rice, Harvey. *Sketches of Western Life.* Boston: Lee and Shepard, 1887.

Rust, Orton Glenn. *History of West Central Ohio.* 3 vols. Indianapolis: Historical Publishing Co., 1934.
   Volume 3 and part of volume 2 include biographical sketches.

Ryan, Daniel Joseph. *A History of Ohio, with Biographical Sketches of Her Governors and the Ordinance of 1787.* Columbus: A.H. Smythe, 1888.

Scamyhorn, Richard and John Steinle. *Stockades in the Wilderness: The Frontier Defenses and Settlements of Southwestern Ohio, 1788-1795.* Dayton, OH: Landfall Press, 1986.

Smith, William Ernest. *History of Southwestern Ohio: The Miami Valleys*. 3 vols. New York: Lewis Historical Publishing Co., 1964.
    Volume 3 contains biographical sketches and is subtitled *Family and Personal History*. Indexed.

Southern Ohio and Its Builders: A Biographical Record of Those Personalities Who by Reason of their Achievements Have Merited a Permanent Place in the Story of Twentieth-Century Southern Ohio. Southern Ohio Biographical Association, 1927.
    Biographical sketches and portraits of prominent citizens.

Stagg, Abraham. *Biographical Sketches of the Fifty-sixth Ohio House of Representatives, Convened January 4th, 1864*. Columbus: Glenn & Heide, 1865.

Stevens, Harry Robert. "A Study of Notable Ohioans." *Ohio State Archaeological and Historical Quarterly* 47 (1938): 159-67.

Stewart, John Struthers. *History of Northeastern Ohio*. 3 vols. Indianapolis: Historical Publishing Co., 1935.
    Volumes 2 and 3 contain biographical sketches of prominent citizens of Northeastern Ohio.

Stille, Samuel Harden. *Ohio Builds A Nation: A Memorial to the Pioneers and the Celebrated Sons of the "Buckeye" State*. 5th ed. Chicago: Arlendale Book House, 1962.
    Biographical sketches of Ohioans and Ohio local history.

Stivison, David V., comp. *The Lord's Shepherds in the Ohio Hills: Biographies of 175 Ministers and Wives of the Southeastern Ohio Conferences of the United Brethren and the Evangelical United Brethren Churches, 1901-1974*. Philadelphia: privately printed, 1987.

Summers, Ewing, comp. *Genealogical and Family History of Eastern Ohio*. New York: Lewis Publishing Co., 1903.
    Detailed biographical sketches and some portraits. See name index compiled by Mrs. Howard W. (Bernice H.) Simon, *Name Index for Genealogical and Family History of Eastern Ohio* (Chagrin Falls, OH, 1973).

Taylor, C.W., Jr. *Bench and Bar of Ohio, 1939-1940*. San Francisco: C.W. Taylor, Jr., 1939.

Taylor, William Alexander. *Ohio in Congress from 1803 to 1901, with Notes and Sketches of Senators and Representatives*. Columbus: Century Publishing Co., 1900.

_____. *Ohio Statesmen and Hundred Year Book from 1788 to 1892 Inclusive*. Columbus: Westbote Co., 1892.

University of Akron. College of Law. "Ohio Judges: A Biographical Index." 1967. Typescript at Ohio Historical Society.

Upton, Harriet Taylor. *History of the Western Reserve*. 3 vols. Chicago: Lewis Publishing Co., 1910.
> Volumes 2 and 3 contain biographical sketches and portraits. This work is one of the major regional histories of the Western Reserve.

Van Tassel, Charles Sumner, comp. *Familiar Faces of Ohio: A Souvenir Collection of Portraits and Sketches of Well-known Men of the Buckeye State*. Bowling Green, OH: C.S. Van Tassel Publisher, 1896.
> Portraits and sketches of prominent Ohioans.

_____. *Men of Northwestern Ohio: A Collection of Portraits and Biographies*. Bowling Green, OH: C.S. Van Tassel, 1898.

_____, comp. *The Ohio Blue Book, or Who's Who in the Buckeye State: A Cyclopedia of Biography of Men and Women of Ohio*. Norwalk, OH: American Publishers' Co., 1917-18; Toledo, OH: C.S. Van Tassel, 1917-1918.
> Brief biographical sketches of prominent Ohio residents. Also has the title *Who's Who in the Buckeye State*.

_____. *Story of the Maumee Valley, Toledo, and the Sandusky Region*. 4 vols. Chicago: S.J. Clarke Publishing Co., 1929.
> Volumes 3 and 4 contain biographical sketches and portraits.

Van Tassel, David D. and John J. Grabowski, eds. *The Dictionary of Cleveland Biography*. Bloomington, IN: Indiana University Press, 1996.

Vietzen, Raymond Charles. *Yesterday's Ohioans*. Elyria, OH: Indian Ridge Museum, 1973.

Walden, Blanche L. *Pioneer Families of the Midwest*. 1939. Reprint. Baltimore: Clearfield, 1998.
> Brief genealogical sketches of Ohioans and other Midwesterners.

Wheeler, Kenneth W. *For the Union: Ohio Leaders in the Civil War*. Columbus: Ohio State University Press, 1968.

Who Is Who in and from Ohio. Cincinnati: Queen City Publishing Co., 1912.

Who's Who in Ohio: A Biographical Dictionary of Leading Men and Women of the Commonwealth. Chicago: Larkin, Roosevelt & Larkin, Ltd., 1947.

Who's Who in Ohio: A Compilation of Biographical Information on Outstanding Citizens of the State of Ohio. n.p., 1974.

Who's Who in Ohio: Those Who Have Achieved Prominence in their Respective Lines of Endeavor. Cleveland: Biographical Publishing Co., 1930.
   Brief biographical sketches of prominent Ohioans.
Williamson, C.W. *History of Western Ohio and Auglaize County, with Illustrations and Biographical Sketches of Pioneers and Prominent Public Men.* Columbus: W.M. Linn, 1905.
Winter, Nevin Otto. *A History of Northwest Ohio: A Narrative Account of Its Historical Progress and Development from Its First European Exploration of the Maumee and Sandusky Valleys and the Adjacent Shores of Lake Erie, down to the Present Time.* 3 vols. Chicago: Lewis Publishing Co., 1917.
   Volumes 2 and 3 contain biographical sketches and portraits.
Wright, George Frederick. *Representative Citizens of Ohio: Memorial, Biographical.* 7 vols. Cleveland: Memorial Publishing Co., 1914-26.
   Detailed biographical sketches of prominent Ohio residents, includes many portraits.
Young American Patriots: The Youth of Ohio in World War II. Richmond, VA: National Publishing Co., 1947.

Churches and Religious Organizations

Allbeck, Willard D. *A Century of Lutherans in Ohio*. Yellow Springs, OH: Antioch Press, 1966.

Amstutz, P.B. *Historical Events of the Mennonite Settlement in Allen and Putnam Counties, Ohio*. 1925. Reprint. Toronto, Ontario, 1978.

Backman, Milton V., Jr. *The Heavens Resound: A History of the Latter-day Saints in Ohio, 1830-1838*. Salt Lake City: Deseret Book Co., 1983.

Barker, John Marshall. *History of Ohio Methodism: A Study in Social Science*. Cincinnati: Curts & Jennings, 1898.

Beachy, Leroy. *Cemetery Directory of the Amish Community in Eastern Holmes and Adjoining Counties in Ohio*. n.p., 1975.

Beggs, S.R. *Pages from the Early History of the West and Northwest, Embracing Reminiscences and Incidents of Settlement and Growth and Sketches of the Material and Religious Progress of the States of Ohio, Indiana, Illinois, and Missouri, with Especial Reference to the History of Methodism*. Cincinnati: Methodist Book Concern, 1868.

Bell, Raymond Martin, et al. *Methodism on the Upper Ohio before 1812*. Washington, PA: R.M. Bell, 1963.

_____. "More on Early Methodist Circuits on the Upper Ohio." Washington, PA: 1983. Typescript. WRHS.

Berry, Ellen Thomas and David A. Berry, Jana Sloan Broglin, ed. 2nd ed. *Our Quaker Ancestors: Finding Them in Quaker Records*. Baltimore: Genealogical.com, 2022.

Bowers, Roy E. "The Historic Rural Church." *Ohio Archaeological and Historical Society Quarterly* 51 (June 1942): 89-100.

Brien, Lindsay Metcalfe. *Abstracts from History of the Church of the Brethren in Ohio*. Fort Wayne, IN: Allen County Public Library, 1983. Typescript.

Brown, James Haldane. "United Church Work in Ohio." *Journal of the Presbyterian Historical Society* 30 (June 1952): 73-94.

Burke, James L. and Donald E. Bensch. "Mount Pleasant and the Early Quakers of Ohio." *Ohio History* 83 (Autumn 1974): 220-25.

_____. *Mount Pleasant and the Early Quakers of Ohio*. Columbus: Ohio Historical Society, 1975.

Burton, Katherine. *Make the Way Known: The History of the Dominican Congregation of St. Mary of the Springs, 1822 to 1957.* New York: Farrar, Straus & Cudahy, 1959.

Church Histories of Tri-State Conference, the Ohio District, the American Lutheran Church 1812-1984. n.p., Tri-State Conference, 1984. WRHS.

Cowles, Henry. *A Defence of Ohio Congregationalism and of Oberlin College.* n.p., n.d.

Davis, Eileen A. and Judith S. Ireton. *Quaker Records of the Miami Valley of Ohio.* Owensboro, KY: McDowell Publications, 1981.

Denlinger, Carolyn Teach. *Every Name Index for History of the Church of the Brethren of the Southern District of Ohio.* Dayton, OH: Southern Ohio District, Church of the Brethren Historical Committee, 1982.

Diehm, Edgar G., ed. *The Church of the Brethren in Northeastern Ohio.* Elgin, IL: The Brethren Press, 1965.

Dolle, Mrs. Percy A., comp. *Ohio Churches: Their Incorporation Dates As Shown in the Laws of Ohio.* Columbus: Mrs. P.A. Dolle, 1957.

Doyle, Joseph Beatty. *The Church in Eastern Ohio.* Steubenville, OH: H.C. Cook, 1914.

Dunlevy, A.H. *History of the Miami Baptist Association.* Cincinnati: George S. Blanchard & Co., 1869.

Durnbaugh, Donald F. "Strangers and Exiles: Assistance Given by the Religious Society of Friends to the Separatist Society of Zoar in 1817-1818." *Ohio History* 109 (Winter-Spring 2000): 71-92.

Eaton, S.J.M. *History of the Presbytery of Erie.* New York: Hurd and Houghton, 1868.

Ebeling, Harry. *The Diocese of Southern Ohio.* Cincinnati: Diocese of Southern Ohio, Communications Office, 1988.
A history of the Episcopal Church in Southern Ohio.

Eberly, William R. *The History of the Church of the Brethren in Northwestern Ohio, 1827-1963.* Hartville, OH: Northern Ohio District, 1982.

Eby, Lela, comp. *Every Name Index, Church of the Brethren in Southern Ohio.* Mill Valley, CA: The compiler, 1955.

Edwards, Martha L. "Ohio's Religious Organizations and the War." *Ohio Archaeological and Historical Quarterly* 28 (1919): 208-24.

Eltscher, Susan M. *The Records of American Baptists in Ohio, and Related Organizations.* Rochester, NY: American Baptist Historical Society, 1981.

Ernsberger, C.S. *A History of the Wittenberg Synod of the General Synod of the Evangelical Lutheran Church, 1847-1916.* Columbus: Lutheran Book Concern, 1917.

Finley, James Bradley. *Sketches of Western Methodism: Biographical, Historical and Miscellaneous, Illustrative of Pioneer Life.* W.P. Strickland, ed. Cincinnati: Methodist Book Concern, 1856.

The First Regular Baptist Church and Other Baptist Churches of Columbus and Central Ohio, 1825-1884. Abstracted by Genevieve M. Obetz, ed. Margaret Hiles Scott, ed. Columbus: Franklin County Genealogical Society, 1984.

Fortman, Edmund J. *Lineage: A Biographical History of the Chicago Province.* Chicago: Loyola University Press, 1987.
The Chicago Province, Society of Jesus; includes Ohio.

The Friends Church. Ohio Yearly Meeting. *Observing Our 150th Yearly Meeting.* Damascus, OH: 1962.

Gill, Charles Otis and Gifford Pinchot. *Six Thousand Country Churches.* New York: Macmillan Co., 1919.

Gray, Elma E. and Leslie Robb Gray. *Wilderness Christians: The Moravian Mission to the Delaware Indians.* Toronto: Macmillian Co., 1956.

Hall, Barbara Yoder. *Born Amish.* Randolph, OH: Jacbar Publications, 1980.

Hamilton, Albert. *The Catholic Journey through Ohio.* Columbus: Catholic Conference of Ohio, 1976.

Harter, Frances D., comp. *Guide to the Manuscripts of Early Ohio Methodism: United Methodist Church of Ohio.* Delaware, OH: United Methodist Archives Center, Ohio Wesleyan University, 1981.

Hayden, Amos Sutton. *Early History of the Disciples in the Western Reserve, Ohio, with Biographical Sketches of the Principal Agents in their Religious Movement.* Cincinnati: Chase & Hall, 1875. Indexed by Georgene Morris Sones.

Hildreth, Samuel Prescott. *Contributions to the Early History of the Northwest, Including the Moravian Missions in Ohio.* Cincinnati: 1864.

Hinshaw, William Wade. *Ohio Quaker Genealogical Records,* vols. 4-5 of *Encyclopedia of American Quaker Genealogy.* 6 vols. 1936-1950. Reprint. Baltimore: Genealogical Publishing Co., 1969. Volumes 4 and 5 cover Ohio Quaker meetings. This is one of the major reference sources for Quaker genealogy.

Historical Records Survey (Ohio). *Inventory of the Church Archives of Ohio Presbyterian Churches.* Columbus: Ohio Historical Society, 1940. Original records at the Presbyterian Historical Society, Philadelphia. Microfilm, FSL.

History of the Central Ohio Conference of the Methodist Episcopal Church, 1856-1913. Cincinnati: Press of the Methodist Book Concern, n.d.

History of the Church of the Brethren of the Southern District of Ohio. Dayton, OH: Otterbein Press, 1920. See *Every Name Index,* comp. by Carolyn Teach Denlinger (Dayton, OH, 1982).

Holmes, John. *Historical Sketches of the Missions of the United Brethren.* 2nd ed. London: John Holmes, 1827.

Houck, George Francis. *A History of Catholicity in Northern Ohio and in the Diocese of Cleveland from 1749 to December 31, 1900.* 2 vols. Cleveland: Press of J.B. Savage, 1903. Volume 1 is historical, volume 2 contains biographical sketches and portraits.

Hynes, Michael J. *History of the Diocese of Cleveland, Origin and Growth (1847-1952).* Cleveland: Diocese of Cleveland, 1953.

Kennedy, William Sloane. *The Plan of Union, or, A History of the Presbyterian and Congregational Churches of the Western Reserve, with Biographical Sketches of the Early Missionaries.* Hudson, OH: Pentagon Steam Press, 1856.

Kem, Richard, ed. *A History of the Ohio Conference of the Churches of God, General Conference, 1836-1986.* Nappanee, IN: Evangel Press, 1986.

Kimball, Stanley B. "Sources on the History of the Mormons in Ohio, 1830-38." *BYU Studies* 4 (Summer 1971): 524-540.

King, I.F. *Introduction of Methodism in Ohio.* Columbus: Ohio Archaeological and Historical Society Publications, 1989.

Kraybill, Donald B. *What the Amish Teach Us.* Baltimore: Johns Hopkins University Press, 2021.

Krumm, Delbert R. *A History of the Scioto, Southeast, and Ohio Southeast Conferences.* Circleville, OH: Ohio Southeast Conference, Evangelical United Brethren Church, 1958.

Krumm, John M. *Flowing Like A River.* Cincinnati: Forward Movement Publications, 1989.

Leedy, Roy B. *The Evangelical Church in Ohio, 1816-1951.* Cleveland: Ohio Conference of the Evangelical United Brethren Church, 1959.
Typescript index compiled by Jana Sloan Broglin.

Leonard, Rev. Delavan L. *A Century of Congregationalism in Ohio, 1796-1896.* Oberlin, OH: Pearce & Randolph, 1896.

Lubbers, Ferne Reedy and Margaret Dieringer, eds. *Advent of Religious Groups into Ohio.* Mansfield, OH: Clark County Chapter, Ohio Genealogical Society, 1978.
A study of the major religious groups in Ohio; includes useful maps.

MacLean, John Patterson. *Shakers of Ohio.* Columbus: F.J. Heer Printing Co., 1907.

McCormick, Virginia E. and Robert W. McCormick. "Episcopal Versus Methodist: Religious Competition in Frontier Worthington." *Ohio History* 107 (Winter-Spring 1998): 5-21.

McKinney, William Wilson, ed. *The Presbyterian Valley.* Pittsburgh: Davis & Warde, 1958.

Manning, Barbara. *Genealogical Abstracts from Newspapers of the German Reformed Church, 1840-1843.* Bowie, MD: Heritage Books, 1995.

Mechling, George Washington. *History of the Evangelical Lutheran District Synod of Ohio Covering Fifty-three Years, 1857-1910.* n.p., 1911.

Miller, Marcus. *Roots by the River: The History, Doctrine, and Practice of the Old German Baptist Brethren in Miami County, Ohio.* Covington, OH: Hammer Graphics, 1973.

Moherman, T.S., et al. *A History of the Church of the Brethren, Northeastern Ohio.* Elgin, IL: Brethren Publishing House, 1914.

Monfort, J.G. *Presbyterianism North of the Ohio, Containing a Statement of the Planting and Progress of the Presbyterian Church in Ohio from 1790 to 1822.* Cincinnati: Elm Street Printing Co., 1872.

Morlan, Charles P., comp. *A Brief History of Ohio Yearly Meeting of the Religious Society of Friends (Conservative).* Barnesville, OH: The Representative Meeting, 1959.

Morton, Sunny Jane and Harold A. Henderson. *How to Find your Family History in U.S. Church Records: A Genealogist's Guide.* Baltimore: Genealogical Publishing Co., 2019.

Mote, Luke Smith. *Early Settlement of Friends in the Miami Valley.* Willard Heiss, ed.. Indianapolis, 1961.

New Order Amish Directory. Millersburg, OH: Abana Books, 1999.

Nolt, Steven M. *A History of the Amish.* 3rd ed. NY: Good Books, 2015

Ohio Church History Society. *Papers of the Ohio Church History Society.* Oberlin, OH: The Society, 1890-1901.

Ohio Federation of Churches. *Survey Report of Churches and Community.* Columbus: 1921-22.

Ohio Lutheran Church Women. *A Century of Roots of Ohio Lutheran Church Women.* n.p., 1978.

Ohio. Sesquicentennial Commission. Religious Participation Committee. *Churches in the Buckeye Country: A History of Ohio's Religious Groups Published in Commemoration of the State's Sesquicentennial, 1953.* (Columbus): The Commission, 1953.

Ohio State Christian Convention. "Proceedings of the First Ohio State Christian Convention." *The Ohio Convention Reporter* 1 (1870).

Ohio's Religious Groups of Historical Interest. Columbus: Columbus Blank Book Co., 1965.

Parkin, Max H. "Conflict at Kirtland: A Study of the Nature and Causes of External and Internal Conflict of the Mormons in Ohio between 1830 and 1838." M.A. thesis, Brigham Young University, 1966.

_____. "Mormon Political Involvement in Ohio." *BYU Studies* 9 (Summer 1969): 484-502.

Peters, Mildred Hull. *Every Name Index for Church of the Brethren in Southern Ohio, 1955.* Elgin, IL: Brethren Publishing House, 1955.

Pike, Kermit J. *A Guide to Shaker Manuscripts in the Library of the Western Reserve Historical Society.* Cleveland: Western Reserve Historical Society, 1974.

Presbyterian Church in the U.S.A. *Historical Sketch of the Synod of Ohio (New School) from 1838 to 1868.* Cincinnati: Elm Street Printing Co., 1870.

History of Presbyterianism in Ohio.

___. *One Hundred and Fifty Years of Presbyterianism in the Ohio Valley,1790-1940.* Cincinnati: n.p., 1941.

___. *The Churches of Miami Presbytery.* By Virginia Rainey. N.p., 1989.

Rainey, Virginia F. *How Firm a Foundation: A Historical Directory of the Congregations of the Miami Presbytery, Presbyterian Church, USA, 1799-1991.* n.p., 1992.

Reed, John H. *Guide to the Manuscripts of Early Ohio Methodism, United Methodist Church of Ohio.* Delaware, OH: West Ohio Conference, United Methodist Church, Commission on Archives and History, 1981.

Reichel, Edward H. *An Historical Sketch of the Church and Missions of the United Brethren, Commonly Called Moravian.* Bethlehem, PA: J.&W. Held, 1848.
Includes a history of Brethren missions in Ohio.

Robinson, Elmo Arnold. *The Universalist Church in Ohio.* Akron: Ohio Universalist Convention, 1923.
Includes biographical notes of Ohio ministers.

Robison, Elwin C. *The First Mormon Temple: Design, Construction, and Historic Context of the Kirtland Temple.* Provo, UT: Brigham Young University Press, 1997.

Rodabaugh, James H. and Mary Jane Rodabaugh. *Schoenbrunn and the Moravian Missions in Ohio.* 3rd ed. Columbus: Ohio Historical Society, 1961.

Sesquicentennial History of the Lancaster-Zanesville Presbytery, 1808-1958. n.p., n.d.

Shaker Membership Card Index. Western Reserve Historical Society, Cleveland. Microfilm, WRHS, FSL.

Shaw, Henry K. *Buckeye Disciples: A History of Disciples of Christ in Ohio.* St. Louis, MO: Christian Board of Publications, 1952.

Sheatsley, C.V. *History of the Evangelical Lutheran Joint Synod of Ohio and Other States from the Earliest Beginnings to 1919.* Columbus: Lutheran Book Concern, 1919.

Sinnema, John R. *German Methodism in Ohio: Its Leaders and Institutions.* Berea, OH: American-German Institute of Baldwin Wallace College, 1983.

Smith, Joseph. *Old Redstone, or, Historical Sketches of Western Presbyterianism, its Early Ministers, its Perilous Times, and its First Records.* Philadelphia: Lippincott, Grambo & Co., 1854.

Smith, Ophia Delilah. "'The Beginnings of the New Jerusalem Church in Ohio." *Ohio State Archaeological and Historical Quarterly* 61 (July 1952): 235-61.

_____. "The Rise of the New Jerusalem Church in Ohio." *Ohio State Archaeological and Historical Quarterly* 61 (Oct. 1952): 380-409.

Smith, Timothy L. "The Ohio Valley: Testing Ground for America's Experiment in Religious Pluralism." *Church History* 60 (1991): 461-79.
A history of Methodism in early Ohio.

Smucker, Isaac. *History of the Moravian Missions of Ohio, and Sketches of Its Missionaries.* Columbus: 1876.

Smythe, George Franklin. *A History of the Diocese of Ohio Until the Year 1918.* Cleveland: The Diocese, 1931.

A history of the Episcopal Church in Ohio.

Snarr, D. Neil. *Claiming Our Past: Quakers in Southwest Ohio and Eastern Tennessee.* Wilmington, OH: D. Neil Snarr, 1992.

Society of Friends. Ohio Yearly Meeting. *Observing Our 150th Yearly Meeting: Ohio Quaker Sesquicentennial, 1812-1962.* Damascus, OH: The Friends Church, Ohio Yearly Meeting, 1962.

Stivison, David V., comp. *The Lord's Shepherds in the Ohio Hills: Biographies of 175 Ministers and Wives of the Southeastern Ohio Conferences of the United Brethren and the Evangelical United Brethren Churches, 1901-1974.* Philadelphia: privately printed, 1987.

Stoltzfus, Grant Moses. *Mennonites of the Ohio and Eastern Conference from the Colonial Period in Pennsylvania to 1968.* Scottdale, PA: Herald Press, 1969.

History of pioneer Mennonite communities in Ohio. Includes a list of congregations and leaders. Concludes with a bibliographical essay for the subject.

Taylor, James W. *History of the State of Ohio, First Period, 1650-1787.* Cincinnati: H.W. Derby & Co. Publishers, 1854.

Includes a history of early Jesuit Missions.

Terrell, C. Clayton. *Quaker Migration to Southwest Ohio.* N.p., n.d.

Umble, John Sylvanus. *Ohio Mennonite Sunday Schools.* Goshen, IN: Goshen College, 1941.

Historical background of Mennonites in Ohio; includes a map of Amish and Mennonite churches in the state.

United Methodist Archives (Ohio). *Methodist Ministers Card Index, All Ohio Conferences, 1797-1981.* United Methodist Archives Center, Ohio. Microfilm, FSL.

The United Methodist Church 1992 East Ohio Conference Journal. 2 vols. Lakeside, OH, 1992.

United Presbyterian Synod of Ohio. *Buckeye Presbyterian.* n.p., 1968.

Vaughan, B.F. *A Centennial History of the Miami Ohio Christian Conference, 1819-1919.* Dayton, OH: Christian Publishing Association, 1919.

Versteeg, John M. and John D. Green, eds. *Methodism: Ohio Area (1812-1962).* Cincinnati: Ohio Area Sesquicentennial Committee, 1962.

A history of Methodism in Ohio; includes official rosters.

Wallen, Ed G. *United Methodism Takes Root in the Black Swamp.*
    Fremont, OH: Lesher Printers, 1981.
Welsh, E.B., ed. *Buckeye Presbyterianism.* United Presbyterian
    Synod of Ohio, 1968.
    A history of seven Presbyterian denominations and their twenty-one synods.
Whitlock, Elias D., et al. *History of the Central Ohio Conference of the
    Methodist Episcopal Church, 1856-1913.* Cincinnati: Press of the
    Methodist Book Concern, 1914.
Yeager, Helen F. "The Rise, Spread, and Influence of Religion in Ohio from
    1783 to 1815." M.A. thesis, University of Cincinnati, 1942.

Ethnic Sources

Abajian, James de T. *Blacks in Selected Newspapers, Censuses and Other Sources: An Index to Names and Subjects.* Boston: G.K. Hall, 1976.

Black, Lowell Dwight. *The Negro Volunteer Militia Units of the Ohio National Guard, 1870-1954: The Struggle for Military Recognition and Equality in the State of Ohio.* Manhattan, KS: Military Affairs/Aerospace Historian Publishing, Kansas State University, 1976.

"Blacks in Ohio in 1870 Who Were Born in Ohio." *The Report* 40 (Winter 2000/2001): 169-176; *The Report* 41 (Spring 2001): 4-10.

Blockson, Charles L. and Ron Fry. *Black Genealogy.* Englewood Cliffs, NJ: Prentice-Hall, 1977.
A general guidebook for African American genealogical research. Includes many addresses and a bibliography.

Brickner, Barnett Albert. *The Jewish Community of Cincinnati, Historical and Descriptive, 1817-1933.* Ph.D. diss., University of Cincinnati, 1933.

Bunch-Lyons, Beverly A. *And they Came: The Migration of African-American Women from the South to Cincinnati, Ohio, 1900-1950.* n.p., 1995.

Byers, Paula K., ed. *African American Genealogical Sourcebook.* Detroit: Gale Research, 1995.
One of the major guides to African American genealogical research. Discusses migration, genealogical sources, oral history, and related topics. Includes bibliographies and many addresses.

Carmack, Sharon DeBartolo. *A Genealogist's Guide to Discovering Your Immigrant & Ethnic Ancestors.* Cincinnati: Betterway Books, 2000.

Chyet, Stanley F. "Ohio Valley Jewry during the Civil War." *Bulletin of the Historical and Philosophical Society of Ohio* 21 (1963): 179-87.

Clark, Peter H. *The Black Brigade of Cincinnati, Being a Report of Its Labors and a Muster Roll of Its Members.* 1864. Reprint. New York: Arno Press, 1969.

Dabney, Wendell P. *Cincinnati's Colored Citizens: Historical, Sociological, and Biographical.* 1926. Reprint. New York: Negro University Press, 1970.
Biographical sketches of African Americans in Cincinnati.

Davis, Lenwood G. *Blacks in the State of Ohio, 1800-1976: A Preliminary Survey*. Monticello, IL: Council of Planning Librarians, 1977.

Davis, Russel H. *Black America in Cleveland, 1796-1969*. Cleveland: Associated Publishers, 1972.

Encyclopedia of Ohio Indians. 2 vols. St. Clair Shores, MI: Somerset Publishers, 1998.

Erickson, Leonard. "Politics and Repeal of Ohio's Black Laws, 1837-1849." *Ohio History* 82 (Summer-Autumn 1973): 154-75.

Evans, William R. *History of Welsh Settlements in Jackson and Gallia Counties of Ohio*. 1896. Reprint. Columbus: Chatham Communicators, 1988.

Fuller, Sara, et al., eds. *The Ohio Black History Guide*. Columbus: Archives-Library Division, Ohio Historical Society, 1975. Bibliographies, lists of county records, and lists of manuscripts. A useful African American reference source.

Gartner, Lloyd P. *History of the Jews of Cleveland*. 2nd ed. Cleveland: Western Reserve Historical Society, 1987.

Gerber, David Allison. *Black Ohio and the Color Line, 1860-1915*. Urbana, IL: University of Illinois Press, 1976.
A scholarly study of African Americans in Ohio race relations, lifestyle, migration, and similar topics.

Haller, Stephen E. and Robert H. Smith, Jr. *Registers of Blacks in the Miami Valley: A Name Abstract (1804-1857)*. Dayton, OH: Wright State University, 1977.
Shows name of slave or free Black, owner's name, date and place of freedom, date and place residing in Ohio, and sometimes date of birth or age.

Henritze, Barbara K. *Bibliographic Checklist of African American Newspapers*. Baltimore: Genealogical Publishing Co., 1995.

Hickok, Charles Thomas. *The Negro in Ohio, 1802-1870*. Ph.D. diss., Western Reserve University, 1896. Reprint. New York: AMS Press, 1975.

Houdek, G. Robert and Michel S. Perdreau. *Blacks in Ohio: A Selected Bibliography of Materials in the Alden Library*. Athens, OH: Ohio University Library, Reference Department, 1978.

Johnson, Anne E. and Adam Merton Cooper. *A Student's Guide to African American Genealogy*. Phoenix, AZ: Oryx Press, 1996.

Joiner, W.A., comp. *A Half Century of Freedom of the Negro in Ohio*. Freeport, NY: Books for Libraries Press, 1972.

Koehler, Llyle. *Cincinnati's Black Peoples: A Chronology and Bibliography, 1787-1982*. Cincinnati: University of Cincinnati, 1986.
: A chronology and history of African Americans in Cincinnati.

Laffoon, Polk IV. "Cincinnati's Jewish Community." *Cincinnati Magazine* 10 (April 1977): 46-57.

Litwack, Leon F. *North of Slavery: The Negro in the Free States, 1790-1860*. Chicago: University of Chicago Press, 1961.

McCluskey, John A., ed. *Blacks in Ohio*. Cleveland: New Day Press, Karamu House, 1976.
: Slavery in Ohio, flight to freedom, Black memories in Ohio.

McGinnis, Frederick A. *The Education of Negroes in Ohio*. Wilberforce, OH: 1962.

Malvin, John. *North Into Freedom: The Autobiography of John Malvin, Free Negro, 1795-1880*. 1879. Reprint. Kent, OH: Kent State University Press, 1988.
: A biography and history of African Americans in Ohio.

Newman, Debra L., comp. *Black History: A Guide to Civilian Records in the National Archives*. Washington, DC: National Archives Trust Fund Board, 1984.

Nitchman, Paul E. *Blacks in Ohio, 1880*. 10 vols. Decorah, Iowa: Anundsen Publishing; Mansfield, OH: Ohio Genealogical Society, 1985-97.
: Identifies African Americans and Mulattoes in the 1880 Ohio census. Each volume is separately indexed.

Ohio. Auditor of State. Special Enumeration of Blacks Immigrating to Ohio, 1861-1863. Columbus. Microfilm.

Ohio. Adjutant General's Office. *Official Roster of the Colored Troops of the State of Ohio in the War of the Rebellion*. Microfilm.
: Original muster in and muster out rolls of the Civil War.

Ohio. Governor's Commission on Socially Disadvantaged Black Males. *Ohio's African-American Males: A Call to Action*. Columbus: Ohio Office of Black Affairs, 1990.

Philipson, David. "Jewish Pioneers of the Ohio Valley." *Publications of the American Jewish Historical Society* 8 (1900): 43-57.

Phillips, Kimberly L. *Heaven-Bound: Black Migration, Community, and Activism in Cleveland, 1915-1945*. n.p., 1992.

Sama, Jonathan D. and Nancy H. Klein. *The Jews of Cincinnati*. Cincinnati: Center for the Study of the American Jewish Experience, Hebrew Union College-Jewish Institute of Religion, 1989.

Streets, David H. *Slave Genealogy: A Research Guide with Case Studies*. Bowie, MD: Heritage Books, 1986.

Tanner, Helen Hornbeck, ed. *Atlas of Great Lakes Indian History*. Norman, OK: University of Oklahoma Press, 1987.

Tolzmann, Don Heinrich, ed. *Dayton's German Heritage: Karl Karstaedt's Golden Jubilee History of the German Pioneer Society of Dayton, Ohio*. Bowie, MD; Heritage Books, 2010.

_____. *Ohio's German Heritage*. Bowie, MD: Heritage Books, 2011.

Turpin, Joan. *Register of Black, Mulatto, and Poor Persons in Four Ohio Counties, 1791-1861*. Bowie, MD: Heritage Books, 1985.

Varady, David P. "Migration and Mobility Patterns of the Jewish Population of Cincinnati." *American Jewish Archives* 3 (1980): 79-88.

Weisman, Kay, comp. *Selected Bibliography of Black History Sources at the Ohio Historical Society*. Columbus: Ohio Historical Society, n.d.

Wesley, Charles Harris. *Negro-Americans in Ohio: A Sesquicentennial View*. Wilberforce, OH: Central State College, 1953.

_____. *Ohio Negroes in the Civil War*. Columbus: Ohio State University Press, 1962.

Weston, Rubin Francis, ed. *Blacks in Ohio History*. Columbus: Ohio American Revolution Bicentennial Advisory Commission, Ohio Historical Society, 1976.

Historical essays regarding the Black experience in Ohio.

Whiteman, Max. "Black Genealogy." *RQ [Research Quarterly]* 11 (1972).

Witcher, Curt Bryan. *African American Genealogy: A Bibliography and Guide to Sources*. Ft. Wayne, IN: Round Tower Books, 2000.

Woodson, Carter G. *A Century of Negro Migration*. Washington, DC: Association for the Study of Negro Life and History, 1918.

Wright, Richard R. *The Negroes of Xenia, Ohio*. United States Department of Labor Bulletin No. 37. n.p., n.d.

Young, Tommie Morton. *Afro-American Genealogy Sourcebook*. New York: Garland Publishing, 1987.

Identifies sources for African American genealogical research. Includes bibliographies and many addresses.

Guidebooks and Methodology

Adams, Marilyn, comp. *Ohio Local and Family History Sources in Print*
    Clarkston, GA: Heritage Research, 1984.
Arnold, Lisa Perry. *Thee & Me, A Beginner's Guide to Early Quaker*
    Records. n.p., 2014.
Balhuizen, Anne Ross. *The History of Your Heritage: Ohio.*
    Centerville, UT: Advanced Resources, 1993.
Bell, Carol Willsey. *Ohio Genealogical Guide.* 6th ed. Youngstown, OH:
    Bell Books, 1995.
    A summary and description of Ohio genealogical records;
    illustrated with examples and maps.
_____. *Ohio Guide to Genealogical Sources.* Baltimore: Genealogical
    Publishing Co., 1988.
    A summary of many genealogical records available for each
    Ohio county, alphabetically arranged by county.
Brannick, John A. "Buried Treasures: Ohio's Unusual County Records."
    Preview Ohio Historical Society 5 (Summer 1996): 13-16.
Clark, Donna K. *Ohio State Directory of Genealogical Records.* Arvada,
    CO: Ancestor Publishers, 1986.
Colket, Meredith Bright. *The Widely Known "Western Reserve" of Ohio.*
    Salt Lake City: Genealogical Society, 1969. Cuyahoga West
    Chapter, Ohio Genealogical Society.
Cuyahoga County, Ohio: Genealogical Research Guide. Fairview Park,
    OH: Cuyahoga West Chapter, 1989.
Douthit, Ruth Long. *Ohio Resources for Genealogists with Some*
    References for Genealogical Searching in Ohio. Rev. ed. Detroit:
    Detroit Society for Genealogical Research, 1972.
    See *Supplement* Mrs. Carl Main, ed..
Eichholz, Alice, ed. *Ancestry's Red Book: American State, County & Town*
    Sources. Rev. ed. Salt Lake City: Ancestry Publishing, 1991.
Elliott, Wendy L. *Ohio Genealogical Research Guide.* Rev. ed.
    Bountiful, UT: American Genealogical Lending Library, 1988.
Fenley, Ann. *The Ohio Connection Formula for Finding Elusive*
    Ancestors. Dayton, OH: Ohio Connection, 1985.
_____. *The Ohio Open Records Law and Genealogy: Researching Ohio*
    Public Records. Dayton, OH: Ohio Connection, 1989.
    A history of Ohio's open records law and accessing Ohio records;
    partially outdated.

Filby, P. William, comp., *American and British Genealogy and Heraldry,* 3rd ed. Boston: New England Historic Genealogical Society, 1983. *1982-1985 Supplement* Boston: New England Historic Genealogical Society, 1987.

Though dated, this work is a comprehensive bibliography of American and British genealogical titles.

Flavell [Bell], Carol Willsey and Florence Clint. *Ohio Area Key.* Denver, CO; Area Keys, 1977.

Although partially dated, this reference guide describes Ohio records of genealogical value and includes useful state maps, historical sources, bibliographies, and other reference materials.

Gagel, Diane VanSkiver. "Researching in Ohio." *The Genealogical Helper* 45 January-February 1991: 10-16.

_____. *Ohio Courthouse Records,* Ohio Genealogical Society Research Guide No. 1; Rev. ed. Mansfield, OH: The Society, 2006.

Gilkey, Elliot Howard. *The Ohio Hundred Year Book.* Columbus: Fred J. Heer, 1901.

Lists of members of the General Assembly, senators, representatives, and biographical sketches. This is a revised and enlarged edition of *Taylor's Ohio Statesmen and Hundred Year Book,* 1892.

The Handybook for Genealogists. 10th ed. Draper, UT: Everton Publishers, 2002.

Harter, Mary (McCollom). "Ohio." In American Society of Genealogists, *Genealogical Research: Methods and Sources,* vol. 2. Rev. ed., Kenn Stryker-Rodda, ed. Washington, DC: The Society, 1983, pp. 22-28.

Harter, Stuart. *Ohio Genealogy and Local History Sources Index.* Fort Wayne, IN: CompuGen Systems, 1986.

Heisey, John W. *Ohio Genealogical Research Guide.* Indianapolis, IN: Heritage House, 1987.

Lists of Ohio sources, bibliographies, and addresses.

Hochstetter, Nancy, ed. *Travel Historic Ohio: A Guide to Historic Sites and Markers.* Madison, WI: Guide Press Co., 1986.

Local history, biography, historical markers, Ohio maps.

Hoffman, Marian, comp. *Genealogical and Local History Books in Print: Family History Volume,* 5th ed., 4 vols. (Baltimore: Genealogical Publishing Co., 1996).

Kalette, Linda Elise. *The Papers of Thirteen Early Ohio Political Leaders: An Inventory to the 1976-77 Microfilm Editions* Columbus: Ohio Historical Society, 1977.

Khouw, Petta. *Genealogy: Helping You Climb Your Family Tree.*
    Occasional Paper, series 3, no. 2. Columbus: State Library of
    Ohio, 1990.
    A valuable guide to the genealogy collection of the State
    Library of Ohio, Columbus, and its services, and an overview of
    Ohio genealogical sources.
McCay, Betty L. *Sources for Genealogical Searching in Ohio.* Rev. ed.
    Indianapolis: The author, 1973.
Main, Florence (Mrs. Carl), ed. *Ohio Genealogical Records: A Supplement
    to Some References for Genealogical Searching in Ohio...Based
    on Material at the Western Reserve Historical Society.* Cleveland:
    Genealogical Advisory Committee of the Western Reserve
    Historical Society, 1968.
Maki, Carol L. "Ohio." In *Ancestry's Red Book: American State, County &
    Town Sources.* Edited by Alice Eichholz. Rev. ed. Salt Lake City:
    Ancestry, 1992, pp. 572-88.
    An overview chapter describing Ohio genealogical sources;
    includes a useful county outline map of the state and county
    information.
Mettle, Suzanne Wolfe, et al., comps. *Genealogical Researcher's Manual:
    With Special References for Using the Ohio Historical Society
    Library.* Columbus: Franklin County Chapter, Ohio Genealogical
    Society, 1981.
National Society of the Colonial Dames of America in the State of Ohio. *A
    Guide to Historic Houses in Ohio.* 2nd ed. Compiled by Elizabeth
    P. Allyn, et al. Westerville, OH: The Society, 1996.
Neel, Thomas Stephen. *Ohio County Courthouse Guide.* Ashland, OH:
    Ashland County Chapter, Ohio Genealogical Society, 1985.
Ohio Factsheet. Online **https://www.ancestry.com**.
The Ohio Genealogical Helper: Vital Records Research. Columbus:
    Maxwell Publications, n.d.
Ohio Genealogical Society. *Guide to Cemetery Preservation.* Mansfield,
    OH: The Society, 1987.
Ohio Public Information Laws. Columbus: Ohio Attorney General.
Ohio Research Outline. Online **https://www.familysearch.org**.
    Briefly outlines Ohio genealogical sources and includes some
    bibliographies. See "Research Helps" at this Internet site.
Parker, Jimmy B. *A Definitive Study of Major U.S. Genealogical Records:
    Ecclesiastical and Secular, Part1, Ohio.* Salt Lake City:
    Genealogical Society, 1969.

Reed, John H. *Guide to the Manuscripts of Early Ohio Methodism, United Methodist Church of Ohio.* Delaware, OH: West Ohio Conference, United Methodist Church, Commission on Archives and History, 1981.

Research Outline: Ohio. Salt Lake City: Family History Department, 1988. A valuable overview of Ohio genealogical sources. For an expanded and updated version see **http://www.familysearch.org**.

Schreiner-Yantis, Netti, comp. *Genealogical and Local History Books in Print,* 4th ed., 4 vols. Springfield, VA; Genealogical Books in Print, 1985-1990.

Schulz, Margaret J., comp. *Sources of Genealogical Help in Ohio.* Burbank, CA: Southern California Genealogical Society, 2000.

Schweitzer, George K. *Ohio Genealogical Research.* Knoxville, TN: The author, 1994.
Bibliographies and descriptions of Ohio sources arranged by subject (church records, etc.) and Ohio by counties.

Sperry, Kip. "Genealogical Research in Ohio." *National Genealogical Society Quarterly* 75 June 1987: 81-104.

_____. "Finding Your Ohio Ancestors." *Everton's Genealogical Helper* 52 1998: 10-15.

Szucs, Loretto Dennis and Sandra Hargreaves Luebking, eds. *The Source: A Guidebook of American Genealogy.* Rev. ed. Salt Lake City: Ancestry Inc., 1997.
This is one of the premier reference sources for American genealogists. Well illustrated.

Terheiden, Connie Stunkel and Kenny R. Burck, comps. *Guide to Genealogical Resources in Cincinnati & Hamilton County, Ohio.* 3rd ed. Cincinnati: Hamilton County Chapter of the Ohio Genealogical Society, 2001.

Wright, David K. *Ohio Handbook.* Emeryville, CA: Moon Publications, 1999.
Includes Ohio history, an overview of Ohio's canals, and other state and local information.

History

Abbott, John Stevens Cabot. *The History of the State of Ohio from the Discovery of the Great Valley to the Present Time.* Detroit: Northwestern Publishing Co., 1875.
One of the major early histories of the state. Illustrated. Online: **https://archive.org/details/historystateohi00abbogoog**

Ambler, Charles Henry. *A History of Transportation in the Ohio Valley.* Glendale, CA: Arthur H. Clark, 1931.

Andrews, E.B. "The Early History of Ohio." *New Englander* 12 (Aug. 1854): 384-408.

Atwater, Caleb. *A History of the State of Ohio, Natural and Civil.* 2nd ed. Cincinnati: Glezen & Shepard, 1838.
See *Index to A History of the State of Ohio, Natural and Civil,* indexed by Marilyn Sims Vadakin (Marietta, OH: Lemon Tree Press, 1993); a personal name, subject, and locality index to this state history.

Aumann, Francis R. and Harvey Walker. *The Government and Administration of Ohio.* New York: Thomas Y. Crowell Co., 1956.

Balhuizen, Anne Ross. *The History of Your Heritage: Ohio.* Centerville, UT: Advanced Resources, 1993.

Banta, Richard Elwell. *The Ohio Valley: A Students' Guide to Localized History.* New York: Teachers College Press, 1966.
Ohio Valley history and bibliographies.

Barclay, Morgan and Charles N. Glaab. *Toledo: Gateway to the Great Lakes.* Tulsa, OK: Continental Heritage Press, 1982.

Barker, Joseph. *Recollections of the First Settlement of Ohio.* George Jordan Blazier, ed. 1958. Reprint. Marietta, OH: Richardson Printing, 1982.

Barnhart, John D. *Valley of Democracy: The Frontier Versus the Plantation in the Ohio Valley, 1775-1818.* Lincoln, NE: University of Nebraska Press, 1953.

Belote, Theodore Thomas. *The Scioto Speculation and the French Settlement at Gallipolis: A Study in Ohio Valley History.* 1907. Reprint. New York: Lenox Hill, 1971.

Berquist, Goodwin F. and Paul C. Bowers, Jr. *The New Eden: James Kilbourne and the Development of Ohio.* Lanham, MD: University Press of America, 1983.
Early Ohio state history and migration history.

Bigham, Darrel E. *Towns & Villages of the Lower Ohio.* Lexington, KY: University Press of Kentucky, 1998.
    A scholarly study of lower Ohio River settlements, with pictures, maps, notes, and a bibliography.

Black, Alexander. *The Story of Ohio.* Boston: D. Lothrop Co., 1888. An early history of the beginnings of Ohio and the Northwest Territory. Illustrated.

Blanchard, Rufus. *The Discovery and Conquests of the Northwest, Including the Early History of Marietta, Cincinnati, Cleveland.* Chicago: 1880.

Bloom, John Porter, ed. *The American Territorial System.* Athens, OH: Ohio University Press, 1973.

Bond, Beverely Waugh, Jr. *The Civilization of the Old Northwest: A Study of Political, Social, and Economic Development, 1788-1812.* New York: Macmillan Co., 1934.

_____. *The Foundations of Ohio.* Columbus: Ohio State Archaeological and Historical Society, 1941.

Booth, Russell H., Jr. *The Tuscarawas Valley in Indian Days, 1750- 1797.* Cambridge, OH: Gamber House Press, 1994.

Boryczka, Raymond. *No Strength without Union.* Columbus: Ohio Historical Society, 1982.

Bowman, David W. *Pathway of Progress: A Short History of Ohio.* New York: American Book Co., 1951.
    An overview history of the state. Illustrated.

Brennan, Joseph Fletcher. *A Biographical Cyclopaedia and Portrait Gallery of Distinguished Men, with an Historical Sketch of the State of Ohio.* 2 vols. Cincinnati: Yorston, 1879.

Brown, Jeffrey P. "The Ohio Federalists, 1803-1815." *Journal of the Early Republic* 2 (1982): 261-82.

_____ and Andrew R.L. Cayton, eds. *The Pursuit of Public Power: Political Culture in Ohio, 1787-1861.* Kent, OH: Kent State University Press, 1994.
    Especially useful are the footnotes, historical background, Ohio timeline, and bibliographic essay.

Bryan, John A. *The Ohio Annual Register, Containing a Condensed History of the State.* Columbus: J. Gilbert & R.C. Bryan, 1835.

Buley, R. Carlyle. *The Old Northwest: Pioneer Period, 1815-1840.* Bloomington, IN: Indiana University Press, 1978. A major historical study of the Northwest Territory.

Burke, James L. and Kenneth E. Davison. *Ohio's Heritage Revised.* Salt Lake City: Peregrine Smith Books, 1989.
Ohio history, ethnic composition, state government, and life in Ohio.

Burke, Thomas Aquinas. *Ohio Lands: A Short History.* 9th ed. Columbus: Auditor of State, 1997.
https://homepages.rootsweb.com/~maggieoh/Land/ohla1.html

Burnet, Jacob. *Notes on the Early Settlement of the Northwestern Territory.* Cincinnati: D. Appleton, 1847.

Butler, Joseph G., Jr. *History of Youngstown and the Mahoning Valley, Ohio.* 3 vols. Chicago: American Historical Society, 1921.

Butler, Mann. *Valley of the Ohio.* Frankfort: Kentucky Historical Society, 1971.

Butler, Margaret M. *A Pictorial History of the Western Reserve, 1796-1860* Cleveland: World Publishing Co., 1963.

Carpenter, Allan. *The Encyclopedia of the Midwest.* New York: Facts On File, 1989.
Includes brief sketches of Ohio history and biography.

Carpenter, W.H. and T.S. Arthur, eds. *The History of Ohio from Its Earliest Settlement to the Present Time.* Philadelphia: J.B. Lippincott & Co., 1858.

Carter, Clarence Edwin, ed. *The Territorial Papers of the United States.* 26 vols. Washington, DC: Government Printing Office, 1934.

Cayton, Andrew R.L. "Land, Power, and Reputation: The Cultural Dimension of Politics in the Ohio Country." *William and Mary Quarterly,* 3rd series. 47 (1990): 276-82.

_____. *The Frontier Republic: Ideology and Politics in the Ohio Country, 1780-1825.* Kent, OH: Kent State University Press, 1986.
Discusses politics, early settlements in Ohio, and historical background. The footnotes and bibliographic essay are especially helpful for Ohio history. See the useful map, "The Ohio Country."

Chaddock, Robert Emmet. *Ohio Before 1850: A Study of the Early Influence of Pennsylvania and Southern Populations in Ohio.* 1908. Reprint. New York: AMS Press, 1967.

Chater, Melville. "Ohio: The Gateway State." *The National Geographic Magazine* 61 (May 1932): 525-91.

Cherry, Peter Peterson. *The Western Reserve and Early Ohio.* Akron, Ohio: R.L. Fouse, 1920.

Collins, William R. *Ohio: The Buckeye State.* 6th ed. Englewood Cliffs, NJ: Prentice-Hall, 1980.

Comley, William J. and W. D'Eggville. *Ohio: The Future Great State, Her Manufacturers and a History of Her Commercial Cities, Cincinnati and Cleveland.* Cincinnati: Comley Brothers, 1875.
   Local and manufacturing history, with biographies and portraits.
Crout, George C. and W.E. Rosenfelt. *Ohio: Its People and Culture.* Minneapolis: T.S. Denison & Co., 1977.
   Ohio history, maps, migration, biographies, pioneer history.
Curtis, Henry B. "Pioneer Days in Central Ohio." *Ohio Archaeological and Historical Publications* I (1887-88): 240-51.
Cutler, Julia Perkins. *The Founders of Ohio.* Cincinnati: Robert Clarke & Co., 1888.
Cutler, Manasseh. *An Explanation of the Map of Federal Lands.* 1787. Reprint. Readex Microprint, 1966.
Daughters of the American Revolution. Dolly Todd Madison Chapter. *Ohio: Early State and Local History.* Tiffin, OH: 1915.
Dowler, John F., ed. *Centennial History, Ohio State Grange, 1873- 1973.* Ashville, OH: Ohio State Grange, n.d.
   A history of the Grange in Ohio, with biographies and some portraits.
Downes, Randolph Chandler. *Council Fires on the Upper Ohio: A Narrative of Indian Affairs in the Upper Ohio Valley Until 1795.* Pittsburgh: University of Pittsburgh Press, 1940.
_____. *Frontier Ohio, 1788-1803.* Columbus: Ohio State Archaeological and Historical Society, 1935.
   An early history of Ohio and its settlers.
_____. *History of Lake Shore, Ohio.* 3 vols. New York: Lewis Historical Publishing Co., 1952.
   Volume 3 contains biographical sketches; indexed.
Duff, William Alexander. *History of North Central Ohio, Embracing Richland, Ashland, Wayne, Medina, Lorain, Huron, and Knox Counties.* 3 vols. Topeka-Indianapolis, Ind.: Historical Publishing Co., 1931.
Educational Research Council of America. *The State of Ohio, Part One, Ohio: From Settlement to 1910.* Cleveland: 1970.
Elkins, Stanley and Eric McKitrick. "A Meaning for Turner's Frontier: Democracy in the Old Northwest." *Political Science Quarterly* 69 (1954): 321-53.
Encyclopedia of Ohio: A Volume of Encyclopedia of the United States. St. Clair Shores, MI.: Somerset Publishers, 1982.
   Ohio state history, biographies, gazetteer of Ohio placenames, and descriptions of historical places.

The Evolution of Ohio. Online: **https://www.oplin.org/evolution/**.
For each geographical region in Ohio, this site shows history (chronology), migration, economy, and population.

Faber, Don. *The Toledo War, The First Michigan-Ohio Rivalry.* Ann Arbor, MI: The University of Michigan Press, 2008.

Fernow, Berthold. *The Ohio Valley in Colonial Days.* Albany, NY: Joel Munsell's Sons, 1890.

Fess, Simeon Davidson. *Ohio: A Four-Volume Reference Library on the History of a Great State.* 5 vols. Chicago: Lewis Publishing Co., 1937.
Historical details for each Ohio county, physical features, first settlements, transportation, economic interests, institutions, notable persons, population statistics, biographies, and portraits. Illustrated.

Fleischman, John. *The Ohio Lands.* San Francisco: Browntrout Publishers, 1995.

Folsom, W.H.C. *Fifty Years in the Northwest, Containing Reminiscences, Incidents and Notes.* Pioneer Press Co., 1888.

Foster, Emily, ed. *The Ohio Frontier: An Anthology of Early Writings.* Lexington: University Press of Kentucky, 1996.
Diaries, letters, travel accounts, and early Ohio history.

Frary, I.T. *Early Homes of Ohio.* New York: Dover Publications, 1970.
Historical background, and some genealogy, along with photographs of homes, courthouses, churches, and other Ohio buildings.

Fry, Mildred Covey. "Women on the Ohio Frontier: The Marietta Area." *Ohio History* 90 (Winter 1981): 55-73.

Galbreath, Charles Burleigh. *History of Ohio.* 5 vols. Chicago: American Historical Society, 1925.
A detailed and useful history of Ohio. See *Cross Index, Charles B. Galbreath's 1925, 5 Volume, History of Ohio,* 2 vols., comp. by Robertalee Lent, Post Falls, Idaho: Genealogical Reference Builders, 1969 and *Index to Charles B. Galbreath's History of Ohio,* indexed by Fay Maxwell Columbus: 1973.

Garrison, Webb. *A Treasury of Ohio Tales.* Nashville: Rutledge Hill Press, 1993.
A guide to Ohio local history and biography.

Giglierano, Geoffrey J. and Deborah A. Overmyer. *The Bicentennial Guide to Greater Cincinnati: A Portrait of Two Hundred Years.* Cincinnati: Cincinnati Historical Society, 1988.

Gilkey, Elliot Howard. *The Ohio Hundred Year Book.* Columbus: Fred J. Heer, 1901.
    Lists of members of the General Assembly, senators, representatives, and biographical sketches. Includes portraits. This is a revised and enlarged edition of *Taylor's Ohio Statesmen and Hundred Year Book* (1892).

Goulder, Grace. *This Is Ohio: Ohio's 88 Counties in Words and Pictures.* Rev. ed. Cleveland: World Publishing Co., 1965.
    A brief history of Ohio's counties and regions. Illustrated.

Gregory, William M. and William B. Guitteau. *History and Geography of Ohio.* New edition. Boston: Ginn and Co., 1935.

Griffiths, D., Jr. *Two Years' Residence in the New Settlements of Ohio, North America.* London: Westley and Davis, 1835.

Gruenwald, Kim M. "Marietta's Example of a Settlement Pattern in the Ohio Country: A Reinterpretation." *Ohio History* 105 Summer-Autumn 1996: 125-44.

Gunckel, John E. *The Early History of the Maumee Valley.* 2nd ed. Toledo: Henry M. Schmit, 1913.

Hansen, Ann Natalie. *Westward the Winds: Being Some of the Main Currents of Life in Ohio, 1788-1873.* Columbus: 1974.

Harris, Charles H. *The Harris History: A Collection of Tales of Long Ago of Southeastern Ohio and Adjoining Territories.* Athens, OH: Athens Messenger, 1957. See *Surname Index to the Harris History,* indexed by Mrs. Jane Whiteman Tulsa, OK: 1978.

Harte, Brian. "Land in the Old Northwest: A Study of Speculation, Sales, and Settlement on the Connecticut Western Reserve." *Ohio History* 101 Summer-Autumn 1992: 114-39.

Hatcher, Harlan Henthorne. *The Buckeye Country: A Pageant of Ohio.* New York: G.P. Putnam's Sons, 1947. An illustrated general history of the state.

_____. *The Western Reserve: The Story of New Connecticut in Ohio.* Rev. ed. Cleveland: World Publishing Co., 1966.

Havighurst, Walter. *Ohio: A Bicentennial History.* New York: W.W. Norton & Co., 1976.
    A popular and general history of Ohio; illustrated.

_____. *The Heartland: Ohio, Indiana, Illinois.* Rev. ed. New York: Harper & Row, 1974.
    Historical background, pioneer settlements, and local history.

Hildreth, Samuel Prescott. *Contributions to the Early History of the Northwest.* Cincinnati: Poe & Hitchcock, 1864.

_____. *Pioneer History: Being An Account of the First Examinations of the Ohio Valley and the Early Settlement of the Northwest Territory.1848.* Reprint. New York: Arno, 1971.
: See *Index to Pioneer History,* indexed by Marilyn Sims Vadakin. Marietta, Ohio: It's My Business, n.d.

Himes, H.E. *A History of Miami-Land, 1770-1990.* Wilmington, DE: H.E. Himes, 1990.

Hinsdale, Burke Aaron and Mary L. Hinsdale. *History and Civil Government of Ohio and the Government of the United States.* Chicago: Werner School Book Co., 1896.

Hintzen, William. *The Border Wars of the Upper Ohio Valley, 1769-1794.* Manchester, CT: Precision Shooting, 1999.

History of Hocking Valley, Ohio. 1883. Reprint. Mt. Vernon, IN: Windmill Publications, 1991. *Surname Index* 1980.

History of Lower Scioto Valley, Ohio. Chicago: Inter-State Publishing Co., 1884.

History of the Upper Ohio Valley, with Family History and Biographical Sketches. 2 vols. Madison, WI: Brant & Fuller, 1890-91.
: See Leila S. Francy, *Surname Index to History of the Upper Ohio Valley.* Apollo, PA: Closson Press, 1993 and Mrs. Jane Whiteman, comp., *Surname Index to History of the Upper Ohio Valley* Tulsa, OK: 1978.

Hochstetter, Nancy, ed. *Travel Historic Ohio.* Madison, WI: Guide Press Co., 1986.
: Useful for a study of Ohio history, early 1800s to the early 1900s.

Hopkins, Charles Edwin. *Ohio: The Beautiful and Historic.* Boston: L.C. Page & Co., 1931.

Hover, John C., et al., eds. *Memoirs of the Miami Valley.* 3 vols. Chicago: Robert O. Law Co., 1919.
: A detailed early history of southwestern Ohio, with biographical details.

Howe, Henry. *Historical Collections of Ohio.* 2 vols. Cincinnati: State of Ohio, 1888-1904. (Publisher varied).
: One of the popular histories of the state. See "Index to Historical Collections of Ohio," index compiled by Fresno Genealogical Society, Fresno, CA. Typescript. See also *Index to Historical Collections of Ohio by Henry Howe,* compiled by Sandra Hudnall Books, 1979.

Kellogg, Louise Phelps, ed. *Early Narratives of the Northwest, 1634-1699.* New York: Charles Scribner's Sons, 1917.

Kennedy, Aileen Elizabeth. *The Ohio Poor Law and its Administration.* Chicago: University of Chicago Press, 1934.

Kern, Kevin F. and Gregory S. Wilson. *Ohio: A History of the Buckeye State.* Malden, MA: Wiley-Blackwell, a John Wiley & Sons, Inc., Publication, 2014.

King, Rufus. *Ohio: First Fruits of the Ordinance of 1787.* 1903. Reprint. New York: AMS Press, 1973.

Kinkead, Charles B. *Ohio Diary: The Saga of Raccoon Valley.* New York: Exposition Press, 1953.

Klauprecht, Emil. *German Chronicle in the History of the Ohio Valley and its Capital City, Cincinnati in Particular.* Don Heinrich Tolzmann, ed. Translated by Dale V. Lally, Jr. Bowie, MD: Heritage Books, 1992.

    A German-American history of the Ohio Valley.

Knapp, H.S. *History of the Maumee Valley.* Toledo: Blade Mammoth Printing, 1872.

    An early history of the Maumee Valley and early settlements.

Knepper, George W. *An Ohio Portrait.* Columbus: Ohio Historical Society, 1976.

    An illustrated general history of Ohio, with historical photos.

_____. *Ohio and its People.* 2nd ed. Kent, OH: Kent State University Press, 1997.

    A valuable history of the state. The Ohio maps in this volume are particularly useful.

Kolehmainen, John I. *A History of the Finns in Ohio, Western Pennsylvania, and West Virginia.* Ohio Finnish-American Historical Society, 1977.

Lawyer, J.P. *History of Ohio from the Glacial Period to the Present Time.* 3rd ed. Columbus: Press of Fred J. Heer, 1904.

Lewis, Thomas William. *History of Southeastern Ohio and the Muskingum Valley, 1788-1928.* 3 vols. Chicago: S.J. Clarke Publishing Co., 1928.

Lieberman, Carl, ed. *Government and Politics in Ohio.* Lanham, Md.: University Press of America, 1984.

Lindsey, David, et al. *An Outline History of Ohio.* Rev. ed. Cleveland: Howard Allen, 1960.

Lossing, Benson J. *A Pictorial Description of Ohio, Comprising a Sketch of Its Physical Geography, History, Political Divisions, Resources, Government and Constitution, Antiquities, Public Lands, etc.* New York: Ensign & Thayer, 1848.

McConagha, John. *Ohio Local History in the Bicentennial Year.* Columbus: State Library of Ohio, 1978.

McConnell, Michael Norman. *A Country Between: The Upper Ohio Valley and Its Peoples, 1724-1774*. Lincoln: University of Nebraska Press, 1992.
    A scholarly study of Native Americans and early settlements in the Ohio region; includes valuable maps of the area.
Madison, James H., ed. *Heartland: Midwestern History and Culture*. Bloomington, IN: Indiana University Press, 1988.
    See especially the chapter, "Ohio: Gateway to the Midwest."
Mahoning Valley Historical Society. *Historical Collections of the Mahoning Valley*. 1876. Reprint. Knightstown, IN: The Bookmark, 1977.
Maizlish, Stephen E. *The Triumph of Sectionalism: The Transformation of Ohio Politics, 1844-1856*. Kent, Ohio: Kent State University Press, 1983.
Marshall, Carrington Tanner, ed. *A History of the Courts and Lawyers of Ohio*. 4 vols. New York: American Historical Society, 1934. Biographical sketches of prominent Ohio lawyers and judges.
Martzolff, Clement Luther. *Fifty Stories from Ohio History*. Columbus: Teacher Publishing Co., 1917.
Marzulli, Lawrence J. *The Development of Ohio's Counties and Their Historic Courthouses*. Columbus: County Commissioners Association of Ohio, 1982.
    A brief history of each Ohio county and its courthouse.
Mathews, Alfred. *Ohio and Her Western Reserve, with a History of Three States*. New York: D. Appleton and Co., 1902.
    A regional history of the Western Reserve in Ohio.
Maxwell, Fay, comp. *Irish Refugee Tract Abstract Data & History of the Irish Acadians*. Columbus: Maxwell Publications, 1974.
Michels, Greg, ed. *Governments of Ohio, 1986*. n.p., 1985.
Miller, James M. *The Genesis of Western Culture: The Upper Ohio Valley, 1800-1825*. Columbus: Ohio State Archaeological and Historical Society, 1938.
Mitchener, Charles Hollowell, ed. *Ohio Annals: Historic Events in the Tuscarawas and Muskingum Valleys and in Other Portions of the State of Ohio*. 1876. Reprint. Strasburg, Ohio: Gordon Printing, 1975. Reprint. Bowie, MD: Heritage Books, 1993.
Moorehead, Warren King. *The Indian Tribes of Ohio Historically Considered*. 1899. Reprint. New York: AMS Press, 1983.
Morrison, Olin Dee. *Ohio, "Gateway State": A History of Ohio, Social, Economic, Political*. 4 vols. Athens, OH: E.M. Morrison, 1962.
    A typescript general history of the state.

Muller, Edward K. "Early Industrialization in the Ohio Valley: A Review Essay." *Historical Geography Newsletter* 3 (Fall 1973): 19-30.
Murdock, Eugene C. *The Buckeye Empire: An Illustrated History of Ohio Enterprise*. Northridge, CA: Windsor Publications, 1988.
Newton, Jim. *Today in Ohio History*. Hamilton, OH: Fort Hamilton Press, 1964.
Noble, Allen G., et al. *Ohio: An American Heartland*. Columbus: State of Ohio, Division of Geological Survey, 1975.
Ohio: An Empire within an Empire. 2nd ed. Columbus: Ohio Development and Publicity Commission, 1950.
Ohio History Central: An Online Encyclopedia of Ohio. Online: **https://www.ohiohistorycentral.org/**
Ohio Historical Society. *Building Ohio: The Historic Settlement and Development of Ohio*. Columbus: Ohio Historical Society, 1998. CD-ROM
"Ohio History Books," Mount Pleasant, SC: Arcadia Publishing, offers a variety of towns or city histories
Ohio Memory: An Online Scrapbook of Ohio History. Online **https://ohiomemory.ohiohistory.org/**
Ohio's Progressive Sons, A History of the State: Sketches of Those Who have Helped to Build up the Commonwealth. Cincinnati: Queen City Publishing Co., 1905.
  Biographical sketches and portraits of prominent Ohioans.
Ohio Women (OPLIN). Online: **https://oplin.org/famousohioans/women/puzzler.html**
Onuf, Peter S. *Statehood and Union: A History of the Northwest Ordinance*. Bloomington, IN: Indiana University Press, 1987.
  A scholarly study of Ohio and the Northwest Ordinance.
Overman, William D., comp. *Select List of Materials on Ohio History in Serial Publications*. Columbus: Ohio State Archaeological and Historical Society, 1941.
Page, Henry Folsom. *The Law of Warrants, Entries, Surveys and Patents in the Virginia Military District in Ohio*. Columbus: J.H. Riley & Co., 1850.
  Describes the history of Virginia military titles in Ohio.
Particular Places: A Traveler's Guide to Inner Ohio. 2 vols. Wilmington, OH: Orange Frazer Press, 1990-93.
  Local history and tours of Ohio.
Pathways to the Old Northwest: An Observance of the Bicentennial of the Northwest Ordinance. Indianapolis: Indiana Historical Society, 1988.

Perry, Dick. *Ohio: A Personal Portrait of the 17th State.* Garden City, NY: Doubleday & Co., 1969.

Peters, William Edwards. *Ohio Lands and their History.* 3rd ed. 1930. Reprint. New York: Arno Press, 1979.
   A detailed history of Ohio lands and early settlements in the state. Includes maps of Ohio land divisions.

Phillips, W. Louis. *Jurisdictional Histories for Ohio's Eighty-Eight Counties, 1788-1985.* Bowie, MD: Heritage Books, 1986.

Pioneer History. Cincinnati: H.W. Derby, 1848.

Randall, Emilius Oviatt and Daniel J. Ryan. *History of Ohio: The Rise and Progress of an American State.* 6 vols. New York: Century History Co., 1912-15.

_____, ed. *Ohio: Centennial Anniversary Celebration.* Columbus: Press of Fred J. Heer, 1903.
   Includes lists of Ohioans, judges, and others.

Reichert, W.O. and S.O. Ludd, eds. *Outlook on Ohio.* n.p.,1983.

Rerick, Rowland H. *History of Ohio.* Madison, WI: Northwestern Historical Association, 1905.

_____. *State Centennial History of Ohio.* Madison, WI: Northwestern Historical Association, 1902.

Richards, Wilfrid Gladstone. *The Settlement of the Miami Valley of Southwestern Ohio.* Chicago: n.p., 1948.

Richardson, Robert H. *A Time and Place in Ohio: A Chronological Account of Certain Historical and Genealogical Miscellany in Eastern Ohio.* Smithtown, NY: Exposition Press 1983.

Roberts, Carl H. and Paul R. Cummins. *Ohio: Geography, History, Government.* Laidlaw Brothers, 1961.

Rohrbough, Malcolm J. *The Land Office Business: The Settlement and Administration of American Public Lands, 1789-1837.* New York: Oxford University Press, 1968.

_____. *The Trans-Appalachian Frontier: People, Societies, and Institutions, 1775-1850.* 1978. Reprint. Belmont, CA: Wadsworth Publishing Co., 1990.
   A scholarly history of the trans-Appalachian frontier, 1775-1850, experiences of the people, rise of societies, social history, and development of institutions. Includes useful maps of the frontier, including Ohio.

Roseboom, Eugene Holloway and Francis Phelps Weisenburger. *A History of Ohio.* 2nd ed. Columbus: Ohio Historical Society, 1969.
   A popular and well-illustrated history of the state.

Rust, Orton Glenn. *History of West Central Ohio*. 3 vols. Indianapolis: Historical Publishing Co., 1934.

Ryan, Daniel Joseph. *A History of Ohio, with Biographical Sketches of Her Governors and the Ordinance of 1787*. Columbus: A.H. Smythe, 1888.

Santmyer, Helen Hoover. *Ohio Town*. Columbus: Ohio State University Press, 1962.

Scamyhom, Richard and John Steinle. *Stockades in the Wilderness: The Frontier Defenses and Settlements of Southwestern Ohio, 1788-1795*. Dayton, OH: Landfall Press, 1986.

An early history of settlements in southwestern Ohio.

Scheiber, Harry N. *Ohio Canal Era: A Case Study of Government and the Economy, 1820-1861*. Athens, OH: Ohio University Press, 1969.

_____, ed. *The Old Northwest: Studies in Regional History, 1787-1910*. Lincoln: University of Nebraska Press, 1969.

Development of the Old Northwest, frontier history, regional history, and studies of migration in the Old Northwest.

Searight, Thomas B. *The Old Pike: A History of the National Road with Incidents Accidents, and Anecdotes Thereon*. Uniontown, PA: the Author, 1894; reprint, Bowie, MD; Heritage Books, 1990.

Shannon, Timothy J. "The Ohio Company and the Meaning of Opportunity in the American West, 1786-1795." *The New England Quarterly* 64 (1991): 393-413.

_____. "This Unpleasant Business: The Transformation of Land Speculation in the Ohio Country, 1787-1820." In *The Pursuit of Public Power: Political Culture in Ohio, 1787-1861*. Jeffrey P. Brown and Andrew R. L. Cayton, eds. Kent, OH: Kent State University Press, 1994.

Sherman, Christopher Elias. *Original Ohio Land Subdivisions*. 1925. Reprint. Columbus: 1982.

Siebert, Wilbur H. *The Underground Railroad in Ohio*. 1895. Reprint. A.W. McGraw, 1993.

Skaggs, David Curtis, ed. *The Old Northwest in the American Revolution: An Anthology*. Madison, WI: State Historical Society of Wisconsin, 1977.

Slocum, Charles Elihu. *History of the Maumee River Basin*. Defiance, OH: The author, 1905.

_____. *The Ohio Country between the Years 1783 and 1815*. 1910. Reprint. Bowie, MD: Heritage Books, 1991.

Smith, Thomas H., ed. *An Ohio Reader: 1750 to the Civil War*. Grand Rapids, MI: William B. Eerdmans, 1975.

_____, ed. *An Ohio Reader: Reconstruction to the Present.* Grand Rapids, MI: William B. Eerdmans, 1975.
    The above two volumes are a documentary history of the development of Ohio.
Smith, William Ernest. *History of Southwestern Ohio: The Miami Valleys.* 3 vols. New York: Lewis Historical Publishing Co., 1964.
    Regional and local history of southwestern Ohio, with many biographies and portraits.
Soltow, Lee. "Inequality Amidst Abundance: Land Ownership in Early Nineteenth Century Ohio." *Ohio History* 88 (Spring 1979): 133-51.
Stewart, John Struthers. *History of Northeastern Ohio.* 3 vols. Indianapolis: Historical Publishing Co., 1935.
Stille, Samuel Harden. *Ohio Builds a Nation: A Memorial to the Pioneers and the Celebrated Sons of the "Buckeye" State.* 5th ed. Chicago: Arlendale Book House, 1962.
    Ohio local history and brief biographical sketches.
Taylor, James Wickes. *History of the State of Ohio, First Period, 1650-1787.* Cincinnati: H.W. Derby & Co. Publishers, 1854.
Taylor, Robert M., Jr., ed. *The Northwest Ordinance, 1787: A Bicentennial Handbook.* Indianapolis: Indiana Historical Society, 1987.
    A detailed history and chronology of the Northwest Ordinance. Includes valuable maps of the region.
Taylor, William A. *Ohio Statesmen and Annals of Progress.* 2 vols. Columbus: Westbote, 1899.
Thwaites, Reuben Gold and Louise Phelps Kellogg, eds. *Frontier Defense on the Upper Ohio, 1777-1778.* Madison: Wisconsin Historical Society, 1912.
Traylor, Jeff and Nadean Disabato Traylor. *The Great Ohio Roundabout.* Monroeville, OH: King of the Road Press, 1998.
    Ohio local history, settlements, maps, and guides to cemeteries and historical sites.
Utter, William T. *The Frontier State, 1803-1825.* Columbus: Ohio State Archaeological and Historical Society, 1942.
Van Aken, William R. *Buckeye Barristers: A Centennial History of the Ohio State Bar Association.* Ohio State Bar Association, 1980.
Van Fossan, William Harvey. *The Story of Ohio.* New York: Macmillan Co., 1937.

Van Tassel, Charles Sumner. *The Book of Ohio and Its Centennial, or One Hundred Years of the Buckeye State.* 20 parts. Bowling Green, OH: C.S. Van Tassel, 1901.
    A well-illustrated general history of the state.
_____. *Story of the Maumee Valley, Toledo, and the Sandusky Region.* 4 vols. Chicago: S.J. Clarke Publishing Co., 1929.
Van Tassel, David D. and John J. Grabowski, eds. *The Encyclopedia of Cleveland History.* 2 vols. 2nd ed. Bloomington, IN: Indiana University Press, 1996. Online **http://www.ech.cwru.edu**.
Venable, W.H. *Footprints of the Pioneers in the Ohio Valley.* Reprint. Bowie, MD: Heritage Books, 1987.
Vexler, Robert I. and William F. Swindler, eds. *Chronology and Documentary Handbook of the State of Ohio.* Dobbs Ferry, NY: Oceana Publications, 1978.
    Includes a chronology of events in Ohio from 1669 to 1977, biographies of prominent citizens, and selected documents.
Wade, Richard. *The Urban Frontier: Pioneer Life in Early Pittsburgh, Cincinnati, Lexington, Louisville, and St. Louis.* Cambridge: Harvard University Press, 1959.
Walker, Byron H. *Frontier Ohio: A Resource Guide for Teachers.* Columbus: Ohio Historical Society, 1972.
    Ohio history and migration, teaching aids, and social history.
Walker, Richard. *Wolf Creek and the Muskingum: Notes on the Settlement of Southeastern Ohio.* Baltimore: Gateway Press, 1996.
Walker, Timothy. *Discourse on the History and General Character of the State of Ohio.* Columbus: 1838.
Ward, Nahum. *A Brief Sketch of the State of Ohio.* Glasgow: J. Neven, 1822.
Warner, Hoyt Landon. *Progressivism in Ohio, 1897-1917.* Columbus: Ohio State University Press, 1964.
Weisenburger, Francis P. *The History of the State of Ohio.* 3 vols. Carl Wittke, ed. Columbus: Ohio State Archaeological and Historical Society, 1941.
_____. *The Passing of the Frontier, 1825-1850.* Columbus: Ohio State Archaeological and Historical Society, 1941.
West, A.W. and J.L. Hunt *A Short History of Ohio.* Dayton, OH: United Brethren Publishing House, 1888.
Wheeler, Robert A. "The Literature of the Western Reserve." *Ohio History* 100 (Summer-Autumn 1991): 101-28.

_____, ed. *Visions of the Western Reserve: Public and Private Documents of Northeastern Ohio, 1750-1860*. Columbus: Ohio State University Press, 2000.

Whitaker, William E. "Land Surveys of Ohio, Historically Considered." Master's thesis, Ohio State University, 1901.

Whittlesey, Charles Barney. *Topographical and Historical Sketch of the State of Ohio*. Philadelphia: Jas. B. Rodgers Co., Printers, 1872.

Willard, Eugene B., et al., eds. *A Standard History of the Hanging Rock Iron Region of Ohio*. 2 vols. 1916. Reprint. Marceline, MO: Walsworth, n.d.

Williams, W.W., ed. *History of the Firelands, Comprising Huron and Erie Counties, Ohio*. 1879. Reprint, Evansville, IN: Unigraphic, 1973.

Williamson, C.W. *History of Western Ohio and Auglaize County*. Columbus: Press of W.M. Linn & Sons, 1905.
See *Index to History of Western Ohio and Auglaize County*. Cridersville, OH: Susanna Russell Chapter, DAR, 1974.

Wills, Charles A. *A Historical Album of Ohio*. Brookfield, CT: Millbrook Press, 1996.
A summary of Ohio history and facts. Illustrated.

Wilson, Ellen Susan. "Gaining Title to the Land: The Case of the Virginia Military Tract." *The Old Northwest* 12 (1986): 65-82.

_____. "Speculators and Land Development in the Virginia Military Tract: The Territorial Period." Ph.D. diss., Miami University, 1982.

Wilson, Frazer Ells. *Advancing the Ohio Frontier: A Saga of the Old Northwest*. Blanchester, OH: Brown Publishing Co., 1937.

Winkle, Kenneth J. *The Politics of Community: Migration and Politics in Antebellum Ohio*. Cambridge: Cambridge University Press, 1988.

Winter, Nevin Otto. *A History of Northwest Ohio*. 3 vols. Chicago: Lewis Publishing Co., 1917.
A detailed history of northwestern Ohio, with many biographical sketches.

Wittke, Carl Frederick, ed. *The History of the State of Ohio*. 6 vols.1941-44. Reprint. Columbus: Ohio Historical Society, 1968. A detailed history of Ohio; illustrated and includes many maps.

Indexes and Genealogical Sources

The American Genealogical-Biographical Index to American Genealogical, Biographical, and Local History Materials. 206 vols. Middletown, CY: Godfrey Memorial Library, 1952-2000. *Supplement,* vols. 1- , 2000- .

Known as AGBI, this is an extensive index to many published genealogies and other sources. Online **http://www.ancestry.com**.

Baldwin, Henry R. *Henry R. Baldwin Genealogical Records Collection.* 75 vols. Youngstown, OH: Public Library of Youngstown and Mahoning County, 1963.

Typescript and handwritten copies of genealogical records for western Pennsylvania and eastern Ohio, cemetery and church records, probate records, genealogies, etc. Separately indexed, *Index to the Henry R. Baldwin Genealogical Records,* 8 vols. Youngstown, OH: Public Library of Youngstown and Mahoning County, 1961-62.

Bell, Carol Willsey, et al., eds. *Master Index, Ohio Society Daughters of the American Revolution Genealogical and Historical Records, Volume 1.* Westlake, OH: Ohio Society Daughters of the American Revolution, 1985.

Useful in identifying Ohio DAR records.

_____. *Ohio Divorces: The Early Years.* Boardman, OH: Bell Books, 1994.

Identifies many early divorces in Ohio; indexed.

_____. *Ohio Genealogical Periodical Index: A County Guide.* 6th ed. Youngstown, OH: Bell Books, 1987.

_____. *Ohio Wills and Estates to 1850: An Index.* Youngstown, OH: Bell Books, 1981. Reprint. Baltimore: Genealogical Publishing Co., 2012.

One of the major personal name indexes for Ohio researchers.

_____. *Ohio Lands: Steubenville Land Office, 1800-1820.* Youngstown, OH: The author, 1983.

Shows name of proprietor, residence in Ohio or elsewhere, year, certificate number, legal description of land.

Berry, Ellen Thomas and David A. Berry. *Early Ohio Settlers: Purchasers of Land in East and East Central Ohio, 1800-1840.* 1989. Reprint. Baltimore: Clearfield, 2000.

_____. *Early Ohio Settlers: Purchasers of Land in Southeastern Ohio, 1800-1840.* Baltimore: Genealogical Publishing Co., 1984.

_____. *Early Ohio Settlers: Purchasers of Land in Southwestern Ohio, 1800-1840*. Baltimore: Genealogical Publishing Co., 1986.

Bowman, Mary L. *Abstracts and Extracts of the Legislative Acts and Resolutions of the State of Ohio, 1803-1821*. Mansfield, OH: Ohio Genealogical Society, 1994.

Gives information on individuals mentioned in Ohio's legislative acts and resolutions; provides details on acts and resolutions. This Ohio reference source is indexed. See next volume cited below.

_____. *Abstracts and Extracts of the Legislative Acts and Resolutions of the State of Ohio, Volumes 20 to 29, 1821-1831*. Mansfield, OH: Ohio Genealogical Society, 1996.

Brien, Lindsay Metcalfe. *A Genealogical Index of Pioneers in the Miami Valley, Ohio*. Dayton, OH: Dayton Circle, Colonial Dames of America in the State of Ohio, 1970.

Shows names of family members, Ohio residence and previous place of residence, dates, and other genealogical details. Covers Miami, Montgomery, Preble, and Warren counties, Ohio. See *Every Name Index to Miami Valley Ohio Pioneers*, indexed by Marjorie Dodd Floyd (Dayton, OH, 1980).

_____. *Miami Valley Will Abstracts from the Counties of Miami, Montgomery, Warren & Preble in the State of Ohio, 1803-1850*. Dayton, OH: 1940.

Burton, Conrad and Ann Burton. *Born in Ohio: Living in Southwest Michigan in 1860*. Decatur, MI: Glyndwr Resources, 1986.

Caccamo, James F. *Marriage Notices from the Ohio Observer Series, 1827-1855*. Apollo, PA: Closson Press, 1994.

Carmean, Barbara J. Carman, comp. *1860 Mortality Schedule, Ohio*. Hillsboro, OH: Southern Ohio Genealogical Society, 1983.

Carter, Clarence Edwin, comp. "The Territorial Papers of the United States, Volume III: The Territory Northwest of the River Ohio, 1787-1803." *The Report* 41 (Fall 2001): 131-34.

A Census of Pensioners for Revolutionary or Military Services, 1840. 1841. Reprint. Baltimore: Genealogical Publishing Co., 1967.

Lists of Revolutionary War pensioners residing in Ohio, and elsewhere, arranged by county. Shows name of pensioner, age, name of head of family with whom residing on 1 June 1840, township, and county. See *A General Index to A Census of Pensioners for Revolutionary or MilitaryService,1840* Baltimore: Genealogical Publishing Co., 1965.

Clark, Marie Taylor. *Ohio Lands: Chillicothe Land Office, 1800-1829*. Chillicothe, OH: The author, 1984.

_____. *Ohio Lands South of the Indian Boundary Line.* Chillicothe, OH: The author, 1984.

Cleveland Public Library. *Index to Family Genealogical Information in Various Books and Periodicals Owned by Cleveland Public Libraries.* 2 vols. Cleveland: n.d.
Photocopies of a card file to genealogies in periodicals and books in the Cleveland Public Library. Arranged by surname. Gives Cleveland Public Library call number.

Colorado Chapter, Ohio Genealogical Society. *County-by-County Research Being Done by Members of the Colorado Chapter of the Ohio Genealogical Society.* Longmont, CO: The Society, 1998.

Cunningham, Miriam L. *Every-Name Index: Together with Abstracted Items of Genealogical Interest Found in Ohio Legislature, 1787-1806.* Columbus: The author, 1980.
A name index to *Journals of the House of Representatives, Journals of the Senate, and Acts of Ohio, 1787-1806.*

Daughters of the American Revolution. Ohio Society. *Early Marriage Bonds of Ohio.* n.p., n.d. (published various years).
Typescripts at State Library of Ohio, Columbus, OH. DAR records are cataloged under each individual Ohio county. Title varies; some carry a series title, *Early Vital Records of Ohio.* Many typescript copies of Bible, cemetery, and vital records are housed at the State Library of Ohio, the DAR Library in Washington, DC, and on microfilm at the Family History Library, Salt Lake City. Most volumes indexed.

_____. *Early Vital Recordsof Ohio: Bible and Cemetery Records.* n.p., n.d. (published various years).
Typescripts available at the Ohio State Library, Columbus, Ohio. DAR records are cataloged under each individual Ohio county.

_____. *Early Vital Records of Ohio: Family Records.* n.p., n.d.
Typescripts at the Ohio State Library, Columbus, Ohio. DAR records are cataloged under each individual Ohio county.

_____. *Early Vital Records of Ohio: Ohio Bible Records.* n.p., n.d.
Typescripts at the Ohio State Library, Columbus, Ohio. DAR records are cataloged under each individual Ohio county.

_____. *Early Vital Records of Ohio: Ohio Cemetery and Church Records.* n.p., n.d.
Typescripts at the Ohio State Library, Columbus, Ohio. DAR records are cataloged under each individual Ohio county.

_____. *Early Vital Records of Ohio: Ohio Family Histories.* n.p., n.d.
Typescripts at the Ohio State Library, Columbus, Ohio. DAR records are cataloged under each individual Ohio county.

_____. Middle Western Section, *Colonial and Genealogical Records Committee.* DAR, 1955.

Day, Sandra Hudnall, comp. *Index to Historical Collections of Ohio by Henry Howe.* Steubenville, Ohio: Jefferson County Chapter, Ohio Genealogical Society, 1990.

Diefenbach, H.B. Mrs., comp. *Index to the Grave Records of Soldiers of the War of 1812 Buried in Ohio.* 1945. Ann Arbor, MI: University Microfilms 1991.

Dyer, Albion Morris. *First Ownership of Ohio Lands.* 1911. Reprint. Baltimore: Genealogical Publishing Co., 1969. Online: **http://www.ancestry.com**.

Early Ohio Settlers, 1700s-1900s, CD-ROM (Family Tree Maker).

The 1812 Census of Ohio: A Statewide Index of Taxpayers. Miami Beach, FL: T.L.C. Genealogy, 1992.

An alphabetical list of all land owners in Ohio as found in the Ohio tax duplicates for 1812 (1814 for Wayne County).

Firelands Pioneer Obituary Index, 1857-1909. n.p., n.d.

Gardner, Frank W. "Central Ohio Genealogical Notes and Queries." Columbus: Sunday Journal Dispatch, n.d.

Photocopies available at State Library of Ohio; indexed.

Genealogical Data Relating to Women in the Western Reserve before 1840 [1850], compiled by Women's Department, Cleveland Centennial Commission. Cleveland: 1943. See separate *Index* cited below.

Green, Karen Mauer. *Pioneer Ohio Newspapers.* 2 vols. Galveston: Frontier Press, 1986.

Hanna, Charles Augustus. *Ohio Valley Genealogies.* New York: J.J. Little & Co., 1900.

Harfst, Linda L. *Local History and Genealogy Resources Guide to Southeastern Ohio.* Wellston, OH: Ohio Valley Area Libraries, 1984.

Harter, Stuart. *Ohio Genealogy and Local History Sources Index.* Fort Wayne, IN: CompuGen Systems, 1986.

Identifies many genealogy and local history sources for Ohio- books, periodical articles, newspaper articles, etc.; arranged by county. Useful for identifying pre-1986 titles.

Index and Abstract of Obituaries for Individuals with Ties to the State of Ohio Published in Colorado Newspapers. Denver: Colorado Chapter of the Ohio Genealogical Society, 1995-.

Index of the Firelands Pioneer from June 1858 to 1937. Norwalk, OH: Firelands Historical Society, 1939.

Index to the Henry R. Baldwin Genealogical Records. 8 vols. Youngstown, OH: Public Library of Youngstown and Mahoning Co., 1961-62.

Index to the Microfilm Edition of Genealogical Data Relating to Women in the Western Reserve before 1840 (1850). Cleveland: Genealogical Committee, Western Reserve Historical Society, 1976.

Jackson, Ronald Vern, et al., eds. *Index to Ohio Tax Lists, 1800-1810.* 2 vols. Bountiful, UT: Accelerated Indexing Systems, 1977-85.

_____ and G. Ronald Teeples. *Early Ohio Census Records.* Bountiful, UT: Accelerated Indexing Systems, 1974.

_____. *Mortality Schedule, Ohio, 1850.* North Salt Lake: Accelerated Indexing Systems International, 1979.

_____. *Ohio Tax Lists, 1800-1810.* 2 vols. North Salt Lake, UT: Accelerated Indexing Systems, 1985.

Klauprecht, Emil. *German Chronicle in the History of the Ohio Valley and Its Capital City Cincinnati in Particular.* Bowie, MD: Heritage Books, 1992.

Koleda, Elizabeth Potts. *Some Ohio & Iowa Pioneers: Their Friends and Descendants.* Prineville, OR: The author, 1973.

Lee, Susan Dunlap, comp. *The Ohio Genealogical Society Periodicals Index: Topical by Location, 1960-2000.* Mansfield, OH: Ohio Genealogical Society, 2002.

Indexes topics (subjects) in periodicals published by OGS; arranged by localities in Ohio.

Library of Congress, *National Union Catalog of Manuscript Collections.* Washington, DC, 1962.

McMullin, Phillip W., ed. *Grassroots of America: A Computerized Index to the American State Papers, Land Grants and Claims 1789-1837.* Salt Lake City: Gendex Corp., 1972.

A personal name index to the *American State Papers* (Land Grants and Claims). Includes many references to Ohio lands. Miami Valley Genealogical Index (Computerized Heritage Association). Online: **https://www.ogs.org**

National Society Colonial Dames of the XVII Century. Ohio Society. *Our Ancestors' Families.* n.p., The Society, 1988.

National Society, United States Daughters of 1812. *Burial Places of Ohio Soldiers of the War of 1812.* 20 vols. The Society, 1927. Volumes housed at the State Library of Ohio, Columbus. Title varied, *Ohio Burial Places of Soldiers of the War of 1812.* See index edited by Phyllis Brown Miller, *Index to the Grave Records of Servicemen of the War of 1812, State of Ohio.*

Northwest Library District (Ohio). *Genealogical Resources Guide: Northwest Ohio Libraries.* Bowling Green, OH: Northwest Library District, 1983.

Ohio. Adjutant General's Dept. *The Official Roster of the Soldiers of the American Revolution Buried in the State of Ohio.* 3 vols. Reprint. 1929-1959. Kokomo, IN: Selby Publishing, 1988.

Ohio Cemetery Records Extracted from the "Old Northwest" Genealogical Quarterly. Baltimore: Genealogical Publishing Co., 1984.

Ohio Company. *The Records of the Original Proceedings of the Ohio Company.* Archer Butler Hulbert, ed. Marietta, OH: Marietta Historical Commission, 1917.

Ohio Genealogical Society. Ancestor Card File. Mansfield, OH. Microfilm, FSL.

_____. *Ancestor Charts of Members of the Ohio Genealogical Society.* Mansfield, OH: The Society, 1987.

Pedigree charts of OGS members; with a surname index. A major genealogical reference source for the state.

_____. *First Families of Ohio Roster, 1964-2000.* Sunda Anderson Peters and Kay Ballantyne Hudson, eds. Mansfield, OH: The Society, 2001.

Arranged alphabetically by surname of ancestor and cross-indexed to name of OGS member. This is one of the major personal name finding aids for the state.

_____. *Official Roster of the Soldiers of the State of Ohio in the War with Mexico, 1846-1848.* Indexed by Jana Sloan Broglin, Mansfield, OH: The Society, 1991.

_____. *The Ohio Genealogical Society Periodicals Index, Topical by Location, 1960-2000.* Mansfield, OH: The Society, 2002.

A subject index to Ohio genealogical periodicals; arranged by localities and surnames, such as families and names of pensioners.

_____. *Ohio Marriages Recorded in County Courts through 1820: An Index.* Jean Nathan, chairman. Mansfield, OH: The Society, 1996.

A monumental index to pre-1820 Ohio marriages. Updated by OGS, *Ohio Marriages, 1821-1830.*

Ohio Records & Pioneer Families: Ten Year Surname Index, 1985-1994 (and 1960-1984). Mansfield, OH: The Society, 1996.

_____. *Surname Index of the Ohio Genealogical Society.* Mansfield, OH: The Society, 1967-69.

Indexes in this reference source show name of person, year of birth, birthplace (state or country), spouse's name, year married, year of death, and state where buried.

Ohio. Secretary of State. *Annual Report of the Secretary of State to the Governor of Ohio: Appendix B, Return of the Number of Deaf and Dumb, Blind, Insane, and Idiotic Persons, May 1856.* 1856. Reprint. Bowie, MD: Heritage Books, 1987.
    Shows county, township, person' name, nature of affliction (blind, dumb, insane, etc.), age, sex, occupation, birthplace (state or country), parents' names and their birthplace, and other details.

_____. *Annual Report of the Secretary of State to the Governor of Ohio: Jail Reports, 1854 and 1855.* Bowie, MD: Heritage Books, 1988.

Ohio Society, Colonial Dames XVII Century, *Our Ancestors' Families* (The Society, 1988).

Ohio Society, Daughters of the American Revolution. *Master Index, Ohio Society, Daughters of the American Revolution Genealogical and Historical Records.* 1985.

Ohio Society, Sons of the American Revolution. *Centennial Register, 1889 to 1989.* Dayton, OH: The Society, 1988.
    Shows name of SAR member, name of his patriot ancestor, date accepted, and SAR membership details.

_____. *Register, Ohio Society Sons of the American Revolution,* comp. by Charles A. Jones. Columbus: F.J. Heer Printing Co., 1956-64.

Ohio Society, United States Daughters of 1812. *Index to the Grave Records of Servicemen of the War of 1812, State of Ohio.* Phyllis Brown Miller, ed.. Huber Heights, OH: Ohio Society, United States Daughters of 1812, 1988.
    Shows name of soldier, birth and death dates, wife's name, and where buried.

Ohio Source Records from the Ohio Genealogical Quarterly. Baltimore: Genealogical Publishing Co., 1986. Indexed.

Ohio State Journal Index, 1913-40.
    WPA card file on microfilm at the Ohio Historical Society, 1913-1926 & 1940. Bound index volumes at OHS prepared by Work Projects Administration in Ohio, Columbus.

Ohio Surname Index. Compiled by the Ohio Society of the Daughters of the American Revolution. Columbus: Ohio Historical Society, 1928-1936. Microfilm, FSL.
    A statewide index to local histories and other Ohio sources. Cards are arranged alphabetically by surname.

Ohio Veteran's Home Death Records, January 3, 1889 through December 31, 1983. Sandusky, OH: Erie County Chapter of the Ohio Genealogical Society, 1984.

Ohioans in the California Census of 1850. San Diego: Southern California Chapter of the Ohio Genealogical Society, 1988.

"Oldest Inscriptions, with Revolutionary and War of 1812 Records, of the Cemeteries of Trumbull, Mahoning, and Columbiana Counties, Ohio, and Lawrence, Mercer, and Beaver Counties, Pennsylvania." 7 vols. in 1. 1913. Typescript.

Page, Henry F. *Virginia Military District of the Law of Warrants, Entries, Surveys and Patents in the V.M.D. of Ohio.* Columbus: J.H. Riley & Co., 1850.

Periodical Source Index. Edited by Michael B. Clegg, Curt B. Witcher, et al. Fort Wayne, IN: Allen County Public Library Foundation, 1987-Annual. Retrospective volumes dated 1847-1985. Internet, CD-ROM, published volumes, and microfiche. See especially U.S. Places-OH (Ohio), Research Methodology, and Family Records (surnames). Periodicals indexed are housed in the Genealogy Department, Allen County Public Library, Fort Wayne, Indiana. PERSI is a retrospective and annual index to American genealogical periodicals and includes many Ohio titles. It indexes personal names, source records, and methodology.

Petty, Gerald McKinney, comp. *Index of the Ohio Girls Industrial School: Inmates' Case Records, 1869-1911.* Columbus: Petty's Press, 1984.

_____, comp. *Index of the Ohio Squirrel Hunters Roster.* Columbus: G.M. Petty, 1984.

_____, comp. *Index of the Ohio 1825 Tax Duplicate.* Columbus: Petty's Press, 1981.

_____, comp. *Index of the Ohio 1835 Tax Duplicate.* Columbus: Petty's Press, 1987.

_____, comp. Name Index, 1812 Ohio Tax Duplicate. Microfilm.

_____. comp. *Ohio 1810 Tax Duplicate.* Columbus: G.M. Petty, 1976.

Phillips, W. Louis. *Index to Ohio Pensioners of 1883.* Bowie, MD: Heritage Books, 1987.
An index to the list of pensioners, male and female, who were residing in Ohio as of 1 January 1883.

_____. *Jurisdictional Histories for Ohio's Eighty-eight Counties, 1788-1985.* n.p., n.d.

Powell, Esther Weygandt, comp. *Early Ohio Tax Records.* 1971. Reprint. Baltimore: Genealogical Publishing Co., 1985.

Reel Index to the Microform Collection of County and Regional Histories of the Old Northwest, Series II, Ohio. New Haven, CT: Research Publications, 1975.
Includes an index to atlases, biographies, and histories of Ohio.

Riegel, Mayburt Stephenson, comp. *Early Ohioans' Residences from the Land Grant Records*. Mansfield, OH: Ohio Genealogical Society, 1976.

Identifies many pre-1825 Ohio pioneers who purchased land from the federal government at early land offices in Ohio.

A Roster of Honorably Discharged Ex-Pupils of the Soldiers' and Sailors' Orphans' Home, Xenia, Ohio. Xenia, OH: Home Weekly Printing, 1898.

Sacchini, Joseph Louis. *Italian Family Genealogy of the Mahoning Valley, 1874-1994: A Genealogy Guide*. Boardman, OH: The author, 1994.

Short, Anita (Mrs. Don R.) and Mrs. Denver Eller. *Ohio Bible Records*. 2 vols. Greenville, OH: Fort Greenville Chapter, DAR, 1970-71.

Shennan, Christopher Elias. *Original Ohio Land Subdivisions*. 1925. Reprint. Columbus: 1982.

Simon, Bernice H., comp. *Name Index for Genealogical and Family History of Eastern Ohio*. Chagrin Falls, OH: B.H. Simon, 1973.

Smith, Alma Aicholtz. *The Virginia Military Surveys of Clermont and Hamilton Counties, Ohio, 1787-1849*. Cincinnati: The author, 1985.

Smith, Clifford Neal. *Federal Land Series*. 4 vols. Chicago: American Library Association, 1972-86. Reprint. Baltimore: Genealogical Publishing Company, 2007.

See especially volume 4, parts 1 and 2.

Smith, Marjorie, ed. *Ohio Marriages Extracted from the Old Northwest Genealogical Quarterly*. 1977. Reprint. Baltimore: Genealogical Publishing Co., 1980.

Snyder, Michael G., ed. *Ohio Genealogy and Local History: A Resource Guide to the Holdings of Twenty-three Member Libraries*. Mansfield, OH: North Central Library Cooperative, 1984.

Society of Colonial Wars in the State of Ohio. *Register*. 1902.

Society of Mayflower Descendants in the State of Ohio. n.p., 1913, 1938.

Southern Ohio Genealogical Society. *Family Bible Records of Southwestern Ohio*. Hillsboro, OH: The Society, n.d.

_____. *Surname/Locality Index*. 4 vols. Hillsboro, Ohio: The Society, n.d.

Indexes pedigree charts on file in the library of the Southern Ohio Genealogical Society, Hillsboro, OH.

Sperry, Kip. "Published Indexes." In Kory L. Meyerink, ed., *Printed Sources: A Guide to Published Genealogical Records*. Salt Lake City: Ancestry, 1998, pp. 193-214.

Sprague, Stuart Seely. *Kentuckians in Ohio and Indiana*. Baltimore: Genealogical Publishing Co., 1986.
   An index to biographies in local histories of Kentuckians residing in Ohio and Indiana.

_____. *Kentuckians in Missouri, Including Many Who Migrated by Way of Ohio, Indiana, or Illinois*. Baltimore: Genealogical Publishing Company, 1983.

Stillahn, Marlene. *Surname Index to the Surname File Cards and Five-generation Charts of the Colorado Chapter, OGS*. Longmont, CO: Colorado Chapter of the Ohio Genealogical Society, 1996.

Strong, Donald H., comp. *Southeastern Ohio Genealogies: Allied Families*. 2 vols. Preston, ID: D.H. Strong, 1992.

Summers, Ewing. *Genealogical and Family History of Eastern Ohio*. New York: Lewis Publishing Co., 1903.
   See *Name Index*, comp. by Mrs. Howard W. Simon (1973).

Tolzmann, Don Heinrich. *Ohio Valley German Biographical Index*. Bowie, MD: Heritage Books, 1992.
   An index to several German-American histories and biographies covering the Ohio Valley-Ohio, Indiana, and Kentucky.

Webb, David K., ed. *Ohio Tombstones (Including Adjoining States)*. Chillicothe, OH: W.O. Francis, 1936. Incomplete work.

Workman, Jeanne Britton. *1880 Ohio Mortality Records: Counties Adams through Geauga*. North Olmsted, OH: S & J Workman, 1991.
   An index to 1880 mortality schedules for these counties.

Maps, Atlases, Gazetteers, and Geographical Finding Aids

All About Ohio Almanac. Hartland, MI: Instant Information Co., 1995.

Andriot, Jay, comp. *Township Atlas of the United States.* McLean, VA: Documents Index, 1991.
>Lists minor civil divisions (townships, etc.) and includes a township map for each county in Ohio and other states.

Atlas of Historical County Boundaries, Ohio. John H. Long, ed. compiled by Peggy Tuck Sinko. New York: Charles Scribner's Sons, 1998.
>Historical maps and chronology of Ohio counties. This atlas is scholarly and well documented.

Atlas of Ohio. Rockford, IL: W.W. Hixson & Co:, 1925.
>Maps show land ownership by township in 1925.

Atlas of Ohio. Madison, WI: American Publishing Co., 1975.

Bailey, A. *Bailey's Northern Ohio Gazetteer and Directory, 1871-72.* Cleveland: A. Bailey, Publisher, 1871.

Baldwin, C.C. *Early Maps of Ohio and the West.* Western Reserve Historical Society Tract No. 25.

_____. *Geographical History of Ohio.* Cleveland: 1880.

Brown, Lloyd Arnold. *Early Maps of the Ohio Valley: A Selection of Maps, Plans and Views Made by Indians and Colonials from 1673-1783.* Pittsburgh: University of Pittsburgh Press, 1959.

Brown, Samuel R. *The Western Gazetteer, or Emigrant's Directory, Containing A Geographical Description of the Western States and Territories...Ohio.* Auburn, NY: H.C. Southwick, 1817.

Burke, Thomas Aquinas. *Ohio Lands: A Short History.* 9th ed. Columbus: Auditor of State, 1997.
https://freepages.rootsweb.com/~maggie/history/ohio-lands/ohl10.html

CitMap Corporation. *The Complete City Maps of Ohio.* Traverse City, MI: CitMap, 1990.
>Detailed city maps for Ohio, arranged by city.

Clagg, Sam E. *Ohio Atlas.* Huntington, WV: The author, 1959.
>Origin of Ohio county names, maps showing population, land subdivisions, early settlements, forts, railroads, Ohio Court of Appeals districts, and other useful maps.

Clements, John. *Ohio Facts: A Comprehensive Look at Ohio Today, County by County.* Dallas: Clements Research II, 1988.

Collins, Charles W. *Ohio: An Atlas*. Madison, WI: American Printing & Publishing, 1975.
    Maps showing physical features, population, economy, and statistical data.

Cutler, Jervis. *A Topographical Description of the State of Ohio, Indiana Territory, and Louisiana*. Boston: Charles Williams, 1812.

Cutler, Manasseh. *An Explanation of the Map of Federal Lands*. Readex Microprint, 1966.

DeLorme Mapping Company. *Ohio Atlas & Gazetteer*. 5th ed. Yarmouth, ME: DeLorme Mapping Co., 1995.
    Detailed modem maps of Ohio showing cities and townships, roads, rivers and creeks, county boundaries, and other useful details.

Dictionary of Ohio Historic Places. 2 vols. St. Clair Shores, MI: Somerset Publishers, 1999.

Downes, Randolph Chandler. *Evolution of Ohio County Boundaries*. 1927. Reprint. Columbus: Ohio Historical Society, 1970.
    A historical description of Ohio's eighty-eight counties.

The 1833 Ohio Gazetteer. 11th ed. 1833. Reprint. Knightstown, IN: Bookmark, 1981.
    Describes Ohio counties and towns, with early population statistics.

Everts, L.H. & Co. *Illustrated Historical Atlas of Miami County, Ohio, with an Atlas of Ohio*. Philadelphia: L.H. Everts & Co., 1875.

Encyclopedia of Ohio: A Volume of Encyclopedia of the United States. St. Clair Shores, MI: Somerset Publishers, 1982. See "Dictionary of Places-Ohio."

Fess, Simeon Davidson. *Ohio: A Four-Volume Reference Library on the History of a Great State*. 5 vols. Chicago: Lewis Publishing Co., 1937.
    Historical details for each Ohio county, physical features, first settlements, transportation, economic interests, institutions, notable persons, and population statistics. Volume 3 entitled *Historical Gazetteer of Ohio*.

Fitak, Madge R., comp. *Place Names Directory: Northeast Ohio*. Columbus: State of Ohio, Department of Natural Resources, 1976.

_____, comp. *Place Names Directory: Southeast Ohio*. Columbus: State of Ohio, Department of Natural Resources, 1980.

_____, comp. *Place Names Directory: Southern Ohio*. Columbus: State of Ohio, Department of Natural Resources, 1986.

Gallagher, John S. and Alan H. Patera. *The Post Offices of Ohio.*
Burtonsville, MD: The Depot, 1979.
Arranged by county. Lists name of post office and date established and discontinued. Indexed by name of post office. Illustrated.

Hargett, Janet L., comp. *List of Selected Maps of States and Territories.*
Washington, DC: National Archives and Records Service, 1971.
See especially the Ohio map section.

Hawes, George W., comp. *Ohio State Gazetteer and Business Directory for 1859 and 1860.* Cincinnati: G.W. Hawes, 1859.

_____. *Ohio State Gazetteer and Business Directory for 1860 and 1861.*
Indianapolis: G.W. Hawes, 1860.
Lists of professions, trades, etc. arranged by locality. Online:
https://babel.hathitrust.org/cgi/pt?id=miun.aja 2907.0001.001&view=1up&seq=9&skin=2021

Hayes, E.L. *Illustrated Atlas of the Upper Ohio River and Valley, from Pittsburgh, Pa., to Cincinnati, Ohio.* Philadelphia: Titus, Simmons & Titus, 1877.

Hough, B. and A. Bourne. *A Map of the State of Ohio from Actual Surveys.*
Chillicothe, OH: 1815.

Howison, William L. *Indian Trails & War Records in Southwestern Ohio.*
Rev. ed. Columbus: W.L. Howison & Associates, 1980.

Izant, Grace Goulder. *This Is Ohio: Ohio's 88 Counties in Words and Pictures.* Cleveland: World Publishing Co., 1953.

Jenkins, Warren. *The Ohio Gazetteer and Traveller's Guide.* Rev. ed.
Columbus: Isaac N. Whiting, 1841.
An early gazetteer of Ohio place-names. The revised edition includes an appendix with the census of Ohio for 1840. Includes a useful list of early Ohio post offices.

Kent, Robert B., et al., eds. *Region in Transition: An Economic and Social Atlas of Northeast Ohio.* Akron, OH: University of Akron Press, 1992.

Kilbourn, John. *The Ohio Gazetteer, or Topographical Dictionary.* 11th ed.
1833. Reprint. Knightstown, Ind.: Bookmark, 1978.
An early gazetteer of the state. Continued by Warren Jenkins' *Gazetteer* cited above.

Marzulli, Lawrence J. *The Development of Ohio's Counties and Their Historic Courthouses.* Columbus: County Commissioners Association of Ohio, 1980.

Maxwell, Fay, comp. *Ohio Indian and Revolutionary Trails: Indexes Ohio Counties, Townships and Dates of Erection.* Columbus: Maxwell Publications, 1974.

Miller, Larry L. *Ohio Place Names*. Bloomington, IN: Indiana University Press, 1996.
A valuable gazetteer that describes Ohio cities, towns, villages, hamlets, and communities.

Morrison, Olin Dee. *Ohio "Gateway State": A History of Ohio*. 4 vols. Athens, OH: E.M. Morrison, 1962.
Volume 3, *Historical Atlas of Ohio*, contains sketch maps of Ohio history, boundaries, and settlements.

_____. *Ohio in Maps and Charts: A Historical Atlas, Social, Economic, Political*. Athens, OH: E.M. Morrison, 1956.
Historical Ohio maps showing early newspapers, emigrant routes, settlements, boundary changes, and other details.

Newberry Library. *Historical Atlas and Chronology of County Boundaries, 1788-1980*. John H. Long, ed. and Stephen L. Hansen, comp. Boston: G.K. Hall, 1984.
See especially the Ohio boundary chronology section and county maps in volume 2. See also *Atlas of Historical County Boundaries*.

The Ohio Almanac: An Encyclopedia of Indispensable Information About the Buckeye Universe. Michael O'Bryant, ed. Wilmington, OH: Orange Frazer Press, 1997.
A detailed gazetteer of Ohio and its counties.

Ohio. Cooperative Topographic Survey. *Final Report (in Four Volumes) Ohio Cooperative Topographic Survey*. By Christopher Elias Sherman. 4 vols. Bellville, Ohio: Press of the Ohio State Reformatory, 1916-33.
Maps of original Ohio lands, historical background, description of lands in Ohio. See especially volume 3, *Original Ohio Land Subdivisions* 1925; reprint, Columbus: 1982.

Ohio. Department of Highways. *Individual Maps of Ohio's 88 Counties*. Columbus: 1969-70.

Ohio Department of Transportation. *Ohio County Maps*. Columbus, 1983-87.
Maps of Ohio's 88 counties, with principal highways and towns.

Ohio. Development and Publicity Commission. *Ohio: An Empire within An Empire*. 2nd ed. Columbus: Ohio Development and Publicity Commission, 1950.

Ohio Gazetteer. Wilmington, DE: American Historical Publications, 1985.
A historical gazetteer of Ohio place-names; includes a Biography Index.

Ohio Geographic Names Information System: Finding List. Reston, VA: U.S.G.S. Topographic Division, Research & Technical Standards, 1984.

Ohio: Her Counties, Her Townships, and Her Towns. Indianapolis: Researchers, 1979.

Ohio Historical Review. *The 88 County Maps of Ohio.* Columbus: Ohio Historical Review, n.d.

Ohio Maps (OPLIN). Online:
https://www.oplin.ohio.gov/search/node?keys=ohio+maps

Ohio Place Names, Including Origin of Counties, Creeks, and Rivers, Post Offices, Towns, and Townships in the Western Reserve. Typed by Joanne Rowe. Cleveland: 1975.

The Ohio State Gazetteer, Shippers' Guide, and Classified Business Directory for 1864-1865. Indianapolis: Hawes & Redfield, 1864.

Ohio, Trailways to Highways, 1776-1976. Columbus: Ohio Department of Transportation, 1976.

"100 Largest Townships in Ohio According to the 2000 Census." *OGS Genealogy News* 34 (January/February 2003): 20.

Overman, William D. *Ohio Place Names: The Origin of the Names of Over 500 Ohio Cities, Towns, and Villages.* Akron, OH: The author, 1951.
    Gives the county and brief history of many Ohio localities.

_____. *Ohio Town Names.* Akron, OH: Atlantic Press, 1959.
    A description of Ohio towns; includes a list of Ohio towns which changed names.

Overton, Julie Minot. *Ohio Towns and Townships to 1900: A Location Guide.* Kay Ballantyne Hudson and Sunda Anderson Peters, eds. Mansfield, Ohio: Ohio Genealogical Society, 2000.
    A monumental alphabetical listing of Ohio towns and townships before 1900, giving location in county, year founded, and other related information. An essential reference work for Ohio genealogists and librarians. See also Kay Ballantyne Hudson, comp., "Ohio Towns and Townships to 1900, Addendum I." *The Report* 41 (Summer 2001): 87-90.

Peacefull, Leonard, ed. *A Geography of Ohio.* Rev. ed. Kent, OH: Kent State University Press, 1996.
    A scholarly look at Ohio settlement, land divisions, geography, and cities. Includes valuable maps.

Peters, William E. *Ohio Lands and their Subdivision.* 2nd ed. Athens, OH: Messenger Printery Co., 1918.

Phillips, W. Louis. *Jurisdictional Histories for Ohio's Eighty-eight Counties, 1788-1985.* Bowie, MD: Heritage Books, 1986.

Place Names in Ohio and County of Location. n.p., 1994. Typescript.

Puetz, C.J., comp. *Ohio County Maps.* Lyndon Station, WI: County Maps, 1996.

Sanborn Map Company. *Sanborn Fire Insurance Maps: Ohio*. Teaneck, NJ: Chadwyck-Healey, 1983. Microfilm.
>Original Sanborn Fire Insurance Maps are located in the Geography and Map Division, Library of Congress.

Smith, Thomas H. *The Mapping of Ohio*. Kent, OH: Kent State University Press, 1977.
>A valuable collection of early Ohio maps, with detailed descriptions and extensive footnotes and bibliographies.

Swanson, Hal, comp. *The Ohio Township Helper: An Aid to Locating Counties and Townships in the State of Ohio*. Longmont, CO: Colorado Chapter, Ohio Genealogical Society, n.d.

State Maps on File, Midwest (Ohio). New York: Facts On File, 1984.

Thorndale, William and William Dollarhide. *Map Guide to the U.S. Federal Censuses, 1790-1920*. Baltimore: Genealogical Publishing Co., 1987.

Thomas Publications. *Ohio County Maps & Recreation Guide*. 1982.

U.S. Geological Survey *Map Locations for Ohio Cemeteries*. **https://www.usgs.gov/**

Vonada, Damaine. *Amazing Ohio*. Wilmington, OH: Orange Frazer Press, 1989.
>Historical facts about Ohio and Ohioans, and biographical sketches.

_____, ed. *The Ohio Almanac*. Wilmington, OH: Orange Frazer Press, 1992-93.
>Historical background, education, religion, and profiles of each county giving date established, county seat, and statistics.

Walling, Henry Francis. *Atlas of the State of Ohio*. 1868. Reprint. Knightstown, IN: Bookmark, 1983.
>One of the major and most useful atlases of Ohio.

Whittlesey, Charles. *Topographical and Historical Sketch of the State of Ohio, with an Historical Map*. Philadelphia: Jas. B. Rogers & Co., 1872.

Williams, C.S. *Williams' Ohio State Register and Business Mirror for 1857*. Cincinnati: C.S. Williams, 1857.

Williams & Company, comp. *Ohio State Directory*. Cincinnati: Williams & Co., 1868-82.

Writers' Program (Ohio). *The Ohio Guide*. New York: Oxford University Press, 1940.
>See especially Part II, "Cities."

Migration, Emigration, and Immigration

Allen, Michael. *Western Rivermen, 1763-1861.* Baton Rouge: Louisiana State University Press, 1990.
    A socio-cultural history of Ohio and Mississippi River boatmen.
Ambler, Charles H. *History of Transportation in the Ohio Valley.* Glendale, CA: Arthur H. Clark Co., 1932.
Aughenbaugh, Gloria L., comp. *Gone to Ohio.* York, PA: South Central Pennsylvania Genealogical Society, 1990-96.
    A listing of people who migrated from selected Pennsylvania counties to selected Ohio counties. Indexed.
Baldwin, Charles Candee. *Early Indian Migration in Ohio.* Cleveland: 1878.
Banta, Richard Elwell. *The Ohio.* 1949. Reprint. Lexington: University Press of Kentucky, 1998.
Barnhart, John D. "Sources of Southern Migration into the Old Northwest." *Mississippi Valley Historical Review* 22 (June 1935): 49-62.
_____. "The Southern Influence in the Formation of Ohio." *Journal of Southern History* 3 (Feb. 1937): 28-42.
Bell, Margaret Van Horn. *A Journey to Ohio in 1810.* 2 vols. New Haven: Yale University Press, 1912.
Berquist, Goodwin F. and Paul C. Bowers, Jr. *The New Eden: James Kilbourne and the Development of Ohio.* Lanham, MD: University Press of America, 1983.
    A study of migration from Connecticut to Ohio.
Berry, Ellen Thomas and David A. Berry. *Early Ohio Settlers: Purchasers of Land in East and East Central Ohio, 1800- 1840.* Baltimore: Genealogical Publishing Co., 1989.
_____. *Early Ohio Settlers: Purchasers of Land in Southeastern Ohio, 1800-1840.* Baltimore: Genealogical Publishing Co., 1984.
_____. *Early Ohio Settlers: Purchasers of Land in Southwestern Ohio, 1800-1840.* Baltimore: Genealogical Publishing Co., 1986.
    Each of the above three volumes gives, in addition to the name of the land purchaser, the date and locality, the person's residence, often in another state. Useful in tracing migration.
Betzler, Allen F. *New Jersey Transplants: A Genealogical Record of Some of the Pioneer Families Who Came from New Jersey to Settle in the Miami Valley of Ohio.* Franklin, OH: 1982.
Bigham, Darrel E. *Towns & Villages of the Lower Ohio.* Lexington: University Press of Kentucky, 1998.

Billington, Ray Allen and Martin Ridge. *Westward Expansion: A History of the American Frontier.* 5th ed. New York: Macmillan Publishing, 1982.

Blunt, Edmund M. *Traveller's Guide to and through the State of Ohio, with Sailing Directions for Lake Erie.* New York: 1833.

Bogue, Donald Joseph. *A Methodological Study of Migration and Labor Mobility in Michigan and Ohio in 1947.* Oxford, OH: Scripps Foundation, Miami University, 1952.

Bond, Beverely Waugh, Jr. *The Foundations of Ohio.* Columbus: Ohio State Archaeological and Historical Society, 1941.

Bradbury, John. *Travels in the Interior of America in the Years 1809, 1810, and 1811, Ohio.* Liverpool: The author, 1817.

Brien, Lindsay Metcalfe. *A Genealogical Index of Pioneers in the Miami Valley, Ohio.* Dayton, OH: Dayton Circle, Colonial Dames of America in the State of Ohio, 1970.
Shows names of family members, Ohio residence and previous place of residence, dates, and other genealogical details. Covers Miami, Montgomery, Preble, and Warren counties, Ohio. See *Every Name Index to Miami Valley Ohio Pioneers,* indexed by Marjorie Dodd Floyd Dayton, OH, 1980.

Bullock, W. *Sketch of a Journey through the Western States of North America from New Orleans, by the Mississippi, Ohio, City of Cincinnati.* London: John Miller, 1827.

Bunch-Lyons, Beverly A. *And they Came: The Migration of African-American Women from the South to Cincinnati, Ohio, 1900-1950.* n.p., 1995.

Carmack, Sharon DeBartolo. *A Genealogist's Guide to Discovering Your Immigrant & Ethnic Ancestors.* Cincinnati: Betterway Books, 2000.

Cayton, Andrew R.L. "A Quiet Independence: The Western Vision of the Ohio Company." *Ohio History* 90 (Winter 1981): 5-32.

Chaddock, Robert E. *Ohio Before 1850: A Study of the Early Influence of Pennsylvania and Southern Populations in Ohio.* 1908. Reprint. New York: AMS Press, 1967.
Discusses westward migration into Ohio, Germans, Quakers, canals in Ohio, social life, and other migration topics.

Cincinnati, Columbus, Cleveland & Erie Railroad Guide. Dayton, OH: Landfall Press, 1986.

Clark, Thomas Dionysius. *Frontier America: The Story of the Westward Movement.* 2nd ed. New York: Charles Scribner's Sons, 1969. See especially Chapter 6, "The Frontier on the Ohio and Mississippi."

Coomer, James. *Life on the Ohio.* Lexington: University Press of Kentucky, 1997.

Crouse, D.E. *The Ohio Gateway.* New York: Charles Scribner's Sons, 1938.
Ohio migration trails are described; includes useful maps.

Dana, E. *Description of the Principal Roads and Routes, by Land and Water, through the Territory of the United States.* Cincinnati: Looker, Reynolds & Co., 1819.
Illustrates roads in Ohio, pp. 97-99.

_____. *Geographical Sketches of the Western Country.* Cincinnati: Looker, Reynolds & Co., 1819.
See pp. 64-87 for Ohio sketches.

Dannenbum, Jed. "Immigrants and Temperance: Ethnocultural Conflict in Cincinnati, 1845-1860." *Ohio History* 87 (Spring 1978): 125-39.

Dollarhide, William. *Map Guide to American Migration Routes, 1735-1815.* Bountiful, Utah: Heritage Quest, 1997.
Shows maps of some Ohio rivers, trails, and other migration routes.

_____, *American Migration Routes: Part I - Indian Paths, Post Roads & Wagon Roads.* Orting, WA: Family Roots Publishing, 2022.

_____, *American Migration Routes: Part II - Stagecoach, Steamboat, Canal & Early Railroad Routes.* Orting, WA: Family Roots Publishing, 2022.

Dolle, Mrs. Percy A., comp. *Abstracts of Items of Genealogical Interest to be Found in the Laws of Ohio.* Columbus: Mrs. P.A. Dolle, 1957.

_____. *Geographical Origins of Early Ohioans As Shown in Land Office Records.* Columbus, 1963.
Shows previous place of residence of Ohioans in another state.

Easterlin, Richard. "Population Change and Farm Settlement in the Northern United States." *Journal of Economic History* 36 (March 1976): 53-54.

Ellis, William Donohue. *The Cuyahoga.* New York: Holt, Rinehart and Winston, 1966.
A history of the Western Reserve and the Cuyahoga River.

Evans, William R. *History of Welsh Settlements in Jackson and Gallia Counties of Ohio.* Columbus: Chatham Communications, 1988.

The Evolution of Ohio.
Online: **https://www.oplin.org/evolution/**
For each geographical region in Ohio, this site shows history (chronology), migration, economy, and population.

Eyre, John. *Travels: Comprising a Journey from England to Ohio, Two Years in that State.* New York: 1852.

Feather, Carl E. *Mountain People in a Flat Land: A Popular History of Appalachian Migration to Northeast Ohio, 1940-1965.* Athens, OH: Ohio University Press, 1998.
An illustrated popular history of Appalachian migration into northeastern Ohio.

Finn, Chester E. "The Ohio Canals: Public Enterprise on the Frontier." *Ohio State Archaeological and Historical Quarterly* 51 (Jan.- March 1942): 1-41.

Frost, Sherman L. and Wayne S. Nichols. *Ohio Water Firsts.* Columbus: Water Resources Foundation of Ohio, 1985.

Gard, R. Max and William H. Vodrey, Jr. *The Sandy and Beaver Canal.* East Liverpool, OH: East Liverpool Historical Society, 1952.

Gephart, William F. "Transportation and Industrial Development in the Middle West." Ph.D. diss., Columbia University, 1909.
Development of roads, canals, and railways in Ohio and the Midwestern states.

Gieck, Jack. *A Photo Album of Ohio' Canal Era, 1825-1913.* Kent, OH: Kent State University Press, 1988.
Ohio maps, photographs, and historical background of canals in the state for the time period 1825-1913.

Grabb, John R. *The Marietta & Cincinnati Railroad, and Its Successor, the Baltimore & Ohio: A Study of This Once Great Route Across Ohio, 1851-1988.* Chillicothe, OH: 1989.

Grant, H. Roger. "Erie Lackawanna: An Ohio Railroad." *Ohio History* 101 (Winter-Spring 1992): 5-20.

_____. *Ohio on the Move: Transportation in the Buckeye State.* Athens, OH: Ohio University Press, 2000.

Havighurst, Walter. *River to the West: Three Centuries of the Ohio.* New York: G.P. Putnam's Sons, 1970.

Hawley, Zerah. *A Journal of a Tour through Connecticut, Massachusetts, New York, the North Part of Pennsylvania and Ohio.* New Haven, CT: S. Converse, 1822.

He, Jian. *Ohio Migration Patterns: State and Counties (1980-1990 and 1990-1994).* Columbus: Ohio Department of Development, Office of Strategic Research, 1996.

Heiser, Alta Harvey. *West to Ohio.* Yellow Springs, OH: Antioch Press, 1954.
A major study of migration to Ohio and migration routes.

Hite, Richard. "The Canals of Ohio." *Preview* (Ohio Historical Society) 5 (Summer 1996): 10-13.

Holbrook, Stewart H. *The Yankee Exodus: An Account of Migration from New England.* New York: Macmillan, 1950.

Hood, Marilyn G. *Canals of Ohio, 1825-1913*. Columbus: Ohio Historical Society, 1971.

"How We Came to Ohio." *The Report* 19 (Summer 1979): 61-67.

Hulbert, Archer Butler. "The Methods and Operations of the Scioto Group of Speculators." *Mississippi Valley Historical Review* 1 (March 1915): 502-15 and 2 (June 1915): 56-73.

_____. *The Ohio River: A Course of Empire*. 1906. Reprint. Salem, MA: Higginson Book Co., n.d.
A history of migration on the Ohio River; illustrated.

_____. "The Old National Road: The Historic Highway of America." *Ohio Archaeological and Historical Publications* 9 (1901): 405-519.

Jenkins, Warren. *The Ohio Gazetteer and Traveller's Guide*. Rev. ed. Columbus: Isaac N. Whiting, 1841.
Useful as an early migration source for the state.

Jones, R.R. "The Ohio River, 1700-1914." Cincinnati: U.S. Engineers Office, 1914. Typescript.

Jordan, Wayne. "The People of Ohio's First County." *Ohio Archaeological and Historical Society* 49 (Jan. 1940): 1-40.

King, Horace. *Granville, Massachusetts to Ohio: A Story of Migration and Settlement*. Granville, OH: Granville Sentinel Publishing, 1989.
A detailed study of migration from Massachusetts to central Ohio. Includes valuable Ohio maps.

Klein, Benjamin F., ed. *The Ohio River: Handbook and Picture Album*. Rev. ed. Cincinnati: Young and Klein, 1969.

Koleda, Elizabeth Potts. *Some Ohio & Iowa Pioneers: Their Friends and Descendants*. Prineville, OR: The author, 1973.

Lang, Elfrieda. "Ohioans in Northern Indiana before 1850." *Indiana Magazine of History* 49 (Dec. 1953): 391-404.

Laher, Franz. *Geschichte und Zustiinder der Deutschen in Amerika*. Cincinnati: Berlag von Eggers und Wulkop, 1847.
History and account of Germans in America, chiefly Ohio and the west.

Loomis, Linn. *Here and Now, Ohio's Canals: The Background of Ohio's Canal System*. Newcomerstown, OH: The author, 1991.

Lubbers, Ferne Reedy and Margaret Dieringer, eds. *Advent of Religious Groups into Ohio*. Mansfield, OH: Clark County Chapter, Ohio Genealogical Society, 1978.
A discussion of major religious groups in Ohio, with maps. Useful for tracing migration to Ohio, and reasons for migration.

McClelland, C.P. and C.C. Huntington. *History of the Ohio Canals*. Columbus: Ohio State Archaeological and Historical Society, 1905.

McCormick, Virginia E. and Robert W. McCormick. *New Englanders on the Ohio Frontier: The Migration and Settlement of Worthington, Ohio.* Kent, OH: Kent State University Press, 1998. A well-researched and documented Ohio local history and migration history. Extensive notes and bibliography.

McNeil, David. *Railroad with 3 Gauges: The Cincinnati, Georgetown & Portsmouth RR and Felicity & Bethel RR.* Cincinnati: The author, 1986.

Marchioni, Michael P. "Economic Development and Settlement Patterns in the Flood Plain of the Upper Ohio Valley." Ph.D. diss., University of Cincinnati, 1971.
Discusses the exploration and settlement of the Ohio Valley, internal transportation, and national expansion. Illustrated.

Merk, Frederick. *History of the Westward Movement.* New York: Alfred A. Knopf, 1980.

Michaux, Francois Andre. *Travels to the West of the Alleghany Mountains in the States of Ohio, Kentucky, and Tennessee, 1802.* London: B. Crosby & J.F. Hughes, 1805.

Muller, Edward K. "Selective Urban Growth in the Middle Ohio Valley, 1800-1860." *Geographical Review* 66 (April 1976): 178-99.

Ohioans in the California Census of 1850. Los Alamitos, CA: Southern California Chapter, Ohio Genealogical Society, 1988.

Ohio Genealogical Society Quarterly. Quarterly of the Ohio Genealogical Society, Bellville, Ohio.
Formerly *The Report,* many of the issues include articles which identify Ohioians residing in other states, or whose previous place of residence was Ohio, record abstracts, lists, genealogies with an Ohio connection, book notices, and other articles of interest to Ohio genealogists.

Ohio State Archaeological and Historical Society. *History of the Ohio Canals.* Columbus: Press of F.J. Heer, 1905.

Ohio State Library. *Ohio Canals.* C.B. Galbreath, comp Springfield, OH: Springfield Publishing Co., 1910.

Papers Relating to the First White Settlers in Ohio. Western Reserve Historical Society, Historical and Archaeological Tracts, No. 6. Cleveland, 1871.

Peacefull, Leonard, ed. *A Geography of Ohio.* Rev. ed. Kent, OH: Kent State University Press, 1996.
Discusses settlement patterns and population patterns. Nicely illustrated.

Pearce, John. *The Ohio River.* Lexington: University Press of Kentucky, 1989.

Peck, J.M. *A New Guide for Emigrants to the West, Containing Sketches of Ohio.* Boston: Gould, Kendall, and Lincoln, 1836.

Phillips, Kimberly L. *Heaven-Bound: Black Migration, Community, and Activism in Cleveland, 1915-1945.* N.p., 1992.

Porter, Burton P. "Old Canal Days." Columbus: Heer Printing Co., 1942.

The Report. See *Ohio Genealogical Society Quarterly.*

Riegel, Mayburt Stephenson, comp. *Early Ohioans' Residences from the Land Grant Records.* Mansfield, Ohio: Ohio Genealogical Society, 1976.
    Identifies many pre-1825 Ohio pioneers who purchased land from the federal government at early land offices in Ohio.

Rittinger, Martha Gerber. *Ohio and Erie Canal Motor Tour.* Chillicothe, OH: Ross County Genealogical Society, 1997. History and pictures of the Ohio and Erie Canal.

Scheiber, Harry N. *Ohio Canal Era: A Case Study of Government and the Economy, 1820-1861.* Athens, OH: Ohio University Press, 1969.

Schneider, Norris Franz. *The National Road: Main Street of America.* Columbus: Ohio Historical Society, 1975.

Siebert, Wilbur Henry. *The Mysteries of Ohio's Underground Railroads.* Columbus: Long's Book, 1951.

Simonis, Louis A. *Maumee River, 1835.* Defiance, OH: Defiance County Historical Society, 1979.

Smith, Clifford Neal. *Early Nineteenth-Century German Settlers in Ohio (Mainly Cincinnati and Environs).* McNeal, AZ: Westland Publications, 1984. Reprint. Baltimore: Genealogical Publishing Company, 2009.

Smithson, Christopher T. *Marylanders to Ohio.* Westminster, MD: Willowbend Books, 2002.

Soltow, Lee and Margaret Soltow. "A Settlement That Failed: The French in Early Gallipolis, an Enlightening Letter and an Explanation." *Ohio History* 94 (Winter-Spring 1985): 46-67.

Sperry, Kip. "Births of British Subjects in Ohio." *The Report* 37 (Fall 1997): 122-24.

Sprague, Stuart Seely. *Kentuckians in Ohio and Indiana.* Baltimore: Genealogical Publishing Co., 1986.
    A valuable index to biographies in local histories of Kentuckians residing in Ohio and Indiana.

_____. *Kentuckians in Missouri, Including Many Who Migrated by Way of Ohio, Indiana, or Illinois.* Baltimore: Genealogical Publishing Company, 1983.

Steckmessar, Kent L. *The Westward Movement: A Short History.* New York: McGraw-Hill, 1969.

Stover, John F. *Iron Road to the West: American Railroads in the 1850s.* New York: Columbia University Press, 1978.

Terrell, C. Clayton. *Quaker Migration to Southwest Ohio.* n.p., 1967.
A brief study of Quaker migrations and reasons for migration to southwest Ohio.

Thompson, Warren Simpson. *Migration Within Ohio, 1935-40: A Study in the Re-distribution of Population.* Oxford, OH: Scripps Foundation for Research in Population Problems, Miami University, 1951.

Trevorrow, Frank W. *Ohio's Canals.* Oberlin, OH: The author, 1973.
A collection of articles and maps relating to the Ohio canal system; includes some biographical sketches.

Unruh, John D., Jr. *The Plains Across: The Overland Emigrants and the Trans-Mississippi West, 1840-60.* Urbana, IL: University of Illinois Press, 1979.

Vedder, Richard K. and Lowell E. Gallaway. "Migration and the Old Northwest." In *Essays in Nineteenth Century Economic History: The Old Northwest,* David C. Klingaman and Richard K. Vedder, eds.. Athens, OH: Ohio University Press, 1975.

Weinberg, Daniel E. "Ethnic Identity in Industrial Cleveland: The Hungarians, 1900-1920." *Ohio History* 86 (Summer 1977): 171-86.

Wheeler, Robert A., ed. *Visions of the Western Reserve: Public and Private Documents of Northeastern Ohio, 1750-1860.* Columbus: Ohio State University Press, 2000.

Wilcox, Frank Nelson. *Ohio Indian Trails: A Pictorial Survey of the Indian Trails of Ohio.* William A. McGill, ed. Kent, OH: Kent State University Press, 1970.
History and sketches of Ohio Indian trails. Lists historic Indian towns in Ohio.

_____. *The Ohio Canals.* William A. McGill, ed. Kent, OH: Kent State University Press, 1969.
A well-illustrated discussion of canals in Ohio.

Wilhelm, Hubert G.H. The Origin and Distribution of Settlement Groups: Ohio, 1850. Athens, OH: Ohio University, 1982.
A migration analysis of the 1850 United States census taken for Ohio. Useful for nineteenth-century Ohio migration studies.

Winkle, Kenneth J. *The Politics of Community: Migration and Politics in Antebellum Ohio.* Cambridge: Cambridge University Press, 1988.
Examines political life in antebellum Ohio and the relationship between migration and politics. A scholarly study of migration to Ohio, with extensive footnotes, bibliographies, maps, and charts.

Wolf, Donna M. *Irish Immigrants in Nineteenth Century Ohio: A Database.* Apollo, PA: Closson Press, 1998.

_____. comp. *Irish Immigrants in Ohio.* n.p., 1996.

Military Records and Military History

Adams, Marilyn, comp. *Index to Civil War Veterans and Widows in Southern Ohio, 1890 Federal Census.* Columbus: Franklin County Genealogical Society, 1986.
Shows names of Southern Ohio Civil War veterans or widows, county and township, and census page numbers.

Alphabetical Index to Ohio Official Roster,Mexican War, 1846-1848. Cleveland: WPA, 1938. Typescript.

Arnold, Gary J., comp. *Civil War Guide Project: Primary Collections at Ohio Historical Society, with Index.* Columbus: Ohio Historical Society, 1996.

Bell, Annie Walker Burns. *Records of Abstracts of Soldiers Who Applied for Pensions While Residing in Ohio.* n.p., n.d.

Bowman, Mary L., comp. *Some Ohio Civil War Manuscripts: A Finding Tool.* Mansfield, OH: Ohio Genealogical Society, 1997.
Describes many Ohio Civil War manuscripts at major repositories-Ohio Historical Society, and others.

Broglin, Jana Sloan, comp. *Index to Official Roster of Ohio Soldiers in the War with Spain, 1898-1899.* 1989. Reprint. Mansfield, OH: Ohio Genealogical Society, 1999.

Carrington,, Henry Beebee. *Ohio in the Civil War.* Columbus, n.d.
History of Ohio during the Civil War, 1861-65.

Clark, Murtie June, comp. *The Pension Lists of 1792-1795 With Other Revolutionary War Pension Records.* Baltimore: Genealogical Publishing Co., Inc., 1996.

Clay, Paul, et al., comps. *The Men and Women of Camp Chase.* Columbus: Hilltop Historical Society, 1990.

Clutters, Kathy and Tom Clutters, eds. *Confederate Soldiers Buried in Ohio.* Ironton, OH: The authors, n.d.

_____. *Ohio Battle Deaths in the Civil War (1861-1865).* Ironton, OH: The authors, n.d.

_____, eds. *Ohio Casualties in the Civil War.* 3 vols. Ironton, OH: The authors, n.d.

Crow, Amy Johnson. "Researching Civil War Ancestors: Examples from Ohio's State and Local Records." Lecture, Fort Wayne, Indiana, July 2000. Audiotape. Hobart, Indiana: Repeat Performance, 2000.

_____. "The Virginia Military District: A Study in Contradictions." *NGS Newsmagazine* 28 (July/August 2002): 208-209, 246.

Dailey, Mrs. Orville D., comp. *The Official Roster of the Soldiers of the American Revolution Who Lived in the State of Ohio.* Columbus: State Society, Daughters of the American Revolution, 1938.

Daughters of the American Revolution. Cincinnati Chapter. *Index of Patriots, Revolutionary War Heroes and their Families.* Jeraldyne Beets Clipson and Katherine Brewer Brinkdopke, comps. Cincinnati: 1983.

Daughters of the American Revolution of the State of Ohio. *Official Roster Ill, Soldiers of the American Revolution Who Lived in the State of Ohio.* Painesville, OH: Painesville Publishing Co., 1959.

_____. *Ohio State History of the Daughters of the American Revolution.* 2 vols. n.p., 1945.

Diefenbach, Mrs. H.B. and Mrs. C.O. Ross, comps. *Index to the Grave Records of Soldiers of the War of 1812 Buried in Ohio.* n.p., 1945.

Dornbusch, C.E., comp. *Military Bibliography of the Civil War.* 4 vols. New York: New York Public Library, 1961-72. Vol. 4, Dayton, OH: Morningside House, 1987.
Extensive bibliographies of Civil War unit histories.

Dyer, Frederick Henry. *A Compendium of the War of the Rebellion.* 1908. Reprint. Dayton, OH: Morningside Bookshop, 1978.
See especially historical background of Ohio regiments during the Civil War. One of the classic reference books on the Civil War.

Frohman, Charles E. *Rebels On Lake Erie.* Columbus: Ohio Historical Society, 1965.
A history of Civil War Confederates on Johnson's Island, Lake Erie.

Frontier Retreat on the Upper Ohio, 1779-1781, Louise Phelps Kellogg, ed. 1917. Reprint. Bowie, MD: Heritage Books, 1994.

Funk, Arville L. *The Morgan Raid in Indiana and Ohio (1863).* Corydon, IN: ALFCO Publications, 1971.

Garner, Grace, comp. *Index to Roster of Ohio Soldiers, War of 1812.* Spokane, WA: Eastern Washington Genealogical Society, 1974.

Harper, Robert S. *Ohio Handbook of the Civil War.* Columbus: Ohio Historical Society, 1961.
An overview of Ohio in the Civil War.

Hatcher, Patricia Law. *Abstract of Graves of Revolutionary Patriots.* 4 vols. Dallas: Pioneer Heritage Press, 1987-88.

Hutchinson, William Thomas. *The Bounty Lands of the American Revolution in Ohio.* 1927. Reprint. New York: Arno Press, 1979.
   An Index of Soldiers of the American Revolution Buried in Ohio. Card index available at the Western Reserve Historical Society Library, Cleveland, Ohio. Microfilm.
Index to Roster of Ohio Soldiers in the War of 1812. Indexed by Bill Oliver. Bowling Green, OH: Wood County Chapter of the Ohio Genealogical Society, 1997.
Jackson, Ronald Vern, ed. *Ohio Military Land Warrants, 1789-1801.* North Salt Lake, UT: Accelerated Indexing Systems, 1988.
Jones, Robert Leslie. *Ohio Agriculture during the Civil War.* Columbus: Ohio State University Press, 1962.
Keifer, J. Warren. *Ohio's Contribution, Sacrifice and Service in the [Civil] War.* Springfield, OH: Republic Printing Co., 1878.
Kellogg, Louise Phelps, ed. *Frontier Advance on the Upper Ohio, 1778-1779.* Madison: State Historical Society of Wisconsin, 1916.
_____. *Frontier Retreat on the Upper Ohio, 1779-1781.* 1917. Reprint. Bowie, MD: Heritage Books, 1994.
Latham, Allen and B.G. Leonard. *A Roll of the Officers in the Virginia Line of the Revolutionary Anny, Who Have Received Land Bounty in the States of Ohio and Kentucky.* Louisville, KY: Lost Cause Press, 1969.
Linscott, Jeff A., comp. *An Organized Listing of the Soldiers of Ohio Who Served in the War of 1812.* Colorado Springs, CO: J.A. Linscott, 1993.
A List of the Civil War Regimental Histories on Microfilm at the State Library of Ohio. n.p., n.d.
List of Pensioners on the Roll, January 1, 1883: Ohio. Washington: Government Printing Office, 1883.
Luttner, Ken, comp. *Ohio's Virginia Military Tract: Index of 1801 Tax List.* Austin, MN: Ohio Genealogy Center, 1991.
   Index of Virginia militiamen who served in the American Revolution; the tract is located west of the Scioto River.
Maxwell, Fay. *Ohio 1840 Census of Revolutionary War Soldiers.* Austin, MN: Ohio Genealogy Center, 1985.
The Military History of Ohio: Its Border Annals, Its Part in the Indian Wars, in the War of 1812, in the Mexican War and in the War of the Rebellion. New York: H.H. Hardesty, 1887.
   Ohio military history, unit histories, biographies, portraits.

Military Order of the Loyal Legion of the United States. *Ohio Commandery: Roll of Members of the Ohio Commandery.* Cincinnati: The Commandery, 1884.

Miller, Charles D. *Report of the Great Reunion of the Veteran Soldiers and Sailors of Ohio Held at Newark, July 22, 1878.* Newark, OH: Clark & Underwood, 1879.

National Society, Daughters of the American Revolution. *DAR Patriot Index: Centennial Edition.* 3 vols. Washington, DC: The Society, 1994.

> Alphabetically arranged by surname. Shows name of patriot ancestor, birth and death dates, state of birth and death, wife's name, rank, state served from (information varies). This is one of the major genealogical indexes for this time period in American history.

_____. *Index of the Rolls of Honor (Ancestor's Index) in the Lineage Books of the National Society of the Daughters of the American Revolution.* 1916-40. Reprint. 4 vols. in 2. Baltimore: Genealogical Publishing Co., 1988.

National Society, Sons of the American Revolution. *Revolutionary War Graves Register.* Comp., Clovis H. Brakebill, ed. Dallas: db Publications, 1993.

National Society, United States Daughters of 1812. *Index to the Grave Records of Servicemen of the War of 1812, State of Ohio.* Phyllis Brown Miller, ed.. Huber Heights, OH: Ohio Society, United States Daughters of 1812, 1988.

> Indexes *Roster of Ohio Soldiers in the War of 1812.*

National Society, United States Daughters of 1812. Ohio Society. *Burial Places of Ohio Soldiers of the War of 1812.* 20 vols. The Society, 1927.

> Volumes housed at the State Library of Ohio, Columbus. Title varied, *Ohio Burial Places of Soldiers of the War of 1812.* See index edited by Phyllis Brown Miller, *Index to the Grave Records of Servicemen of the War of 1812, State of Ohio.*

_____. *Index to the Grave Records of Servicemen of the War of 1812, State of Ohio.* n.p., 1969.

_____. *Index to the Roster of Ohio Soldiers in the War of 1812.* n.p., n.d.

The Military History of Ohio: Its Border Annals, Its Part in the Indian War, in the War of 1812, in the Mexican War, and in the War of the Rebellion. New York: H.H. Hardesty, 1887.

Neill, Michael John. "World War II Draft Cards." *OGS Genealogy News* 33 (July-August 2002): 124-27.

Niedringhaus, David A. "Dress Rehearsal for World War I: The Ohio National Guard Mobilization of 1916." *Ohio History* 100 (Winter-Spring 1991): 35-56.

The Official Roster of Ohio Soldiers in the War with Spain, 1898-1899. Columbus: Edward T. Miller Co., 1916
https:www.ancestry.com. Consult Jana Sloan, Broglin, comp., *Index to Official Roster of Ohio Soldiers in the War with Spain, 1898-1899* 1989, Reprint. Mansfield, OH: Ohio Genealogical Society, 1999.

The Official Roster of the Soldiers of the American Revolution Buried in the State of Ohio. 3 vols. Columbus: F.J. Heer Printing Co., 1929- 59.

Official Roster of the Soldiers of the State of Ohio in the War of the Rebellion, 1861-1865. 12 vols. Akron, OH: Werner Co., 1893, and Norwalk, OH: Laning Co., 1895 (publisher varied). Titles vary. Microfilm.

Arranged by unit, shows names of soldiers, rank, age, date entered service, period of service, remarks (date mustered out), appointments, promotions, if wounded or killed, if captured, date of death, and other details. Volume 12 includes a roster of Ohio soldiers in the War with Mexico, 1846-48. Indexed by Works Progress Administration of Ohio, comps., *Alphabetical Index to Official Roster of the Soldiers of the State of Ohio in the War of the Rebellion,* 9 vols. (Cleveland: Warks Progress Administration, 1938). See also index by Jana Sloan Broglin (OGS).

Official Roster of the Soldiers of the State of Ohio in the War with Mexico, 1846-1848. 1897. Reprint. Mansfield, OH: Ohio Genealogical Society, 1991. Reprint edition is indexed.

Official Roster of the Soldiers of the State of Ohio, Spanish American War. Muster in and muster out rolls. Microfilm.

Ohio. Adjutant General's Dept. *Roster of Ohio Soldiers in the War of 1812.* 1916. Reprint. Baltimore: Genealogical Publishing Co., 1968.

Arranged by company, shows name of soldier and rank.
https://www.ohiohistory.org/resource/database/rosters.html

Ohio. Adjutant General's Office. *Grave Registrations of Soldiers Buried in Ohio.* Microfilm.
    This is one of the major personal name finding aids for Ohio.

———. *The Official Roster of Ohio Soldiers, Sailors, and Marines in the World War, 1917-1918.* 23 vols. Columbus: F.J. Herr Printing Co., 1926-29. Microfilm.
    Includes rosters of soldiers, sailors, and marines for World War I.

———. *The Official Roster of the Soldiers of the American Revolution Buried in the State of Ohio.* 3 vols. Columbus: F.J. Heer Printing Co., 1929-1959. Vol. 2 has the title, *The Official Roster of the Soldiers of the American Revolution who Lived in the State of Ohio.*

———. *Official Roster of the Soldiers of the State of Ohio in the War of the Rebellion.* Microfilm.
    Original muster in and muster out rolls of Ohio military organizations in the Civil War. Arranged by regiment.

———. *Roster of Soldiers of the Ohio National Guard, 1874-1917.* Microfilm.

———. *Soldiers from Ohio, War of 1812.* Microfilm.

———. *World War I, Service Cards of the State of Ohio.* Microfilm.

Ohio: Department of Health. *Veteran's Records, 1941-1964.* Microfilm.
    Grave reports regarding deceased veterans in Ohio.

"Ohio Roster of Soldiers in the War of 1812." Akron, OH, n.d. Typescript. Indexes *Roster of Ohio Soldiers in the War of 1812.*

Ohio Veteran's Home Death Records, January 3, 1889 through December 31, 1983. Sandusky, OH: Erie County Chapter of the Ohio Genealogical Society, 1984.

"Oldest Inscriptions, with Revolutionary and War of 1812 Records, of the Cemeteries of Trumbull, Mahoning, and Columbiana Counties, Ohio, and Lawrence, Mercer, and Beaver Counties, Pennsylvania." 7 vols. in I. 1913. Typescript at State Library of Ohio, Columbus.

Oyos, Matthew. "The Mobilization of the Ohio Militia in the Civil War." *Ohio History* 98 (Summer-Autumn 1989): 147-74.

Page, Henry F. *Virginia Military District of the Law of Warrants, Entries, Surveys and Patents in the V.M.D. of Ohio.* Columbus: J.H. Riley & Co., 1850.

Petty, Gerald M. *Index of the Ohio Squirrel Hunters Roster.* Columbus: Petty's Press, 1984.

Phillips, William Louis. *Annotated Bibliography of Ohio Patriots: Revolutionary War & War of 1812.* Bowie, MD: Heritage Books, 1985.

_____. *Index to Ohio Pensioners of 1883.* Bowie, Md.: Heritage Books, 1987.

Indexes Civil War and War of 1812 veterans and their widows who received federal pensions and were residing in Ohio in 1883.

Pitcavage, Mark. "Burthened in Defence of Our Rights: Opposition to Military Service in Ohio during the War of 1812." *Ohio History* 104 (Summer-Autumn 1995): 142-62.

Piton, Mrs. Phillip. *Confederate Cemeteries in Ohio: Camp Chase & Johnson Island.* Columbus: Franklin County Chapter, Ohio Genealogical Society, 1980.

The Plain Dealer. *Official History of the Ohio National Guard and Ohio Volunteers.* Cleveland: Plain Dealer Publishing Co., 1901.

Lists of soldiers, portraits, history, and biographical sketches.

Poland, Charles A., comp. *Army Register of Ohio Volunteers in the Service of the United States.* Columbus: Ohio State Journal Printing Co., 1862.

Porter, George. "Ohio Politics During the Civil War Period." *Columbia University Studies in History, Economics, and Public Law* 50 (1911): 18-21.

Reed, Beverly Todd. *Military Pension Applications, 1875-1889, Buchanan & MacGahan Law Finn, Toledo, Ohio.* Toledo: Lucas County Chapter of the Ohio Genealogical Society, 1997.

Reid, Whitelaw. *Ohio in the War: Her Statesmen, Generals, and Soldiers.* 2 vols. 1895. Reprint. Columbus: Bergman Books, 1996.

A history of Ohio during the Civil War, 1861-65. Detailed history of Ohio regiments and other military organizations, rosters of soldiers, and biographical sketches. Includes many portraits of soldiers.

A Reprint of Official Roster of the Soldiers of the American Revolution Buried in the State of Ohio. Mineral Ridge, OH: Ohio Genealogical Society, 1973.

Roseboom, Eugene H. *The Civil War Era, 1850-1873.* Columbus: Ohio State Archaeological and Historical Society, 1944.

Roster of Ohio Volunteers in the Service of the United States, War with Spain. Columbus: J.L. Trauger, 1898.

Ryan, Daniel Joseph. *The Civil War Literature of Ohio: A Bibliography with Explanatory and Historical Notes.* 1911. Reprint. Mattituck, NY: Peconic Co., 1994.

———. *Ohio in Four Wars: A Military History.* Columbus: Heer Press, 1917.

History of Ohio in the War of 1812, Mexican War, Civil War, and Spanish American War.

Shriver, Phillip R. and Donald J. Breen. *Ohio's Military Prisons in the Civil War.* Columbus: Ohio State University Press, 1964.

Smucker, Isaac. *The Military Expeditions of the Northwest Territory.* Columbus: 1876.

Society of Mayflower Descendants, State of Ohio. *Mayflower Descendants of Ohio.* n.p., 1913.

Sons of the American Revolution. Ohio Society. *Centennial Register, 1889 to 1989.* Dayton, OH: Ohio Society, SAR, 1988.

Shows name of patriot ancestor, member's name, SAR chapter, and state SAR number. Cross indexed by member's name.

———. *Register, 1922-1928.* Columbus: The Society, 1928.

———. *Year Book of the Ohio Society of the Sons of the American Revolution.* Columbus: The Society, 1896-1909.

Sons of the Revolution (Ohio). *Year Book of the Ohio Society of the Sons of the Revolution.* Cincinnati: The Society, 1897-.

Includes a history of this Society and biographical sketches of soldiers showing rank, unit, and other details. Microfilm.

Starr, Stephen Z. "The Third Ohio Volunteer Cavalry: A View from the Inside." *Ohio History* 85 (Autumn 1976): 306-18.

Thwaites, Reuben Gold and Louise Phelps Kellogg, eds. *Frontier Defense on the Upper Ohio, 1777-1778.* 1912. Reprint. Millwood, NY: Kraus Reprint Co., 1973.

———, eds. *The Revolution on the Upper Ohio, 1775-1777.* 1908. Reprint. Bowie, MD: Heritage Books, 1992.

Two Hundred Years: The Military History of Ohio. New York: H.H. Hardesty, 1886.

United States War Department. *The Pension List of 1820.* Indexed ed. (Baltimore: Genealogical Publishing Company, 2000).

United Spanish War Veterans. Department of Ohio. *Deaths and Graves Registration,* ca. 1900-1980. Microfilm.

United States. Adjutant General's Office. *Index to Compiled Service Records of Volunteer Union Soldiers Who Served in Organizations from the State of Ohio.* Microfilm.

United States. General Land Office. *Registers of Revolutionary War Land Warrants, Act of 1788: Military District of Ohio, 1789-1805.* United States. *List of Pensioners on the Roll, January 1, 1883.* Washington, DC: Government Printing Office. Volume 3 Volume 3 includes Ohio.

United States Sanitary Commission. Soldiers' Aid Society of Northern Ohio, Cleveland. *Our Acre and Its Harvest: Historical Sketch of the Soldiers' Aid Society of Northern Ohio.* Cleveland: Fairbanks, Benedict & Co., 1869.

United States. Selective Service System. *World War I Selective Service System Draft Registration Cards, 1917-1918.* Microfilm. Cards are arranged by state, county, city, and then by surname.

Waldenmaier, Inez. *Revolutionary War Pensioners Living in Ohio before 1834.* Tulsa, OK: The author, 1983. Alphabetically arranged by surname. Shows age, residence, and military service.

War Department. *World War II Honor List of Dead and Missing, State of Ohio.* Washington, DC: 1946.

Wheeler, Kenneth W., ed. *For the Union: Ohio Leaders in the Civil War.* Columbus: Ohio State University Press, 1968.

White, Virgil D. *Genealogical Abstracts of Revolutionary War Pension Files.* 4 vols. Waynesboro, TN: National Historical Publishing Co., 1990.

_____. *Index to Old Wars Pension Files, 1815-1926* Rev. ed. Waynesboro, TN: National Historical Publishing Co., 1993.

_____. *Index to Volunteer Soldiers in Indian Wars and Disturbances, 1815-1858.* 2 vols. Waynesboro, TN: National Historical Publishing Co., 1993.

_____. *Index to Volunteer Soldiers, 1784-1811.* Waynesboro, TN: National Historical Publishing Co., 1987.

_____. *Index to War of 1812 Pension Files.* 2 vols. Waynesboro, TN: National Historical Publishing Co., 1992.

Whittlesey, Elisha. *War of 1812 in Ohio.* Western Reserve Historical Society, Historical and Archaeological Tracts, No. 7.

Wolfe, Barbara Schull. *An Index to Mexican War Pension Applications.* Indianapolis: Heritage House, 1985.

Young American Patriots: The Youth of Ohio in World War II. Richmond, VA: National Publishing Co., 1947.

Periodicals and Newsletters

The American Genealogist., P.O. Box 11, Barrington, RI 02806

Black Swamp Heritage. Grace Luebke, Martin, OH (continues *Sandusky County Heritage*).

Buckeye Californian. Southern California Chapter, Ohio Genealogical Society, El Cajon, CA. Discontinued.

Bulletin of the Historical and Philosophical Society of Ohio. Historical and Philosophical Society of Ohio, Cincinnati. *Cumulative Index* Cincinnati, 1957. Discontinued.

Cities & Villages. Bimonthly. Ohio Municipal League, 175 South Third Street, Suite 510, Columbus, OH 43215.

County News. Quarterly. County Commissioners Association of Ohio, 37 West Broad Street, Suite 650, Columbus, OH 43215.

Echoes. Bimonthly. Ohio Historical Society, 1982 Velma Ave., Columbus, OH 43211.

The Firelands Pioneer. Firelands Historical Society, 4 Case Ave., Norwalk, OH 44857 (vol. 1, June 1858-).

Gateway to the West. 1967-78. Quarterly. Compiled by Ruth Bowers and Anita Short. Reprint, 2 vols. Baltimore: Genealogical Publishing Co., 1989; Baltimore: Clearfield Co., 2001. Covers a wide range of genealogical source materials and records. Well-indexed.

Journal of the Historical and Philosophical Society of Ohio. 1838. Reprint. Cincinnati: Robert Clarke & Co., 1872.

The Library News. Western Reserve Historical Society, 10825 East Boulevard, Cleveland, OH 44106.

The Local Historian. Bimonthly. Ohio Association of Historical Societies and Museums, Ohio Historical Society, 1982 Velma Avenue, Columbus, OH 43211.

National Capital Buckeye Quarterly. P.O. Box 105, Bladensburg, MD 20710. Discontinued.

National Genealogical Society Quarterly. National Genealogical Society, 4527 17th Street North, Arlington, VA 22207.

Northwest Ohio Quarterly. Lucas County/Maumee Valley Historical Society, 1031 River Road, Maumee, OH 43537.

OAH Newsletter. Published 3 times a year. Ohio Academy of History, Youngstown State University, Youngstown, OH 44555.

OGS Genealogy News. Ohio Genealogical Society, 611 State Route 97 West, Bellville, OH 44913.
(Began publication in January/February 2002 as Volume 33 Number 1.)

Ohio Academy of History Newsletter. Published three times a year by the Ohio Academy of History, Ohio Wesleyan University, Delaware, Ohio.

Ohio Archaeological and Historical Quarterly [Ohio Archaeological and Historical Publications].
Established in June 1887. Ohio State Archaeological and Historical Society, Columbus. Continued by *Ohio State Archaeological and Historical Quarterly, Ohio Historical Quarterly,* and *Ohio History* (q.v.). Microfiche (University Microfilms). See *Cumulative Table of Contents,* vols. 1-62 (1954).

Ohio Archivist. Semiannual. Society of Ohio Archivists, Ohio Historical Society, 1982 Velma Avenue, Columbus, OH 44195.

Ohio Civil War Genealogy Journal. Quarterly. Ohio Genealogical Society, 611 State Route 97 West, Bellville, OH 44913.

Ohio Clues. Maumee Valley Historical Society, 1031 River Road, Maumee, OH 43537.

The Ohio Genealogical Helper. Maxwell Publications, P.O. Box 83, Columbus, OH. 43216. Discontinued.

The Ohio Genealogical Quarterly. 1937-44. Reprinted in *Ohio Source Records from the Ohio Genealogical Quarterly* (Baltimore: Genealogical Publishing Co., 1986).

The Ohio Genealogical Society Newsletter. Ohio Genealogical Society, Bellville, Ohio. Discontinued. Replaced by *OGS Genealogy News.*

Ohio Genealogical Society Quarterly. Ohio Genealogical Society, 611 State Route 97 West, Bellville, OH 44913.
Quarterly.
This is the major genealogical periodical for the state. Includes First Families of Ohio rosters, Society of Civil War Families of Ohio, Ohio source material, compiled genealogies, biographies, family Bibles, members' ancestor charts, lists of Ohioans in other states, ethnic sources, related articles, and book reviews.

Ohio's Heritage. Quarterly. Ohio Department of Aging, 50 West Broad Street, Columbus, OH 43215.

Ohio's Historical Detective. Quarterly newsletter for genealogists researching Ohio. Dukeman Publications Company, 4111 Yellowood St., Lima, OH 45806.

Ohio History. Ohio History Connection, 800 E. 17th Ave., Columbus, OH 43211. Online and indexed at the Ohio History Connection website **https://www.ohiohistory.org**.

Ohio-Indiana-Iowa Queries. Pioneer Publications, P.O. Box 1179, Tum Tum, WA 99034.

Ohio Libraries. Published three times a year. Ohio Libraries, 35 East Gay Street, Suite 305, Columbus, OH 43215.

Ohio Magazine, 62 East Broad Street, Columbus, OH 43215.

Ohio Palatine Heritage. Palatines to America, 611 East Weber Road, Columbus, OH 43211.

Ohio Queries. Pioneer Publications, P.O. Box 1179, Tum Tum, WA 99034.

Ohio Records and Pioneer Families. Ohio Genealogical Society, 611 State Route 97 West, Bellville, OH 44913. Quarterly. Available by subscription from Ohio Genealogical Society.

The Ohio Researcher. 4 vols. Murray, UT: Allstates Research Co., 1962-66. Discontinued.

Ohio Valley History Journal. Cincinnati Museum Center, Cincinnati, OH 45203.

Ohio's Last Frontier. Newsletter. Williams County Genealogical Society, P.O. Box 293, Bryan, OH 43506.

Ohio Records. Edwards Brothers, 2500 South State Street, Ann Arbor, MI 48104.

Ohioana News. Ohioana Library Association, 274 East First Avenue, Columbus, OH 43201

Ohioana Quarterly. Ohioana Library Association, 274 East First Avenue, Columbus, OH 43201.

Ohionetwork. Monthly newsletter of OHIONET, 1500 West Lane Avenue, Columbus, OH 43221.

The Old Northwest: A Journal of Regional Life and Letters. Quarterly. Miami University, Oxford, OH 45056.
Biographies, memoirs, diaries, history of the Old Northwest, social history, book reviews.

The "Old Northwest" Genealogical Quarterly 15 vols. The ""Old Northwest" Genealogical Society, Columbus, Ohio, 1898-1912. Cemetery records, notes and queries, vital records, genealogies, local history, and biographies. See "Index of the Granville Centennial Issue, the 'Old Northwest' Genealogical Quarterly, 1905." Typescript.

Our Family Heritage: A Journal of Genealogy and History of the Ohio River Valley and Central Kentucky. Genealogical Research, Fairborn, OH, 1973-75. Discontinued.

The Palatine Immigrant. Quarterly. Palatines to America, 611 East Weber Road, Columbus, OH 43211.

Preview. Ohio Historical Society. Discontinued.
Describes records and the Ohio Historical Society collections of interest to genealogists.

Quarterly Bulletin. The Historical Society of Northwestern Ohio, 1932-33. Discontinued.

Quarterly Publication of the Historical and Philosophical Society of Ohio. Cincinnati, Ohio. Discontinued.

The Report. See *Ohio Genealogical Society Quarterly.*

The Researcher: A Family Heritage Newsletter. Family Heritage, 3105 Petersburg Rd., Jackson, OH 45640.

Rocky Mountain Buckeye. Colorado Chapter, Ohio Genealogical Society, P.O. Box 470189, Aurora, CO 80047-0189.

Roots & Shoots Quarterly. Southern Ohio Genealogical Society, P.O. Box 414, Hillsboro, OH 45133-0414.

State Library of Ohio News. Monthly. State Library of Ohio, 274 East First Avenue, Columbus, OH 43201.

Timeline. Bimonthly. Ohio History Connection, 800 E. 17th Ave., Columbus, OH 43211.

Towpaths. Quarterly. Canal Society of Ohio, 550 Copley Road, Akron, OH 44320.

The Tracer. Quarterly. Hamilton County Chapter, Ohio Genealogical Society, P.O Box 15865, Cincinnati, OH 45215.

Western Reserve Historical Society Genealogical Committee Bulletin. Western Reserve Historical Society, Genealogy Committee, 10825 East Boulevard, Cleveland, OH 44106.

Western Reserve Historical Society News. Western Reserve Historical Society, 10825 East Boulevard, Cleveland, OH 44106.

Western Reserve Magazine. Western Reserve Magazine, 2101 Superior Avenue, Cleveland, OH 44114. Discontinued.
Northern Ohio and Western Reserve local history, collectibles, antiques.

Ohio Maps

Index to Ohio Maps

1. *Map of the State of Ohio,* by Rufus I. Putnam, January 1804.
2. Early Ohio map, n.d. (Ohio Historical Society, Columbus).
3. Early Ohio map, n.d. (Ohio Historical Society, Columbus).
4. Ohio [map] to Accomany Rufus King's *Ohio in American Commonwealths* n.d.
5. Ohio, 1828, Anthony Finley, *A New General Atlas,* Philadelphia: Anthony Finley, 1828.
6. Ohio in 1853 (Jonathan Sheppard Books, Albany, NY).
7. Ohio, Principal Land Grants and Surveys, n.d.
8. *The Ohio Country,* by Robert L. Brewer. In Andrew R.L. Cayton, *The Frontier Republic: Ideology and Politics in the Ohio Country, 1780-1825* Kent, OH: Kent State University Press, 1986. With permission of Kent State University Press.
9. *Original Ohio Land Divisions* Ohio University Cartographic Center. Permission to reproduce the maps "Original Ohio Land Divisions," and "Frontier Settlement Advance," received from Hubert G.H. Wilhelm, Professor of Geography, Ohio University, Athens, OH.
10. *Frontier Settlement Advance* Ohio University Cartographic Center.
11. *Early Migration Routes to Ohio* Ohio map, 1803. Permission to reproduce this Ohio map, published with the article "How We Came to Ohio," *The Report* 19 (Summer 1979), p. 61, received from Phyllis Brown Delaney, former president, Ohio Genealogical Society, Mansfield, OH.
12. *Map of Ohio Canals* State Library of Ohio, Columbus.
13. *Map of the State of Ohio Showing Existing, Abandoned and Proposed Canal Routes and the Lands Granted by the United States to the State of Ohio for Canal Purposes* Ohio Historical Society, Columbus.
14. *Road Map to Ohio, 1810* Survey of Transportation.

15. *Ohio's Transportation Ties* ca. 1840. Permission to reproduce this map, published in *Heavens Resound: A History of the Latter-day Saints in Ohio, 1830-1838,* by Milton V. Backman, Jr. Deseret Book Co., 1983, received from Deseret Book Company, Salt Lake City, UT. Rights to this map are owned by Deseret Book Company.
16. Ohio County Boundary Changes, 1801-1808.
17. Ohio, ca. 1900.
18. *Counties of Ohio.* This map was created for the author by the Geography Department, Brigham Young University, Provo, UT.
19. Map of Ohio Counties, Ohio Department of Transportation, Columbus, n.d.
20. *Ohio Counties and County Seats.* n.d.
21. *The Building of Ohio: 18 Land Grants,* by Thomas E. Ferguson, Auditor of State. Courtesy of the State Library of Ohio, Columbus.

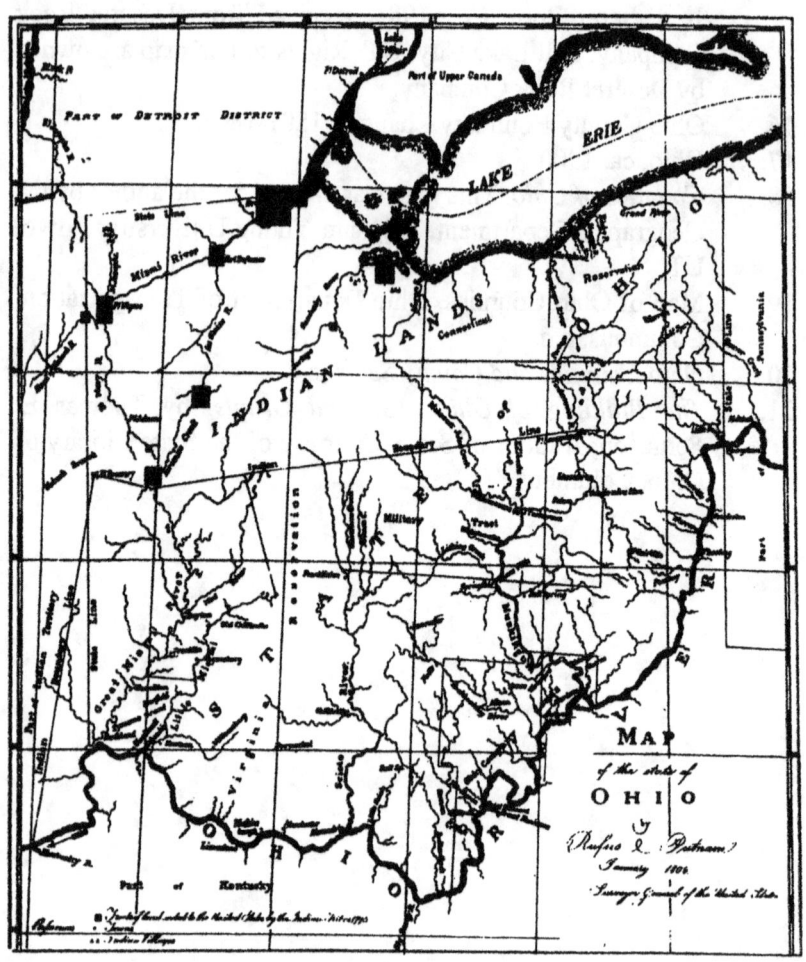

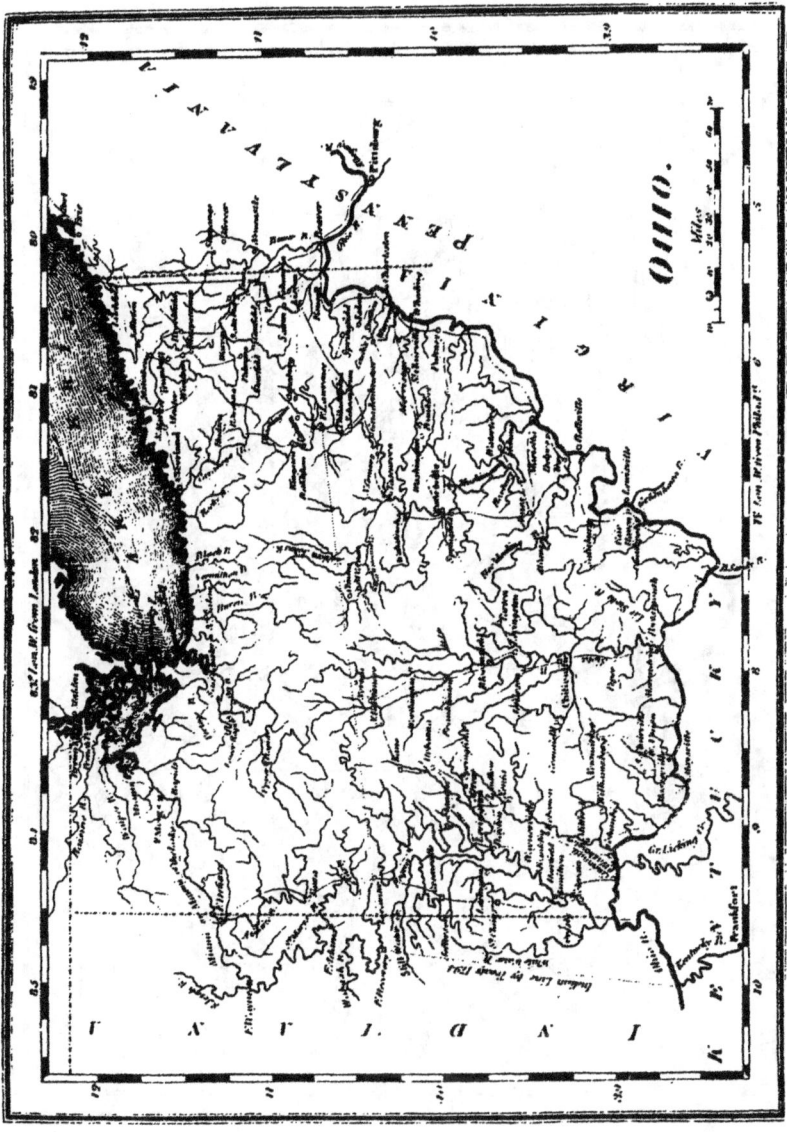

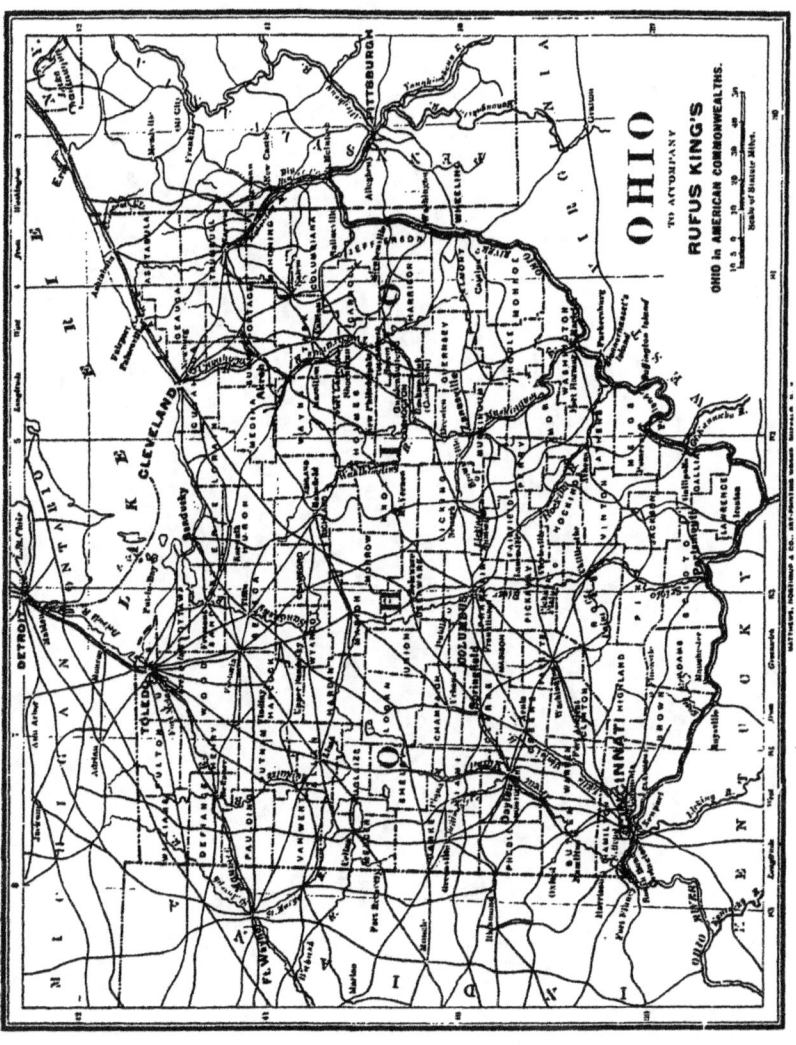

Genealogical Research in Ohio 329

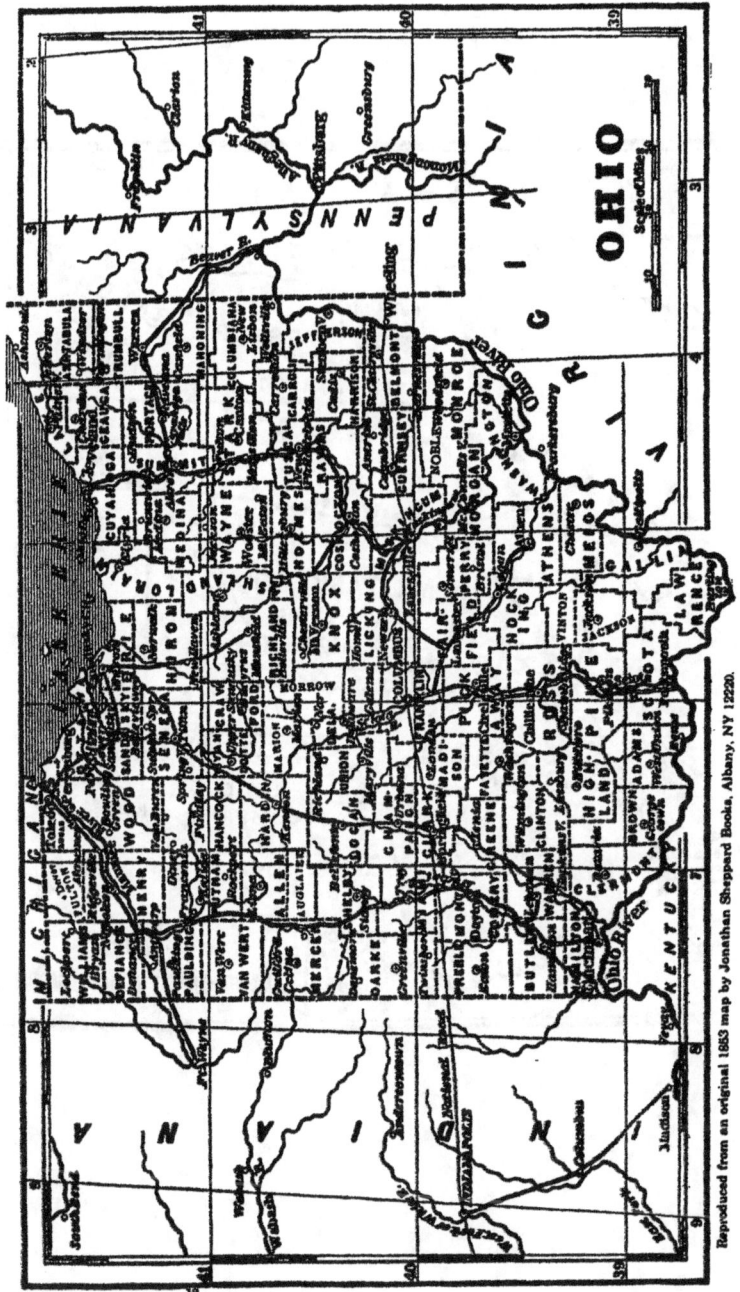

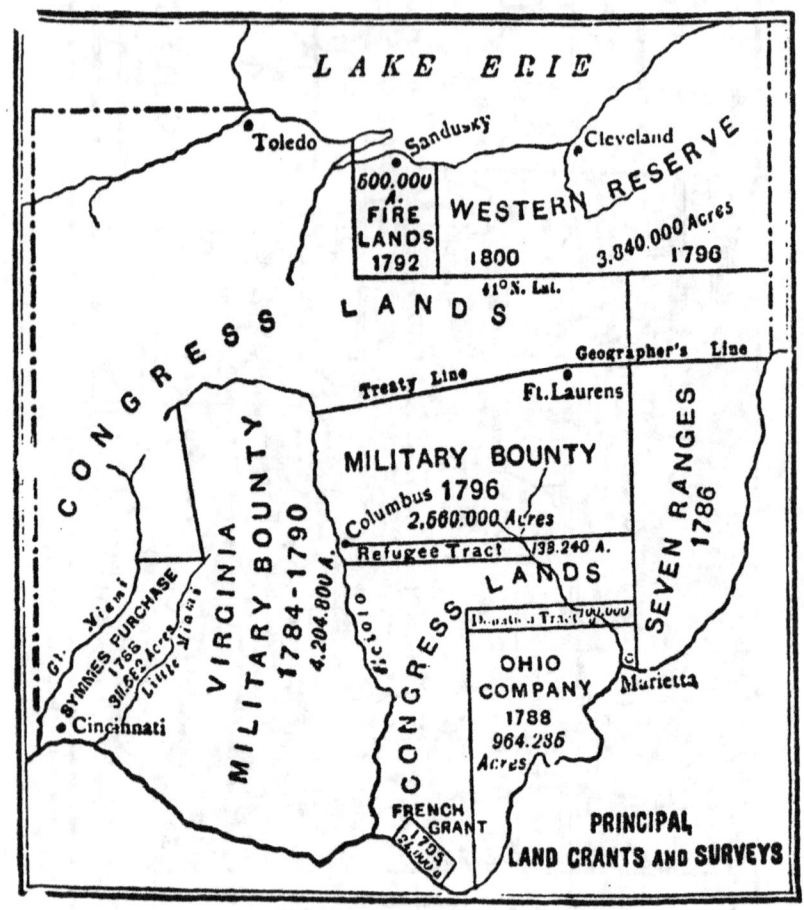

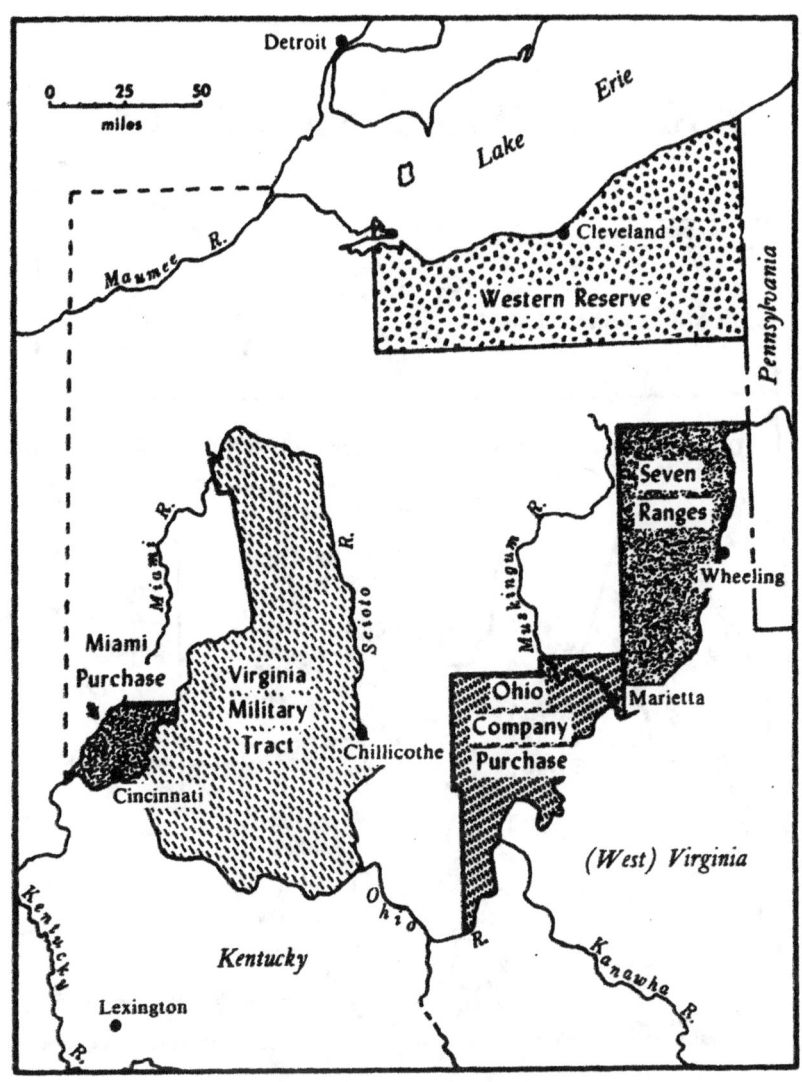

The Ohio Country

Map drawn by Robert L. Brewer.

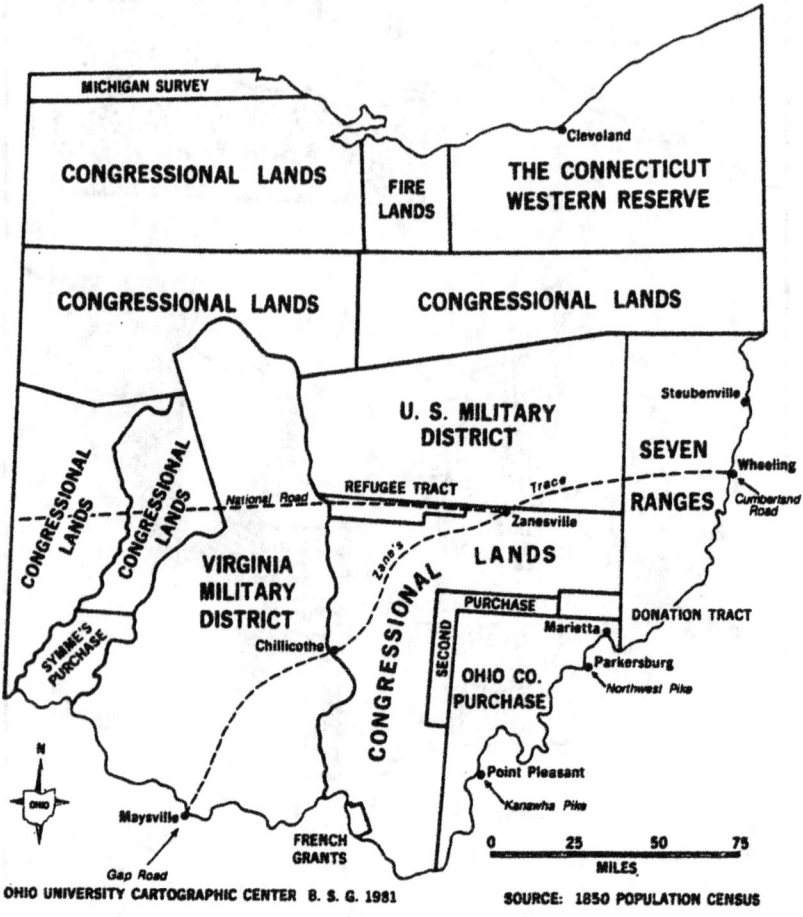

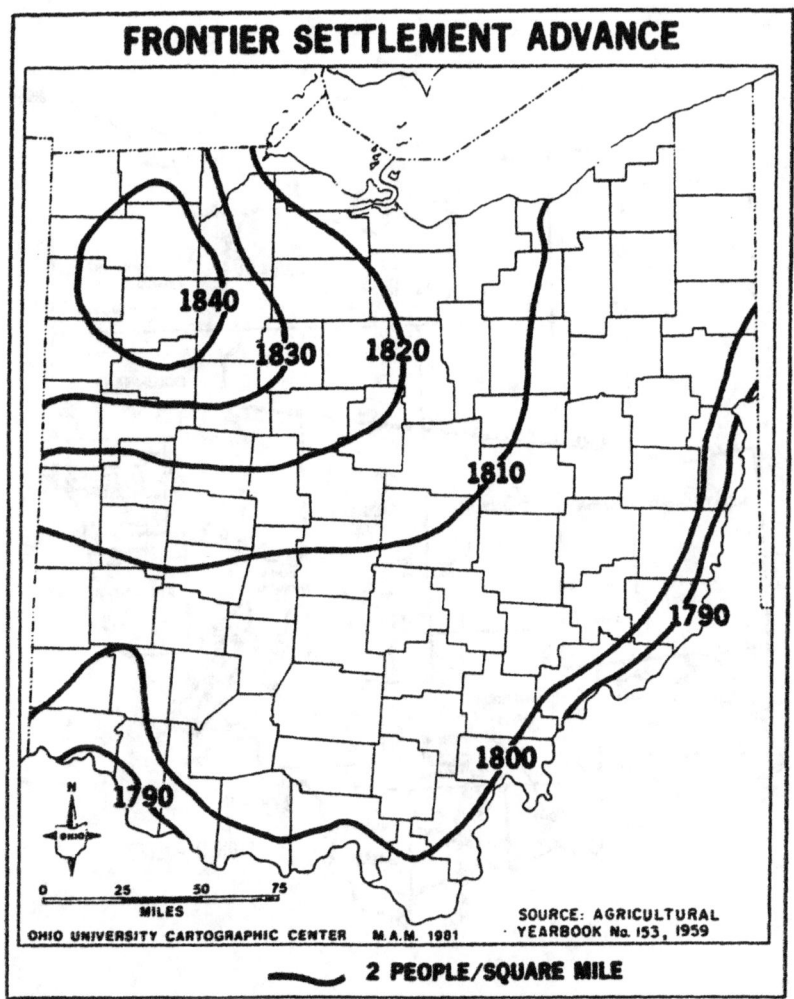

Early Migration Routes to Ohio

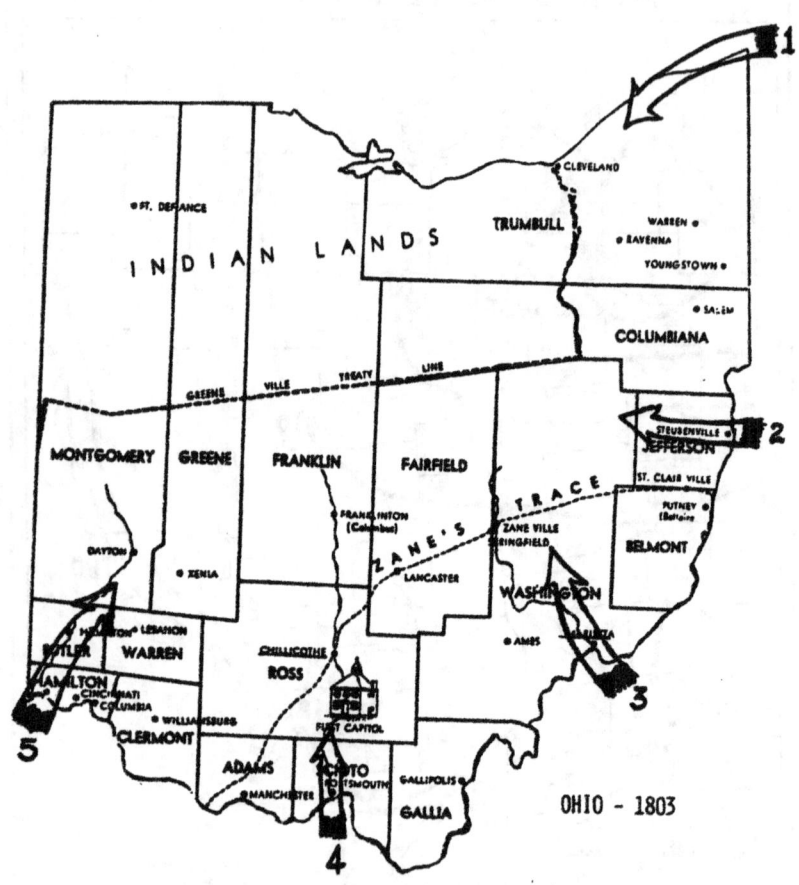

"How We Came to Ohio," The Report 19 (Summer 1979): p. 61
Used with permission of the Ohio Genealogical Society, Mansfield, OH

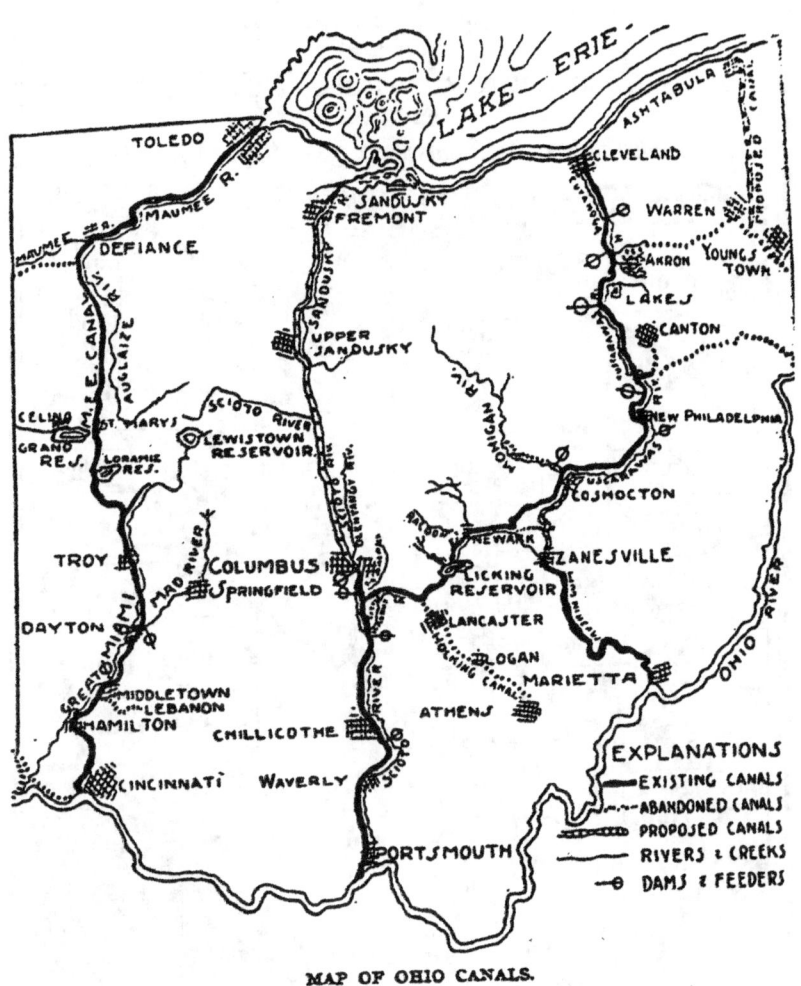

MAP OF OHIO CANALS.

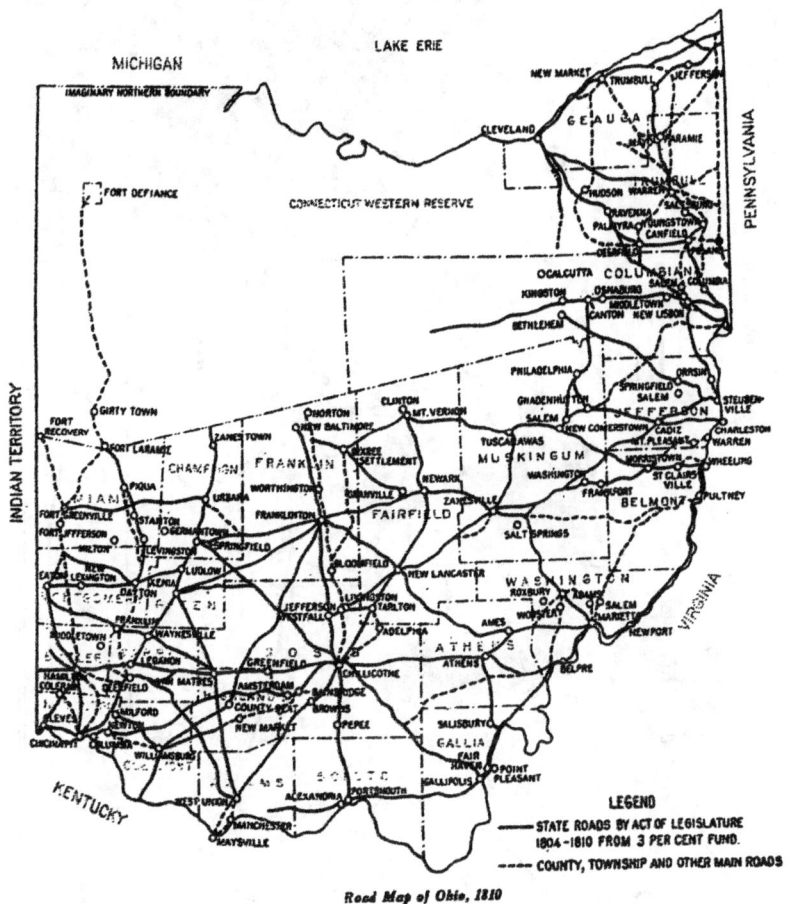

Road Map of Ohio, 1810

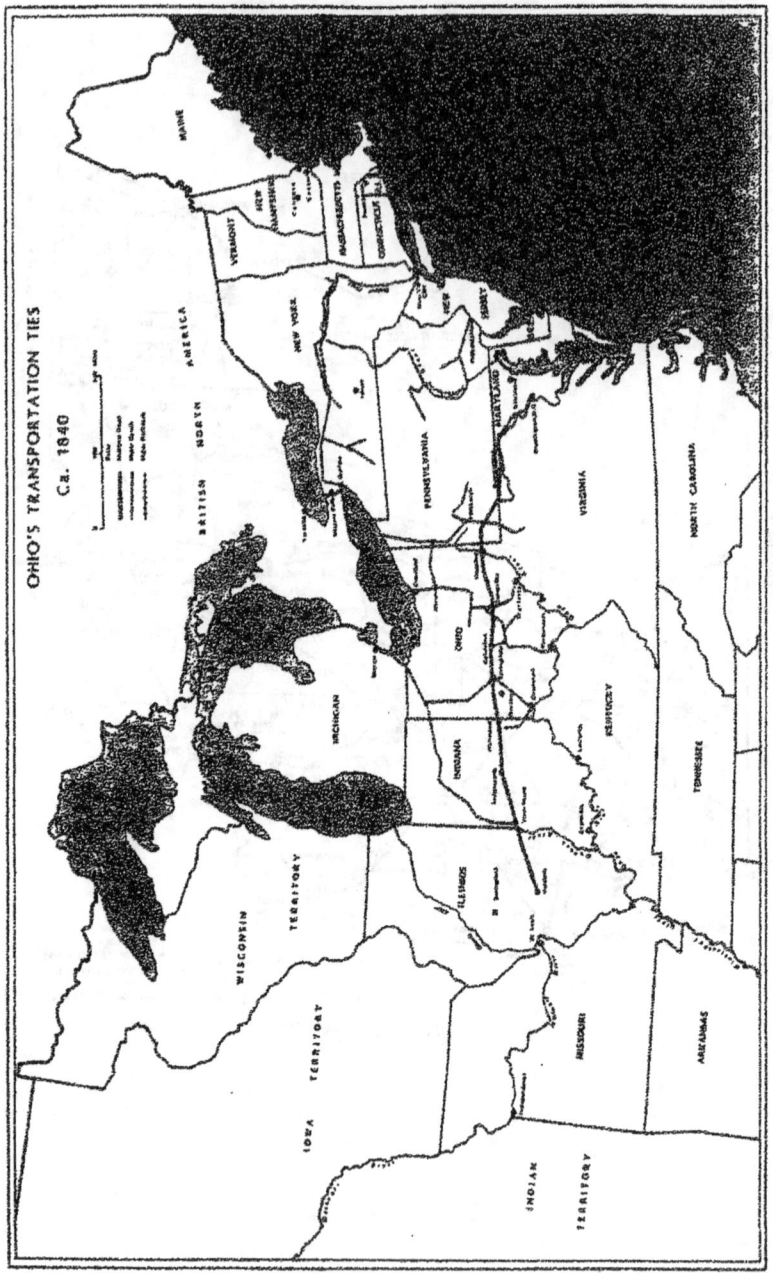

COUNTY BOUNDARY CHANGES

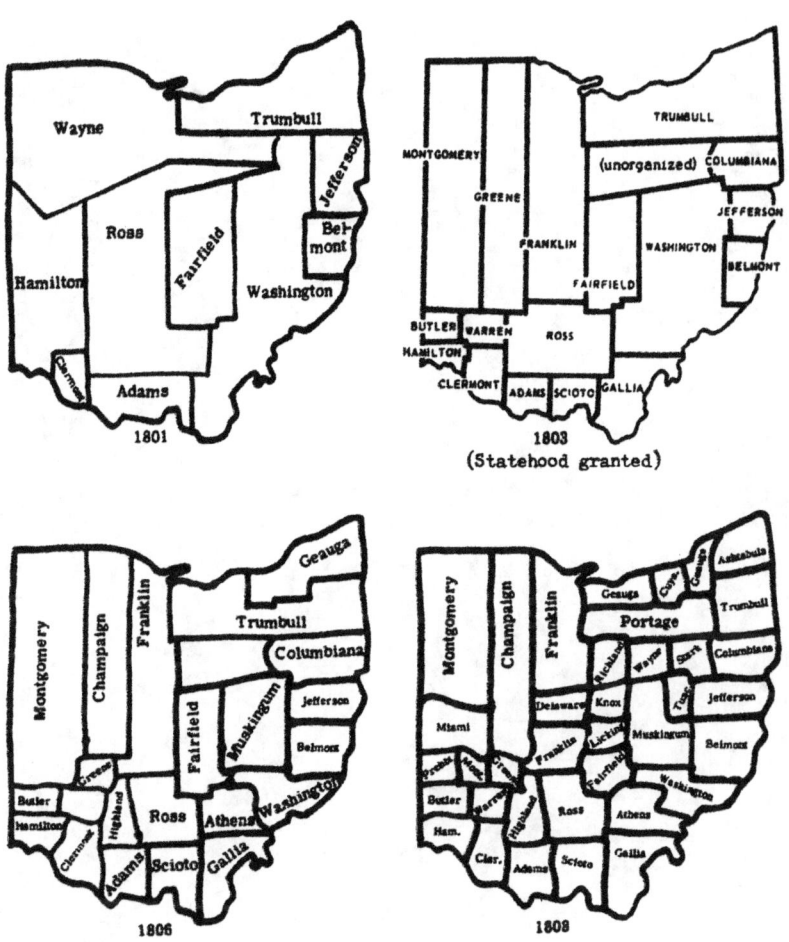

COUNTIES OF OHIO

Ohio Counties & County Seats

General Index

Abbreviations vi
Addresses—Ohio 193
Addresses—Outside Ohio . . 227
Adoptions 75
African Americans 6, 8, 14,
                    93, 144, 153,
                    157, 168
Agricultural census 61,
                    66, 80, 81
Allen County Public Library
    Fort Wayne, IN
  . . . . 66, 130, 165
American Revolution, *See*
    Revolutionary War
Ancestor Card File . 38, 45, 179
Ancestor Charts 38, 70, 179
Ancestral File 25, 179
Archives & Libraries *See*
    Libraries, Repositories
Atlases and maps . . 48, 117, 118
Auditor of State's Tax Duplicate,
    See Tax records
Bible records 38, 39, 45,
         46, 63, 76, 179, 180
Bibliographies . . . . iv, v, 12,
                  70, 94, 112
Bibliographies, Guides, and
    Finding Aids 229
Biographies . . . . ii, iv, 23, 45, 48
         61, 67, 70, 94, 114,
         115, 122, 128, 135,
         152, 158, 162, 168,
         171, 179, 181, 240,
Birth records . . . . i, 8, 9, 22,
      23, 25, 27, 43, 45,
      46, 62, 71, 74, 75, 77,
      96, 102, 115, 122, 123

Bluffton College 9, 855, 99
Boundaries 16
Bowling Green State University
  . . . . v, vi, viii, 9, 18-20,
                99, 100, 149
Brigham Young University,
    Provo, Utah 66, 97
British Records 63
Bureau of Land Management
    (BLM) . . . . vi, 68,
                102, 110, 111
Burials, *See* Cemetery records
Campus Martius Museum,
    Marietta 2, 17
Canals . . . . xiii, 13, 14
Capsule, Ohio xiii
Cemetery records, *See also*
    Graves Registration File
Census indexes 38, 45, 61,
                    68, 80
Census records 23, 71, 79,
                  81, 102
Census substitutes 79, 81-83
Census web sites 84
Chancery records . . . 87, 91, 179
Chronology 1
Church archives 72, 84, 90
Church histories 69, 85
Church of Jesus Christ of Latter-
    day Saints, *See*
    FamilySearch Library,
    FamilySearch Centers
Church records . . iv, 22, 23, 39,
         46, 52, 57, 62, 63,
         84-86, 94, 96, 98, 122
Churches, *See* Religions

Cincinnati Historical Society
.... vi, 17, 99
Cincinnati Public Library, *See*
　　Public Library of
　　Cincinnati and Hamilton
　　County
Cities, Ohio xiii
City directories, *See* directories
Civil War..... vi, 8, 43, 46, 51,
　　54, 56, 60, 62, 65,
　　71, 80, 102, 122,
　　126-128, 137-139,
　　143, 158, 159, 166
Civil War records 62, 65,
　　129-135, 138, 139, 182
Cleveland Public Library
.... vii, xiii, 17, 32, 67,
　　97, 99, 153, 168
Collections.......... iv, v, 15,
　　17-20, 22, 24, 28, 45-49,
　　51, 54-56, 60-66, 69,
　　71-73, 85, 99, 104,
　　113, 126, 128, 146,
　　149-152, 165, 168
College records, *See* School
　　records
Colonial Dames XVII .. 44, 129
Columbus Metropolitan Library
.... xiii, 17, 32, 51-54,
　　56-59, 77, 97, 99, 130, 148
Computer catalogs......... 17
Counties.. xiii, 6, 12, 15, 16, 19,
　　27, 38, 45, 46, 56,
　　61, 63, 78-81, 87, 94,
　　106, 109, 113, 114,
　　116, 119, 120, 143, 146,
　　149, 152, 161-163,
　　169, 170, 176, 181
County courthouses..... 62, 75,
　　87, 88, 98
County directories, *See*
　　Directories

County formation 13, 119,
　　183-187
County record centers 18
Court records....... iii, 45, 46,
　　65, 88, 89, 188-192
Courthouses, *See* County
　　courthouses
Cuyahoga County Public Library
.... vi, 17, 32, 67, 99
DAR, *See* Daughters of the
　　America Revolution
　　Ohio Society of
DAR Library.......... 76, 97
Daughters of the American
　　Revolution records
.... ix, 52, 56, 120,
　　127-129, 176, 180
Death records 8, 9, 23, 27,
　　48, 51, 71, 74, 75, 102,
　　124, 175-177, 181
Deeds, *See* land records
Department of Health, *See* Ohio
　　Department of Health
Directories...... iv, 23, 38, 45,
　　46, 48, 53, 57, 60,
　　61, 66, 67, 70, 82,
　　90, 116, 171, 174
Divorce records.... 91, 92, 143,
　　158, 176, 177
Early settlements.......... 12
Economy................ xiii
Emigration and immigration . 57
Erie Canal 6, 7, 13
Ethnic records ... iv, 16, 57, 61,
　　62, 93-95
Fairview Park Regional Library
.... iv, 17, 32, 67, 99
Family and home sources
.... ii, 76, 94, 96
Family Bibles, *See* Bibles
Family histories, *See* Genealogies

FamilySearch Library 21,
    24, 26, 44, 66, 74,
    76, 77, 80-82, 84,
    87, 89, 97, 98, 109,
    111, 113, 116, 120,
    128, 142, 147, 169,
    171, 174, 175, 177, 178
FamilySearch Library Catalog
    .... 109, 113, 177
Family records.......... 76, 96
FamilySearch
    Affiliates.......... 32
    Centers 29
Federal census schedules, *See*
    Census records
Federal land records, *See* Land
    records
Federal records 68, 132
Finding aids......... 50, 62, 68,
    69, 102, 117, 142
    148, 151, 229, 294
Gazetteers 117, 294
Genealogical collections
    .... 17, 24, 58, 66
Genealogical Society of Utah
    .... 21, 22, 74
Genealogical sources.... 49, 52,
    56, 61, 67, 70,
    72, 75, 89
Genealogies..... 23-27, 38, 45,
    48, 58, 60, 67, 70,
    71, 78, 82, 83, 96
Geographical finding aids .. 294
German-Americans 53, 57,
    99, 116
Government, local 18, 19, 48-50,
    57, 62, 65
Government records 18, 94
    See also National
    Archives
Governor's Office of Veterans
    Affairs.......... 126

Graves Registration File ... 126
Gravestones, *See* Cemetery
    records
Guardianship records
    .... 129, 169
Guidebooks and methodology
    265
Guides..... 15, 47, 49, 50, 62,
    65, 70, 72, 77, 115
Harold B. Lee Library, *See*
    Brigham Young
    University
Historical guides, *See* Guides
Historical societies ..... iv, 17,
    27, 72, 82, 89, 90,
    93, 97, 130, 145,
    148, 163, 168, 171,
    175, 178,179
Histories, *See* Local histories
Home sources, *See* Family
    sources
IGI, *See* FamilySearch
Immigration, *See* Emigration and
    Immigration, Migration
Indexes .... iv, 23, 24,
    26, 27, 39, 50, 61,
    67, 70, 71, 74, 87,
    102, 109, 111, 112,
    116, 122, 125, 126,
    128, 130, 133, 135,
    142, 148, 149, 151-153,
    158, 162, 166, 169,
    173, 174, 177, 180, 181
Institutional records. 72, 97, 180
International Genealogical Index,
    See FamilySearch
Internet addresses 99
Jails, *See* Institutional records
Lake Erie, *See* Migration
Land records 23, 47, 48,
    82, 102, 107-113,
    125, 129, 179, 180

Legal sources.......... 70, 89, 97, 158, 161
Libraries, *See* Repositories
Libraries directories, *See* Guides
Library of Congress..... 50, 89, 128, 130, 134, 150, 153
Library of Virginia 112
Lineage societies.... 43, 44, 46, 129, 181
Local histories........ 23, 38, 46, 48, 51-54, 56-59 60, 61, 66, 67, 69 70, 71, 89, 97, 102, 116, 158, 161, 162, 165, 181
Lodges............... 98, 143
Manuscripts, *See* Collections
Maps, Ohio, index to...... 325
See also Atlases and maps
Marietta, Ohio... 2, 3, 6, 12-14, 17, 37, 42
Marriage records.... 10, 23, 25, 27, 45, 51, 63, 67, 71, 75, 91, 96, 102, 119, 120, 122, 124, 143, 148,149, 152, 176, 177, 179-181
Masons 98
Methodology............ 268
Middle Atlantic states 13
Migration, *See* Emigration and Immigration
Migration routes 14
Military history...... 124, 127, 139, 309
Military index 131, 184

Military records.. iv, 7, 23, , 38, 39, 46-48, 52, 56, 61, 62, 65, 66, 70, 75, 94, 96, 102, 122, 124-126, 128, 130-140, 143, 144, 158,161, 162, 164, 168, 176, 181
Mortality schedules.. 66, 80, 81, 122, 152, 162, 181
Motto, Ohio.............. xiii
Mug books, *See* Biographies
National Archives 79, 95, 110, 111, 124-126, 131-134, 140, 181
National Archives, Chicago 68, 132, 141,142
National Road..... 5, 7, 13, 14
National Society Daughters of the American Revolution, *See* Daughters of the American Revolution
National Union Catalog of Manuscript Collections .... ix, 128
Native American records... 1-3, 44, 46, 93, 95, 156
Naturalization records... iv, 23, 47, 48, 56, 68, 94, 96, 122, 141, 142, 181
Network Centers, *See* Ohio Network of American History Research Centers
New England.......... 12, 17, 23, 54, 63, 71
New England states.. 13, 54, 70
Newsletters 45, 46, 158, 166, 167
Newspapers............. 146
Nickname, Ohio xiii
Northwest Ordinance........ 2, 12, 106

Northwest Territory.... xiv, 1-3
12, 13, 38, 44, 145
Obituaries, *See* Newspapers
Ohio counties 186
Ohio County History Surname
Index........... 116
Ohio county records ... 188-192
Ohio Department of Health... v,
10, 75, 91, 103,
119, 176, 177
Ohio Genealogical Society
.... iv, 38, 59, 86,
120, 128, 158, 160
Chapters 40-42
Library ..... v, 17, 34,
38, 76, 77, 79,
89, 97, 99, 135,
147, 168,171, 179
Lineage Societies
.... 43, 44, 129
Selected holdings 45-46
Ohio genealogy, *See* Guides,
Methodology
Ohio History Connection. v, xiii,
10, 17-20, 47, 48,
50, 55, 74, 77, 81,
84, 89, 100, 104,
108-110, 116, 119, 120,
125, 126, 128, 135, 147,
151, 152, 163, 168, 169,
173, 176-178, 180, 181
OhioLINK......... 17, 54, 55,
69, 100, 149
Ohio Network of American
History Research
Centers 18-20, 49,
100, 183-187
Ohio River, *See* Rivers
Ohio State Library, *See* State
Library of Ohio
Ohio State University ... xiii, 9,
70, 93, 100, 101, 148, 152

Ohio Surname Index, *See* Ohio
County History
Surname Index
Ohio University... 4, 18-20, 100
168, 183-187
Ohioana Library ... 55, 69, 101
Passenger lists, *See* Emigration
and immigration
Passport applications....... 23
Patriotic societies, *See* Lineage
societies
Pedigree Resource File 26
Pension records, *See* Military
records
Pensioners' census....... 7, 80
Periodical Source Index (PERSI)
.... 165, 166, 181
Periodicals............ 21, 38,
46-48, 55-57, 60-62,
66, 67, 69-71, 78, 85,
98, 116, 22,129, 149,
152, 158-167, 181
Population, Ohio, . xiii, 3-10, 15
See also, Census records
Preface................. iv-v
Presbyterian Historical Society
.... 84
Prisons, *See* Institutional records
Probate Court 8, 74, 87,
119, 141, 142, 169,
170, 176, 177
Probate records ..... iv, 23, 62,
75, 123, 143, 144,
152, 158, 169, 170,182
Property records, *See* Land
records
Public libraries 17, 27, 59,
60, 72, 93, 100, 130,
148, 168, 171, 193-228
Public Library of Cincinnati and
Hamilton County
.... xiii, 17, 60, 97, 101

Public Library of Youngstown
and Mahoning County
.... 35, 225
Quadrennial enumerations
.... 48, 81
Railroads .... xiii, 14
Reference books 67, 70
Regional Network Centers, *See*
Ohio Network of
American History
Research Centers
Religions .... xiv, 252-260
Religious organizations, *See*
Church histories,
Religions
Repositories, *See also*, Libraries
Research Centers, *See* Ohio
Network of American
History Research
Centers
Research outlines.......... 96
Revolutionary War 1, 7, 44,
51, 80
Rivers, (in Ohio) ...... xiii, xiv,
2, 13
SAR, *See* Sons of the American
Revolution
School records......... 62, 65,
82, 83, 97
Serials, *See* Periodicals
Settlement patterns, *See also*
Migration
Settlements in Ohio.... 1, 2, 12,
15, 16, 121, 146
Sexton records........... 122
Shaker records......... 63, 65
Social Security Death Index
.... 182
Sons of the American Revolution
.... 129
Southern states.......... 8, 13

Statehood, Ohio.......... xiv,
44, 91, 146
State Land Office 109
State Library of Ohio... v, xii, 5,
17, 51-57, 69, 81,
89, 97, 100, 101
Substitutes for vital records, *See*
Vital record substitutes
Tax records..... iv, 46, 51, 82,
158, 173-175
Toledo-Lucas County Public
Library ...... xiii, 37,
70, 97, 101
Tombstones, *See* Cemetery
records
Township records .... iv, 62, 65
123, 162, 175
Tract books 109-111, 113
United States—Emigration and
immigration.... 23, 57,
62, 67, 68, 93, 300
Universities......... 8, 17, 18
University of Akron..... 8, 20,
183-187
University of Cincinnati 5,
18-20, 199, 101, 183-187
University records, *See* School
records
Veterans 9, 44, 68, 80
Veterans Administration 68
Virginia.... 1-3, 5, 8, 13, 14, 60
Virginia Military District... 2, 3,
8, 106, 109, 111
Vital record substitutes . 179-182
Vital records, *See also*, Births,
Marriages, Deaths
Vital statistics office, *See* Ohio
Department of Health
Voting records........... 81
War of 1812, *See* Military
history, Military records
Warnings out............ 175

Web sites, *See* Internet resources
Western Reserve Historical
       Society .... xii, 17, 18,
       20, 38, 61, 63-65,
       77, 85, 93, 97, 101
       125, 128, 136, 152, 168
Wills, *See* Probate records
Work Projects Administration
       (WPA)........... 84
World War I records 9, 51
Wright State University..... 18,
       20, 101, 183-187
Youngstown Historical Center of
       Industry and Labor
       .... 18, 20, 183-187

www.ingramcontent.com/pod-product-compliance
Lightning Source LLC
Chambersburg PA
CBHW071149300426
44113CB00009B/1142